INTERPRESS
THE SOURCE
BOOK

*"Optimus atque
Interpres legum
sanctissimus."*

JUVENAL

INTERPRESS
THE SOURCE
BOOK

Steven J. Harrington
Robert R. Buckley

Xerox Corporation

A Brady Book
New York, New York 10023

B R A D Y

A Brady Book
Simon & Schuster, Inc.
Gulf + Western Building
One Gulf + Western Plaza
New York, New York 10023

XEROX®, Interpress, and all Xerox product names are trademarks of Xerox Corporation. Macintosh® is a trademark of Apple
Computer, Inc. Unix is a trademark of AT&T. DEC,VMS, DECVax, and Microvax are trademarks of Digital Equipment Corporation.
IBM, MVS/370, MVS/XA, and IBM-PC are trademarks of International Business Machines Corporation. Kodak is a trademark of
Eastman Kodak Company. Pantone® is a trademark of Pantone, Inc. Wang is a trademark of Wang Laboratories, Inc.

Printed in the United States of America

10 9 8 7 6 5 4 3 2 1

Library of Congress Cataloging-in-Publication Data

Harrington, Steven.
    Interpress, the source book/Steven Harrington, Robert Buckley.
        p. cm.
    "A Brady book."
    Includes index.
    1. Electronic publishing. 2. Interpress (Computer program
language) I. Buckley, Robert, 1950– . II. Title.
Z286.E43H37 1988
686.2'2—dc19   88-3149
                                                             CIP

ISBN 0-13-475591-X

Dedicated to

Brett, Randy, Sean, Geoffrey, Logan
and
Holly

CONTENTS

CREDITS

Interpress: The Source Book represents the culmination of the research and practical experience of many individuals at Xerox Corporation who work with the Interpress page- and document-description language every day. Without their participation and assistance, this book would not have been possible and it is a pleasure to acknowledge their contributions.

Much of the original input for this book came from Xerox papers written by the following staff: Jerry Mendelson on the Interpress operators and imaging model; Michael Plass, Maureen Stone, and Steve Strasen on text and graphics; Caesar Chavez and Mary Ann Dvonch on practical details and troubleshooting; and Abhay Bhushan and Dennis Frahmann on market use and page-description language requirements. Some sections of the book are taken from the *Introduction to Interpress* by Robert Sproull and Brian Reid.

Mary Ann Dvonch, Jerry Mendelson, Danielle Battut, Michael Plass, Caesar Chavez, Marian Suggs, Eric Nickell, and Dave Rumph reviewed the manuscript; Debra Tasseff, Maureen Turner, and Laura Ingersoll typed it. Sean Cotter coordinated the editing and proofreading, and Dianne Jacob proofed the final manuscript.

Mike Tiffany designed the book. The figure illustrations were done by Steven Wallgren and Rob Buckley. Wendy Harrison and Diane Spelman did the page layouts.

The manuscript and illustrations were merged in Interpress and used to generate camera-ready page images. Richard Sauvain, Linda Burley, and Dave Rumph handled special font requirements. Henry Moon supplied the scanned images. Tim Diebert and Bridget Scamporrino produced the final page images on a 1200-spot-per-inch Interpress output device at the Xerox Palo Alto Research Center.

We would like to thank all these people for their help in ensuring that this book not only describes Interpress well, but also represents a model use of the document description language.

FOREWORD

It wasn't too many years ago that the seers of the marketplace were predicting a paperless office. That has yet to be seen; in fact, the opposite has happened. The proliferation of personal computers, desktop publishing, and laser printers has only increased the volume of paper produced.

Why is that? Why is the printed word more important today than ever before? I think it is because new technologies have made printed information more valuable. Through technology, printed information can be generated in a more timely and effective manner.

Let's look at some examples. People have long said that a picture is worth a thousand words, and typical corporate office documentation is beginning to prove it. Casual correspondence, day-to-day memorandums, reports, and proposals are increasingly taking advantage of business graphics, scanned artwork, and high-quality typography to make their point. As a result, the value of printed information goes up.

At Xerox, electronic publication centers accept information directly from a writer's workstation and print a small press run on a high-speed laser printer. The turn-around time on documentation drops from months to days. Multi-national customers print documents in 45 different languages all on the same laser printer, often with two or more languages on the same page. Customers store electronic documents and print needed copies on demand, not only avoiding warehousing costs but also ensuring that a user always receives the most current version. In many ways, the value of printed information is indeed going up.

In the early seventies, Xerox anticipated that new technologies in printing and computing would have a major impact on the way our society uses information. We established a program at our Xerox Palo Alto Research Center (PARC) to explore ways to use the potential of new technology in many environments.

The challenge was to find inexpensive and convenient ways to enable workers to process documents and to share information quickly, efficiently, and over geographically dispersed areas. This required easy-to-use workstations and effective network communications that can integrate workstations, printers, and other office products to share files, distribute documents, and make common use of other limited office resources.

Many new technologies poured out of PARC: laser xerographic printing in 1971; high-resolution bit-map workstations incorporating icons, windows, pull-down menus, and the mouse in 1973; Ethernet, the industry standard local area network in 1975; and Interpress, the industry's first page description language, in 1981.

Interpress, the Xerox page and document description language developed from that research, is now one of the keystone technologies for integrating Xerox systems products and for enabling Xerox printers to print complex page images.

Interpress, like other networking standards and protocols developed by Xerox within the Xerox Network Systems architecture, was placed in the public domain as part of a Xerox commitment to an open system. As part of that commitment, Xerox has been active in working with groups such as the International Standards Organization and the Corporation for Open Systems to develop formal industry standards. We have encouraged such organizations to look at Interpress as the base for an international standard.

Until such a standard exists, Xerox is committed to Interpress as the page and document description language that will integrate our product lines in electronic printing and publishing. We are also committed to working with other vendors to help them add Interpress support to their product lines.

In this light, it is exciting to see Steve Harrington and Rob Buckley's work in giving a crisp and clear introduction to the Interpress language. It will be even more exciting to see readers of this book utilize the expressive power of an Interpress-output device. Each such reader will, as a result, expand the value of printed information.

Paul Allaire
President, Xerox Corporation

INTRODUCTION

This book has been written to help you understand and take advantage of Interpress, the page- and document-description language developed by Xerox Corporation. It summarizes the research and practical experience of the many individuals at Xerox Corporation who have worked with Interpress for the last five years.

Who Can Use This Book

This book has been written with several technical audiences in mind. The software developer who writes programs to generate Interpress documents is the primary audience. Our goal is to help such a person understand what Interpress can do and how it does it. Examples of Interpress programs appear throughout the book. Because you should have some practical experience in programming software if you are planning to be an Interpress developer, we do not explain the basic programming concepts underlying these examples.

The implementor of an Interpress-accepting printer, typesetter, or display is also likely to find this book useful. Most chapters include discussions of printer-implementation concerns, because these concerns influence how you write efficient Interpress-generating programs. This book is not, however, a theoretical treatise on page-description languages. Discussion of the theory of Interpress and of design decisions in this book focuses only on what is needed to write effective Interpress software.

Finally, if you are interested in the potential of inhouse publishing systems in general, or specifically in their revenue-conserving and quality enhancement functions, this book will show you precisely how Interpress devices produce documents, presentations, and all the other output of an inhouse publishing system.

How to Use This Book

This book, which uses a tutorial approach, begins by explaining basic concepts and models. Then, one by one, those concepts and models are expanded in practical detail.

Chapters 1, 2, and 3 introduce the basic concepts of the Interpress programming language and imaging model. Chapter 4 explains in detail how to control text in an Interpress document. Chapters 5, 6, and 7 describe how to handle synthetic graphics (vector graphics including straight and curved lines), raster graphics (bitmap graphics such as scanned images), and color.

The first seven chapters deal primarily with page-description issues. Chapter 8 focuses on the entire document or print job and explores how Interpress handles document-wide issues like document finishing. Chapter 9 deals with practical issues such as troubleshooting and gives tips on writing efficient programs. Chapter 10 examines the role of Interpress in the growing inhouse publishing market.

Finally, three appendices and a glossary contain various kinds of reference material, supplying a quick source for information about the programming language. The appendices not only summarize the material in the rest of the book but also provide additional information, such as the details of the standard encoding of Interpress and the makeup of the Interpress function sets.

If you are reading this book primarily to gain a better general understanding of the role and value of Interpress, you should focus on Chapters 1 and 10, and then peruse the other chapters in which you might have an interest.

If you are reading this book to prepare yourself to write Interpress-generating software, you should read Chapters 1 through 8. You should also read Chapter 9 and the appendices before you begin your actual development work.

Additional Resources

To ease widespread use of Interpress, Xerox Corporation has developed a number of Interpress tools, which are available at a nominal charge for a variety of environments, both networked and multiuser.

This book is a supplement to, but not a replacement for, the Interpress standards documents for software development. If you intend to write Interpress software, you should acquire the necessary standards documents, which are listed at the end of the book in the section entitled Further Reading. The complete formal specification of the Interpress Electronic Printing Standard, Version 3.0 as well as the Xerox Raster Encoding Standard and other related standards can be obtained from the Xerox Systems Institute, as can specialized Interpress consulting.

For details on obtaining these services, documents, and tools, write to:

Xerox Systems Institute
Xerox Corporation, 475 Oakmead Parkway, Sunnyvale, CA 94086
408/737-7900

Chapter 1
INTERPRESS:
A DOCUMENT
DESCRIPTION
LANGUAGE

*"Would that we
could at once
paint with the eyes!
In the long way
from the eye,
through the arm,
to the pencil,
how much is lost!"*

GOTTHOLD LESSING

L ittle more than a decade ago imaging scientists first began experimenting with laser printers. Yet today laser printers have exploded into the business world. Because of them, the power of the press has moved to the desktop. High-quality typography is creeping into everyday memos and impressive graphics appear in training manuals. Existing artwork is scanned and merged with computer-generated engineering drawings. Once the words and images are created, edited, and stored, laser printers print them all (see Figure 1.1). This accomplishment is possible in part because of document- and page-description languages such as Interpress.

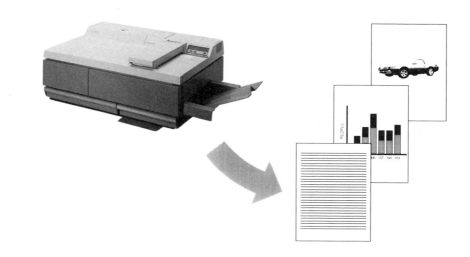

Figure 1.1 Laser printers can print high-quality typography, synthetic graphics, and scanned images.

Interpress is both a document and page-description language. As a page-description language, it makes available the power of laser-printing devices to produce any two-dimensional image on the page (see Figure 1.2). Page-description languages allow pages to be created and formatted, and most of these languages primarily suit smaller-scale office desktop publishing. A page-description language can describe the image on a page but may have little notion of a larger document structure. Information such as what belongs in various copies of the document or how the document should be finished may be difficult to express. That is why a document-description capability is

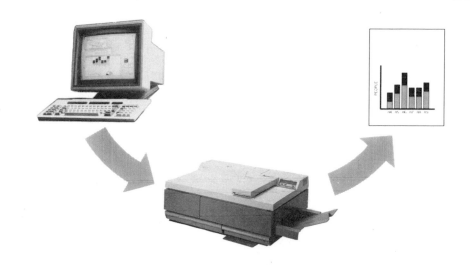

Figure 1.2 A workstation uses a page description language to describe the image on the page to the printer.

needed. As a document-description language, Interpress treats a document as an entity, an important consideration in a publishing environment (see Figure 1.3). Interpress is a document- and a page-description language that allows a variety of document-creating devices to communicate with a variety of document-imaging devices, not only laser printers, but also plotters, digital typesetters, and preview workstations.

Besides a powerful page- and document-description language, Interpress is designed specifically for transmitting to an output device an electronic representation of a document that has been created on a workstation, personal computer, or mainframe. Software employing Interpress is widely used in today's business world. A broad range of printers and digital typesetters use Interpress to control the images they print. To take advantage of these devices, many software and workstation suppliers support Interpress in their products.

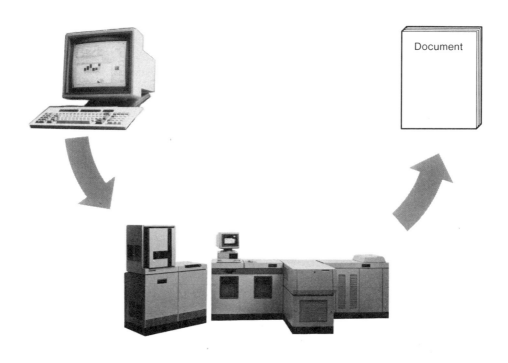

Figure 1.3 A workstation uses a document description language to describe the entire document to the printer.

This chapter summarizes the design goals that underlie the structure of Interpress and introduces the facilities of the three Interpress function sets. The programming language itself is introduced in Chapter 2.

Design Goals

To understand Interpress, you first need to think about the way laser printers and other computer-driven raster printers operate. All computer printers are linked to the computers that control them by an interface that exchanges more information than just the data to be printed (see Figure 1.4). For example, at the beginning of each line, a line printer honors carriage-control codes, which specify vertical spacing. In the past, these interfaces corresponded closely to the capabilities of the printer: if a printer could print characters of different sizes, then the interface offered a command to change size; if a printer could print superscripts, then it offered a way of specifying superscripts. The data flowing through the computer-to-printer interface consisted of device controls, including a command to control every option of the printing device.

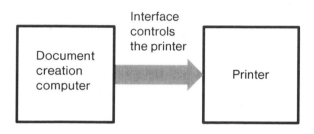

Figure 1.4 The interface between creator and printer.

Raster technology produces an image from a large array of tiny, individually controlled dots that cover the page (see Figure 1.5). Conceptually, a raster printer can print any image simply by arranging the appropriate pattern of dots on paper. It is the interface to that device, not the printer itself, that

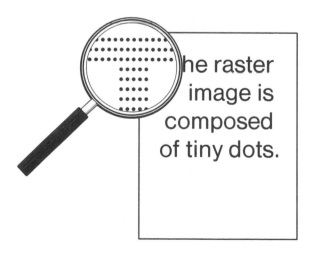

Figure 1.5 Raster printers produce the image from an array of tiny dots.

determines what can be printed (see Figure 1.6). Traditional printing formats were geared to the hardware characteristics of individual printers and could not take advantage of the general software-driven nature of a raster device. With a raster printer, however, it is the expressive power of the interface rather than the capabilities of the printer that limit the range of images that can be printed. Because the nature of the interface is not dictated by the properties of the printing machine, a universal interface–an interchange standard–can represent any document and control any raster printer.

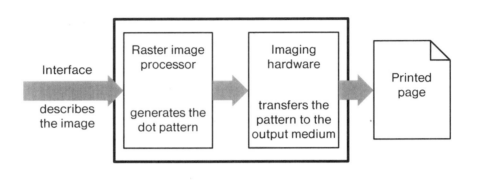

Figure 1.6 The image is limited by what the interface can describe.

This is where Interpress comes in. Fundamentally different from more conventional interfaces, it uses a software approach to control the increasing possibilities in the newest generation of output devices.

One way to define a digital printing standard might be to have the interface mimic a traditional printing press by presenting the printer with a facsimile of what its output is to be. The computer program would prepare data directly in raster format, and the raster printer would print the data verbatim. This scheme has several disadvantages, however:

- Raster data takes up an enormous amount of storage space–often hundreds of millions of bits are needed to represent the image on a single page. A raster representation of a four-color halftone page from a high-quality retail catalog typically takes 50 million bytes to store. This kind of storage inefficiency slows down transmission and increases storage costs. An Interpress document should be as compact as possible.

- Raster data depends on the resolution of the printing device–the number of dots per inch. If the resolution of the raster printer is not the same as the resolution intended by the programmer, then the printed image will have the wrong size or shape. An Interpress document should print equally well on a wide range of printers, regardless of their resolution or scanning direction.

- It is very difficult to do a good job of transforming raster images–rotating them, shrinking them to fit into a particular space, making changes to accommodate a different printer resolution, and so forth. These transformations are vital to an artist or editor assembling high-quality published material.

- If a printed page is to contain text, the computer program that generates it must have access to raster pictures of all the letters in all the fonts that it will be using. This adds a huge burden in complexity and storage to the generating program. The task of creating an Interpress document should be as simple as possible.

For all these reasons and others, Interpress is not a pictorial standard–it does not specify an image of the printed page. Instead, it gives the printing software a set of instructions for generating a certain picture (see Figure 1.7).

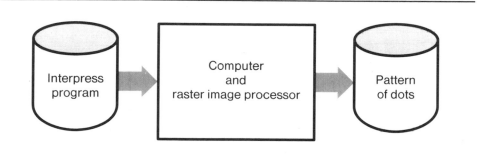

Figure 1.7 Interpress is a program which is run on a computer to generate the dot pattern of the image.

The purpose of Interpress is to describe complex pages that can contain text, line graphics, and photographic images in black and white, gray scale, or full color (see Figure 1.8). A standard for line graphics must not have built-in limitations on its expressive power. All possible pictorial or textual combinations must be specified with it; otherwise, it will eventually become obsolete. An Interpress master is a program, written in the Interpress programming language, that is executed by the printing machine to produce the finished document. Although most Interpress masters consist entirely of simple imperative statements, such as "place the letter 'b' here," the full power of the programming language is available for complex applications. The nature of an Interpress document also implies that the computer program that generates an Interpress master is a program-generating program.

National Service Support

**Xerox Systems Support:
Maximizing your investment
in office automation.**
Before, during, and after the sale, Xerox
Systems Support can help you make
informed decisions and ensure that you
get the most from your systems
investment. There are hundreds of ways
we can help, including the following:

Systems Consulting Services.
An organization of systems professionals
will assist in the design and installation
of large-scale information systems. We
begin with a three-day study to
determine systems requirements, and
follow through with recommendations
that utilize your existing hardware
whenever possible.

Customer Education.
Whether you need training in word
processing or in the operation and
maintenance of large, complex systems,
every Xerox Customer Education course
is designed to give you the maximum
return on your system investment . We
help your staff achieve their greatest
potential by providing a dedicated
learning environment where they can

concentrate on developing their
professional skills and resources.
Customer Education courses vary from
a few hours to intensive week-long
workshops. They're held at Xerox
Training Centers conveniently located
in major U.S. cities from coast to coast.
Courses for printing systems, office
systems, personal computers, word
processors, and publishing systems are
available.

Customer Support Centers.
Highly skilled technical specialists are
available to offer telephone consultation
in the use of Xerox products. They are
capable of dealing with the most
difficult inquiries regarding Xerox office
systems, printing, and publishing
systems products.

Figure 1.8 Interpress can express text, line graphics, and scanned images.

Complex Pages

The fundamental design goal is that Interpress must be able to describe any conceivable printed page. This obviously includes text, line drawings, filled areas, and photographic images–in black and white, gray scale, or even color.

For text, this goal requires the ability to produce the richest typography possible. In other words, Interpress must be able to describe high-quality fonts of different sizes and at different angles of rotation. It must be able to deal with important typesetting requirements, such as ligatures and kerning. For line drawings or computer-generated art, Interpress must describe synthetic graphics completely and efficiently. For example, a curve should be described as a single mathematical construct, not as an approximation composed of many short, straight lines. For photographic images or other bit-mapped images, Interpress must recognize the requirements and problems associated with rotating or changing the resolution. For color, Interpress must develop an imaging model that not only can deal with black and white and single colors, but also is rich enough to support full- or process-color applications.

Device Independence

Different printers clearly have different characteristics, including printing speeds, resolutions, marking-engine technologies, and document-finishing capabilities.

Interpress is designed to be a universal page- and document-description language. In other words, you should be able to print one version of an Interpress document on a variety of output devices, regardless of their characteristics (see Figure 1.9). The same electronic Interpress master should produce equivalent output on all printers.

Thus, the software developer using Interpress works in a device-independent, master coordinate system and generally does not worry about printer specifics.

Although Interpress is designed for raster printers and other high-capability devices, it is not incompatible with less powerful printing devices. An important consideration in the design of Interpress is the choice of image-generation functions that allow printers to exert their best efforts to approximate the ideal appearance and to cope gracefully with masters that contain image-generation functions beyond their capabilities.

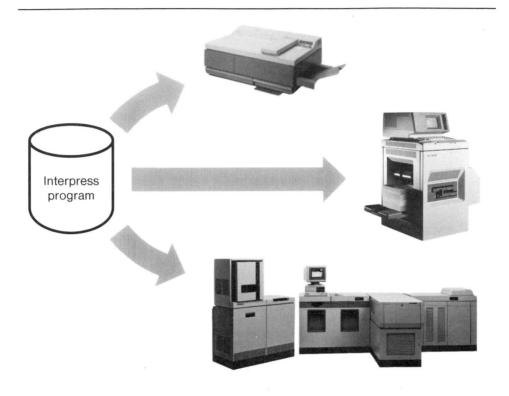

Figure 1.9 Interpress documents are printable on a variety of output devices.

Performance Orientation

There are several primary methods of producing output. One makes use of a master copy for offset printing or duplicating; this typically involves low-speed, high-resolution typesetters and low-speed, low-resolution proofing devices. A second is demand publishing of electronic documents, which involves high-speed, low-resolution devices. A third is networked distribution of documents, which involves using a variety of output devices connected to local- or wide-area networks.

Interpress is designed to be effective in all these areas. Particular care was taken to ensure that high-speed printers can implement Interpress effectively. The designers also ensured that in shared environments, using Interpress on one print job will not affect the next print job. All this guarantees the software developer access to a full range of printing devices.

Document Control

In some printing environments you need to look at printing applications not as a series of pages but as whole documents. This may be because you are concerned with issues such as collating and document finishing (as in demand-publishing applications). Or, perhaps a specific printer needs to print the job's last page first. Interpress views its print jobs as a series of pages that make up a complete document, which makes it possible to embed within the document printing instructions that apply to the whole document (see Figure 1.10). In addition, each page is isolated from the next, which allows the printer software to optimally use its print engine's capabilities. For example, it is relatively easy to write routines for such tasks as two-up printing or printing of selected pages, as shown in Figure 1.11.

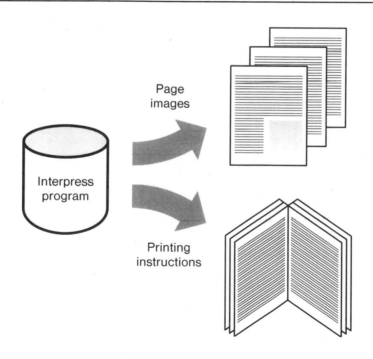

Figure 1.10 Interpress not only describes what pages look like, but also how they form a document.

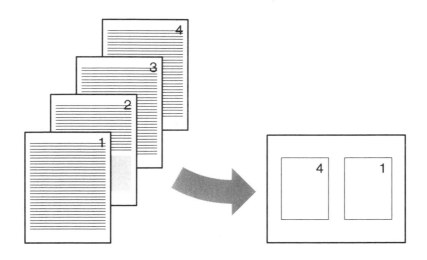

Figure 1.11 Page independence makes it easy to perform page-level operations such as selecting and merging entire pages.

Document Architecture

Naturally, the task of connecting a printer to a workstation to form a publishing system requires far more than a page-description language. We also need to consider how fonts are specified, what character codes are used (particularly in a multi-lingual environment), and how scanned images are integrated. Within a network environment, there are interactions with directory and authentication services for which protocols must be selected. Also, there are questions of the actual physical connection of the two devices, which might be a local-area network such as the IEEE 802.3 standard, a direct connection such as an RS-232 connection or a medium such as magnetic tape.

Interpress, which is designed to open paths to a total architecture, does not attempt to define those items that go beyond the bounds of a page-description language. Instead, it supplies ways of integrating appropriate standards. The initial implementors of Interpress published a standard set of associated protocols for such areas as fonts and character codes. You can adopt these to ease the overall task of system development, provided that they satisfy your requirements.

Extensibility

Over the past few years, the capabilities of electronic printing have grown rapidly. In the next few years, we can expect that growth rate to increase. Any proposed standard for talking to output devices needs to be capable of evolving to take advantage of new techniques. Interpress is designed to support extensibility. As new features are needed, new commands can be added to the language. Xerox Corporation, with the help of other Interpress implementors, formally adds new features to Interpress as technology evolves. This book is based on Version 3.0 of Interpress, released in January 1986.

Interpress Function Sets

As a programmer of software that uses Interpress, you need to consider several distinctions. The first distinction is that between creators and printers. As shown in Figure 1.12, Interpress exists in two places: on the workstation generating documents (the creator), and on the output device preparing the final image (the printer). When writing creator software, you implement only as much of Interpress as you need to describe the kind of document your software handles. For example, if your documents do not generate graphics, you do not need to implement the Interpress commands for graphics. On the other hand, your printer should implement all the features in one of three formally defined function sets.

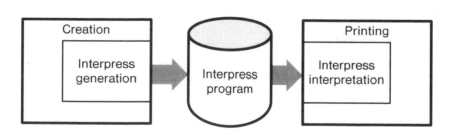

Figure 1.12 Interpress software is used at both the creator and the printer.

To give vendors the option of supplying only as much functionality as their customers require, the Interpress standard defines the following function sets (see Figure 1.13):

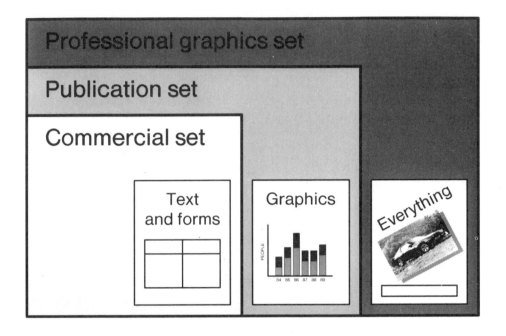

Figure 1.13 Interpress sets.

- The Commercial set supports applications requiring text (with 90-degree rotations), forms, and scanned binary images. It can reproduce typical office documents, as well as text generated by a computer data center.
- The Publication set includes all the facilities of the Commercial set, plus computer-generated graphics, including straight and curved lines (both solid and dashed), filled outlines, uniform grays, and named colors. The Publication set is designed to generate office and technical publications such as reports, proposals, and illustrated engineering manuals.
- The Professional Graphics set includes all of the facilities of the Publication set, and also supplies techniques for creating specialized graphic artwork, including color images. It contains all the imaging facilities of Interpress, including multi-level full color pixels and arbitrary rotations of text and graphics.

Appendix A gives a full description of the operators in each set.

Although a creator needs to implement only as much of Interpress as is necessary to support the documents to be printed, it is generally a good idea to target masters toward one of the three sets. In other words, you should identify which Interpress function set has the minimum level of capabilities needed for your application and then avoid using Interpress commands that are only found in higher-level function set implementations.

Users of your software usually need to know the level at which you have written your program to ensure that they have a printer sufficiently powerful to print all possible documents from your software package. In general, most software should target Publication Set-level printers. Interpress gives a printing instruction (described in Chapter 8) for declaring the set that the printer must support to print a specific document. This can be used to route the document to a printer with sufficient capabilities.

Summary

Interpress is a full-function, general-purpose, device-independent document- and page-description language for printing. With Interpress, the software developer can control the descriptive power of modern raster output devices. As a language, Interpress can describe complex pages composed of text and graphics, and can do so in a way that is device-independent and compatible with high-speed printing, document finishing, and network architectures.

Chapter 2 introduces the basic concepts of the Interpress language.

Chapter 2
THE
PROGRAMMING
LANGUAGE

*"Language is
only the
instrument of
science, and
words are but
the signs
of ideas."*

SAMUEL JOHNSON

As a computer language, Interpress shares many features with more general-purpose programming languages and resembles FORTH. A special-purpose language designed for expressing documents and transferring them between machines, Interpress also contains special operations for creating images and lacks a few general language features that are unnecessary in the context of document and page description.

In this chapter, we begin our exploration of Interpress by considering features it shares with other languages–the *base-language component*. In the following chapters, we will consider the special operations that are supplied for constructing images. We begin with the base language because it is likely to be most familiar. Most "real world" Interpress programs, however, make only light use of this portion of the language. Because the purpose of an Interpress program is to describe the images that make up the pages of a document, heavy use is made of the imaging operations, and efficient programs do little else.

Like most programming languages, an Interpress program is constructed of data values and instructions (called *operators*) that manipulate the data. At the printer, an Interpress interpreter examines the program and applies the operations to the data. Central to the interpreter is an *operand* stack. The stack supplies the data to the operators and stores the results of the operations. An operator such as ADD takes two operands from the top of the stack, adds them, and pushes the result back onto the stack (see Figure 2.1).

The natural way to express program elements for stack machines is *postfix notation;* that is, the operator follows its operands in the program. The interpreter sees a stream of data objects and operators. When it sees a data object, it pushes that data object onto the stack. When it sees an operator, it executes that operator. For example, a program to add 2 and 5 reads (from left to right):

2   5   ADD

On execution, the interpreter first places 2 on the stack, next places 5 on the stack, and then executes the ADD operator, which removes the 5 and 2; it then adds these two values and pushes the result 7 onto the stack (see Figure 2.2).

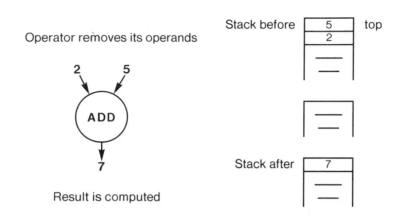

Figure 2.1 Operands are popped from the stack. Results are pushed onto the stack.

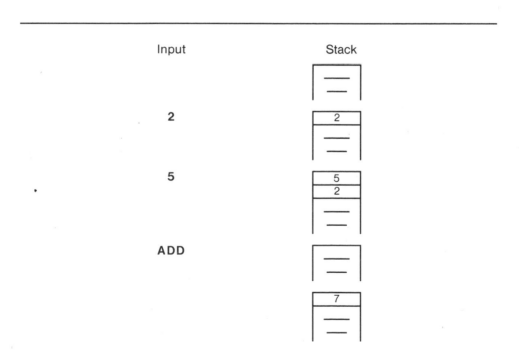

Figure 2.2 Data objects are pushed onto the stack, and operators are executed.

As a second example, calculating $(2 + 1) \times (4 - 3)$ is done as follows:

2   1   ADD   4   3   SUB   MUL

If you wanted to write one of these simple programs, one of the first things you need to know is how to express the numbers and operators so that the printer will understand them. For example, numbers could be a string of ASCII characters or an n-bit two's-complement representation. Operators can be represented as character strings or by special numerical codes. The way in which the program elements are represented is the *encoding* of Interpress. Interpress does not require any particular encoding; it allows you to use any encoding you wish. Of course, to communicate, both the document creator and the printer must agree on the encoding. So, if you wish to construct an Interpress document, you should use an encoding that your printer supports.

To avoid the problem of every printer using a different encoding, the Interpress standard does contain a "standard" encoding, a highly compact machine language, which most printers support. It is the language to use with machines that generate programs for other machines. Like most machine languages, however, it is not very easy for people to use, especially for us in this book. Therefore, for our examples, we shall use an Interpress assembly language–a textual encoding of Interpress that can be easily converted to and from the standard encoding.[†]

Data Types

Of the 11 different data types Interpress supports, only two (*number* and *identifier*) are primitive types that can be expressed as data values in an Interpress program. All other data types are associated with objects that can be constructed by operators.

Numbers are rational numbers:

3   4.5   0.222   –5

All printers should support values between 10^{-30} and 10^{+30}, with an accuracy of 1 part in 10^6. They also should contain all the integers in the range $-(2^{24}-1)$ to $(2^{24}-1)$. Some operators expect their operands to be *cardinals*, not a separate type but rather a proper subset of the type number: a nonnegative integer.

An identifier is expressed as a sequence of lowercase letters, digits, and the minus "–" character. Actually, it may contain uppercase letters, but these are mapped into the corresponding lowercase form. Identifiers are not strings but

---

[†]Programs that convert between the Interpress assembly language used in this book and the standard encoding are available from Xerox Corporation.

rather are treated within the language as atomic entities. They are used to name objects in the printer's environment. Identifiers cannot be decomposed into constituent elements by any operator in the language. If your program specifies identifiers containing the same sequence of characters in two different places, the resulting identifiers will be equal.

Constructed types in the base language component include *vectors* and *composed operators*. An Interpress vector is a sequence of values, referred to as *components* or *elements*. A vector can be manipulated as a single entity, or its components can be read individually, but the components cannot be modified. Because the components of a vector can be read, a new vector can be created that is equivalent to a given vector, but with specific components modified. Vectors are heterogeneous; that is, the components need not be of the same type. A component of a vector is accessed by means of an integer index. The indices of a vector range from some lower-bound cardinal, l, to some upper-bound cardinal, u. Vector operators are available for creating vectors and for reading their components.

Other data types are used to construct graphic objects: *pixel array*, *trajectory*, and *outline*. There are also types that hide the actual representation of some entities, allowing each device to represent them optimally. They include *font, color, transformation*, and *clipper*. We will consider these types further in our discussion of the operators that create and use them.

Each type is assigned a number, and the TYPE operator replaces the top stack item with the numerical code for its type. This allows you to write an Interpress operator that either checks the type of its data or accepts an operand with varying type. For example, you could write an operator that takes as an argument either a number or a vector of numbers. By duplicating the argument and performing the TYPE operation, your operator can determine the type of the operand and take the appropriate action.

The syntax of the TYPE operator can be described as

$$<\text{x:Any}> \text{ TYPE } \rightarrow <\text{c:Cardinal}>$$

This is an example of the way in which operators will be described in this book. The quantities in angle brackets <name:type> are data objects. Those on the left, in this case <x:Any>, precede the operator and are popped from the stack. The leftmost object is deepest in the stack, and the object just before the operator is on top of the stack when the operator begins execution. The objects to the right of the arrow, in this case <c:Cardinal>, describe the results pushed onto the stack by the operator. The names (x and c) are used in describing what the operator does. In this case, x is popped from the stack, its type index c is determined and pushed onto the stack. We also describe the type of the data objects. Usually, this will be one of the types we have discussed, but for the TYPE operator we use "Any" to mean all types are accepted by this operator. We could have said that the result was <c:Number>, but instead we said <c:Cardinal>. Although cardinal is not actually a type (number is), this gives you a little more information about the nature of the operator.

The operands of an operator are always popped off the stack, even for those operators that copy them right back. This is how the operator checks that there are enough operands and that they have the expected type.

Note that, although our notation shows the operands to the immediate left of the operator, this does not mean that they must immediately precede the operator in the input stream. The notation means only that, when the operator is executed, the operands must be on the top of the stack. The operands can be placed on the stack early and other operands can come and go. All that is required is that the stack must have the operands on top by the time the operator arrives.

Marks are special stack objects placed on the stack by special operators, and removed only by special operators. They guard against stack underflow and aid in recovery from errors. Composed operators, the Interpress equivalent of the procedures found in other programming languages, can be saved and copied as data objects, or executed, much as Lisp functions can be.

A Simple Interpress Program

Now let's look at a complete Interpress program to add 1 and 2. (See Example 2.1, the program statements are on the left, and comments in the form --a comment-- are on the right.)

Example 2.1

```
Header "Interpress/Xerox/3.0 "    --header--
BEGIN                             --start of the program--
   { }                            --preamble--
   {                              --start of the page--
      1 2 ADD                     --adding of two numbers--
   }                              --end of the page--
END                               --end of the program--
```

The program begins with a *header*, a string of characters terminated with a space. The header identifies this as an Interpress program. It also tells what encoding is used (Xerox), and what version of Interpress to expect (3.0).

The BEGIN token signals the start of the program, and the END token signals its completion. Braces "{ }" group Interpress instructions. A group of instructions enclosed in braces is called a *body*. Grouping instructions shows which instructions belong to which page. These groups are called *page bodies*.

Our simple program has only one page body; it contains the instructions to add 1 and 2. There is also a *preamble body* immediately following the BEGIN that supplies initial data values for all pages, and which, in this example, contains no instructions.

Our simple program will push 1 and 2 onto the stack, then pop and add them, pushing the result 3 back onto the stack. It will also print a blank page (and the printer will probably complain that we have terminated with a value left on the stack). We have not included any instructions for printing the results. Actually, Interpress does not have any built-in operators for printing computational results. This may seem strange in a language designed for output of information, but the fact is that such operators are not usually needed. Interpress typically images strings, graphics, and pictures, supplied as part of the input program. Computation usually takes place before the creation of the Interpress program, with the results expressed as a string of digit characters.

In fact, it is considered poor form to do computations at the printer when it can be avoided, for two reasons. For one thing, the printer is optimized for imaging, not calculating, and arithmetic may be done less efficiently at the printer than on a more general-purpose machine (or in a more general-purpose language). Second, because one printer may serve a number of document sources, it is rude to tie up this limited resource with computations that can be performed elsewhere.

Printing of computational results is possible, but you must write your own operator to determine the appropriate image to draw for a numerical value. We have done this in Appendix C. By copying these "magic" operators into your Interpress programs, you can experiment with the base-language operations and display the results on the page. (You may also be able to display the results of an experiment with the message mechanism used to report warnings, errors, and comments. See the section on error recovery.)

Arithmetic Operators

The following is a list of the arithmetic operations available in Interpress:

<a:Number> ABS → <c:Number>
<a:Number> <b:Number> ADD → <c:Number>
<a:Number> CEILING → <c:Number>
<a:Number> <b:Number> DIV → <c:Number>
<a:Number> FLOOR→ <c:Number>
<a:Number> <b:Number> MOD → <c:Number>
<a:Number> <b:Number> MUL → <c:Number>
<a:Number> NEG → <c:Number>

$$<\text{a:Number}> \ <\text{b:Number}> \ \text{REM} \rightarrow \ <\text{c:Number}>$$
$$<\text{a:Number}> \ \text{ROUND} \rightarrow \ <\text{c:Number}>$$
$$<\text{a:Number}> \ <\text{b:Number}> \ \text{SUB} \rightarrow \ <\text{c:Number}>$$
$$<\text{a:Number}> \ \text{TRUNC} \rightarrow \ <\text{c:Number}>$$

The actions of these operators are straightforward. (Descriptions of all operators and their actions are provided in Appendix B for reference.) The MOD and REM operators are subtly different. Both produce the remainder when dealing with positive numbers (11 4 MOD gives 3). If a/b is negative, however, the results of the two operators are different:

$$-11 \ 4 \ \text{MOD} \quad \text{produces} \ 1$$

whereas

$$-11 \ 4 \ \text{REM} \quad \text{produces} \ -3$$

The most difficult part of arithmetic operations may be converting from the familiar infix notation to the postfix order. Here are some examples:

Ceiling $((3 + 5) \times 2.1 - 4 / 7.3)$ becomes
    3 5 ADD 2.1 MUL 4 7.3 DIV SUB CEILING
$((1 + 2) \times 3 + 4) \times 5 + 6$ becomes
    1 2 ADD 3 MUL 4 ADD 5 MUL 6 ADD
$6 + 5 \times (4 + 3 \times (2 + 1))$ becomes
    6 5 4 3 2 1 ADD MUL ADD MUL ADD

Stack Operators

Our look at arithmetic operations shows that careful planning is sometimes needed to arrange for the proper operands to reach the proper operators in the proper order at the proper time. This is much easier when we have tools to rearrange the order of objects on the stack. This way, if we need to perform a calculation and the necessary operands are not on the top of the stack or are not in the proper order, we just move them around.

The operators to move stack elements are EXCH and ROLL:

$$<\text{x:Any}> \ <\text{y:Any}> \ \text{EXCH} \rightarrow \ <\text{y}> \ <\text{x}>$$
$$<x_1\text{:Any}>...<x_{\text{depth}}\text{:Any}> \ <\text{depth:Cardinal}> \ <\text{moveFirst:Cardinal}>$$
$$\text{ROLL} \rightarrow \ <x_{\text{moveFirst}+1}>...<x_{\text{depth}}> \ <x_1>...<x_{\text{moveFirst}}>$$

The EXCH operator exchanges the order of the top two objects on the stack. For example, $7 / (2 + 3)$ could be handled as 2 3 ADD 7 EXCH DIV.

The ROLL operator does a cyclic permutation of the top *depth* stack items. A ROLL is handy for moving any item to the top of the stack, or for moving the top item down to some position within the stack. A series of ROLLs can produce any arrangement of the stack items. Just ROLL the deepest item into place, then the second deepest, and so on until all are correctly positioned. Some examples of the ROLL operation are shown in Figure 2.3. An n 1 ROLL will move the nth-from-the-top item to the top. An n n–1 ROLL will move the top item to be the nth-from-the-top item.

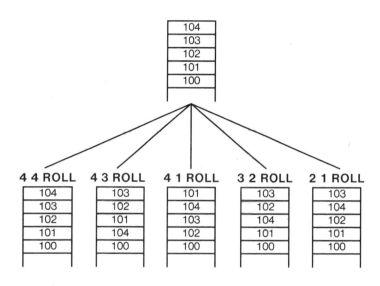

Figure 2.3 Examples of the ROLL operator.

We have also seen that operators often have the nasty habit of consuming their operands. For example, the TYPE operator will tell you what type an object is, but in the process destroys the object. You can test the type, and decide what to do, but you no longer have the original object on which to do it. What is useful here is the ability to duplicate objects on the stack, so that you can test the copy and still retain the original.

The operations to reproduce stack items are DUP and COPY:

$$<x{:}Any> \text{ DUP} \rightarrow <x> \ <x>$$
$$<x_1{:}Any>...<x_{depth}{:}Any> \ <depth{:}Cardinal>$$
$$\text{COPY} \rightarrow <x_1>...<x_{depth}> \ <x_1>...<x_{depth}>$$

DUP makes a copy of the top stack element. COPY uses the top item *depth* to determine how many items to copy, and then makes a copy of the next *depth* items. The following instructions use DUP to calculate $(1+3/7)^2$:

$$1\ 3\ 7\ \text{DIV ADD DUP MUL}$$

The operator POP removes an unwanted item from the stack:

$$<\text{x:Any}>\text{POP} \rightarrow\ <\ >$$

Figure 2.4 illustrates the stack operations.

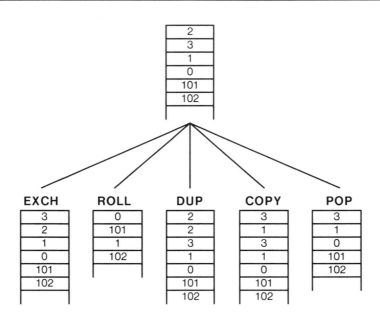

Figure 2.4 Examples of STACK operators.

Frame Variables

Some of our examples may seem a little silly because they involve only operations on numerical constants. "2+1" does not look as useful as "x:=x+1." So you may wonder if there are variables where items may be saved (other than on the stack). The answer is that there is an array of at least 50 such variables, called the *frame*. You can move an object from the stack into a frame variable and save it there. You can also place a copy of a frame-variable value back on the stack when it is needed. Like the stack, frame variables will save data objects of any type. As with variables in other languages, when a frame variable is assigned a new value, the previous value is lost. The operators for moving objects to and from the frame are FSET and FGET (see Figure 2.5).

$$<\text{j:Cardinal}>\ \text{FGET} \rightarrow\ <\text{x:Any}>$$
$$<\text{x:Any}>\ <\text{j:Cardinal}>\ \text{FSET} \rightarrow\ <\ >$$

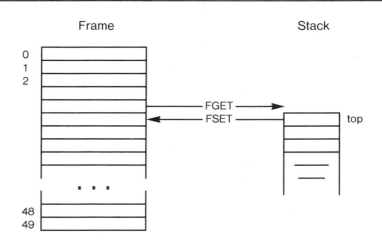

Figure 2.5 Moving items from and to the frame.

The variables in the frame are identified by an index. Printers will support at least 50 variables with indices between 0 and 49 inclusive. 0 FGET gets the value of frame variable 0 and places it on the stack. 5 3 FSET will store the number 5 in frame variable 3. Both the 3 and 5 are removed from the stack. Note that, although FSET consumes the stack data in the process of setting the frame, FGET does *not* alter the frame variable when it copies it onto the stack. This means that you can store an object in the frame just once, and then get copies of it whenever you need them. This is useful for saving objects that may be used in several places during the construction of a page image, such as the set of fonts that are used on the page.

Our example "x: = x + 1," if we let frame variable 7 play the role of x, would become

$$7\ \text{FGET}\ 1\ \text{ADD}\ 7\ \text{FSET}$$

As we shall see later, the frame acts as a set of local variables for composed operators. It also offers a mechanism for communicating a set of initial data items to every page.

Vectors

Interpress supplies a way to bundle a collection of data objects and then treat them as a single object. This feature is heavily used in Interpress. Individual character codes are bundled into a string vector; pixel values are bundled into a sample vector; instructions for printing the document are collected in an instructions vector; and there are many other cases. Basically, whenever it is natural to treat a collection of data as a unit (to save them, to pass them to an operator, or just to give them some structure), it is done with a vector.

Vectors are like arrays, records, or structures in other programming languages; however, there are differences. An Interpress vector is a collection of existing data. You must have the values in hand when you make the vector. You cannot make a vector and fill in the values later. Furthermore, a vector is a read-only object. You cannot change the value of an object in a vector. If you want to change the value of a vector element, you construct an entirely new vector with the desired values. Vectors are heterogeneous; like objects on the stack or in the frame, the elements of a vector can be of assorted types. They are constructed by placing the prospective vector elements on the stack and then applying the MAKEVEC or MAKEVECLU operator.

$$<x_1:Any>...<x_n:Any> <n:Cardinal> \text{ MAKEVEC} \rightarrow <v:Vector>$$

$$<x_1:Any>...<x_n:Any> <l:Cardinal> <u:Cardinal>$$
$$\text{MAKEVECLU} \rightarrow <v:Vector>$$

The vector elements are identified by an index. Each vector contains a *lower bound*, which is the index of the first element. The elements are then numbered sequentially; thus, if l is the index of the first element, and there are n elements, then $u = l + n - 1$ is the index of the last element or the *upper bound*. You specify these bounds when you make the vector. The MAKEVEC operator takes the number of elements n as an operand, as well as the element values. It produces a vector with lower bound 0 and upper bound $n-1$.

The operator MAKEVECLU takes the lower- and upper-bound values as arguments, and produces a vector from the next $n = u - l + 1$ stack items. The lower bound is a cardinal, so 0 is the lowest possible value for the lower bound (negative values are not allowed).

You can find the lower bound and number of elements for a vector by means of the SHAPE operator.

$$<v:Vector> \text{ SHAPE} \rightarrow <l:Cardinal> <n:Cardinal>$$

Note that this operator consumes the vector in determining its shape. So, if you still want to use the vector after determining its shape, you should first duplicate it or store it in the frame.

Vector elements can be extracted with the GET operator:

$$< v{:}Vector> \ \ <j{:}Cardinal> \ \ GET \rightarrow \ <x{:}Any>$$

GET takes the vector and element index as operands and returns the desired element. Again, the vector is consumed by this operation, so it must first be duplicated or saved if more than one element is to be extracted. (Most Interpress interpreters represent vectors internally as a pointer to the component elements, so duplicating the vector is really just duplicating a pointer.)

An example of a series of vector operations is shown in Figure 2.6.

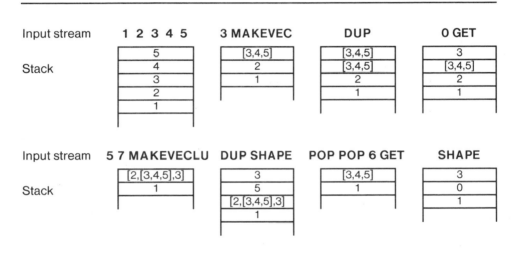

Figure 2.6 A sequence of vector operations.

Property Vectors

One use of vectors is for *property vectors.* These are ordinary vectors, but with a special interpretation placed on their elements. Property vectors contain an even number of elements and the elements are considered in pairs.

The first component of each pair is a *property name.* The second component of each pair is a *value.* A property name should be an identifier, a vector of identifiers, or a cardinal number. Although there is no rule that specifies these types, other types may not be recognized by the operators that deal with property vectors.

The GETP and GETPROP operators are used to extract values from a property vector:

<v:Vector> <propName:Any> GETP → <value:Any>
<v:Vector> <propName:Any>
GETPROP → <0:Cardinal> or <value:Any> <1:Cardinal>

You use GETP when you are certain that the desired property name is in the vector. GETP takes the vector and the desired name as operands and searches the vector for the first occurrence of that name, returning the corresponding value. The name and vector are consumed in the process. An example is shown in Figure 2.7.

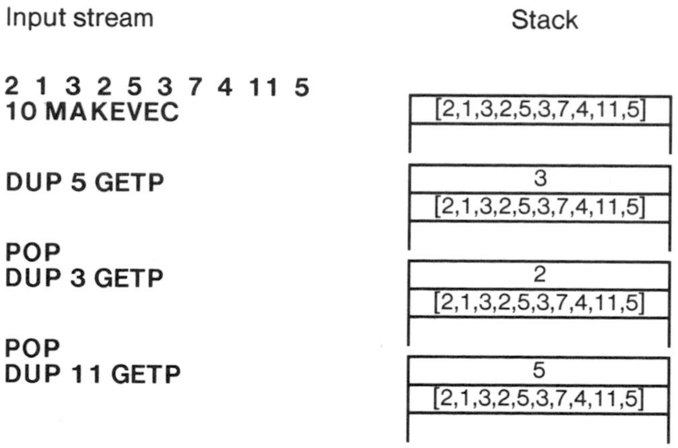

Input stream	Stack
2 1 3 2 5 3 7 4 11 5 **10 MAKEVEC**	[2,1,3,2,5,3,7,4,11,5]
DUP 5 GETP	3 [2,1,3,2,5,3,7,4,11,5]
POP **DUP 3 GETP**	2 [2,1,3,2,5,3,7,4,11,5]
POP **DUP 11 GETP**	5 [2,1,3,2,5,3,7,4,11,5]

Figure 2.7 Accessing a property vector with GETP.

You should use the GETPROP operator when you are uncertain whether the vector contains the property you are seeking. It leaves either a 1 or a 0 on the top of the stack. A 1 means it found the property, and a 0 means it did not. If it did find the property name, the corresponding value is returned beneath the 1. We shall see in later sections how you can test the top item and decide what to do, based on whether GETPROP was successful. Figure 2.8 shows examples of the use of GETPROP.

Property vectors illustrate the usefulness of the identifier type. They allow you to access data items by name, rather than by number. For example, suppose you wanted to associate the names "white," "light-gray," "dark-gray," and "black" with the numerical values 0.0, 0.3, 0.7, and 1.0, respectively. You could build a property vector to do this:

```
Identifier   "white"       0.0
Identifier   "light-gray"  0.3
Identifier   "dark-gray"   0.7
Identifier   "black"       1.0
8 MAKEVEC
```

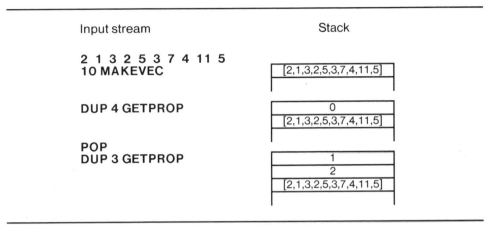

Figure 2.8 Accessing a property vector with GETPROP.

You can now use GETP to access these values by name. For example,

```
Identifier   "light-gray"   GETP
```

acting on the vector would return 0.3 as the result.

Although property vectors typically use identifiers as property names, numbers are sometimes useful. For example, an Interpress fontDescription is a property vector that describes a font. Various properties of the font (its name, version, overall metrics, character drawing operators, character dimensions, and so on) are accessed by identifier names. However, the properties for individual characters (for example, the character's width) are accessed by the numerical character code.

It is possible to construct a property vector that has several entries with the same name:

```
Identifier   "red"     3
Identifier   "blue"    2
Identifier   "red"     4
Identifier   "green"   1
8 MAKEVEC
```

In this vector, we have two entries with the name "red." If you wrote

```
Identifier "red" GETP
```

would you get the value 3 or 4? The answer is 3. The property vector is searched, starting with the lowest index (deepest on the stack when the vector is made). The first entry that matches the name is returned. The "red 3" entry is the first pushed on to the stack, so it will have the lowest index, and will be the first found.

There are occasions when it is useful to combine property vectors, such as when you wish to add a few new characters to a fontDescription. You can create a property vector describing your new characters, and merge it with the property vector describing the characters in the original font. The operator that does this is MERGEPROP.

$$<v_1\text{:Vector}> \ <v_2\text{:Vector}> \ \text{MERGEPROP} \rightarrow \ <v_3\text{:Vector}>$$

The operator will combine two property vectors into one property vector. You may wonder what happens if the two vectors both contain the same property name but with different values. In this case, the elements of the topmost vector are searched before those of the vector below it. The operator acts as though the two vectors were first exchanged, then expanded into their constituent elements, and finally formed into one property vector. In the example in Figure 2.9, the result is 3 because this value is the first matching element of the top vector that underwent the merge.

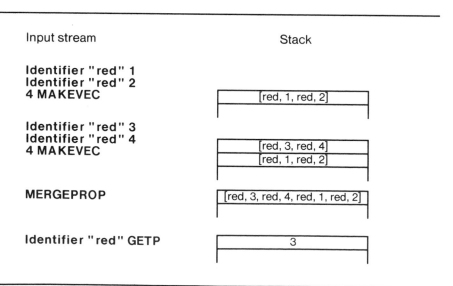

Figure 2.9 Merging property vectors with identical property names.

Interpress leaves the form of merged property vectors up to the printer. One implementation would be simply to append the two vectors, as we have shown in Figure 2.9. Another approach would be to remove elements that can never be reached by GETP and GETPROP. Because this is left open to the particular device, the results of GET and SHAPE on a merged property vector are device dependent. Interpress does not specify the number or order of elements in a merged property vector; it indicates only that the vector must behave properly under GETPROP and GETP.

Universal Names

When you are using identifiers to find items in a property vector, there is a danger of inadvertently using the same name for two different elements in the vector. This may not be as much of a problem for the property vectors you build and control as it is for finding objects in the printer's environment. For example, you might install on your printer two different fonts that happen to have the same name. If this should happen, you would always get one of them, and never reach the other. To help avoid name collisions, a scheme called *universal names* was devised. A universal name is not a single identifier but rather a vector of identifiers.

The first identifier in the vector, called a *universal identifier,* is a name that an organization has registered in the Interpress Universal Registry (for example, "Xerox," "DEC," "Wang"). Only the organization that registered the name should use it in creating new universal names. The organization is responsible for all names that begin with its universal identifier. It can, in turn, form a registry for the second identifier in the vector and allocate responsibility for maintaining unique names, accordingly. The scheme is thus a hierarchical naming system, much like the hierarchical file-directory system that maintains distinct names for files in many computer operating systems. Therefore, you should not be surprised to find a vector of identifiers used as the property name in a property vector.

Boolean and Relational Operators

Interpress supplies operators for Boolean operations (AND, OR, and NOT):

<a:Cardinal> <b:Cardinal> AND → <c:Cardinal>
<a:Cardinal> <b:Cardinal> OR → <c:Cardinal>
<b:Cardinal> NOT → <c:Cardinal>

A value of 0 is regarded as *false,* and any other value means *true.* A true result is expressed as the number 1. The AND operator returns 1 if both a and b are nonzero, and 0 otherwise. The OR operator returns 0 if both a and b are zero, and 1 otherwise. The NOT operator returns 1 if b is zero, and 0 otherwise.

A relational operator allows you to compare quantities to get a Boolean result. The operators GT, GE, and EQ test for greater than, greater than or equal to, and equal to respectively.

$$<a:Number> <b:Number> \text{ GT} \rightarrow <c:Cardinal>$$
$$<a:Number> <b:Number> \text{ GE} \rightarrow <c:Cardinal>$$
$$<a:Any> <b:Any> \text{ EQ} \rightarrow <c:Cardinal>$$

The GT and GE operators require numbers as arguments. The GT operator will return c=1 if a > b and c=0 otherwise. The GE operator tests a ≥ b. The EQ operator compares two numbers or two identifiers but returns 0 (false) if operands of any other type are used. The tests for not equal to, less than or equal to, and less than can be made by following the relational tests with a NOT operator.

The following are some examples of relational and Boolean expressions and the corresponding Interpress code. We assume frame variable 1 acts as x and frame variable 2 acts as y:

x > y becomes
  1 FGET 2 FGET GT

(y > 0) and (x < 1) becomes
  2 FGET 0 GT 1 FGET 1 GE NOT AND

(x = 0) or (x = y) becomes
  1 FGET 0 EQ 1 FGET 2 FGET EQ OR
  or 1 FGET DUP NOT EXCH 2 FGET EQ OR

((x < 3) and (y ≠ 6)) or (x ≥ 4) becomes
  1 FGET 3 GE NOT 2 FGET 6 EQ NOT AND 1 FGET 4 GE OR

Control Operators

Now that you have seen how to compare quantities, you are probably asking how you can use the test results to control the execution of your Interpress program. Interpress supplies an IF operator that will conditionally execute a body of instructions.

$$<i:Cardinal> \text{ IF} <b:Body> \rightarrow <\text{effect on the stack depends on i and b}>$$

where the instructions in b are executed if i is nonzero and are skipped otherwise. Remember that a body is a series of Interpress instructions enclosed in braces:

{Interpress Instructions}

The IF operator removes a cardinal from the stack, and the following body is executed if, and only if, it is true (nonzero). Note that our notation describing this operator is a little different from that used for previous operators in that we have shown the body following the operator. Although the Interpress standard shows the body to the left, as though popped from the stack, Interpress has been designed so that bodies can always follow the operators that use them. There can be no intervening operations between an operator that needs a body and the body itself, guaranteeing that you can send the operator before the body in the token stream.

The Interpress interpreter will encounter the IF operator before it encounters the body. By the time it sees the body, it knows whether to execute that body or to discard it. Thus, the interpreter can deal with the potentially large group of instructions in the body as they are scanned. It does not have to save them on the stack as an argument for the IF. Therefore bodies and the operators that use them are an exception to the postfix-ordering rule. Body operators precede the bodies in the standard Interpress encoding.

The following are examples of IF statements and their Interpress equivalents (again, we assume frame variable 1 is used for x):

if x = 1 then push 3 onto the stack
1 FGET 1 EQ IF {3}

if the top element is a vector, replace it with its first element
DUP TYPE 3 EQ IF {0 GET}

if there are more than 2 elements in a vector, get the third
DUP SHAPE 2 GT IF {2 ADD GET}

One peculiarity about the Interpress IF operator is that changes made to the frame during the execution of the body do not survive beyond the scope of the body, as illustrated by Example 2.2.

Example 2.2

```
  3 1 FSET              --places 3 in frame variable 1--
    1 IF                --executes the following body--
    {
      5 1 FSET          --changes frame variable 1 to 5--
```

```
    1 FGET              --places the number 5 on the stack--
  }
1 FGET                  --places the number 3 on the stack--
                        --because the original frame is restored--
                        --outside of the body--
```

The reason for this strange behavior is that Interpress executes the body of the IF by means of the same mechanism used to execute composed operators, which are described later in this chapter. The frame serves as a set of local variables for composed operators, variables that have no effect beyond the scope of the operator. This restoration of the frame means that any conditional alterations of the frame must be done via the stack. For example, the statement

$$\text{if } x > 0 \text{ then } x: = x - 1$$

would look like Example 2.3 in Interpress.

Example 2.3

```
1 FGET                  --get x--
DUP                     --copy for the test--
0 GT IF                 --if x is positive--
  {
    1 SUB               --then subtract 1--
  }
1 FSET                  --store x back whether or not it changed--
```

The calculation is performed on the stack, and the result is saved back in the frame only after the completion of the IF body, so the change will be permanent.

There is also a mechanism in Interpress for constructing if-then-else statements. It requires the use of the IFELSE operator

$$<\text{i:Cardinal}> \text{ IFELSE } <\text{b:Body}> \rightarrow$$
$$<\text{effect on the stack depends on i and b}> <\text{c:Cardinal}>$$

If $i = 0$, IFELSE discards the body and returns a cardinal $c = 1$ on the stack. If $i = 1$, IFELSE executes the body in the same manner as an IF operator, then returns a cardinal $c = 0$ on the stack.

IFELSE is designed to work in conjunction with IF to produce results equivalent to conventional-language results produced by

$$\text{If i then } B_1 \text{ else } B_2$$

This effect is achieved by the following code in Interpress:

$$\text{i IFELSE } B_1 \text{ IF } B_2$$

Note that if $i=0$, body B_1 is ignored and a 1 is returned to the stack. Therefore, the IF operator will find the stack containing 1, and the body B_2 will be executed. On the other hand, if $i=1$, IFELSE will cause the body B_1 to be executed, and a 0 will be returned to the stack. In this case, the IF operator will find the stack containing 0, and the body B_2 will be ignored.

Similarly, the conventional-language effect produced by

$$\text{If } i_1 \text{ then } B_1 \text{ else if } i_2 \text{ then } B_2 \text{ else } B_3$$

is obtained in Interpress by the code

$$i_1 \text{ IFELSE } B_1 \text{ IF } \{i_2 \text{ IFELSE } B_2 \text{ IF } B_3\}$$

Let's see how this works. If $i_1 = 1$, the first IFELSE causes the body B_1 to be executed and returns a 0 to the stack. This 0 is coupled with the entire body $\{i_2$ IFELSE B_2 IF $B_3\}$ as the operands of the first IF. Therefore, the first IF causes that entire body to be ignored.

If $i_1 = 0$, the first IFELSE causes the body B_1 to be ignored, and returns a 1 to the stack. This 1 is coupled with the entire body $\{i_2$ IFELSE B_2 IF $B_3\}$ as the operands of the first IF. Therefore, the first IF will cause that entire body to be executed. At this point, we have ignored the body B_1 and are faced with the execution of

$$i_2 \text{ IFELSE } B_2 \text{ IF } B_3$$

This is exactly the form previously discussed, and it produces the execution of B_2 if $i_2 = 1$, or B_3 if $i_2 = 0$. The peculiar structure of IFELSE owes to the fact that each body operator can have only one body operand in Interpress.

Assuming frame variables 1 and 2 act as x and y, the following are examples of IF statements written in Interpress:

if $x < 0$ then $y: = -x$ else $y: = x$
   1 FGET DUP 0 GE NOT IF {NEG} 2 FSET

if $x < y$ then $x: = x + 1$ else $y: = y + 4$
   1 FGET 2 FGET GE NOT IFELSE {1 FGET 1 ADD 1} IF {2 FGET 4 ADD 2} FSET

replace a 2-element vector x with lower bound 0 by its largest element
   1 FGET DUP DUP 0 GET EXCH 1 GET GT IFELSE {0} IF {1} GET

if x is a property vector with the property "creation-date," then return the property value; otherwise, return 0
   1 FGET Identifier "creation-date" GETPROP NOT IF {0}

if $x \geq 0$ then (if $y \geq 0$ then push 1 else push 4)
else (if $y \geq 0$ then push 2 else push 3)

1 FGET 0 GE IFELSE {2 FGET 0 GE IFELSE {1} IF {4}}
IF {2 FGET 0 GE IFELSE {2} IF {3}}

Imager Variables

Besides the operand stack and the frame, Interpress has a third, highly specialized storage structure called the *imager variables*, a collection of variables that govern the description of the imaging process. The variables contain information such as the current "pen" position on the page, the width of its strokes, the color of its ink, and the font style for characters. There are 25 of these variables for you to get and set, as listed in Table 2.1. You can access them by their index value using the IGET and ISET functions (see Figure 2.10). Unlike those in the stack and frame, each of these variables has a specific type. The imager variables are not simply data storage, but rather active participants in the imaging process.

Table 2.1 Imager variables.

Name	Index	Type
Persistent:		
DCScpx, DCScpy	0, 1	number
correctMX, correctMY	2, 3	number
Nonpersistent:		
T	4	transformation
priorityImportant	5	cardinal
mediumXSize, mediumYSize	6, 7	number
fieldXMin, fieldYMin	8, 9	number
fieldXMax, fieldYMax	10, 11	number
font	12	font
color	13	color
noImage	14	cardinal
strokeWidth	15	number
strokeEnd	16	cardinal
underlineStart	17	number
amplifySpace	18	number
correctPass	19	cardinal
correctShrink	20	number
correctTX, correctTY	21, 22	number
strokeJoint	23	cardinal
clipper	24	clipper

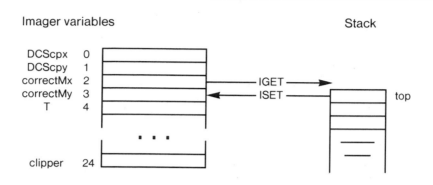

Figure 2.10 Accessing imager variables.

ISET removes an index j and value x from the stack and saves the value in the imager variable with that index:

$$<x{:}Any> \ <j{:}Cardinal> \ \text{ISET} \rightarrow <>$$

IGET copies the value of an imager variable onto the stack:

$$<j{:}Cardinal> \ \text{IGET} \rightarrow <x{:}Any>$$

Many of the imager variables have special "setting" functions that should be used rather than the general ISET. Because using values obtained with IGET sometimes can generally lead to problems, it is not recommended.

The description of the individual variables and their effects will be considered in the chapters on the imaging functions they control. A summary of the variables is given in Appendix B.

Composed Operators

Interpress offers you a way to write your own operators, corresponding to the subroutines, procedures, and functions of other programming languages. Writing your own operators extends Interpress' facilities. It can make the printer absorb some of the work of matching the imaging operators supplied to the imaging operators needed. For example, Interpress does not have a dedicated operator for drawing a circle, but it does have operators for drawing arcs from which a circle can be constructed. If your application draws numerous circles, you may wish to construct a circle-drawing operator. Judicious use of composed operators can result in simpler, more compact Interpress programs.

Constructing a composed operator is quite simple. You need only make the Interpress instructions that define your operator into a body by enclosing them in braces and then place a MAKESIMPLECO operator before the body:

MAKESIMPLECO < b:Body > → < o:Operator >

The resulting operator is left on the stack. The operator can be treated like any other data object (for example, duplicated, rolled, or stored in the frame), and it can be executed. The operator is actually composed of the body and a copy of the frame (see Figure 2.11). This frame copy is made by MAKESIMPLECO and serves as the initial values for the operator's local variables.

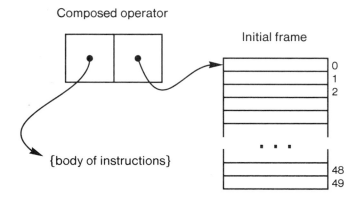

Figure 2.11 Composed operators contain a body of instructions and an initial frame.

To execute your composed operator, you use the DO operator:

< o:Operator > DO → < effect on the stack depends on o >

DO removes the operator o from the stack and executes it (see Figure 2.12).

Like other operators, the operator o can use anything it finds on the stack as its operands and can leave any results on the stack. Consider creating and executing an operator to compute the average of two numbers on the stack, as shown in Example 2.4.

Example 2.4

```
MAKESIMPLECO
{
    ADD
```

```
    2 DIV
}                           --creates the operator--
DO                          --executes it--
```

Because DO consumes the operator, you will usually store it in the frame or duplicate it on the stack before executing it. In Example 2.5 we build our averaging operator, store it in frame variable 3, then later use it to average two numbers.

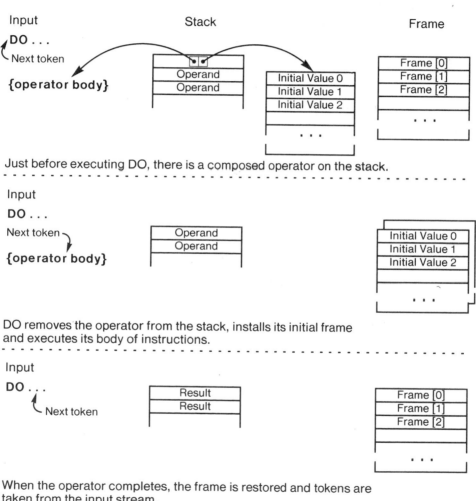

Figure 2.12 Execution of a composed operator by DO.

Example 2.5

```
MAKESIMPLECO
{
   ADD
   2 DIV
}                          --define the operator--
3 FSET                     --save it--
. . .
47 23                      --numbers to be averaged--
3 FGET                     --get the operator--
DO                         --execute it--
                           --the result 35 will be left on the stack--
```

Consider a pseudorandom-number generator that expects a seed value on the stack, and returns a pseudorandom number between 0 and 1, which may be used as the seed for the next number, as shown in Example 2.6.

Example 2.6

```
MAKESIMPLECO
{
   16384 MUL
   509 MUL
   3463 ADD
   16384 MOD
   16384 DIV
}
4 FSET
. . .
0                          --initial seed--
4 FGET
DO                         --first random number--
```

The frame acts as a set of local variables for a composed operator. Thus, your operator can use whatever frame variables you like without fear of colliding with another operator's usage. You can create an operator that stores values in variables 1, 2, and 3. Later, at the time the operator is called, you may have decided to store some other important information in frame variables 1 and 2. No problem! Each operator uses its own private copy of the frame. The frame being used during your operator's execution is different from the one in use when the operator is called; so changes made by the operator disappear when the operator completes execution, and the previous frame is restored. In effect, each operator has its own private copy of at least 50 variables to use however it wishes. This also means that communication of results must be done via the stack. If you try to save the answer in the frame, it will be lost when the operator completes execution.

Because each composed operator has its own copy of the frame, you can specify initial frame values for the operator. Every time the operator is called, it will start with the same values in its frame. By arranging for the constant data and functions that an operator needs to be in the initial frame, you can avoid their inclusion in the operator body. The operator's initial frame is a copy of the frame that existed when the operator was created. To set up an operator frame, simply store the appropriate values just before making the operator. For example, if we wished to get the three constants used in the random-number generator operator from its frame (instead of listing them in the body), we could write the program in Example 2.7.

Example 2.7

```
16384 1 FSET        --save constants in frame--
509 2 FSET
3463 3 FSET
MAKESIMPLECO        --define random-number operator--
{
   1 FGET MUL        --use the frame in effect for this definition--
   2 FGET MUL
   3 FGET ADD
   1 FGET MOD
   1 FGET DIV
}
4 FSET              --save the operator in the frame--
```

It will not matter what values are stored in frame variables 1, 2, and 3 when the operator is called because on execution, first off, a copy of the frame that existed when we defined the operator is installed. During execution, the proper constants are in the frame. After execution, the caller's frame is restored.

The imager variables can act either as global variables (like those in the stack), or as local variables (like those in the frame), depending on how a composed operator is called. If you use the DO operator to execute your function, and it changes the value of an imager variable, then that change will persist after your function has completed execution. This may not always be what you desire. For example, if you create an operator that draws a circle with a 1-millimeter-wide line, then one thing this operator must do is set the imager variable that controls the stroke width to 1 millimeter. Now, if you are also drawing figures with 2-millimeter-wide lines, then every time you finish drawing a circle, you must remember to reset the stroke width to 2 millimeters.

This is annoying enough, but if you copy an operator into your program that someone else created, you may not know what it alters and what must be repaired. To avoid this problem, Interpress has a DOSAVEALL operator:

<o:Operator> DOSAVEALL → <effect on the stack depends on o>

Like DO, DOSAVEALL causes a composed operator to be executed; in addition, it has the bonus of saving a copy of the imager variables just before execution, and of restoring them on completion. When you use DOSAVEALL, the imager variables are protected, just as the frame is. The operator can make all the changes it likes; when it is finished, the values are restored.

There is a third operator called DOSAVE; it saves most, but not all, imager variables.

<o:Operator> DOSAVE → <effect on the stack depends on o>

The first four imager variables save current position and text-line length. They are called *persistent* imager variables, because changes to them persist if an operator is executed with DOSAVE. All other variables are called *nonpersistent* because they are saved and restored, so changes to them do not remain (see Figure 2.13).

DOSAVE is particularly useful in imaging strings of characters. Here we want the shift in position to persist as we move from one character to the next, but we want to be protected from all other changes to the imager state that may occur when characters are drawn.

Sometimes we are mainly interested in the protection to imager variables and the frame that the DOSAVE mechanism offers. We may wish to draw some object, changing imager variables as needed, and then easily restore the imager variables when we are done. We could do this by creating a composed operator and immediately executing it:

MAKESIMPLECO {body to be executed} DOSAVE

If we use this approach, however, the printer must save the instructions in the body somewhere and construct a composed operator that references them. The body must be saved because an operator might be copied and executed many times. If we intend to execute the body only once, and immediately, this is needless overhead. A more efficient approach is to save the frame and imager variables, to execute the body as it is scanned (not saving it), and to restore the frame and imager variables when the end of the body is found. This is what is done by DOSAVESIMPLEBODY.

DOSAVESIMPLEBODY <b:Body> → <effect on the stack depends on b>

DOSAVESIMPLEBODY offers a more efficient approach to the one-time execution of bodies.

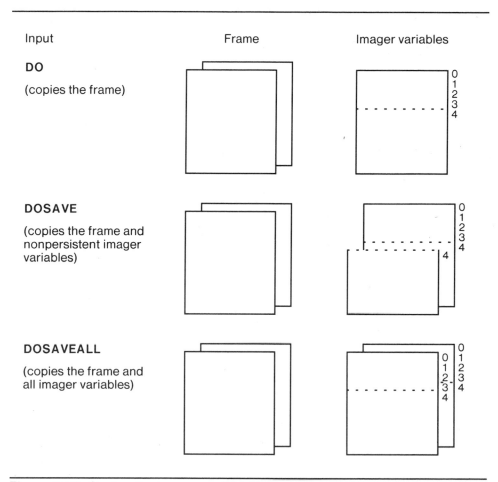

Figure 2.13 Saving the imager variables depends on the version of DO used to execute the operator.

Operators from the Environment

Interpress supplies an excellent selection of built-in primitive operators. We have also seen a mechanism for constructing your own composed operators. One further source of operators is the printer's environment, which gives a standard way of dealing with nonstandard operators. Suppose there is an operator that you would find terribly useful. You might construct a composed operator for it, and then include its definition in every Interpress master. If you are friends with the folks who maintain the printer's software, however, there is an alternative: you can ask them to write the operator for you and install it in the printer's environment. Then, when you need it, you find it at the printer, instead of making it. This is done with the FINDOPERATOR operator:

<v:Vector> FINDOPERATOR → <o:Operator>

The v is a vector of identifiers that gives the universal name for the operator. The printer will compare this name against the operators in its environment and, if it finds a match, place the operator on the stack. Once you have the operator, you can execute it with DO, DOSAVE, or DOSAVEALL.

For example, suppose an operator that draws a logo is installed at the printer. Assume that the operator's universal name is [IPBook, Operator, logo]. To draw the logo, you would use the code in Example 2.8.

Example 2.8

```
Identifier "IPBook"
Identifier "Operator"
Identifier "logo"
3 MAKEVEC
FINDOPERATOR
DOSAVEALL
```

Note that your master needs to find an operator only once, because it can store that operator in the frame. Thereafter, it can fetch a copy of the operator from the frame whenever it needs one.

Recursive Operators

Interpress has no looping operator. Loops are not needed for the representation of documents, and they tend to place the work on the printer (the shared resource), rather than on the creator. You can write recursive operators, though, so the power of repeated execution is available. You will probably never need to generate a recursive operator in a real-life application. Nevertheless, we shall present them here to show how they can be used—because playing with the language can be fun.

A recursive procedure calls itself, and the simplest form in Pascal is that shown in Example 2.9.

Example 2.9

```
program infinite;
procedure foo;            (* define a procedure *)
```

```
BEGIN
   foo                      (* which calls itself *)
END;

BEGIN
   foo                      (* initial call of the procedure *)
END
```

Note that this procedure will continue to call itself indefinitely until the machine breaks, usually with a stack overflow–the counterpart of an infinite loop. The equivalent Interpress expression appears in Example 2.10.

Example 2.10

```
MAKESIMPLECO              --define a procedure--
{
   DUP DO
}                         --that duplicates and calls itself--
DUP DO                    --initial execution--
```

Recursive operators are executed with DUP DO, DUP DOSAVE, or DUP DOSAVEALL. In this way, the operator is executed, but a copy remains on the stack for use in a recursive invocation. You would write the composed operator so that it expects a copy of itself on the top of the stack. If any other operands are needed, they can be placed on the stack beneath the operator, and rolled to the top as needed. Of course, a recursive operator should always contain some stopping test so that it does not call itself forever, as Example 2.10 does.

The classic recursion example is the factorial operator. Example 2.11 shows how it looks in Interpress.

Example 2.11

```
MAKESIMPLECO
{
   EXCH                   --operator on top, so exchange with n--
   DUP 1 GT IFELSE        --test to see if done--
   {
      DUP 1 SUB           --not done, find n-1--
      3 1 ROLL            --stack has factorial op, n-1, n--
      DUP DO              --recursive call on n-1--
      MUL
   }                      --result is n times (n-1)!-
   IF
   {
      EXCH
      POP
```

```
    }                           --done, so remove operator--
  }                             --end of operator--
  1 FSET                        --save the operator in frame[1]--
```

To calculate 5! using this operator you would say

```
                    5 1 FGET
                    DUP DO
```

As a second example, consider an operator that takes a vector and expands it into its individual elements–the opposite of MAKEVEC (see Example 2.12).

Example 2.12

```
    MAKESIMPLECO                --one-time overall operator--
    {
      DUP SHAPE                 --find shape--
      EXCH
      DUP 3 2 ROLL              --set up arguments--
      ADD
      MAKESIMPLECO              --recursive operator for expansion--
      {
        4 3 ROLL                --move the operator out of the way--
        2 COPY
        EQ IFELSE               --compare index to limit to see if done--
        {
          POP
          POP
          POP
          POP
        }                       --if so, remove operands--
        IF                      --otherwise must get an element--
        {
          4 3 ROLL              --move index and vector to top--
          2 COPY
          GET                   --copy to save them and extract element--
          5 4 ROLL              --roll it out of the way--
          1 ADD                 --increment index--
          4 2 ROLL              --put operands back in order--
          DUP DO
        }                       --recursively expand remainder--
      }                         --end of recursive operator--
      DUP DO                    --initial call of recursive operator--
    }
```

Error Recovery

What happens if something goes wrong? What if you divide by zero, or an argument has the wrong type, or a vector has too few elements? Interpress has a mechanism for describing errors. Errors should be reported to you, but the exact means of reporting depends on the printer (an error report might be displayed on a terminal, written in a file, or printed on an error page). There are four types of error reports:

1. *Appearance warning:* an approximation to the ideal image was made, but the content was preserved. A font substitution is an example of an appearance warning.
2. *Appearance error:* the resulting image will not be correct. For example, if the printer cannot print a pictorial image and has omitted that image from the page, an appearance error is generated.
3. *Master warning:* a problem was found in the master, but processing could continue. For example, a printer might handle arithmetic overflow by ignoring the overflow bits and forging ahead. If so, it notifies you through a master warning.
4. *Master error:* the error is so severe that normal processing cannot continue. The printer will try to reset its state (its stack, frame, imager variables, and input stream) to a clean condition, and proceed from there. The process is called *mark recovery*. You actually control this process by indicating what the clean states are, and setting marks.

A mark is a special stack item that serves as a "fire wall" on the stack. Normal operators cannot consume marks, and marks cannot be copied, rolled, or exchanged. Items below a mark on the stack are protected until the mark is removed. You place a mark on the stack with the MARK operator

$$<x_1:Any>...<x_n:Any> <n:Cardinal>$$
$$MARK \rightarrow <m:Mark> <x_1>...<x_n>$$

Note that you do not have to place the mark on the top of the stack, and that you must supply an operand to indicate how deep it should go.

To remove a mark, you have an UNMARK operator:

$$<m:Mark> <x_1:Any>...<x_n:Any> <n:Cardinal>$$
$$UNMARK \rightarrow <x_1>...<x_n>$$

There is also an operator UNMARK0, which is equivalent to 0 UNMARK. UNMARK0 plays a major roll in mark recovery, the process of recovering from an error.

$$<m:Mark> UNMARK0 \rightarrow <>$$

During mark recovery, the stack is popped down to and including a mark. Marks indicate a clean state for the stack. Upon recovery from a master error, the stack is cleared until it contains only the elements that were below the mark.

Cleaning the stack is not sufficient; you should also restore the frame and imager variables to a good state. Marks offer a means of doing so by remembering their *context* (the operator body which created them). During mark recovery, the frame and imager variables are restored to those of the context that set the mark. Therefore, if you set a mark before executing an operator, errors in the execution of the operator cause both the stack and the frame (and also the imager variables if you used DOSAVEALL) to be restored to their state before execution.

Finally, the position in the input stream must be shifted to a point where execution can safely resume. The stream is scanned until an UNMARK0 is found in the same context as the mark. Note that we look for an UNMARK0 operator and not for an UNMARK operator. This is because on mark recovery the stack is cleared down to and including the mark. The general UNMARK operator applies when stack items are to be left above the mark. That will not be the case on mark recovery, however, and it would not be a good point at which to resume execution. Therefore, when using marks for error recovery, remove them with UNMARK0.

Specification of the state for error recovery might look like Example 2.13.

Example 2.13

```
0 MARK
DOSAVESIMPLEBODY
{
                          --body of Interpress instructions--
}
UNMARK0
                          --remaining Interpress instructions--
```

If a master error occurs within the body, mark recovery allows you to resume processing the "remaining Interpress instructions."

Note that, within the body of Interpress instructions in Example 2.13, you can set another mark and create another layer of error-recovery information. You can have several marks on the stack at one time. On mark recovery, the stack is cleared to the top-most mark, where there can be found an UNMARK0 with the same context (see Figure 2.14).

In summary, there are five points that you should remember about mark recovery:

1. The stack is popped until a mark is on top.
2. If the context in which the mark was placed on the stack no longer exists, the mark is popped, and there is another mark recovery.

3. Otherwise, composed operators in execution are exited (restoring frames and imager variables) until the one that placed the mark is executed.
4. The input for this operator is skipped until an UNMARK0 is found.
5. The UNMARK0 removes the mark and execution proceeds.

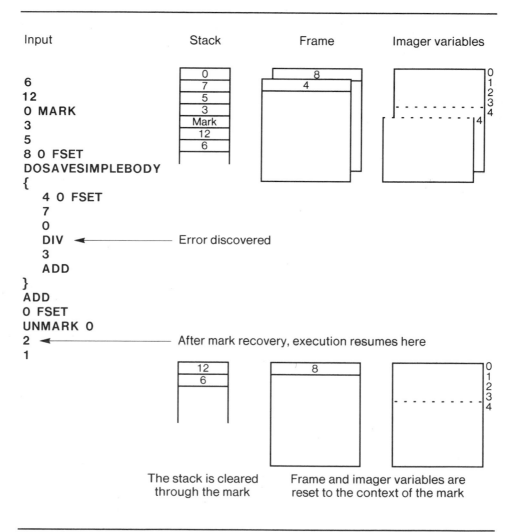

```
Input

6
12
0 MARK
3
5
8 0 FSET
DOSAVESIMPLEBODY
{
    4 0 FSET
    7
    0
    DIV     ◄─────────── Error discovered
    3
    ADD
}
ADD
0 FSET
UNMARK 0
2       ◄─────────── After mark recovery, execution resumes here
1
```

The stack is cleared through the mark

Frame and imager variables are reset to the context of the mark

Figure 2.14 Mark recovery.

Besides facilitating error recovery, marks are handy for protecting from stack underflow, and for counting stack items. A COUNT operator counts how many items are above the mark.

$$<\text{m:Mark}>\ <\text{x}_1\text{:Any}>...<\text{x}_n\text{:Any}>$$
$$\text{COUNT} \rightarrow <\text{m:Mark}>\ <\text{x}_1>...<\text{x}_n>\ <\text{n:Cardinal}>$$

For example, if you had an operator that returned a varying number of results, you could determine how many items were returned by placing a mark, doing the operation, and then using COUNT to count the results. Note that COUNT UNMARK will remove a mark when you do not know its depth, and COUNT MAKEVEC POP removes all items above a mark.

You can also use MARK and COUNT to make a vector of an arbitrary number of elements. You place a mark on the stack, followed by the vector elements. You then count the elements and form the vector. Finally, you remove the mark. The Interpress code is shown in Example 2.14.

Example 2.14

```
0 MARK                --mark the stack--
                      --push the vector elements here--
COUNT                 --tell how many elements are in the vector--
MAKEVEC               --make the vector--
1 UNMARK              --remove the mark from beneath the vector--
```

We have seen how to control error recovery, but not how to generate errors. Of course, some errors are generated automatically by the system if it finds something wrong, but it is handy to be able to make your own tests and to generate your own errors in your own operators. Interpress provides the ERROR operator for this purpose:

$$<\text{message:Vector of Cardinal}>\ <\text{code:Cardinal}>\ \text{ERROR} \rightarrow\ <\ >$$

The operator lets you specify an error message and a number code. The message is a vector of ISO 646 character codes describing the error; the number code indicates the severity of the error. It can have the values:

0	master error
10	master warning
50	appearance error
60	appearance warning
100	comment

Note that this supplies a comment feature, which prints the message in the error log. This can be handy in tracing execution and in debugging. Example 2.15 shows an operator that extracts an element from a vector, but gives a master warning and 0 value if the index is out of range, rather than the master error that GET would cause.

Example 2.15

```
MAKESIMPLECO              --assumes vector v and index i--
{                         --on top of the stack vi--
  2 COPY                  --copy both vector and index vivi--
  DUP                     --copy index vivii--
  3 1 ROLL                --move vector to top viiiv--
  SHAPE                   --get the vector shape viiiln--
  EXCH                    --lower bound to top viiinl--
  DUP 4 3 ROLL            --stack has viilinl--
  ADD                     --calculate upper bound viliiu--
  EXCH GT                 --test upper bound vilib--
  3 2 ROLL                --roll for lower bound test vibli--
  GE                      --test lower bound vibb--
  AND                     --combine the two tests--
  IFELSE                  --if passes both--
  {
    GET                   --get the element--
  }
  IF                      --otherwise--
  {
    POP                   --remove arguments--
    POP
    0                     --and generate error--
    66 65 68 32 73 78 68 69 88   --"BAD INDEX"--
    9 MAKEVEC
    10 ERROR
  }
}
```

The Interpress Virtual Machine

Let us visualize a model for an Interpress machine and review some of the ideas presented in this chapter. Figure 2.15 is a representation of an Interpress interpreter and the associated data structures.

An Interpress master is defined in terms of a collection of Interpress *operators* and *operands*. Every operand has a particular type. Each operand and operator is a *token* and can be made self-defining as to the specific nature of its content and to its length in bytes, so that the token stream can be readily parsed on the fly. You can see the token stream containing a master at the top of Figure 2.15. It flows into the processor as a serial byte stream. You can find

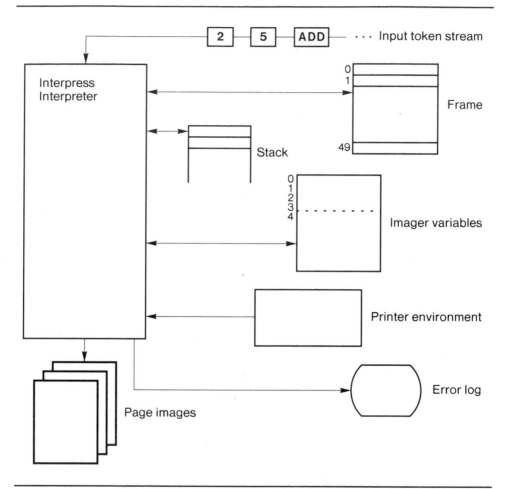

Figure 2.15 The Interpress virtual machine.

more about the encoding of an Interpress master and the structure of tokens in Appendix B.

The *stack* offers a dynamic working space for temporary storage of operands. It operates in much the same manner as a cafeteria-style dish-stacking mechanism. Operands from the token stream and the results of operators are pushed onto the stack. The placing of an operand on top of the stack causes all operands previously pushed onto the stack to be pushed down one level. The stack can contain any mix of operand types in any sequence. Operands are popped off the stack when used as the arguments for an operator's execution.

A second primary functional element is the *frame,* which is a collection of elements that are used for the storage and retrieval of any of the operand types of the Interpress language. Each element has an addressing integer index associated with it. These index values serve as the means for addressing an element for either storage or retrieval operations.

The Interpress language permits a frame to contain an arbitrary (not less than 50) but implementation-specific number of elements. Most Interpress implementations will contain exactly 50 elements in their frame, so let's use that value. Think of these 50 elements as 50 pigeonholes, numbered from 0 to 49, each of which can contain an operand of any type. Interpress includes the operators FSET and FGET that store and retrieve operands from the frame. The type of operand contained within each element of the frame can vary over time; for example, element 0 could contain a number at one time, a vector at another time, and an identifier at still another time. The frame constitutes a space, available in addition to the stack, for the processing operations associated with the printing of a page.

The third main functional element in an Interpress machine is the *imager state.* The imager state is a collection of 25 storage elements, each of which holds a specific *imager variable.* For purposes of discussion, imager variables have names, but their access in the imager state is by means of their associated integer indices. The imager variables are divided into two classes, designated as *persistent* and *nonpersistent,* that behave differently under the various DO operations.

An imager variable is a parameter that controls some facet of the imaging process, such as the thickness of lines and curves or the current font being used. Imager variables generally do not change frequently.

At the beginning of the processing of each page in the document, the imager variables are reset to a standard set of values. These standard values are specified in Appendix B. The current transformation and the medium, field, and clipper variables are initialized to values that depend on the device and page. Interpress includes operators for the modification of these variables during the processing of a page.

The Interpress machine also has access to objects in the printer's environment, such as fonts, colors, and special operators. These objects are installed on the printer, and each printer can have its own set. They are identified by universal names to avoid duplication or confusion in names. The objects are obtained for use by means of operators with FIND in their names, such as FINDOPERATOR.

The Interpress language includes a simple programming language that provides for the conventional manipulation, storage, and retrieval of operands and also offers a limited set of computational and decision-making capabilities. In addition, the Interpress language creates the images to be placed on the output medium. Many of the parameters that control this process are held in the imager state. The imaging model and the operators that define images are described in the following chapters.

The primary output of an Interpress program is a collection of page images. Interpress builds the images that will ultimately be displayed on the output medium in an incremental fashion. These increments are created by imager processes, and then are accumulated in the page image. When all the images that represent the contents of a page have been accumulated, the page image is ready for printing.

Finally, there is a mechanism for displaying or logging messages and errors. The exact form of this message output depends on the printing device.

Summary

You have seen that Interpress contains much of the power of conventional programming languages. You have been shown how to perform arithmetic and logical operations. Data can be manipulated on the stack, stored in the frame, and organized in vectors. Property vectors allow data to be accessed by name as well as by index. The operations that create vectors are summarized in Figure 2.16. You have also seen how to write conditional statements and

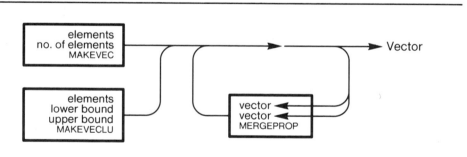

Figure 2.16 Constructing vectors.

construct your own operators. The operations are shown in Figure 2.17. This is a powerful set of capabilities, although the way in which they are expressed may seem awkward at times. Remember that Interpress was designed as a language to be generated by machines for machines. It was intended to communicate document information and page images efficiently, accurately, and in a way that can use a broad class of imaging devices effectively. The following chapters describe how Interpress models images and the features it offers for rendering them.

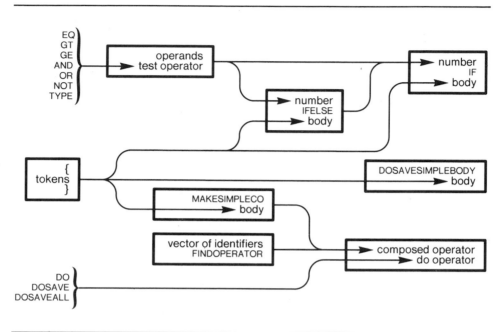

Figure 2.17 Using bodies and composed operators.

Chapter 3
IMAGING
FUNDAMENTALS

*"My ways are
as broad as the
king's high road,
and my means
lie in an
inkstand."*

ROBERT SOUTHEY

The purpose of an Interpress master is to describe the image presented on the page or screen. In Interpress, the page is generated in an incremental fashion, synthesized from a series of primitive images. A complex page is created by making a sequence of simple changes to a blank page image. Each imaging operation adds further primitive images to the page image, until the complete page has been generated. The Interpress master incrementally defines what the image should look like. Because defining the image is not necessarily the same as actually drawing it, this synthesis is independent of how the output device creates the physical image. The physical-image creation could also be incremental, or the full image could be created in a storage medium and then converted to its physical form.

In this and following chapters, we shall consider Interpress facilities for page description. In this chapter, we present the basic Interpress imaging model which governs what is meant by an imaging primitive and how properties such as its shape, size, orientation, and color are specified. It also defines what we mean by a page, how you place new image primitives on a page, and how new imaging primitives interact with previous image components. These basic topics apply to all imaging primitives. In the subsequent chapters, we shall introduce specific imaging primitives for text, line graphics, and raster images.

The Imaging Model

The shape and position of a primitive image is established by what Interpress calls a *mask*. We can conceptualize a mask as follows. Prepare a stencil out of some flat, opaque material by cutting an opening that has the shape, but not necessarily the size or orientation, of the desired primitive image. Stretch the stencil until its opening matches the size of the desired image. (Interpress allows uniform scaling and stretching, which you cannot do with a real paper stencil.) Orient and position the deformed stencil so that the shape that it defines is located at the desired place and at the desired orientation on the medium. A mask has now been created (see Figure 3.1).

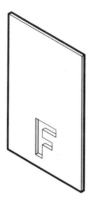

Figure 3.1 A mask.

Interpress supports three classes of masks (see Figure 3.2). The first class consists of masks for geometric graphic constructions (sometimes called synthetic graphics), such as straight lines, arcs, curves, and polygons. These masks are described by the geometrical quantities that define their shape (for example, the endpoints and width of a line segment).

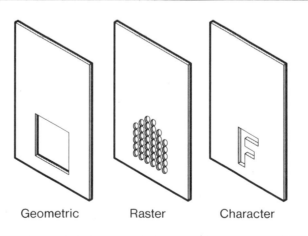

Geometric   Raster   Character

Figure 3.2 Classes of masks.

A second class of masks provides binary raster images or scanned images. These masks define rectangular arrays of spots in which each spot can be either an open or a closed hole in the imaginary stencil.

The third class of masks contains characters. Character masks are defined by the desired font and the character code. A character is a built-in shape that you reference, rather than a shape that you have to construct.

In the Interpress imaging model, ink is pressed onto the page through the mask stencil and a clipping stencil. The ink (Interpress calls it a *color*) can be black, gray, white, red, yellow, or any other color value or pattern.

In Figure 3.3, the color (represented by the parallelogram) is set at a certain value by the Interpress program, and the "F" is added to the page through the clipping region using a mask that defines the character's shape.

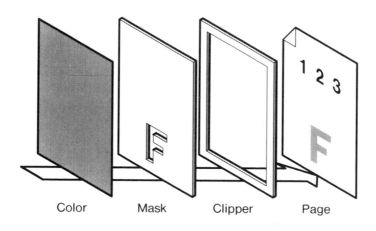

Color   Mask   Clipper   Page

Figure 3.3 The Interpress imaging model.

In summary, the Interpress imaging model involves four objects:

1. *The page image.* A two-dimensional image that accumulates the primitive image being laid down.
2. *The clipper.* A stencil that protects portions of the page from imaging.
3. *The mask.* A specification for the shape, orientation, and position of a primitive image to be added to the page image; that is, it determines precisely where the page image will be modified. In effect, the mask specifies an opening (or stencil) through which ink can be pressed onto the current page image.

4. *The color*. A specification for the ink to be pressed through the mask onto the page image, so that the primitive image can be added to the page image. With one minor exception, Interpress colors are opaque. That is, when a color is pressed onto the page, it completely overprints any color already placed on the page. Colors do not mix; a yellow overprinted on a blue produces yellow, not green or black or white.

Imager Variables

Interpress has 24 imager variables which contain imaging-state information (data used in creating images). Because these variables typically apply to several of the objects imaged, they are set as a state, rather than being individually specified with each object. The imager variables are global in the sense that any composed operator can access them. In Chapter 2, we discussed a mechanism for saving and restoring imager variables. This mechanism is connected with the execution of composed operators, allowing them to alter the imager variables freely, because the variables are restored to their original state as soon as the operation is completed.

Executing a composed operator with DOSAVEALL causes a copy of the imager variables to be saved and then restored after the operation is complete. If you execute a composed operator with a DO, however, the imager variables are not saved or restored, and any changes made by the operator will be preserved.

We explained how clever, if incautious, programmers can save and restore individual imager variables using the Interpress stack and the IGET and ISET operators. We do not recommend this procedure because a printer might also maintain hidden imager variables. These variables describe a printer's internal state; as such, they are saved and restored with DOSAVEALL but are not accessible through the IGET and ISET mechanisms.

The imager variables supply information required in the construction of masks, tell what color should be used, and control the imaging process. For example, one of the imager variables is called *noImage*. In effect, this variable can place an imaginary barrier in front of a page so that that page will not be changed by the mask and color (see Figure 3.4). This control thus can turn off the imaging process without affecting the other behavior of the printer.

If the noImage variable has the value 0, the page image can be altered. If, however, this variable has a nonzero value, the page image cannot be altered. This variable normally is used during the execution of the CORRECT operator (discussed in Chapter 4). It also may be set by direct action in the master. By setting noImage, you can execute Interpress instructions and note their side effects without actually altering the page. This variable is automatically set to the value 0 at the beginning of each page.

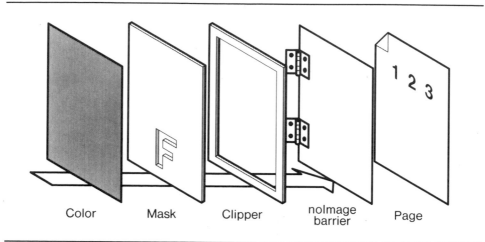

Color   Mask   Clipper   noImage
barrier   Page

Figure 3.4 The noImage variable can prevent the page from being altered.

The Interpress Coordinate System

The ultimate goal of an Interpress master is to create a set of images on an output medium. Because Interpress is independent of the output medium, an Interpress master could be created for skywriting with images measured in tens of feet, for printing on paper or displaying on a cathode-ray tube (CRT) screen with images measured in fractions of an inch, for creating microfilm with images measured in thousandths of inches, and even for describing microcircuit surfaces with images measured in microns. The Interpress operators are independent of these considerations; the only difference is a scaling component in the language. We refer to a document as though it were printed on paper (regardless of the actual output medium), and we will call its images pages.

Every image must be defined in terms of a coordinate system. The general practice is to choose a point of reference in the space of the image, establish a pair of orthogonal axes with that point of reference as its origin, and choose a unit of measurement along each of the two axes. The measurement unit is usually the same along the two axes, but it need not be. The points that are contained within the image can then be defined either by giving their position as measured within this coordinate system, or by providing some rules, expressed with respect to the coordinate system, to determine the points within the image. (For example, you can give the equation of the points of a curve that constitutes a portion of the image, or you can make a statement such as, "All the points that lie within the interior of a closed curve.")

For device independence, the masks in an Interpress master must be expressed in a coordinate system independent of the printing-device coordinates. The designers of Interpress chose to express this coordinate system in terms of meters, with a vertical y axis and a horizontal x axis, and the origin in the lower-left corner of the page, as shown in Figure 3.5. This is called the *Interpress coordinate system* (ICS).

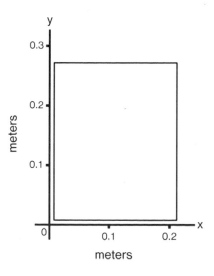

Figure 3.5 The Interpress coordinate system.

You can construct and position an image primitive by using meters as the unit of length. For example, a simple mask creation operator is MASKRECTANGLE.

<x:Number> <y:Number> <w:Number> <h:Number>
MASKRECTANGLE → < >

The numbers x and y give the (x,y) coordinate of the lower-left corner of a rectangle. The w and h numbers provide the rectangle's width and height. To draw a rectangle 2 centimeters high and 4 centimeters wide, with the lower-left corner 5 centimeters from the left and 10 centimeters from the bottom of the paper, you would write the code in Example 3.1 (see Figure 3.6).

Example 3.1

```
Header "Interpress/Xerox/3.0 "
BEGIN
   { }
   {
      0.05 0.1 0.04 0.02 MASKRECTANGLE
   }
END
```

Figure 3.6 The result of Example 3.1.

Example 3.1, a complete Interpress program, contains the mandatory (but empty, in this instance) preamble body and one page body. The page body images one mask, which is a rectangle. The default color is black, and the coordinate units are meters.

A transformation converts from the coordinates in the Interpress program to those the printing device uses. The mapping functions of the transformation make possible the arbitrary translation, rotation, and scaling (sizing) of images from the coordinate systems in which they are defined to the printer's coordinate system. Each printer initializes this transformation to convert from meters to the units it desires in its *device coordinate system* (DCS). The transformation is stored in an imager variable named T and is called the *current transformation*. At the start of each page body, the printer sets T to be the ICS-to-DCS transformation. For the preamble, T is initialized to the identity transformation. (This is not always true. We shall see in Chapter 8 how you can start each page in a page coordinate system, which can, for example, include offsets of the origin from the corner of the page for binding margins.)

Interpress Linear Transformations

The transformations supported by Interpress are represented by the following relationships:

$$x_{to} = a \times x_{from} + b \times y_{from} + c$$
$$y_{to} = d \times x_{from} + e \times y_{from} + f$$

where coordinates are converted from the (x_{from}, y_{from}) system to the (x_{to}, y_{to}) system. We can think of applying the transformation as a way of allowing you to express coordinates in a new system (x_{from}, y_{from}) by giving you a way to convert them to an original or old system (x_{to}, y_{to}). The equations express the image in a new coordinate system, and offer a way to transform results to those of the old system.

The ICS serves as a universal interface coordinate system. This decoupling of the printer's coordinate system from the creator's coordinate system by means of the ICS is one of the major factors that makes the Interpress master device independent. Every printer can use its own coordinate system with the origin placement, axes orientation, and units of measurement best suited to how it images the page. The transformation from the ICS to the printer's DCS is a straightforward one. It may be different for each printer, but each printer knows the specific transformation that it requires for this process.

For the ICS-to-DCS transformation, (x_{from}, y_{from}) will be Interpress coordinates (x_{ICS}, y_{ICS}); and (x_{to}, y_{to}) will be device coordinates (x_{DCS}, y_{DCS}). At the start of each page, the printer establishes the appropriate a, b, c, d, e and f values for the transformation equations.

These equations can be expressed in the form of a matrix multiplication:

$$[x_{to} \; y_{to} \; 1] = [x_{from} \; y_{from} \; 1] \times \begin{bmatrix} a & d & 0 \\ b & e & 0 \\ c & f & 1 \end{bmatrix}$$

where the point in the *to* space is represented by the vector $[x_{to}\ y_{to}\ 1]$ and the point in the *from* space is represented by the vector $[x_{from}\ y_{from}\ 1]$. The transformation is represented by the 3×3 matrix

$$\begin{bmatrix} a & d & 0 \\ b & e & 0 \\ c & f & 1 \end{bmatrix}$$

Performing the vector-by-matrix multiplication shown by the asterisk maps a point in the *from* coordinate system to a point in the *to* coordinate system. This matrix multiplication is accomplished by multiplying and summing the elements of the vector by the elements of each of the matrix columns.

Mapping ICS points into the DCS is expressed in this vector-matrix representation by the following:

$$[x_{DCS}\ y_{DCS}\ 1] = [x_{ICS}\ y_{ICS}\ 1] \times \begin{bmatrix} a_{ID} & d_{ID} & 0 \\ b_{ID} & e_{ID} & 0 \\ c_{ID} & f_{ID} & 1 \end{bmatrix}$$

where the matrix represents the initial T transformation. We shall refer to this as T_{ID}.

To give you the greatest degree of freedom, Interpress permits you to use any coordinate system for the description of the images that you wish to print. Indeed, each image can be expressed in its own most suitable coordinate framework, independent of all other images.

You can adopt the coordinate system that you wish to use in the master by modifying the current transformation T. You must change T so that, instead of converting from the Interpress coordinates to device coordinates (ICS to DCS), it converts from your desired *master coordinate system* (MCS) to device coordinates (MCS to DCS). For example, you can use units of inches, rather than meters, to express your image, provided you first change T such that it transforms from inches to the device coordinates. To decide how to change T, think of performing the transformation in two steps. The first is to convert from your MCS to the ICS, and the second is to convert from the ICS to the DCS (see Figure 3.7). Using P_{MCS} to represent the point in your master coordinates, P_{ICS} for the point in Interpress coordinates, and T_{MI} as the transformation to convert from master to Interpress coordinates, we can write

$$P_{ICS} = P_{MCS} \times T_{MI}$$

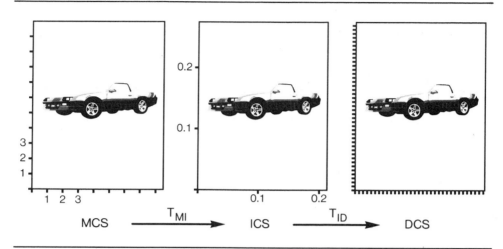

Figure 3.7 Changing coordinate systems.

The transformation to a point P_{DCS} in device coordinates can be written as

$$P_{DCS} = P_{ICS} \times T_{ID}$$

If we now substitute the expression for P_{ICS} from the first expression into the second, we have the following:

$$P_{DCS} = (P_{MCS} \times T_{MI}) \times T_{ID}$$

This expression merely makes the symbolic statement that a point P_{MCS} is mapped to a point P_{DCS} by means of a two-step process.

The preceding expression shows a series of matrix multiplications that we can group differently to read

$$P_{DCS} = P_{MCS} \times (T_{MI} \times T_{ID})$$

If we had a transformation T_{MD} that converted directly from MCS to DCS, we could write

$$P_{DCS} = P_{MCS} \times T_{MD}$$

Comparing these two equations, and remembering that they must be true for all points, we realize that

$$T_{MD} = T_{MI} \times T_{ID}$$

The critical point of this vector–matrix representation is that the two matrices can be "multiplied" using a formal matrix-multiplication process to produce one matrix of the same 3×3 type. The single matrix resulting from the matrix product represents one transformation, T_{MD}, that is the *concatenation* of the transformation T_{MI} with the transformation T_{ID}.

The transformation that converts from some MCS to the DCS is equal to the product of the transformation matrices from master to Interpress, and from Interpress to device coordinates. Because the current transformation T is initialized to T_{ID} at the start of each page, you must multiply T by T_{MI} if you want to switch to some other coordinates (MCS). If you prefer to use inches instead of meters, you must multiply T by the transformation from inches to meters.

We will need two new operations from Interpress: a way to create the T_{MI} transformation, and a way to multiply this transformation into the current transformation T.

Converting from inches to meters is just a change of scale. There are 0.0254 meters per inch, so

$$x_{ICS} = 0.0254\ x_{MCS}$$
$$y_{ICS} = 0.0254\ y_{MCS}$$

This gives a transformation matrix of

$$T_{MI} = \begin{bmatrix} 0.0254 & 0 & 0 \\ 0 & 0.0254 & 0 \\ 0 & 0 & 1 \end{bmatrix}$$

The Interpress operator to build a transformation of this form is SCALE.

$$<\text{s:Number}> \text{SCALE} \rightarrow <\text{t:Transformation}>$$

The SCALE operator constructs the transformation

$$\begin{bmatrix} s & 0 & 0 \\ 0 & s & 0 \\ 0 & 0 & 1 \end{bmatrix}$$

The Interpress operator for multiplying a transformation with T and making the result the current transformation is called CONCATT. The name comes from "concatenating" a transformation onto "T."

$$<\text{t:Transformation}> \text{CONCATT} \rightarrow <\ >$$

The effect of left concatenating a scale onto T is to establish a new coordinate system with units of measure that must be multiplied by s to produce the units of measure of the old coordinate system. The transformation converts coordinates from the new system back to the old one (see Figure 3.8).

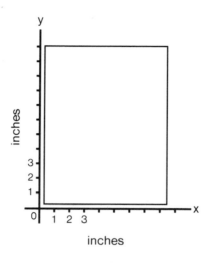

Figure 3.8 A master coordinate system arising from a change of scale.

If you wanted to draw a rectangle 2 inches high and 4 inches wide, with the lower-left corner 1 inch from the left and 3 inches from the bottom of the paper, you could use Example 3.2 (see Figure 3.9).

Example 3.2

```
Header "Interpress/Xerox/3.0 "   --header--
BEGIN                            --start of the master--
   { }                           --preamble--
   {                             --start of the page--
      0.0254 SCALE               --transform inches to meters--
      CONCATT                    --set inches as MCS units--
      1 3 4 2 MASKRECTANGLE      --draw the rectangle--
   }                             --end of the page--
END                              --end of master--
```

Figure 3.9 The result of Example 3.2.

Next consider a shift in coordinate position. Suppose that you do not mind specifying lengths in meters, but prefer the origin to be near the center of the page, rather than in the lower-left corner (see Figure 3.10). You wish to shift the origin up by 0.14 meters and right by 0.11 meters. That means that these values must be added to each point so that a point at (0,0) in the MCS will become (0.11,0.14) in the ICS.

$$x_{ICS} = x_{MCS} + 0.11$$
$$y_{ICS} = y_{MCS} + 0.14$$

We see that this yields the transformation

$$\begin{bmatrix} 1 & 0 & 0 \\ 0 & 1 & 0 \\ 0.11 & 0.14 & 1 \end{bmatrix}$$

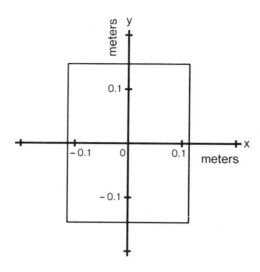

Figure 3.10 A master coordinate system arising from a translation of position.

Transformations of this form, called *translations*, are produced by the TRANSLATE operator in Interpress.

<c:Number> <f:Number> TRANSLATE → <t:Transformation>

This operator creates the transformation

$$
\begin{bmatrix}
1 & 0 & 0 \\
0 & 1 & 0 \\
c & f & 1
\end{bmatrix}
$$

The effect of left concatenating a translation onto T is to establish a new coordinate system, the origin of which is at the point (c, f) in the old coordinate system. The transformation maps coordinates from the new system back to the old one.

If you wanted to translate the origin near the center of the page, and then draw a rectangle 2 centimeters high and 4 centimeters wide with the lower-left corner at (–0.03, –0.01), you would write the program in Example 3.3 (see Figure 3.11).

Example 3.3

```
Header "Interpress/Xerox/3.0 "              --header--
BEGIN                                        --start of the master--
   { }                                       --preamble--
   {                                         --start of the page--
     0.11 0.14 TRANSLATE                     --move the origin for a--
     CONCATT                                 --new coordinate system--
     -0.03 -0.01 0.04 0.02 MASKRECTANGLE     --draw a box--
   }                                         --end of the page--
END                                          --end of master--
```

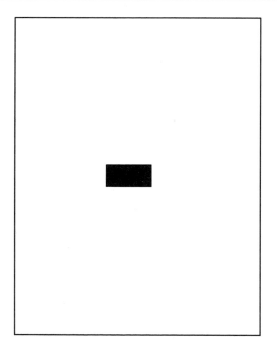

Figure 3.11 The result of Example 3.3.

Now suppose you wished both to translate the origin near the center of the page and to change the units from meters to inches. In effect, each point undergoes two transformations to convert from the master coordinates desired to the Interpress coordinates.

$$P_{ICS} = (P_{MCS} \times T_{scale}) \times T_{translate}$$

The overall transformation to device coordinates is

$$P_{DCS} = P_{MCS} \times T_{scale} \times T_{translate} \times T_{ID}$$

This can be put in place by two adjustments to the current transformation:

```
0.11 0.14 TRANSLATE        --shift origin to the center--
CONCATT
0.0254 SCALE               --and change units of length--
CONCATT
```

Note that the order in which we change T is important. In this example, we start with coordinates in meters, so to shift the origin (which is done first) we give the amount to shift in meters. We then change the scale to inches. If, however, we were to change the scale first, then we would be using inches to measure lengths when we translated. We would have to write

```
0.0254 SCALE               --change units to inches--
CONCATT
4.331 5.512 TRANSLATE      --inches required to place origin--
                           --at (0.11, 0.14) meters--
CONCATT
```

The origin is not at the exact center of the page (4.25, 5.5), because we converted the round numbers (0.11 , 0.14) from meters to inches.

As another example of scale and translation, consider changing to a coordinate system in which the origin is in the upper-left corner, and y increases as you move down, as shown in Figure 3.12. (These coordinates are often used in imaging systems that actually produce their image in this order.)

To reverse the direction of the y axis, we can scale it by –1.

$$x_{ICS} = x_{MCS}$$
$$y_{ICS} = (-1) \times y_{MCS}$$

We have changed y but not x, and the transformation matrix would be

$$\begin{bmatrix} 1 & 0 & 0 \\ 0 & -1 & 0 \\ 0 & 0 & 1 \end{bmatrix}$$

To build this, we need a new Interpress operator, called SCALE2:

$$< a:Number > \ < e:Number > \ \text{SCALE2} \rightarrow \ < t:Transformation >$$

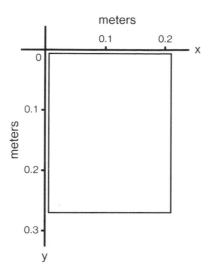

Figure 3.12   A master coordinate system with reversed y direction.

This produces a transformation of the form

$$\begin{bmatrix} a & 0 & 0 \\ 0 & e & 0 \\ 0 & 0 & 1 \end{bmatrix}$$

The effect of left concatenating this scale onto T is to establish a new coordinate system, with units of measure along the x axis that must be multiplied by the operand a, and with units of measure along the y axis that must be multiplied by the operand e to produce the units of measure of the old coordinate system along the corresponding axes.

So, to reverse the y-axis direction, we would write

```
1 -1 SCALE2
CONCATT
```

Note, however, that we are not done. We have not shifted the origin to the upper-left corner. Without this translation, our image will be off the paper and will not be drawn (see Figure 3.13). If we scale first, then we are moving

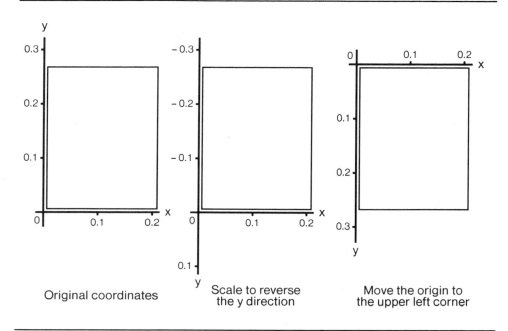

Figure 3.13 Building a transformation to reverse the y direction and move the origin.

the origin in the negative y direction. Assuming a page is 0.2794 meters high, the full transformation would be

```
1 -1 SCALE2
CONCATT
0 -0.2794 TRANSLATE
CONCATT
```

A program to draw a rectangle 2 centimeters high and 4 centimeters wide, with the lower-left corner 5 centimeters from the left and 8 from the bottom of the page using this coordinate system, is shown in Example 3.4 (see Figure 3.14).

Example 3.4

```
Header "Interpress/Xerox/3.0 "       --header--
BEGIN                                --start of the master--
   { }                               --preamble--
   {                                 --start of the page--
      1 -1 SCALE2                    --reverse y axis--
```

```
        CONCATT
        0  -0.2794 TRANSLATE                 --origin to upper left--
        CONCATT
        0.05  0.1794  0.04  0.02 MASKRECTANGLE  --draw the rectangle--
    }                                       --end of the page--
END                                         --end of master--
```

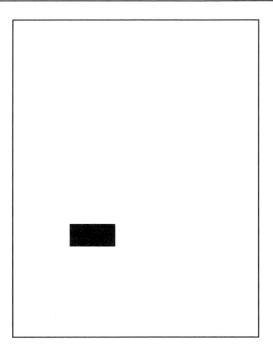

Figure 3.14 The result of Example 3.4.

In these last examples, we have modified the current transformation twice (once with a scale, and once with a translation). This corresponds to writing

$$(T_{translation} \times (T_{scale} \times T_{ID}))$$

This, in turn, is mathematically equivalent to

$$(T_{translation} \times T_{scale}) \times T_{ID}$$

Thus, an alternative way to make this transformation would be first to multiply the translation and scaling transformations together to form a single composite transformation and then to concatenate that result onto the current transformation. We can do this if we have an operator that will multiply two transformations. We do, and it is called CONCAT (with only one T).

$$<t_1:\text{Transformation}> \; <t_2:\text{Transformation}>$$
$$\text{CONCAT} \to \; <t_3:\text{Transformation}>$$

This result, t_3, is the matrix product of $t_1 \times t_2$.

Using CONCAT, we obtain Example 3.5.

Example 3.5

```
Header "Interpress/Xerox/3.0 "              --header--
BEGIN                                       --start of the master--
  { }                                       --preamble--
  {                                         --start of the page--
    0 -0.2794 TRANSLATE                     --move origin--
    1 -1 SCALE2                             --reverse y direction--
    CONCAT                                  --combine transformations--
    CONCATT                                 --fold into T--
    0.05 0.1794 0.04 0.02 MASKRECTANGLE     --draw the rectangle--
  }                                         --end of the page--
END                                         --end of master--
```

Notice how the order in which the transformations are specified is reversed so that they will be on the stack in the proper order for the CONCAT operation.

As the next problem, suppose you want to rotate the coordinates so that the x axis lies along the long edge of the paper, and the y axis lies along the short edge (landscape mode, see Figure 3.15).[†] To do this, Interpress provides an operator that creates transformations for rotations about the origin. It is called ROTATE.

$$<a:\text{Number}> \; \text{ROTATE} \to \; <t:\text{Transformation}>$$

[†]We assume that the printer's normal orientation has the x axis along the short edge. Although usually the case, Interpress does not require it; each device can make a choice as to the size of the medium and how the Interpress coordinates are positioned on it. Interpress does, however, supply a way for you to request a medium with the desired lengths for x and y directions. This can be done with the media printing instruction discussed in Chapter 8.

The resulting transformation is of the form

$$\begin{bmatrix} \cos a & \sin a & 0 \\ -\sin a & \cos a & 0 \\ 0 & 0 & 1 \end{bmatrix}$$

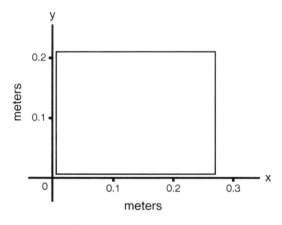

Figure 3.15 Landscape coordinates.

The angle operand a is specified in units of degrees (not radians). This means that you can specify 90-degree rotations exactly. The 90-degree rotation 90 ROTATE results in the transformation

$$\begin{bmatrix} 0 & 1 & 0 \\ -1 & 0 & 0 \\ 0 & 0 & 1 \end{bmatrix}$$

Rotating by a positive angle (measured counterclockwise) results in counterclockwise motion of the *from* coordinates with respect to the *to* (see Figure 3.16). A negative angle causes a clockwise rotation of the axes.

In our MCS, a page would be as pictured in Figure 3.17. If the printer oriented the paper in portrait mode (shorter side horizontal), it would produce the image shown in Figure 3.18.

To form the MCS-to-ICS transformation, we introduce a rotated coordinate system (RCS) as an intermediate step. Notice that the MCS coordinates are

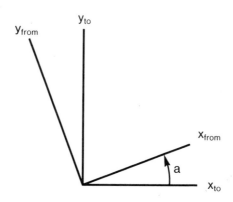

Figure 3.16 A positive angle rotates the new (x_{from}, y_{from}) coordinates.

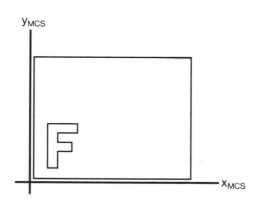

Figure 3.17 The page in master coordinates.

rotated counterclockwise by 90 degrees from the RCS coordinates (see Figure 3.19). So 90 ROTATE creates a transformation T_{MR} to convert from the MCS to RCS.

Notice also that the RCS coordinates are shifted by the width of a page (about 0.2164 meters) from the ICS coordinates (see Figure 3.20). Therefore, a transformation T_{RI} to convert from RCS to ICS would be constructed by 0.2164 0 TRANSLATE.

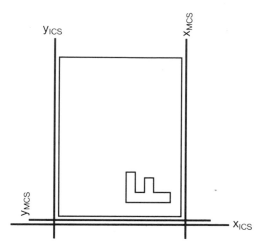

Figure 3.18 The page in Interpress coordinates.

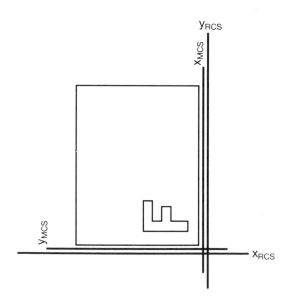

Figure 3.19 The rotated (RCS) and master (MCS) coordinate systems.

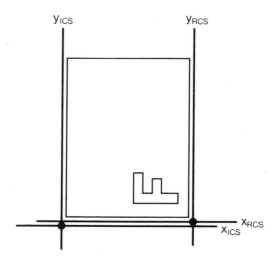

Figure 3.20 The rotated (RCS) and Interpress (ICS) coordinate systems.

The overall transformation we require takes us from master coordinates to device coordinates and has the form

$$T_{MR} \times T_{RI} \times T_{ID}$$

It can be constructed by concatenating first T_{RI} and then T_{MR} onto the current transformation T.

```
0.2164 0 TRANSLATE    --shift origin to lower-right corner--
CONCATT               --gives the RCS coordinates--
90 ROTATE             --rotate counterclockwise 90 degrees--
CONCATT               --gives the MCS coordinates--
```

Interpress provides one more operator for building transformations, called MAKET.

<a:Number> <b:Number> <c:Number>
<d:Number> <e:Number> <f:Number> MAKET → <t:Transformation>

This operator constructs the transformation

$$\begin{bmatrix} a & d & 0 \\ b & e & 0 \\ c & f & 1 \end{bmatrix}$$

MAKET is useful when the desired transformation is not naturally expressed as simple rotations, scales, and translations.

We have described masks as stencils that can be stretched, oriented, and positioned on the page. These actions are performed by transformations, which work in the same way as in changing coordinates, although the interpretation is different. When you scale the points of an object by a value less than 1, you obtain smaller numbers. Of the two interpretations, one, of course, is that we have the same object, but we have changed coordinates. If we start with an object described in inches, the result might be the same object described in meters. The alternative view is that the same coordinates apply in both cases, and the size of the object changes: you start with a length in meters and end up with a smaller length in meters.

The transformation machinery is exactly the same in these two cases; only the interpretation changes. Scaling by a small number can mean either reducing the size of the object or increasing the unit of length. Translating by a positive number can mean either keeping the coordinates fixed and moving the object in the positive direction, or keeping the object fixed and shifting the coordinates in the negative direction. Rotating by a positive angle can mean either turning the object counterclockwise or turning the coordinates clockwise.

Transformations of Masks

The Interpress transformation machinery can be used both to set up an MCS and to scale, orient, and position masks. You can use SCALE, SCALE2, TRANSLATE, ROTATE, MAKET, and CONCAT to build the transformations that you wish to apply to masks. If we call the transformation that adjusts the mask T_{MM}, then each point P_{MASK} on the mask must undergo

$$P_{DCS} = (P_{MASK} \times T_{MM}) \times (T_{MI} \times T_{ID})$$
$$= P_{MASK} \times (T_{MM} \times T_{MI} \times T_{ID})$$

To adjust masks, we must build the appropriate transformation and fold it into the overall transformation that is applied to the shape being drawn. The method for doing this in Interpress depends on the type of mask. For characters, for instance, T_{MM} determines the size and orientation of the characters in a font. The transformation is stored as part of the font and is included automatically whenever a character is shown. For raster-image masks and synthetic graphics, you must explicitly include T_{MM} in the total transformation by means of CONCATT. Let's look at some examples.

Suppose we choose inches as our coordinate units. We can draw a 1- by 1-inch rectangle at the origin as shown in Example 3.6 (see Figure 3.21).

Example 3.6

```
Header "Interpress/Xerox/3.0 "          --header--
BEGIN                                   --start of the master--
  { }                                   --preamble--
  {                                     --start of the page--
    0.0254 SCALE                        --set inches as MCS units--
    CONCATT
    0 0 1 1 MASKRECTANGLE               --draw the rectangle--
  }                                     --end of the page--
END                                     --end of master--
```

Figure 3.21 The result of Example 3.6.

We can position this mask at 3 inches to the right and 5 inches from the bottom with a translation (before drawing), as in Example 3.7 (see Figure 3.22).

Example 3.7

```
Header "Interpress/Xerox/3.0 "    --header--
BEGIN                             --start of the master--
  { }                             --preamble--
  {                               --start of the page--
    0.0254 SCALE                  --set inches as MCS units--
    CONCATT
    DOSAVESIMPLEBODY              --protect the imager variables--
    {                             --body for drawing the mask--
      3 5 TRANSLATE               --include the translation in T--
      CONCATT
      0 0 1 1 MASKRECTANGLE       --draw the rectangle--
    }                             --end of the body, restore T--
  }                               --end of the page--
END                               --end of master--
```

Figure 3.22 The result of Example 3.7.

We have enclosed the rectangle positioning and drawing within the body of a
DOSAVESIMPLEBODY. This will result in automatic saving and restoring of the
imager variables, including the current transformation T. In this way,

changes made to T to position the rectangle will not survive beyond the body that draws the rectangle.

As a second example, we can scale the square to form a rectangle 0.5 inches high and 6 inches wide, centered on an 8.5- by 11-inch page (see Example 3.8 and Figure 3.23). We do this in three steps. First, we will translate the center of the square to the origin ($T_{to\ origin}$); then, we scale it (T_{scale}); finally, we translate the center of the rectangle to the center of the page ($T_{to\ page}$). The points should be transformed according to

$$P_{MCS} = (((P_{square} \times T_{to\ origin}) \times T_{scale}) \times T_{to\ page})$$

Example 3.8

```
Header "Interpress/Xerox/3.0 "   --header--
BEGIN                            --start of the master--
  { }                            --preamble--
  {                              --start of the page--
    0.0254 SCALE                 --set inches as MCS units--
    CONCATT
    DOSAVESIMPLEBODY             --provides protection for T--
    {                            --start of body for mask--
      -0.5 -0.5 TRANSLATE        --move center of square to origin--
      6 0.5 SCALE2               --scale to 6 by 0.5--
      CONCAT                     --combine translate and scale--
      4.25 5.5 TRANSLATE         --move rectangle to center of page--
      CONCAT                     --combine with other transformations--
      CONCATT                    --fold into T--
      0 0 1 1 MASKRECTANGLE      --draw the rectangle--
    }                            --end of the body, restore T--
  }                              --end of the page--
END                              --end of master--
```

Note how this example makes use of CONCAT, which allows us to enter the component transformations in the order in which we picture them occurring. We imagine starting with the square and transforming it into the correctly-placed rectangle. If we had used just CONCATT, we would have had to enter the transformation in the reverse order, which is more natural when thinking about changing the coordinates than when thinking about changing the mask.

We can produce more efficient Interpress code if we determine the overall object transformation ourselves and send this result to the printer, instead of

Figure 3.23 The result of Example 3.8.

making the printer calculate it from the components by means of CONCAT. In Example 3.9, the overall transformation is (see Figure 3.24)

$$
\begin{bmatrix} 1 & 0 & 0 \\ 0 & 1 & 0 \\ -0.5 & -0.5 & 1 \end{bmatrix} \times \begin{bmatrix} 6 & 0 & 0 \\ 0 & 0.5 & 0 \\ 0 & 0 & 1 \end{bmatrix} \times \begin{bmatrix} 1 & 0 & 0 \\ 0 & 1 & 0 \\ 4.25 & 5.5 & 1 \end{bmatrix} = \begin{bmatrix} 6 & 0 & 0 \\ 0 & 0.5 & 0 \\ 1.25 & 5.25 & 1 \end{bmatrix}
$$

To limit numerical errors, Interpress supplies guidelines on the use of transformations. For example, a printer must guarantee accurate results only when no more than eight primitive transformations are concatenated. The Interpress standard also suggests limits on the sizes of the elements within the primitive matrices and the result matrix (see Section 5.6 of the Interpress standard).

In Example 3.10, we rotate the square counterclockwise by 30 degrees and place it in the center of the page. Again, this is a transformation that is most easily pictured as moving the center of the square to the origin, rotating about the origin, and then moving the square to the center of the page (see Figure 3.25).

Example 3.9

```
Header "Interpress/Xerox/3.0 "       --header--
BEGIN                                --start of the master--
   { }                               --preamble--
   {                                 --start of the page--
     0.0254 SCALE                    --set inches as MCS units--
     CONCATT
     DOSAVESIMPLEBODY                --provide protection for T--
     {                               --start of body for mask--
       6 0 1.25 0 0.5 5.25 MAKET     --net transformation for mask--
       CONCATT                       --folded into T--
       0 0 1 1 MASKRECTANGLE         --draw the rectangle--
     }                               --end of the body, restore T--
   }                                 --end of the page--
END                                  --end of master--
```

Figure 3.24 The result of Example 3.9.

Example 3.10

```
Header "Interpress/Xerox/3.0 "      --header--
BEGIN                               --start of the master--
  { }                               --preamble--
  {                                 --start of the page--
    0.0254 SCALE                    --set inches as MCS units--
    CONCATT
    DOSAVESIMPLEBODY                --provide protection for T--
    {                               --start of body for mask--
      -0.5 -0.5 TRANSLATE           --move center of square to origin--
      30 ROTATE                     --rotate square 30 degrees--
      CONCAT
      4.25 5.5 TRANSLATE            --move square to center of page--
      CONCAT
      CONCATT                       --fold this transformation into T--
      0 0 1 1 MASKRECTANGLE         --draw the square--
    }                               --end of the body, restore T--
  }                                 --end of the page--
END                                 --end of master--
```

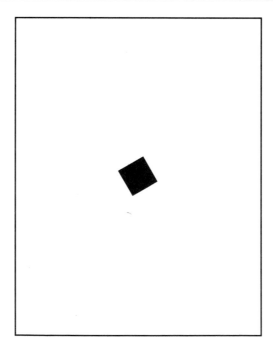

Figure 3.25 The result of Example 3.10.

Character and Pixel-Array Coordinate Systems

We mentioned that transformations scale and rotate fonts to produce the desired size and orientation of characters. This is possible only if you know the font's original size and orientation. If you know the original size, you can decide what scale factor is required to produce the size you want. In Interpress, a font is initially 1 unit high, with "up" pointing in the positive y direction. The height of the font is roughly the distance between single-spacedlines of text in the font. Sometimes called the point size or body size, it often is measured in units of points (72 points = 1 inch).[†]

Suppose you are using inches for your MCS, and you wish to print with a 10-point font. Then you want the font to be 10/72 inch high. The font, now 1 unit high, must be scaled by 10/72. You also can think of this as a mapping between coordinates. The coordinate system in which a font is 1 unit high is called the *character coordinate system* (CCS).

The font designer may find it convenient to work in units other than those of the CCS. If so, another layer of transformation must help convert from the *font-definition coordinate system* (FDCS) of the font designer to the CCS. When a character is imaged, it may be converted from the coordinates used to design it to the CCS to make it a known, uniform size, then transformed to the MCS to make it the size you want, then transformed to the ICS so that it is in coordinates on which every device can rely, and finally to the DCS needed by the actual imaging hardware (see Figure 3.26). This may seem like a lot of work, but fortunately all these transformations can first be multiplied together to yield one overall transformation.

A well-specified coordinate system is also needed when dealing with raster graphics. Each spot in the raster pattern is called a *pixel* (short for picture element), and the entire rectangular image pattern is called a *pixel array*. The natural unit of length for pixel arrays is 1 unit per pixel, but various orientations are possible. The orientation depends on the order in which the pixels in the array are scanned (the order in which the pixel values are stored in memory). Different scanning devices may sample pixel values in different orders. Likewise, different printing devices may image the pixel values in different orders.

We can use transformations on the pixel arrays to handle raster graphics, provided that we have a standard, well-defined scanning order. The creator of the pixel array can provide a transformation to convert from the original pixel ordering to the standard pixel ordering, and the printing device can introduce

---

[†]Throughout this book, we define a point to be 1/72 inch or 0.00035278 meter. Some standards hold that there are 72.3 points to the inch. Since Interpress requires that all measurements ultimately be expressed in meters, the choice of scaling, and hence also of the size of a point, is up to the master. See Chapter 4 for a discussion of fonts.

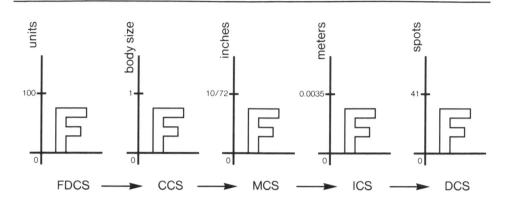

Figure 3.26 Character coordinate transformations from design to image.

a transformation from the standard ordering to the order required for printing. In Interpress, this standard ordering begins with the lower-left corner of the first pixel of the scanned image placed at the origin of the pixel-array coordinate system. Subsequent pixels along the first scan line are placed with their left sides along the y axis of this system. The lower-left corner of the first pixel of the second scan line is placed at the point (1,0), and subsequent pixels on the second scan line proceed up the line x = 1. This process is repeated, with subsequent scan lines being represented along the lines x = 2, x = 3, and so on (see Figure 3.27).

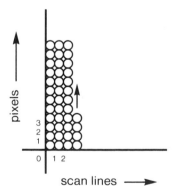

Figure 3.27 Scanning order in the pixel-array coordinate system.

The coordinate system in which pixels are 1 unit in size and have the orientation corresponding to this scanning order is called the *pixel-array coordinate system* (PCS). A pixel array undergoes a transformation to orient it in the PCS, followed by a transformation to give it the desired size, orientation, and position in the MCS you want to use, followed by a transformation to convert to the ICS that all printers understand, followed by a transformation to the DCS for actual printing. Usually, the overall transformation is the identity, so that each pixel maps to a corresponding spot on the page (see Figure 3.28).

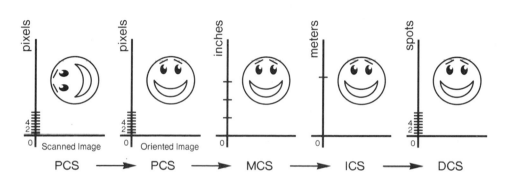

Figure 3.28 Transformations applied to pixel arrays.

To determine proper transformation to map from the original coordinates of the pixel array to the MCS, it may be easier first to transform to a *normalized pixel-array coordinate system* (NPCS) rather than to the PCS. These coordinates support the same scanning order as the PCS does but are scaled so that the upper-left corner of the image is located at the point (0,1) (see Figure 3.29). This mapping causes the pixel array representing the scanned image to behave precisely like a character in a font. This approach provides for homogeneous treatment of fonts and scanned images. Pixel-array coordinates and transformations are discussed in detail in Chapter 6.

Positioning of Masks

There are several ways of specifying where a mask should be on the page. We have seen two of them. One is to specify the position when you create the mask. When you write an x y w h MASKRECTANGLE instruction in Interpress, the x and y numbers specify where the mask should go.

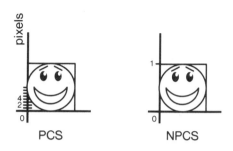

Figure 3.29 Pixel-array and normalized pixel-array coordinate systems.

The second is to use translation transformations to move the object where you want it. Usually you select some reference point on the object and create the mask with the reference point at the origin. Then transformations move the origin (along with the object) to the desired position on the page. For example, if the reference point for a rectangle is the lower-left corner, then you could use 0 0 w h MASKRECTANGLE to draw it. To place it at position (x,y) you would use (see Figure 3.30)

```
x y TRANSLATE CONCATT
0 0 w h MASKRECTANGLE
```

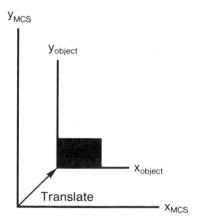

Figure 3.30 Using translation to position an object.

Raster graphic images are positioned in this way. The mask for a pixel array is placed with the lower-left corner at the origin, and you must position the origin where the image belongs on the page before drawing it.

A third method for placement uses a *current position* variable. This is the method used in positioning text. You begin by setting the current position to the starting coordinates for the text string. The first character of the string is imaged at this place, and the current position is shifted by the width of the character. The second character is then imaged at this new place, and the current position is again shifted. This continues until the entire string has been imaged, and the current position is placed at the end. The current position is maintained in imager variables *DCScpx* and *DCScpy* (indices 0 and 1).

The current position is saved in terms of device coordinates. However, you can set the current position in terms of your MCS by using special operators that convert the specification to device coordinates before saving. The reason for saving the current position in device coordinates is that you can then change the MCS whenever you like, and the current position will not get lost. The operators for changing the current position are

$$<\text{x:Number}> \; <\text{y:Number}> \; \text{SETXY} \rightarrow <\,>$$
$$<\text{x:Number}> \; <\text{y:Number}> \; \text{SETXYREL} \rightarrow <\,>$$
$$<\text{x:Number}> \; \text{SETXREL} \rightarrow <\,>$$
$$<\text{y:Number}> \; \text{SETYREL} \rightarrow <\,>$$

The SETXY operator takes its x and y operands to be the coordinates of the new current position. It transforms them by the current transformation T and saves the result in the current-position imager variables.

$$[\text{DCScpx} \; \text{DCScpy} \; 1] = [\text{x} \; \text{y} \; 1] \times T$$

The SETXYREL operator treats its operands as adjustments or offsets, relative to the current position. It will shift the current position over x and up y in the master coordinates. The new value is converted to device coordinates and saved.

The SETXREL and SETYREL commands are special cases of SETXYREL. The SETXREL operator makes an adjustment in the x position, but leaves the y position unchanged. It is equivalent to x 0 SETXYREL. The SETYREL operator changes the y position in the MCS, but leaves the x position alone.

Because the relative-positioning commands use the old position to determine the new position, it is possible for round-off errors in the position value to accumulate. An Interpress printer will guarantee accurate positioning only if a sequence of relative moves has no more than 250 moves.

For accurate placement, because each character in a string is positioned by a relative move, strings should not contain more than 250 characters.

There also is a special operator, called GETCP, for reading the value of the current position.

$$\text{GETCP} \rightarrow \langle \text{x:Number} \rangle \; \langle \text{y:Number} \rangle$$

The GETCP operator applies the inverse of the current transformation to the DCScpx and DCScpy imager variables to yield the current position in terms of the current master coordinates. This result is returned on the stack.

DCScpx and DCScpy are persistent imager variables. If they are changed within a body that is executed by DOSAVE or DOSAVESIMPLEBODY, the change will persist beyond the end of the body. Most other imager variables will be saved at the start of the body and restored at its end; but not these two. Thus, you can construct an operator that does two things: draw something, making free use of imager variables, and alter the current position (perhaps to set it up for the next thing to be drawn). On completion, the changes made to the imager variables for drawing will be removed, but the update of the current position will remain (see Figure 3.31).

We said that text uses the current position for placement; if you wish, however, you can position other types of objects at the current position. You do this by translating the origin of the coordinates to the current position, and then drawing the object at the origin. To make this easy, Interpress supplies an operator that shifts the origin to the current position.

$$\langle\rangle \; \text{MOVE} \rightarrow \langle\rangle$$

The MOVE operator has the effect of GETCP TRANSLATE CONCATT. That is, a transformation is constructed that maps the origin into the current position. This transformation then becomes part of T, the current transformation.

There is also a TRANS operator, which is a variation on MOVE.

$$\langle\rangle \; \text{TRANS} \rightarrow \langle\rangle$$

TRANS first rounds the current position to the nearest device coordinate grid point and then translates the origin there. When this operator is used, the origin is aligned with the spots of the output device and is placed as near as possible to the current position. You would use TRANS to position a pixel array at the current position because it not only moves the pixel array where you wish, but also aligns the first pixel in the array with a dot on the page.

As an example, using the current position for placement, let's construct an operator that draws a small bar at the current position (CP) and shifts the current position to the other end of the bar. We will do this such that, if the

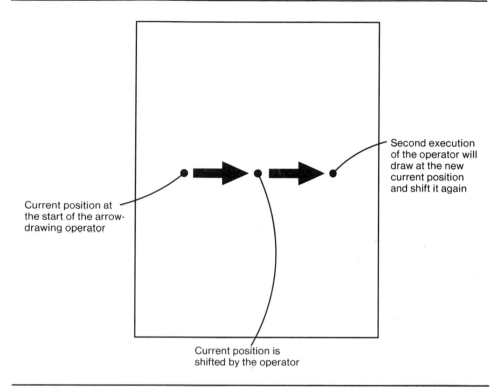

Current position at the start of the arrow-drawing operator

Second execution of the operator will draw at the new current position and shift it again

Current position is shifted by the operator

Figure 3.31 Operators can make persistent changes to the current position if executed with DOSAVE.

operator was called several times in succession, the bars would be placed end to end to form a line. The bar will be 2 millimeters high and 10 millimeters wide. In Example 3.11, we save this operator in frame variable 0, and use it to draw two lines on the page (see Figure 3.32).

Example 3.11

```
Header "Interpress/Xerox/3.0 "        --header--
BEGIN                                 --start of the master--
   { }                                --preamble--
   {                                  --start of the page--
     MAKESIMPLECO                     --operator to draw a bar--
     {                                --start of operator body--
       MOVE                           --move origin to CP--
```

```
        0 0 0.01 0.002 MASKRECTANGLE   --draw the bar--
        0.01 SETXREL                    --update CP to end of bar--
    }                                   --end of the operator body--
    0 FSET                              --save the operator--
    0.04 0.20 SETXY                     --set CP for first line--
    0 FGET DOSAVE                       --draw line out of two bars--
    0 FGET DOSAVE
    0.04 -0.04 SETXYREL                 --shift CP for second line--
    0 FGET DOSAVE                       --draw second line
    0 FGET DOSAVE                       --out of three bars--
    0 FGET DOSAVE
  }                                     --end of the page--
END                                     --end of master--
```

Figure 3.32 The result of Example 3.11.

Color

So far, we have talked mostly about masks. Interpress also allows you to control the "ink" that flows through the mask to form the image. The ink which describes the color of the object, is saved in an imager variable called *color*. This variable determines the current color in which objects are drawn. Here, "color" is used very broadly. It might be black, white, or a shade of gray. It might be some constant hue such as red, pink, green, or turquoise. It also might be a pattern, or a scanned image (either black and white, or full color). In general, it is any pattern of colored spots that can be pressed through the mask and onto the page.

In effect, color is the inkwell into which the operator dips its brush before adding ink to the page. The color applied by the mask replaces what was previously laid down at the same page position. A color pattern might not be specified over the same region of the page that the mask operator wants to fill (see Figure 3.33). If so, the color pattern is extended by tiling (stepping and repeating) the pattern until it covers the mask region, as shown in Figure 3.34.

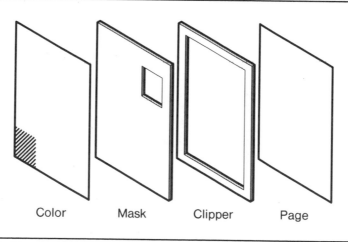

Color   Mask   Clipper   Page

Figure 3.33 The color may be defined for only part of the page.

The default color is black. The operation for creating other colors is described in detail in Chapters 6 and 7; however, we will introduce one method at this point to illustrate the behavior of the imaging model. This method uses an operator called SETGRAY.

$$< f{:}Number > \text{SETGRAY} \rightarrow <\,>$$

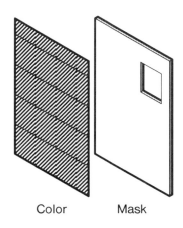

Color   Mask

Figure 3.34 The color pattern is extended by tiling until it covers the mask.

This operator changes the color variable to a gray ink. The operand f tells what shade of gray to use. The value of f can range between 0 (white) and 1 (black). A value of 0.5 would give a 50 percent gray. Example 3.12 draws a rectangle in 50 percent gray (see Figure 3.35).

Example 3.12

```
Header "Interpress/Xerox/3.0 "            --header--
BEGIN                                     --start of the master--
   { }                                    --preamble--
   {                                      --start of the page--
      0.5 SETGRAY                         --change color to gray--
      0.05 0.1 0.04 0.05 MASKRECTANGLE    --draw a rectangle--
   }                                      --end of the page--
END                                       --end of master--
```

Figure 3.35 The result of Example 3.12.

In Example 3.13, we draw two dark-gray squares and one light-gray square (see Figure 3.36).

Example 3.13

```
Header "Interpress/Xerox/3.0 "            --header--
BEGIN                                     --start of the master--
  { }                                     --preamble--
  {                                       --start of the page--
    0.8 SETGRAY                           --change color to dark gray--
    0.05 0.10 0.05 0.05 MASKRECTANGLE     --draw two squares--
    0.09 0.14 0.07 0.07 MASKRECTANGLE
    0.3 SETGRAY                           --change color to light gray-
    0.07 0.05 0.04 0.04 MASKRECTANGLE     --draw a square--
  }                                       --end of the page--
END                                       --end of master--
```

Figure 3.36 The result of Example 3.13.

Example 3.14 is a bit more complex: it uses several of the ideas introduced in Chapters 2 and 3. To draw an 8 by 8 checkerboard with alternating black and gray squares, we construct an operator to draw a square at the current position and shift the current position two squares. This is saved in frame variable 0. A second operator uses the first to lay down four squares of one color. This is placed in frame variable 1 which, in turn, constructs two rows of the checkerboard by an operator saved in frame variable 2. This also shifts the current position up two squares. A fourth operator draws the entire checkerboard at the current position (see Figure 3.37).

Example 3.14

```
Header "Interpress/Xerox/3.0 "    --header--
BEGIN                             --start of the master--
  { }                             --preamble--
  {                               --start of the page--
    MAKESIMPLECO                  --operator to draw a square--
    {                             --start of operator body--
```

```
    MOVE                              --move origin to CP--
    0 0 0.01 0.01 MASKRECTANGLE       --draw the square--
    0.02 SETXREL                      --shift the CP--
  }                                   --end of operator body--
  0 FSET                              --save this operator in frame[0]--
  MAKESIMPLECO                        --operator to draw four squares--
  {                                   --start of operator body--
    0 FGET                            --get the operator for a square--
    DUP DOSAVE                        --save on the stack and do it,--
    DUP DOSAVE                        --saving imager variables--
    DUP DOSAVE                        --except CP--
    DOSAVE                            --do it four times--
  }                                   --end of operator body--
  1 FSET                              --save this operator in frame[1]--
  MAKESIMPLECO                        --operator to draw two rows--
  {                                   --start of operator body--
    1 SETGRAY                         --color is black--
    1 FGET                            --get operator for four squares--
    DUP DOSAVEALL                     --draw four squares, saving CP--
    0.01 SETXREL                      --shift right one square--
    0.5 SETGRAY                       --change color to gray--
    DUP DOSAVEALL                     --draw four more squares--
    0.01 SETYREL                      --shift up one square--
    1 SETGRAY                         --change color to black--
    DUP DOSAVEALL                     --draw four squares--
    -0.01 SETXREL                     --shift left one square--
    0.5 SETGRAY                       --change color to gray--
    DOSAVEALL                         --draw last four squares--
    0.01 SETYREL                      --leave CP up one more square--
  }                                   --end of operator body--
  2 FSET                              --save this operator in frame[2]--
  MAKESIMPLECO                        --operator to draw checkerboard--
  {                                   --start of operator body--
    2 FGET                            --get operator that--
    DUP DO                            --draws two rows--
    DUP DO                            --and do it four times--
    DUP DO                            --to draw eight rows--
    DO
  }                                   --end of operator body--
  3 FSET                              --save this operator in frame[3]--
  0.03 0.1 SETXY                      --place to draw the checkerboard--
  3 FGET DO                           --draw it--
}                                     --end of the page--
END                                   --end of master--
```

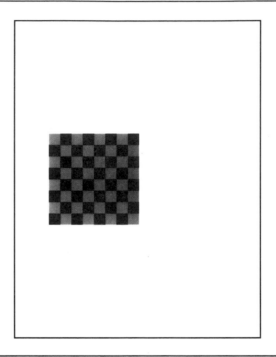

Figure 3.37 The result of Example 3.14.

Priority

In the Interpress imaging model, new objects cover old ones. The order in which the images are created does not matter if the colors are the same or there is no overlap among images. However, if two different colors overlap in some portion of the image, the last one to be laid down will be the one that is visible. This aspect of the model leads to one efficiency problem. The printer should have as much latitude as possible with respect to the order in which it creates images. Allowing the printer to create images in any order, however, is in conflict with the need to preserve the order in the case where different colors overlap. Interpress resolves this conflict with the *priorityImportant* imager variable.

The priorityImportant imager variable controls whether or not the printer must create images within a page in the sequence in which they are presented in the Interpress master. If this imager variable has a value of 0, the printer may create images in any order. If its value is not 0, the printer must generate images in precisely the order that they are generated in the Interpress master. This variable is set to an initial value of 0 at the beginning of every page. The order in which mask operators occur in a page body determines their priority: an operator has a higher priority than those that come before it in the body and a lower one than those that follow it.

Example 3.15

```
Header "Interpress/Xerox/3.0 "          --header--
BEGIN                                   --start of the master--
   { }                                  --preamble--
   {                                    --start of the page--
     1 5 ISET                           --set priorityImportant to 1--
     1 SETGRAY                          --set color to black--
     0.03 0.05 0.1 0.1 MASKRECTANGLE
     0.5 SETGRAY                        --set color to medium gray--
     0.08 0.09 0.1 0.1 MASKRECTANGLE
   }                                    --end of the page--
END                                     --end of master--
```

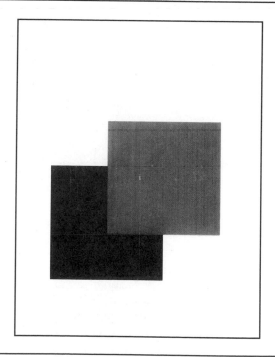

Figure 3.38 The result of Example 3.15.

The command 1 5 ISET in Example 3.15 sets priorityImportant to 1, so that the mask operators are executed in the order in which they appear in the master, with the result shown in Figure 3.38. If this line is removed, then priorityImportant is 0, its default value at the beginning of the page body. Without priority, the master could produce either of the pages shown in Figure 3.39, depending on the way in which the printer orders the masks: for example, top to bottom on the page (a) or left to right, or in order of decreasing lightness (b).

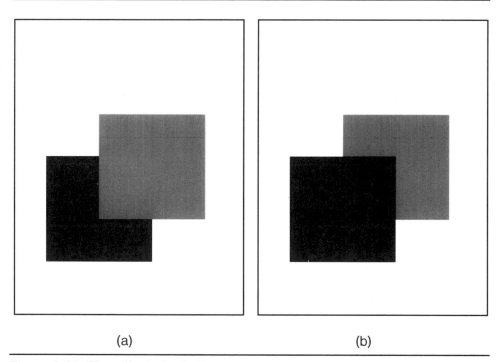

(a)   (b)

Figure 3.39 The effect of priority.

Priority allows precise control of the placement of objects on the page. Interpress preserves the priority order of all ordered masks (those defined when priorityImportant is 1), but may alter the priority among unordered masks (those created when priorityImportant is 0) and between ordered and unordered masks. Leave priorityImportant set to 0 whenever possible, because the imager usually must work harder to preserve priority than it must to ignore it.

Medium and Field

In our examples, we have treated a page as if it were 8.5- by 11-inch paper, but there is no reason why this must be the case. Each printing device is free to select the size and type of medium that it will use. Interpress allows this freedom, and it also gives you a means to learn the size of the medium being used. With this information, your Interpress program could create a transformation that scales and rotates your image for a best fit on the page, or you could leave the image at a fixed size and request that the program issue a warning if the image does not fit.

The imager variables *mediumXSize* and *mediumYSize* define the size of the medium on which the printing will take place, expressed in units of meters. These variables are set at the start of each page. The only function of these variables is to give you information. Changing the value of these variables does not alter the size of the medium used, and trying to do so causes an error.

Some printing systems cannot print to the edge of the printing medium. The imager variables *fieldXMin*, *fieldYMin*, *fieldXMax*, and *fieldYMax* define the ranges for the x and y coordinates of the printable field on the page (see Figure 3.40).

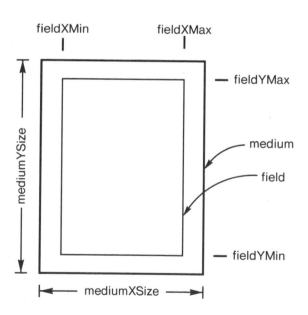

Figure 3.40 Medium size and field size.

Like mediumXSize and mediumYSize, these variables only give information and cannot be changed. However, there is an imager variable called *clipper* that controls the area of the page used (see Figure 3.41). At the start of each page, the clipper is set to the full field area. You can change the clipper to be the intersection of its current region and another shape that you specify. Thus, every change in the clipping region causes the area to be reduced (see Figure 3.42). With this handy property, you can apply a clipping region to an operator that already makes use of the clipper, without danger of expanding the clipping region and ruining the operator. It does *not* mean that, once you make the clipping area small, it can never be large again. The clipper is an imager variable, so it can be saved and restored by the DOSAVE mechanism. You can start with a large clipping region and execute an operator with DOSAVE. If that operator reduces the clipping region, the region will stay small through its execution. Upon completion of the operator, however, the imager variables will be restored, and clipper will be restored to the old, large-area value. Methods for changing the clipper will be discussed in Chapter 5.

In computer graphics, scaling and clipping are often used to show a small portion of a large structure. There may be no limit to the size of the overall structure, because the clipping window restricts the portion shown to an area that fits on the display device. Interpress, however, does limit the size of the unclipped image. A printer must support accurately only those images that exceed the largest field dimension by no more than 10 percent. This allows printer implementors to use fast integer representations for device coordinates, without the danger of arithmetic overflow.

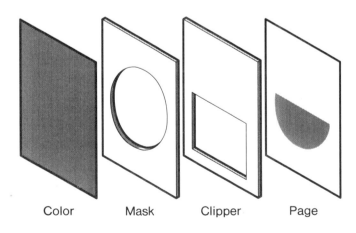

Color   Mask   Clipper   Page

Figure 3.41 The effect of the clipper.

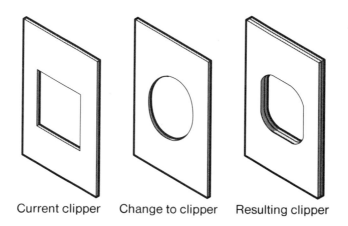

Current clipper   Change to clipper   Resulting clipper

Figure 3.42 Changing the clipper.

Summary

In this chapter, we have seen how complex images can be constructed from a sequence of primitive images. The shape and location of each primitive image is described by a mask. The image is formed by pressing a color through the mask and onto the page, covering up any previous color. The current color is specified by the color imager variable. The last-on-top rule assigns the priority of the primitive images. There also is a priorityImportant imager variable that allows the printer to reorder the primitive images for efficiency, if priority does not matter. The mask undergoes transformations that specify its coordinates of definition; to scale, orient, and position it; and to convert it into the units required by the display device. The overall current transformation is saved in the imager variable T. Some masks also may be placed using a current position that is saved in imager variables DCScpx and DCScpy.

We learned how to build and use transformations and how to set and get the current position. The operators for building transformations are shown in Figure 3.43. Finally, we saw how the medium and field imager variables can tell us the size of the printable area of the page and how the clipper variable can help reduce the drawing region.

In the next chapter, we shall look at imaging text, and see how to find a font of character masks, adjust them to the proper size and orientation, and use them to image a string. We shall also see how to solve common typographical problems and learn how to correct for problems that arise from font substitutions. Finally, we shall discuss how to build a font of our own.

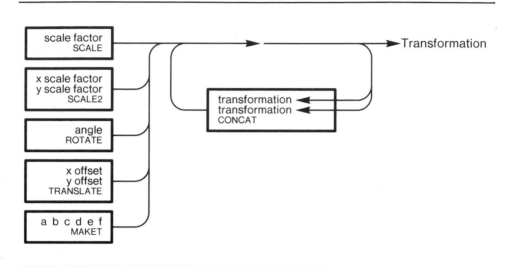

Figure 3.43 Operators that produce transformations.

Chapter 4
FONTS AND TEXT

*"You shall
see them on a
beautiful
quarto page,
where a neat
rivulet of text shall
meander through
a meadow of
margin."*

RICHARD SHERIDAN

In this chapter, we begin our examination of the special operators provided by Interpress for describing images. We start with fonts and characters, the constructs used to image text. We shall learn what a font is, how it can be specified, and even how to build one. We shall see how character strings can be imaged and how special typographical effects can be obtained. We shall also learn about the Interpress features for coping with font approximations, which can arise as font libraries evolve or when documents are transferred to different printing sites.

Letterforms and Fonts

Although Interpress can specify almost any image on a printed page, images containing letters, numbers, and other text characters are common enough that Interpress has a special mechanism for dealing with them, patterned after the mechanism of movable type. Much of the vocabulary necessary to understand and use the language comes from typesetting.

To draw a character on a page, we add an image of the character to the page, drawn in a certain way, in a certain size and orientation. A character's shape is called a *letterform,* and placing a character on a page is called *imaging a letterform* (see Figure 4.1). Most of the earliest models of phototypesetting machines make use of mechanical letterforms–photographic negatives–that are imaged by shining a bright light through them onto photographic paper, one letter at a time. Interpress does not use photographic negatives or mechanical letterforms, of course, but you can think about the mechanism in the same way.

A a a a A A

Figure 4.1 Letterforms.

Interpress accommodates letterform definitions of many different sorts and can take advantage of the high-quality typefaces designed for photocomposition and printing. The letterform definition includes several pieces of information. One is a representation of the shape of the character. But the definition also includes information about how the character should be positioned relative to other characters in a line, and the effective "width" of the character (see Figure 4.2).

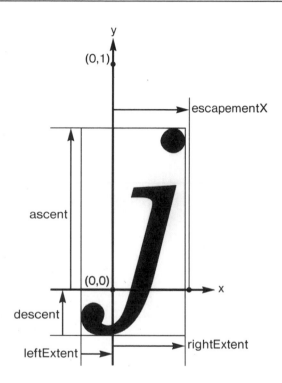

Figure 4.2 Letterform definitions include positioning and width information.

A font, a collection of letterforms designed to be used together, contains a complete set of letterforms designed so that the various characters in the font appear pleasing when printed together in words and lines; their shapes have stylistic consistency and are easy to read, their sizes are consistent, each one's escapement (the amount of movement of the current position) is chosen so that all possible juxtapositions of characters look pleasing, and so on. In the printing industry, a font is given a name, such as Times Italic, Helvetica

Light, or Bodoni Condensed Bold. There are thousands of fonts, with more being designed all the time.

Besides containing the information for each component letterform, an Interpress font may also contain information that applies to the whole collection of letterforms, such as the font's name and version number or the optimum interline spacing or suggested placement of subscripts and underlines.

An Interpress font describes the shape of each letterform, but the actual size and orientation of the printed characters depends on the transformations that are in effect. In Chapter 3, we described how transformations affect the size, orientation, and position of graphic objects; they also affect these aspects of letterforms. Interpress uses transformations to specify size and orientation of the printed characters. Thus, the font only needs to define each letterform for a single "standard" size, and can be scaled to any size required for actual printing (see Figure 4.3). (For high-quality typography we may actually use slightly different shapes for small sizes than for large sizes. This is easily handled by considering the different letterforms as different fonts.)

Figure 4.3 Transformations scale and orient letterforms.

The Letterform-Imaging Process

In Interpress, the imaging of characters is a three-step process. The first step is to identify which font you wish to use. The second step is to specify the size and orientation for the letterforms taken from the font (that is, how the letterforms should be transformed before imaging). The third step is to select and position the individual letterforms (see Figure 4.4). You must indicate which characters you want printed and where they should be placed on the page. To see how this is done, we shall present and explain a simple example.

1. Select a font

ABCDEFGH...

2. Transform to size and orient

A B C...

3. Select and position individual letterforms

THE

Figure 4.4 Steps in imaging characters.

The Interpress master in Example 4.1 places the single word "Interpress" on one page. The word begins at a point 2.9 inches from the left edge of the page and 9.4 inches from the bottom of the page. The characters are in 18-point type. Figure 4.5 shows the top portion of the page at half scale.

Example 4.1

```
Header "Interpress/Xerox/3.0 "    --header--                      --1--
BEGIN                             --start of the master--        --2--
  { }                             --preamble--                   --3--
  {                               --start of the page--          --4--
    Identifier "xerox" Identifier "XC1-1-1" Identifier "times"   --5--
    3 MAKEVEC                     --font name--                  --6--
    FINDFONT                      --get font from printer--      --7--
    0.00635 SCALE                 --transform to 18-point size-- --8--
    MODIFYFONT                    --include it in the font--     --9--
    0 FSET                        --save font in frame[0]--      --10--
    0 SETFONT                     --make it the current font--   --11--
    0.07366 0.23876 SETXY         --position the string--        --12--
```

```
      73 110 116 101 114 112 114 101 115 115                          --13--
      10 MAKEVEC                    --vector of character codes--  --14--
      SHOW                          --image the string--           --15--
    }                               --end of the page--            --16--
  END                               --end of the master--          --17--
```

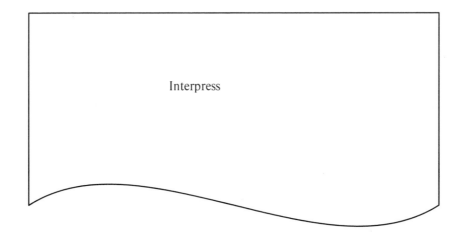

Figure 4.5 The result of Example 4.1.

This example prints one page. The page body begins by establishing a character font and setting up an imager variable that describes the current font. It then sets the current position to x = 2.9 inches, y = 9.4 inches. Because we did not choose to introduce a master coordinate system in this example, we are implicitly using the Interpress coordinate system. Therefore, we must present these measurements in meters. Finally, it constructs a vector of character codes for the word "Interpress," and shows it using the current font, starting at the current position.

The current position is like a cursor, identifying a point on the image at all times. The SHOW operator uses the current position to indicate where to place something on the page image. When SHOW is called, it places an image of the first character, "I," at the current position. (Actually it places the origin of the character's coordinate system at this point.) Then SHOW moves the current position to the right to account for the *width* or *escapement* of the character just shown. Then the process is repeated for the second and all subsequent characters in the character string passed as an argument to SHOW. When

SHOW is finished, the current position ends up just to the right of the final "s." The current position behaves much like a typewriter: as each character is typed, the current position moves to the location where the next character should appear.

Setting Up a Font

Interpress has a comprehensive and, consequently, complex, set of facilities for handling fonts. Because Interpress is designed to deal with high-quality "typeset" documents, the font machinery must be sufficiently general to deal with most or all of the typesetter's needs and to accommodate characters from many different printed languages.

For each kind of character that can be placed in the page image, an Interpress printer has a *character-mask* operator and *character metrics*. The character mask describes the shape of a letterform. Part of the purpose of SHOW is to invoke appropriate character-mask operators. When a character-mask operator is executed, it places an image of its character on the page image. SHOW places the image at the current position. The SHOW operator then moves the current position to the spot where the next character in a string of characters should appear.

An Interpress printer is expected to maintain a library of fonts. A master can copy a font from the library onto the stack so that the master can make use of the letterforms it defines. The FINDFONT operator finds a font in the library and places it on the stack:

$$< v{:}Vector > \text{ FINDFONT} \rightarrow < f{:}Font >$$

The "name" of the font is passed to FINDFONT as a vector of identifiers. In Example 4.1 the font requested is named [xerox, XC1-1-1, times]. The result of executing the following instructions is to leave on the stack an object of type font:

```
Identifier   "xerox"
Identifier   "XC1-1-1"
Identifier   "times"
3 MAKEVEC
FINDFONT
```

To allow a creator to predict the appearance of characters it places on the page, Interpress fonts adhere to rigid conventions governing the precise actions taken when an individual character is placed on the page by SHOW. However, the Interpress treatment of fonts is deliberately flexible in two important areas: the naming conventions used, and the choice of a character set for a font–that is, the correspondence between character codes and shapes.

In the areas of character sets and font names, the Interpress standard accommodates a wide range of current practice in the computing and printing industries, rather than imposing new standards. Both of these areas are characterized by long and interesting histories that have led to diverse practices. Rather than choosing a particular practice and making that a standard, Interpress allows arbitrary character sets to be used and offers a framework in which almost arbitrary font names can be used. For a representative sample of typefaces, Autologic's *Digital Types and Non-Latin Alphabets* (1985) is superlative.

Font Names

Interpress names a font with a universal name that is a vector of identifiers, for example [itc, ascii, times]. Names of arbitrary complexity are handled by extending the vector to contain any number of identifiers. The name may capture any or all aspects of a font, such as its style, the name of its designer, or a version number. Font names used in the printing industry can be mapped quite easily into this framework. Thus, Bodoni Bold Condensed might become [itc, ascii, bodoni, bold, condensed], and similarly, Caslon Demi-Bold might become [itc, ascii, caslon, demibold].

In these examples, the identifiers "itc" and "ascii" precede the identifiers for what might conventionally be considered the font name. These identifiers, examples of hierarchical naming conventions, are the only aspect of font names required by Interpress. Interpress insists on universal names so that different Interpress users and applications can devise unique font names that do not conflict with anyone else's invented names. The way that hierarchical universal names are organized was described in Chapter 2. Once past the first few identifiers that satisfy hierarchical name requirements, however, you are free to organize font names as you wish. Naturally, the font-naming scheme must allow masters to refer to fonts by name and Interpress printers to find and use the fonts.

A font name does not contain information about the geometric properties of a font, such as its size and orientation. These are controlled not by the name but rather by the geometric transformations performed on the font. However, the highest-quality typographic practice requires that letterforms of different sizes have different shapes; letterforms are not simply magnified or reduced. Here the different type designs are given different names. For example, a common technique is to define different letterform designs for footnotes, common body text, and headline or display type. These properties could be part of the font name, as in [itc, ascii, caslon, demibold, display]. However, the optimum letterform design relates to the viewing angle it subtends at the eye, not to its physical size. Characters on a billboard may be most legible if they are 50 centimeters high, whereas the characters on this page are only 0.35

centimeters high. These two uses of characters take advantage of the same letterform design but have different geometric transformations applied.

Xerox Font Names

Fonts that have hierarchical names beginning with [xerox, . . .] are subject to a naming standard developed by Xerox Corporation. The Interpress masters in this book all use the following convention:

1. The first identifier is "xerox."
2. The second identifier specifies the character set used by the font, which is the Xerox Character Code and Rendering Code Standards, and is denoted by "XC1-1-1."
3. The third identifier is the typographical name of the font, encoded in a single identifier. Examples are "modern," "modern-italic," and "modern-bold."

Font Transformations

All the fonts saved in a printer's library have a standard size: they are 1 unit high. That means that each operator is defined so that the text will be readable if lines of text are spaced 1 unit apart. The characters in the font are thus slightly less than one unit high in the character coordinate system (CCS). If one of these character operators were to be executed in the page body of Example 4.1, the character would be almost a meter high! That is because the conventions in the page body are that distances are measured in meters, and a distance of one unit in the CCS will means a distance of 1 meter in the ICS. This is clearly not what we want.

To obtain characters of the proper size, we make use of Interpress' ability to perform linear *transformations*. We want to *scale* each character as it is placed on the page image. To obtain 18-point text, each character needs to be scaled such that its height (originally one unit) becomes 18 points; each character needs to be scaled by a factor of $18 \times 0.00035278 = 0.00635$.

Each object of type font contains a transformation for converting from the CCS to the MCS. As part of the process of imaging a letterform, the SHOW operator transforms it by both the CCS-to-MCS transformation (from the font) and the MCS-to-DCS transformation (from the T imager variable). When a font is freshly obtained from the printer's environment by FINDFONT, the CCS-to-MCS transformation is initialized to the identity. To alter the size or orientation of the font, you must multiply by an additional transformation. In this case, you may find it easier to think of the transformation as changing the object (the letterform) and keeping the coordinates fixed, rather than as changing coordinates. The change in transformation is done by the MODIFYFONT operator:

$$<f_1:Font> \ <m:Transformation> \ \text{MODIFYFONT} \rightarrow \ <f_2:Font>$$

If the CCS-to-MCS transformation in font f_1 is m_1, then the CCS-to-MCS transformation in font f_2 will be $m_2 = m_1 \times m$.

In lines 5 through 9 of Example 4.1, MODIFYFONT builds a font object for an 18-point font named [xerox, XC1-1-1, times]. This font object is left on the stack. Line 10 saves the font in the frame element with index 0 for future reference. If we were to use several different fonts in a document, each would be saved in a different frame element.

Current Font

A font typically helps image many strings of characters, so the font is specified with a current-font imager variable named *font* (index = 12).

Line 11 of Example 4.1 establishes the font that has been saved in frame element 0 as the current font. To set the font variable, we could execute

0 FGET 12 ISET

However, because the sequence n FGET 12 ISET may be executed quite frequently, the primitive operator SETFONT is defined so that the sequence n SETFONT can be used instead:

$$<n:Cardinal> \ \text{SETFONT} \rightarrow \ <>$$

Simply a convenience operator, this has exactly the same effect as

n FGET 12 ISET

You can use lines 5 through 10 of Example 4.1 as a template for setting most fonts. Find a font of a given name, scale the font's CCS-to-MCS transformation, and save the font in a frame element. Thus, the template is

name FINDFONT *size* SCALE MODIFYFONT *frameIndex* FSET

where *name* is the name of the font, expressed as a vector of identifiers, such as [xerox, XC1-1-1, times]; *size* is the height of the font measured in master coordinates (recall that the height is actually the minimum distance between lines of text that allows comfortable reading, sometimes called the *body size* of the characters); and *frameIndex* is the numeric index of the frame element in which to save the font object. Note that this template only saves the font object in the frame; it does not set the font-imager variable.

Once fonts have been set with this template, we can set the current font to the one we desire with

$$frameIndex \text{ SETFONT}$$

This second template actually sets the font imager variable so that the font is invoked with SHOW.

Character Imaging

The task of imaging characters falls on the SHOW operator:

$$< v{:}\text{Vector of Cardinal} > \text{ SHOW} \rightarrow\ < >$$

This operator takes a vector of cardinal numbers as its operand. Each number, interpreted as a code for a character, accesses the letterform in the font. For each number, the SHOW operator must find the corresponding character mask and transform that mask by the font's CCS-to-MCS transformation to the proper size and orientation. The SHOW operator also transforms the mask by the current transformation to express it in device coordinates. It places the mask at the current position and causes the character to be imaged. The SHOW operator must then look up the escapement of the character and shift the current position by this amount so that the next character will be properly placed (see Figure 4.6).

Because the overall shift in the current position is a result of the accumulated displacements for the characters, round-off errors in escapement values can lead to inaccuracies in placements. To prevent such errors from reaching unacceptable levels, the vector consumed by the SHOW operator should have no more than 250 character codes.

Because a vector of cardinals represents a string of character codes, any cardinal value can be used as the code for a character. You are not restricted to numbers between zero and 255; you have a much larger selection of possible code values, so you can assign unique character codes to a large number of symbols. For example, the Xerox character code standard uses 16-bit numbers to assign codes to the symbols for most languages, including Japanese, Chinese, and those of technical disciplines such as mathematics and engineering. For English text, however, most strings use characters from only a small subset of the possible symbols. By assigning the small numbers as the codes for those symbols, it is possible to devise compact encodings for strings. Such a compaction scheme, *sequenceString*, is supplied in the Xerox encoding of Interpress.

Using the sequenceString encoding, the vector of 16-bit character codes is represented as a sequence of bytes. Each byte is the low-order 8 bits of a character code. At the start of the string, each character code is assumed to

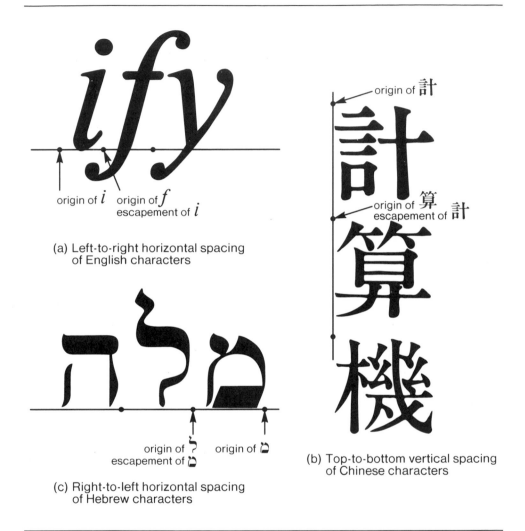

(a) Left-to-right horizontal spacing of English characters

(b) Top-to-bottom vertical spacing of Chinese characters

(c) Right-to-left horizontal spacing of Hebrew characters

Figure 4.6 Spacing character masks.

have zero in the high-order 8 bits. This can be changed to some other value, h, by including an escape byte (a byte with value 255), followed by the high-order byte value h. If this change is made, then h will be used as the high-order half of each character code until it is changed to something else or until you start a new sequenceString. The encoding scheme also lets you change to a mode in which 16-bit words represent characters. You would use this mode when the high-order byte changes frequently (as for Kanji text). The details of the encoding scheme are described in the Interpress standard and the Xerox character code standard. Our examples assume an assembler that can create the sequenceString encoding from quoted text, similar to the handling of identifiers. Thus, using the sequenceString encoding, we have Example 4.2.

Example 4.2

```
Header "Interpress/Xerox/3.0 "     --header--
BEGIN                              --start of the master--
  { }                              --preamble--
  {                                --start of the page--
    Identifier "xerox" Identifier "XC1-1-1" Identifier "times"
    3 MAKEVEC                      --font name--
    FINDFONT                       --get font from printer environment--
    0.00635 SCALE                  --transform to 18-point size--
    MODIFYFONT                     --include in the font--
    0 FSET                         --save the font in frame[0]--
    0 SETFONT                      --make it the current font--
    0.07366 0.23876 SETXY          --position the string--
    String "Interpress"            --vector of character codes--
    SHOW                           --image the string--
  }                                --end of the page--
END                                --end of the master--
```

Note that, in this format, we do not need the MAKEVEC operator. The sequenceString is an encoding for a vector of numbers, so the vector is made automatically. The sequenceString encoding is both more compact and more efficient than the vector of numbers constructed on the stack. It is the preferred way of encoding strings, and most printers optimize the handling of strings in this form.

As an example of the power of the Interpress machinery, we shall construct a composed operator to print text in a spiral. The operator expects the stack to contain an initial orientation, initial size, and the string to be printed. It prints the string spiraling in, starting at the current position. Each character is 93 percent of its predecessor's size and rotated 30 degrees.

The procedure that does this is stored in frame variable 2. It first finds the number of elements in the vector of character codes and then uses a recursive procedure to step through the vector, imaging each character. It calculates the angle and scale to be used on the next character and rolls them out of the way. Then it calls an operator in frame variable 1 to image one character. This second operator scales and rotates the font, extracts a character code, wraps it in a vector, and SHOWs it. The base font is stored in frame variable 0.

The operators are called for a sample string in Example 4.3 (see Figure 4.7).

Example 4.3

```
Header "Interpress/Xerox/3.0 "      --header--
BEGIN                              --start of the master--
 { }                               --preamble--
 {                                 --start of the page--
  Identifier "xerox" Identifier "XC1-1-1" Identifier "modern"
  3 MAKEVEC FINDFONT
  0 FSET                           --store the basic font in frame[0]--

  MAKESIMPLECO                     --the operator to image a character--
  {                                --expects the scale, angle, character code--
   SCALE
   EXCH
   ROTATE
   CONCAT                          --build the transformation for the font--
   0 FGET                          --get the font--
   EXCH
   MODIFYFONT                      --and transform it--
   12 ISET                         --make it the current font--
   1 MAKEVEC SHOW                  --show the character--
  } 1 FSET                         --store this operator in frame[1]--

  MAKESIMPLECO                     --operator to print a string in a spiral--
  {                                --expects initial size, angle and string--
   DUP SHAPE EXCH POP              --get number of characters in the string--
   DUP 3 FSET                      --save this count in frame[3]--
                                   --make a recursive operator--
   MAKESIMPLECO                    --to traverse the string--
   {                               --size, angle, string, count and operator--
    5 4 ROLL                       --roll the operator out of the way--
    DUP IF                         --check if all characters imaged--
    { 2 COPY                       --if not, determine index of next character--
      3 FGET
      EXCH
      SUB
      GET                          --get the character code--
      5 2 ROLL 2 COPY              --now get and copy the scale and angle--
      0.93 MUL 7 6 ROLL            --next time scale is reduced by 0.93--
      30 SUB 7 6 ROLL              --next time rotate -30--
```

```
       1 FGET DO              --show the character--
       1 SUB                  --decrement the count--
       5 1 ROLL               --roll the operator to the top--
       DUP DO                 --recursive call for the rest of the string--
     }
   } DUP DO                   --do the recursive operator--
                              --to show the string--
  POP POP POP POP POP         --remove the leftover arguments--
 } 2 FSET                     --save this operator in frame[2]--

 0.06 0.17 SETXY              --position of the first character--
 90                           --angle of the first character--
 0.06                         --size of the first character--
 String "Interpress**Interpress**Interpress**Interpress**Interpress"
 2 FGET DO                    --print the string in a spiral--
 }                            --end of the page--
END                          --end of the master--
```

Figure 4.7 The result of Example 4.3.

Note that each character in Example 4.3 is imaged with a font that has undergone a different transformation. The positioning is done by the normal mechanism of each character following the last, but because of the change in size and orientation of the characters, the path of the string curves around in a spiral.

Character Sets

We have said that the SHOW operator uses the character code to look up the mask for a corresponding letterform, but we have not said what the correspondence between code and letterform must be. The term *character set* refers to this correspondence. The notion of character set is clearly vital to Interpress, which must make graphic images on a page according to digitally-encoded instructions. Many different character sets are used today, and some have been standardized (for example, ASCII, ISO 646, EBCDIC), but each of these standards is unacceptable for some applications, and none has become dominant. As a result, Interpress is carefully designed not to depend in any way on the choice of character set for a font.

An Interpress printer treats all characters the same way, with no knowledge of what a character code signifies. It is the master that controls both the choice of character codes passed to SHOW and the choice of the font of letterforms to use; thus, the character set is of no consequence to an Interpress printer.

An analogy may help to clarify the nature of a character set. Consider a typewriter that uses the daisywheel printing technology. Let us ignore the labels printed on the typewriter keys, and instead print on each key a number from 1 to 96 that corresponds to a position on the wheel. The typewriter mechanism responds to a keystroke on key N by rotating the wheel to position N and striking the wheel to imprint whatever character shape has been cast into the wheel at that position. The typewriter is completely insensitive to the identity of the characters in the images it makes. Instead, the user controls the character selection because he or she controls the selection of both the keys struck and the wheel used. This situation corresponds exactly to that in Interpress: the identity of the character images is controlled entirely by the master. The character codes in the operand passed to SHOW correspond to key numbers, and the font established by SETFONT corresponds to a wheel selection.

The analogy also helps to illustrate another aspect of character sets. In a daisywheel typewriter, keys are labeled with characters (for example, A, B, C) because most, but far from all, daisywheels use the same character set. A wheel for Roman type and one for italic type uses the same character set; this avoids confusion and is convenient because keys can be labeled in a meaningful way. Some wheels, however, contain many special symbols that do not correspond to the key labels. In this case, a plastic chart overlaid on the keyboard tells the typist which key to strike to obtain each special character. This chart is somewhat like a character set, in that it defines the correspondence between character codes (typewriter keys) and printed symbols. However, it is not completely analogous to a character set, because it is a mapping between the special key meanings and the regular key meanings, rather than a mapping between the special key meanings and the printwheel positions.

Interpress imposes no standard character set when printing character images. If the master selects a font designed to use the ASCII character set, calls to SHOW must have operands containing ASCII character codes. If the same master later selects a font designed to use the EDCDIC character set, subsequent calls to SHOW must provide EBCDIC character codes. Still other fonts may use no standardized character set, but instead simply choose character codes at will, like the daisywheel for special characters. Fonts of arbitrary character set can be used within the same master, just as daisywheels of arbitrary character set can be used to type on the same page.

For example, a font might be designed so that the letterform with index 1 generates an "A," the letterform with index 2 a "B," and so on. If such a font becomes the current font, the sequence [1, 2, 3] SHOW would print the string "ABC." However, another font might be designed so that the letterform with index 65 generates an "A," the letterform with index 66 a "B," and so on. When this font is the current font, the sequence [65, 66, 67] SHOW will be used to generate the string "ABC."

In our examples, we will assume that all fonts are designed with the same conversions, and that the encoding of literals written as string "ABC" is consistent with these conventions. Thus, string "ABC" will encode as [1, 2, 3] if the first set of conventions is used, and as [65, 66, 67] if the second set is used.

Limitations. Two practices in some existing character sets cannot be achieved with Interpress characters:

1. *Formatting characters.* Many character sets contain formatting characters other than spaces that are used to control the format and presentation of text. Examples from ASCII are carriage-return, tab, form-feed, and vertical-tab. A character imaged by the SHOW operator cannot achieve the effect of these characters. The reason is that the current position cannot be reset to a particular value (carriage-return) or to one of a number of fixed values (tab, vertical-tab). These formatting operations are achieved in Interpress with positioning commands, such as SETXY, rather than by interpretation of character codes.

2. *Automatic ligatures.* High-quality typography often makes use of ligatures–special graphic forms showing sequences of characters in a row. For example, two *f* characters in a row may appear as a ligature, "*ff*," rather than as two separate characters. You may have to look closely to see the difference in text, but it should be more visible in the enlarged characters in Figure 4.8. The master, rather than invoking [102, 102] SHOW to obtain two separate *f* characters, might image the ligature, which is simply another character in the font. Automatic ligatures cannot be achieved by Interpress SHOW operators because each character is processed by MASKCHAR, which uses DOSAVEALL and stack protection. Therefore, a character operator cannot convey any information–such as its identity–to neighboring characters, nor can it have any effect on the current position, as would be needed for automatic ligatures. This is not a serious restriction, because the creator can recognize character pairs as it outputs them and perform the appropriate substitution. Moreover, this strategy adheres to an important design goal of Interpress: all decisions about presentation and formatting should be made by the creator, not by the printer. The creator can get information about the font's ligatures and can use them where appropriate.

Interpress Use of Character Sets. Although the Interpress language does not have a standard character set, the encoding of Interpress uses a standard character set in three cases: the encoding of identifiers, of certain messages to the printer operator and error log, and of the header uses the ISO 646 character set to obtain a numeric code for the characters. This use of a standard character set, however, has nothing to do with character sets of fonts or with making images of characters; it merely provides a standard way of interpreting names, writing to CRT displays, and producing a readable transcription of the header.

Two characters   Ligature

Figure 4.8 A ligature.

Font Names and Character Sets. Font names can be devised to communicate character-set properties. For example, a system might incorporate the character-set name into the hierarchical font name. Xerox Corporation's computer printing products adopt this convention, so fonts with names of the form [xerox, ascii, . . .] use an ASCII character set, those of the form [xerox, ebcdic, . . .] use the EBCDIC character set, and those of the form [xerox, XC1-1-1, . . .] use Xerox Character Codes.

Multifont Text

Example 4.4 shows how you can obtain text in several different fonts on one page. The font set-up template is used several times to obtain different fonts, and then SETFONT is used to switch among them. This example prints two lines of text, as shown in Figure 4.9.

Example 4.4

```
Header "Interpress/Xerox/3.0 "      --header--
BEGIN                               --start of the master--
  { }                               --preamble--
  {                                 --start of the page--
    Identifier "xerox"
    Identifier "XC1-1-1"
    Identifier "times"
    3 MAKEVEC FINDFONT              --find Times Roman font--
    0.00352778 SCALE                --10 points=0.00352778 meters--
    MODIFYFONT                      --set size to 10 point--
    0 FSET                          --font 0 is 10-point Times Roman--
    Identifier "xerox"
    Identifier "XC1-1-1"
    Identifier "times-italic"
    3 MAKEVEC FINDFONT              --find Times italic font--
    0.00352778 SCALE
    MODIFYFONT                      --also 10 point--
    1 FSET                          --font 1 is 10-point Times Italic--
    0.0254 0.254 SETXY              --current position is x=1", y=10"--
    0 SETFONT                       --use font 0--
    String "The "
    SHOW                            --image the string "The "--
    1 SETFONT                       --use font 1--
    String "Interpress Electronic Printing Standard "
    SHOW                            --image the string--
    0 SETFONT                       --back to font 0--
```

```
        String "is a standard for interfacing raster"
        SHOW                         --image the string--
        0.0254 0.2494139 SETXY       --position at x=1", y= 10"-13 pts--
        String "printers to digital computers. A raster printer is"
        SHOW                         --image the string--
    }                                --end of the page--
END                                  --end of the master--
```

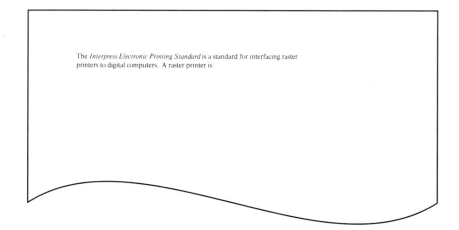

Figure 4.9 The result of Example 4.4.

Note that the second line is positioned 13 points (0.0045861 meters) below the first one. Extra space between lines, called *leading*, helps to make long lines easier to read.

A Line-Printer Listing

A common computer output is the listing of a text file. Example 4.5 shows how you might generate a listing with Interpress.

Example 4.5

```
    Header "Interpress/Xerox/3.0 "      --header--
    BEGIN                               --start of the master--
      { }                               --preamble--
      {                                 --start of the first page--
        Identifier "xerox" Identifier "XC1-1-1" Identifier "terminal"
```

```
3 MAKEVEC FINDFONT
0.00282222 SCALE
MODIFYFONT
0 FSET                         --set font 0 to 8-point terminal--
0 SETFONT                      --make it the current font--
0.0254 0.2667 SETXY            --heading at x=1", y=10.5"--
String "Listing of GPO.PAS at 14:32 on 31 January 1982 Page 1"
SHOW
0.0254 0.254 SETXY             --top line at x=1", y=10"--
String "1  (* GP.PAS -- Simple PASCAL graphics package. *)"
SHOW
0.0254 0.2497667 SETXY         --lines are 12 points apart--
String "2  const EnterGraphicsMode=29; LeaveGraphicsMode=31;"
SHOW
0.0254 0.2455333 SETXY
String "3  var xlast,ylast: integer; v: InquiryResponse;"
SHOW
0.0254 0.2413000 SETXY
String "4"
SHOW
0.0254 0.2370667 SETXY
String "5  procedure TransmitCoords (x,y: real);"
SHOW
--more lines of text for the first page would be added here--
}                                   --end of the first page--
{                                   --start of the second page--
Identifier "xerox" Identifier "XC1-1-1" Identifier "terminal"
3 MAKEVEC FINDFONT
0.00282222 SCALE
MODIFYFONT
0 FSET                         --set font 0 again--
0 SETFONT                      --make it the current font--
0.0254 0.2667 SETXY            --heading at x=1", y=10.5"--
String "Listing of GPO.PAS at 14:32 on 31 January 1982 Page 2"
SHOW
0.0254 0.254 SETXY             --top line at x=1", y=10"--
String "51  procedure DrawText (s: string);"
SHOW
--more lines of text for the second page would be added here--
}                                   --end of the second page--
--more page bodies for more pages would be added here--
END                                 --end of the master--
```

The first few lines of the first page of this listing would look like this:

```
Listing of GPO.PAS at 14:32 on 31 January 1982   Page 1
1   (* GP.PAS -- Simple PASCAL graphics package. *)
2   const EnterGraphicsMode=29; LeaveGraphicsMode=31;
3   var xlast,ylast: integer; v: InquiryResponse;
4
5   procedure TransmitCoords (x,y: real);
```

This example illustrates an important point: the contents of the frame are not saved from one page to the next. At the beginning of each page, the frame is reset to an initial value. Therefore, in Example 4.5, the font to be used is looked up anew on each page. We will see in Chapter 8 that duplicate lookups can be avoided by placing appropriate information in the preamble.

This example also illustrates that it is quite easy to prepare a master that will produce a "listing" of a text file that requires no special formatting. The listing program reads the text file and writes the encoded master in one pass over the text. As each new line of text begins, an appropriate SETXY call is placed in the master, or a new page body is started if the text has reached the bottom of the page. Then, the character codes from the text file are copied into the master, encoded as a string. (The codes can be copied, provided that the character set assumed in the text file is the same as the character set of the chosen font. Otherwise, character-code values may have to be changed as the string is placed in the master to conform to the font's conventions.) After each string, a call to SHOW is placed in the master. It is quite a simple job, so the creator program can be very fast.

Even for a simple case of a listing, Interpress requires that the creator control formatting by preparing an appropriate master. Interpress makes no formatting or typographical decisions; there are no facilities for "automatically" formatting or paginating a text file.

There are other listing formats that you might desire to use, such as rotating text 90 degrees so that it reads the long way on an 8.5- by 11-inch page. Although Interpress does this too, the easy way is to rely on transformations.

Although the masters in this section will print correctly on an Interpress printer, they depart from good Interpress style in two ways:

1. Each page of a multipage document duplicates font definitions. Judicious use of the *preamble*, explained in Chapter 8, avoids this duplication.

2. The use of transformations that define the MCS allows masters to be expressed in units of measurement that are more convenient than meters. By picking coordinates in which positions can be expressed as

integers, you can make the masters a bit more compact than the ones illustrated here.

In Example 4.6, we have revised the Interpress code of Example 4.2 to show the use of an alternate MCS.

Example 4.6

```
Header "Interpress/Xerox/3.0 "      --header--
BEGIN                                --start of the master--
   { }                               --preamble--
   {                                 --start of the page--
      0.000035278 SCALE              --set MCS to 1/10-point units--
      CONCATT                        --the scale factor in the page body--
      Identifier "xerox" Identifier "XC1-1-1" Identifier "times"
      3 MAKEVEC FINDFONT             --find Times Roman font--
      180 SCALE                      --derive the 18-point size--
      MODIFYFONT
      0 FSET                         --font 0 is 18-point Times Roman--
      0 SETFONT                      --set current font to font 0--
      2088 6768 SETXY                --start string at x=2.9", y=9.4"--
      String "Interpress"
      SHOW                           --image the string--
   }                                 --end of the page--
END                                  --end of the master--
```

Note that, at the start of the page body, we concatenate a scaling transformation onto the current transformation. The particular scaling factor we have chosen changes the MCS units to 1/10 of a point. Thus, all coordinates specified in the page body are expressed in 1/10-point units, not meters. This change of units allows us to use integers to express the coordinates. This is desirable because the encoding for integers is more compact and efficient than that for rationals.

You also should note that the scale given to MODIFYFONT changes from 0.00635 in Example 4.2 to 180 in Example 4.6. This is because MODIFYFONT converts from the CCS to the MCS. In Example 4.6, the MCS in effect when the font is used has 1/10-point units. So, to scale a 1-unit-high font to be an 18-point font when the units are 1/10 points, we need a scale factor of 180.

Using Interpress for Typography

Typography is the fine art of designing letterforms and placing them so as to have a legible and pleasing effect. Although many forms of computer output are so crude that worrying about typographic quality is futile, Interpress can describe documents of extremely high resolution and quality and thus can represent documents with fine typography.

In the following pages, we describe how various typographic effects can be best achieved in Interpress. We do not attempt to instruct you in the principles of good typography; such a task is far too ambitious for this book, and the subject has been covered in other texts. The beginner is urged to consult James Craig's *Designing with Type* (1980), which contains many useful hints for simple typography.

Interpress has been designed specifically to accommodate high-quality typography. Probably the single most important design feature in Interpress is that *the printer makes no typographic decisions; all decisions are made by the creator*. Thus, for example, Interpress contains no notion of a "subscript," because if a master were to specify that a text string is a subscript, the printer would have to decide exactly where the subscript should appear–that is, how far below the normal baseline the subscript's baseline should be. Instead, in the master instructions that control the precise placement of all text, the creator specifies whether subscripts, superscripts, or normal text should be used.

Because you, as the creator, make all typographical decisions, Interpress can represent documents that have been formatted according to many different sets of typographical rules or styles. Different creators may embody different typographical rules in their programs and still be able to express the results as Interpress masters.

Typographic Facilities

Before exploring the various ways to achieve high-quality typography in Interpress, we will review the Interpress facilities that apply:

- *Letterform definitions*, expressed as operators in a font. These definitions may be extracted from a printer's font library or may be defined in the master itself. There are no restrictions on the shape of a letterform.

- *Geometric transformations* that can scale, rotate, and translate a letterform so that it can appear in an arbitrary size, rotation, and position on the page. In general, scaling and rotation are handled by MODIFYFONT and the page coordinate system, while translation is handled by SETXY and SHOW.

- *Additional graphic operators* to define rules, underlines, strikethroughs, and the like.

This set of facilities is small yet surprisingly versatile because Interpress places so few restrictions on how these primitive facilities can be used. There are no limits, for example, on the number of characters in a "line" of text;

characters can appear at arbitrary positions or can be spaced close to each other, far apart or even overlap.

Although a master can represent a document with high typographic quality, not all printers can achieve high-quality results. Some printers have insufficient resolution; some use a coarse printing method that leaves specks or other forms of noise in the image; some place limits on a page's maximum complexity or on the sizes of characters that can be printed. It is important to understand that these are printer, not Interpress, limitations. A high-resolution, high-quality printer imposes no restrictions on the Interpress masters it prints.

Positioning of Characters

A conceptually simple method for setting type in Interpress is to specify precisely the position of each character on the page. Character positions can be specified with the SETXY operator, and characters can be printed with the SHOW operator. In Example 4.7, each character in the string "Interpress" is individually positioned.

Example 4.7

```
Header "Interpress/Xerox/3.0 "        --header--
BEGIN                                 --start of the master--
  { }                                 --preamble--
  {                                   --start of the page--
    0.000035278 SCALE                 --set MCS to 1/10-point units--
    CONCATT
    Identifier "xerox" Identifier "XC1-1-1" Identifier "times"
    3 MAKEVEC FINDFONT
    180 SCALE
    MODIFYFONT
    0 FSET                            --font 0 is 18-point Times--
    0 SETFONT                         --make font 0 the current font--
    2088 6768 SETXY String "I" SHOW   --print "I" at x=2.900", y=9.4"--
    2155 6768 SETXY String "n" SHOW   --print "n" at x=2.993", y=9.4"--
    2257 6768 SETXY String "t" SHOW   --print "t" at x=3.135", y=9.4"--
    2313 6768 SETXY String "e" SHOW   --print "e" at x=3.212", y=9.4"--
    2398 6768 SETXY String "r" SHOW   --print "r" at x=3.331", y=9.4"--
    2465 6768 SETXY String "p" SHOW   --print "p" at x=3.424", y=9.4"--
    2567 6768 SETXY String "r" SHOW   --print "r" at x=3.565", y=9.4"--
    2634 6768 SETXY String "e" SHOW   --print "e" at x=3.658", y=9.4"--
    2719 6768 SETXY String "s" SHOW   --print "s" at x=3.776", y=9.4"--
    2786 6768 SETXY String "s" SHOW   --print "s" at x=3.869", y=9.4"--
```

```
        }                                      --end of the page--
        END                                    --end of the master--
```

This method of setting type clearly shows Interpress' flexibility. You can position each character carefully and precisely to obtain the most pleasing effect. One drawback, though, is that it is not particularly device independent; that is, the text will not look good if even a slight font approximation is made, because the spacing between characters is controlled by the master rather than by the character operators themselves. Another is that it leads to quite lengthy Interpress masters and, as a result, to a slow interpretation by a printer.

The examples of typesetting in earlier sections all relied on the character operators to achieve proper character-to-character spacing, using SETXY only for positioning the first character in a line of text. In Example 4.6, the entire string "Interpress" is printed with one call to SHOW. The position of the origin of the first character, "I," is x = 2.9 inches, y = 9.4 inches, the position set by the call to SETXY. The SHOW operator modifies the current position to account for the width of the "I." The next character, "n," will be positioned so that its origin is at the modified current position. The SHOW operator moves the current position still further, and so on. The effect is the same as that of Example 4.7, but the spacing is performed by the SHOW operator rather than by explicit calls to SETXY. Besides yielding a more compact master, this technique does better with font approximation: the intercharacter spacing will be correct for the font that is chosen rather than for the font the master requested.

The approach of Example 4.6 still has a minor deficiency with respect to device independence. Although the placement of the beginning of the "Interpress" string is always x = 2.9 inches, y = 9.4 inches, and the intercharacter spacings are those of the actual font, the overall length of the string may be greater or less than the master intended if font approximation is required. If the objective is to center the string on the page, this error will be objectionable. We shall see later how to solve this problem so that strings of text will be centered even in the presence of font approximation.

Font Descriptions

When a master is prepared, the creator needs to know a good deal about its fonts to format the document properly. To decide how many characters will fit on a line or to justify a line of text, the creator must know the "width" of each character.

All the information about a font in a printer's library is captured in a property vector called a *fontDescription*, which contains information about the font as a whole—such as the name and version. A fontDescription can

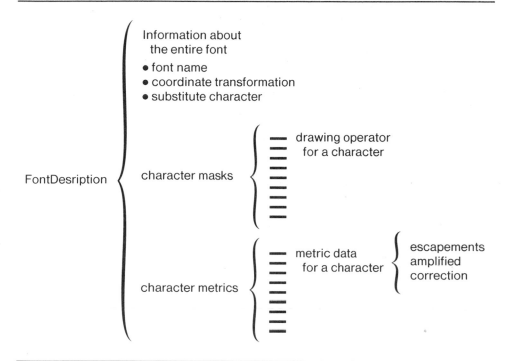

Figure 4.10 Rough structure of a font description.

contain a transformation to convert from some letterform-definition coordinates to the standard character coordinates. This allows you to define the letterforms in whatever coordinate system is most convenient. There may be a *substituteIndex,* which indicates a substitute for characters missing from the font. The fontDescription also contains the description of the letterforms in two elements (see Figure 4.10). The elements are:

- *characterMasks:* A vector of composed operators: these are the character operators themselves. Execution of an operator will draw a character shape. The index of an operator in the characterMask's vector is called the *character index*, or the *character code*.
- *characterMetrics:* A vector of property vectors, designed so that certain metric properties can be given and others can be omitted. Each character has its own property vector of metric information. The most important character metrics, which Interpress records about every character, are *escapementX* and *escapementY*. These two numbers give the width of the character. If escapementX or escapementY is not specified, it is assumed to have value zero. Figure 4.11 shows examples of escapements for several characters.

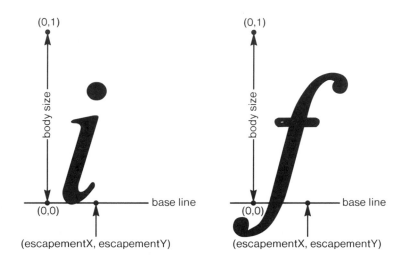

(a) Metrics for left-to-right horizontal spacing

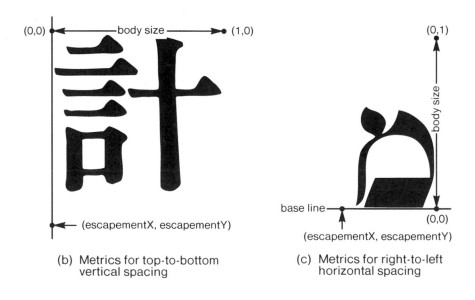

(b) Metrics for top-to-bottom vertical spacing

(c) Metrics for right-to-left horizontal spacing

Figure 4.11 Character metrics for characters with different spacing directions.

Two other properties that we shall use in the following sections are *amplified* and *correction*. An amplified character's escapements can be scaled automatically. We will use this property in adjusting the spacing of words. The correction metric describes how the character behaves under the adjustments that compensate for font approximation.

Character metrics can also contain information about ligatures in the font. For example, in the character-metric information for the letter "f," a ligature table says that if this character is followed by one specific character, an "f," a ligature for the two-character sequence is available as character code 136; or, if this character is followed by another specific character, an "l," another ligature is available.

Although a creator does not need to know all details of a font to create a master, it must have a certain amount of metric information about each character. Font metric information, represented as property vectors, can be made available to the creator as a *metric master,* an Interpress master that has a preamble but no page bodies. The execution of the preamble of the metric master leaves on the stack one or more fontDescription property vectors, each corresponding to a font in the printer's library. Usually, these vectors contain only the characterMetrics, overall metrics for the font, and name properties. To simplify interpretation of the metric master, there are restrictions on the set of Interpress primitive operators it may contain.

A portion of a metric master is shown in Example 4.8. It describes a font library containing two fonts, [xerox, ascii, times] and [xerox, ascii, times-italic]. The first font has character indices from 32 to 126 inclusive; the second has from 32 to 136. Besides the character escapements, the metrics also contain the amplified property, which is used in justification, and the second font shows how ligatures might be recorded for the character "ff." Amplified characters and ligatures are discussed in later sections.

Example 4.8

```
BEGIN                              --start of the metric master--
{                                  --start of the preamble--

  --FontDescription vector for [xerox, ascii, times]--
                                   --characterMetrics property vector--
  Identifier "characterMetrics"    --property name--
                                   --property value is property vector--
                                   --of character metric information--
  32                               --property name is character index--
    Identifier "escapementX" 0.34  --metric information for char 32--
    Identifier "escapementY" 0
    Identifier "amplified" 1
  6 MAKEVEC                        --vector of metric properties--
```

```
33                                    --metric information for char 33--
  Identifier "escapementX" 0.24       --escapementY=0, amplified=0--
2 MAKEVEC                             --by default--
34                                    --metric information for char 34--
  Identifier "escapementX" 0.28
2 MAKEVEC
  . . .                               --and so on, for characters--
                                      --35 through 126--
190 MAKEVEC                           --make characterMetrics property--
                                      --vector; since each character uses--
                                      --two elements, size of vector is--
                                      --190=(126-32+1)*2--
Identifier "name"                     --property name for font name--
  Identifier "xerox" Identifier "ascii" Identifier "times"
3 MAKEVEC                             --property value is universal name--
4 MAKEVEC                             --construct FontDescription vector--

--FontDescription vector for [xerox, ascii, times-italic]--
Identifier "characterMetrics"     --property name--
  32
    Identifier "escapementX" 0.36
    Identifier "amplified" 1
  4 MAKEVEC                           --metrics for char 32--
  33
    Identifier "escapementX" 0.26
  2 MAKEVEC                           --metrics for char 33--
  34
    Identifier "escapementX" 0.30
  2 MAKEVEC                           --metrics for char 34--
    . . .                             --metrics for chars 35 to 101--
  102                                 --character code 102 ("f")--
    Identifier "escapementX" 0.30
                                      --property vector for ligatures--
    Identifier "ligatures"           --property name--
      102 136 2 MAKEVEC              --"ff" ligature is code 136--
      108 135 2 MAKEVEC              --"fl" ligature is code 135--
    2 MAKEVEC                         --property value--
  4 MAKEVEC                           --metrics for char 102--
    . . .                             --metrics for chars 103 to 135--
  136
    Identifier "escapementX" 0.58
  2 MAKEVEC                           --metrics for char 136--
210 MAKEVEC                           --characterMetrics property vector--
```

```
Identifier "name"                    --property name for font name--
  Identifier "xerox" Identifier "ascii" Identifier "times-italic"
3 MAKEVEC                            --property value is universal name--
4 MAKEVEC                            --construct FontDescription vector--
}                                    --end of the preamble--
END                                  --end of metric master--
```

The metric master, unlike most Interpress masters, conveys information from the printer (or font library) to the creator (see Figure 4.12). Interpress does not define how metric masters are created or how a creator obtains access to one. The idea is that each printer should be able to produce a metric master that describes its font library and to record that master on transportable media or transmit it to the computer on which the creator runs. There the master presumably will be stored as a file that the creator can access repeatedly (see Figure 4.13).

Figure 4.12 A metric master conveys information about the printer's fonts to the creator.

The metric master is encoded with the same rules as for making ordinary masters. Although such standard encoding is easy to describe, it may not be particularly convenient to use. If it is deemed unsuitable for a creator to contain software that can interpret Interpress operators in a metric master, then a simple conversion program can perform this evaluation once and write the font information into a file in a private format; the creator can then read this file to find its font metrics. This scheme is pictured in Figure 4.14. Interpress neither defines nor prohibits metric representations other than the metric master.

Table 4.1 provides metric information (such as would be extracted from a metric master) for some characters from the Times Roman and Times Italic fonts.

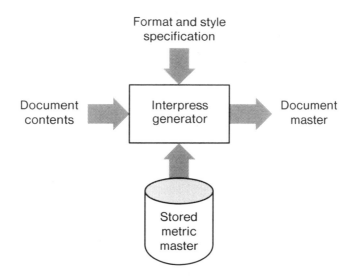

Figure 4.13 Information required to generate an Interpress master.

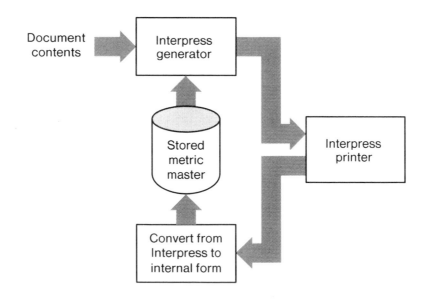

Figure 4.14 Converting the metric master to an internal form.

Table 4.1 Width table for Times Roman and Times Italic characters.

	ampli-fied	EscapementX Roman	EscapementX Italic		ampli-fied	EscapementX Roman	EscapementX Italic
a	0	0.469	0.500	A	0	0.749	0.719
b	0	0.564	0.500	B	0	0.656	0.689
c	0	0.439	0.439	C	0	0.719	0.719
d	0	0.564	0.500	D	0	0.814	0.781
e	0	0.469	0.439	E	0	0.656	0.689
f	0	0.344	0.314	F	0	0.656	0.625
g	0	0.500	0.500	G	0	0.844	0.719
h	0	0.564	0.535	H	0	0.816	0.844
i	0	0.281	0.281	I	0	0.375	0.439
j	0	0.281	0.281	J	0	0.439	0.439
k	0	0.531	0.564	K	0	0.818	0.750
l	0	0.281	0.281	L	0	0.656	0.689
m	0	0.844	0.788	M	0	0.969	0.965
n	0	0.563	0.540	N	0	0.824	0.781
o	0	0.531	0.500	O	0	0.781	0.781
p	0	0.564	0.500	P	0	0.594	0.656
q	0	0.564	0.500	Q	0	0.781	0.781
r	0	0.375	0.375	R	0	0.751	0.719
s	0	0.375	0.375	S	0	0.564	0.625
t	0	0.314	0.318	T	0	0.656	0.656
u	0	0.564	0.535	U	0	0.813	0.781
v	0	0.500	0.439	V	0	0.719	0.719
w	0	0.719	0.656	W	0	1.000	1.000
x	0	0.500	0.564	X	0	0.751	0.719
y	0	0.500	0.469	Y	0	0.749	0.719
z	0	0.437	0.439	Z	0	0.656	0.719
0	0	0.500	0.500	.(period)	0	0.248	0.250
1	0	0.500	0.500	,(comma)	0	0.248	0.250
2	0	0.500	0.500	(space)	1	0.250	0.250
3	0	0.500	0.500				
4	0	0.500	0.500				
5	0	0.500	0.500				
6	0	0.500	0.500			All characters have	
7	0	0.500	0.500			escapementY = 0	
8	0	0.500	0.500				
9	0	0.500	0.500				

Text Measuring

A creator often must calculate the space required to print a text string–the string's *measure*. The measure of a string is simply the sum of the widths (the escapements) of the characters in the string. This calculation breaks up a long sequence of words into lines of a certain length, and decides where to position a string so that it will be centered and so on.

While the measure of a string can be computed in many different units, it usually is most convenient for the creator to compute the measure in the MCS, which is the same system used to position the string. The measure is thus the sum of the character escapements as measured in the MCS.

Font metric information offers escapements in the character coordinate system units, so we must convert from the CCS to the MCS when computing widths. This transformation is precisely the one supplied to MODIFYFONT when a font is prepared, but we are interested only in the scaling component of the transformation. Let's define the *scale* of a font to be the SCALE argument in the transformation (or the product of the SCALE arguments, if there is more than one). Thus, the *scale* of font 0 in Example 4.6 is 180.

We therefore can compute the measure of a string in the x direction in the MCS with the following *MeasureX* algorithm (s[i] is the ith character of the string s and length(s) is the number of characters in the string):

```
procedure MeasureX(s:string):real;
  var m:real; i:integer;
  begin
  m:=0;
  for i:=1 to length(s) do
    m:=m + (escapementX of s[i] from metric master)
           * (scale of the font to which s[i] belongs);
  MeasureX:=m;
  end
```

For example, the measure of the string "Interpress" in Example 4.6 is 765.72. (Because the scale of all the characters is 180 in this case, we can sum the escapementX value for the 10 characters in "Interpress" from Table 4.1, obtaining 4.254, and then multiply by 180 to obtain 765.72.) The MeasureX algorithm properly computes the measure when characters from different fonts or of different sizes are mixed in a string.

Precision in Character Escapement

Adequate precision is important in calculating the measure of text lines. At a viewing distance of about 12 inches, the eye can detect a 1/400-inch positioning difference between two objects sufficiently close together. For example, the eye could detect such differences in the horizontal positions of the following two vertical bars:

|
|

When a line is measured, many character escapements are summed; the Interpress precision rules indicate that up to 250 character escapements can be summed safely. Therefore, you should be sure the absolute error in a character width is less than $(1/2) \times (1/400) \times (1/250)$ inch. For 10-point characters, that means keeping character widths to about one part in 30,000. For larger characters, more precision may be required, although it is probably safe to assume that far fewer than 250 round-off errors will accumulate.

When to Use Absolute and Relative Positioning

In setting the current position for the start of a string, you can either set it to an absolute location by using SETXY, or move it somewhere relative to where you find it by using SETXYREL, SETXREL, or SETYREL. There are no hard and fast rules about the use of positioning operators, but good Interpress style leads to the following guidelines:

- Use relative positioning when the relationship between two adjacent objects is important. Characters within a word, or words within a line, should be positioned relative to one another. This is why all character operators use relative positioning.

- Use absolute positioning to locate unrelated or loosely-related objects on the page. Thus, an entire line of text or an entry in a column of a table should be positioned globally.

- Never allow more than about 250 relative-positioning operators between absolute-positioning operators. The reason is that small numerical errors usually accompany each relative addition to the current position. If too many of these errors accumulate, the positioning error will be noticeable. Printers must obey precision rules that guarantee that the error will not be noticeable, provided fewer than 250 relative motions are used.

When relative positioning is used for closely-related objects, an Interpress master is more device independent; that is, it is more immune to the ill effects of font approximation. Thus, Example 4.7 may print badly if a font approximation is made, because characters may collide or overlap if the widths of the actual character operators are greater than those assumed when the master was created. Example 4.6, which prints the same text, is more immune to font approximation.

By contrast, absolute positioning achieves global or long-distance positioning relationships. For example, if several lines of text are to align at the left side of the text column (so-called *flush left*), it is best to set the starting position of each line with an absolute position.

When you are deciding whether to use absolute or relative positioning, ask yourself the question, "If the printer does not have the font requested, and uses an approximate font in which characters have very different escapements, what will happen to the printed result?" Usually, you will be able to decide how you want the image to degrade when font approximations occur.

Font Approximation

A master extracts fonts from a printer's font library using the FINDFONT operator. Normally, the font requested by the master is available in the printer's library. But what happens if the font named in the call to FINDFONT is not available? In this case, a printer does not just give up or summarily reject the master; instead, it searches for an approximate font to substitute. The printer then can print the document represented by the master, although the product's appearance will not precisely match the images specified by the master.

The way in which an approximate font is located is not defined by Interpress. The intention is that a printer retains, as an adjunct to its font library, some information that helps it to approximate font requests. It might, for example, keep for each font in the library a list of the fonts it approximates. Or it might have algorithms for finding the approximate font, such as rules for examining the identifiers in the name of the requested font and matching them to names available in the font library. For example, if a font name includes an identifier that indicates a font's character set, the printer could limit its search to those fonts with the same character-set identifier.

When a printer does not have a font and is forced to find a substitute, it issues an *appearance warning* to alert the user that the appearance of the printed document will not be precisely as specified in the master.

In practice, font approximation will seldom occur. You usually know what fonts are available on the printer when you construct the master. The need for approximation arises if a master is prepared for one printer and then transmitted to another printer, one that has a different font library. Similarly, if in the course of maintenance and upgrades an obsolete font is removed from a printer's library, masters may still be stored that request the font. If one of these masters is sent to the printer, an approximate font will have to be found; often, the approximation is simply the newer version of the missing font.

Font Tuning

A printer may use an approximate font to increase image quality. This seemingly paradoxical situation arises when the printer's font has been tuned for the best possible appearance or legibility on that particular device. Although Interpress allows a single character operator to be scaled to arbitrary sizes, converting a standard definition into an array of dots to expose on a raster printer may introduce jagged edges, stroke-weight irregularities, and other artifacts that reduce the font's legibility. To avoid these effects, a printer may retain separate character definitions for each size, with each definition carefully tuned to the printer's imaging properties.

Font tuning may also alter the escapements of characters very slightly, so that each width is an integral number of dots on the printing device. Again, this modification is sometimes necessary to guarantee pleasant and legible juxtapositions of letterforms. Although even small deviations from the character escapements used by the creator could potentially spoil the appearance of text, the CORRECT operator can compensate for any ill effects of font tuning.

The CORRECT Operator

The Interpress master precisely defines the position of every image on the printed page. For textual information, the master specifies the starting point of a line of text, but the final positioning of each succeeding character in a string is a function of the character-escapement metrics of the font being used by the printer. The creator of the master uses its knowledge of the character escapements to compute where the printer will place every character of the string. Synchronism between the actual placement of the text and the creator's computation of that placement of the text will be maintained only if the printer's character metrics are exactly the same as those known to the creator. In practice, the two sets of metrics may be different for a number of reasons, including the following:

1. The printer may have a version of the font different from the one used by the creator. The metrics of fonts tend to "drift" over time as font designers fine-tune their creations. Different printers may have different releases of a font. Even if all printers have the same release of the font, the document may have been archived for some time, and the release number currently in place may be different from the release number that existed when the document was created.

2. The printer may not be able to offer the font called for in the document, and may have to substitute another font with different font metrics in order to print the document. The printer may not have the required font at all, in which case it may use a different font of the

same size but with different metrics; or the printer may have the required font, but not in the exact size required by the master, in which case it might use the nearest size that it can supply, again with different metrics.

If either of these conditions occur, the images of the text string, and of any other images whose positions are tied to those of the string, will not be placed on the printed page in the *correct* positions. This incorrect positioning is further aggravated if the text, and any other associated images, is justified to fit a specified space on the page.

Suppose you are concerned about proper intercharacter spacing *and* the total length of a line, as in justification. If no font approximations occur, you can anticipate exactly the printer's intercharacter spacings, and therefore can anticipate exactly where the line will end by summing the widths of all the characters. If a font approximation occurs, however, one of two things happens:

1. If the master has used *relative* positioning automatically given by character operators, intercharacter spacings will be correct, but the total length of the line will be incorrect.

2. If the master has used *absolute* positioning of characters, the total length of the line will be correct, but the intercharacter spacings will be inappropriate for the font.

If you seldom care about the total length of the line, you can use relative positioning for maximum device independence. When you justify text lines, however, you care about *both* intercharacter spacing for maximum legibility and total line length so that left and right edges of lines align. The problem occurs often enough to cause concern (see Figure 4.15).

Interpress provides the CORRECT operator to cope with this case:

$$\text{CORRECT} <b:\text{Body}> \rightarrow <>$$

CORRECT precedes an Interpress body that prints a line of text. CORRECT also has access to the proper measure for the line via the imager variables. By setting imager variables you can specify the measure you expect the line to have. The CORRECT operator adjusts the positions of characters intelligently within the line, if necessary, to ensure that the line fits exactly in the specified measure. Thus, when you care where lines end, as well as where they begin, you should use CORRECT so that the master will print reasonably, even in the presence of font approximations. For efficiency, however, it is inadvisable to use CORRECT in less constrained circumstances, such as for making listings of computer files, or for ragged right text, when the creator is not vitally concerned where a text line ends.

When CORRECT prints a line, it may need to contract or expand the spacing within that line. To retain the text's legibility, even with substantial

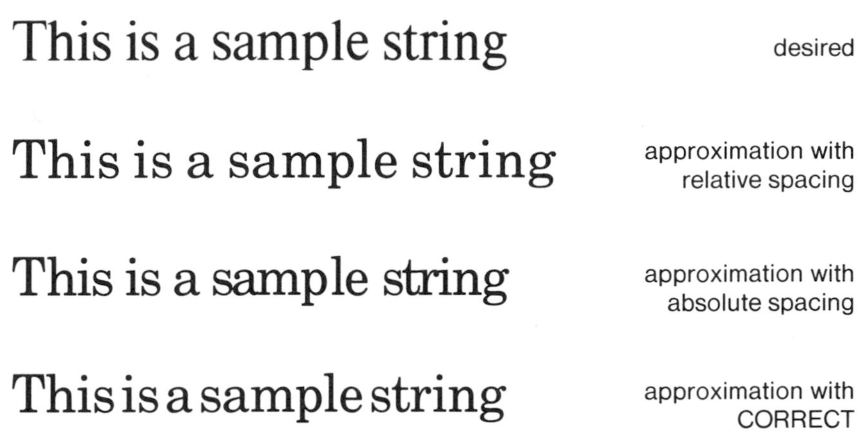

This is a sample string — desired

This is a sample string — approximation with relative spacing

This is a sample string — approximation with absolute spacing

This is a sample string — approximation with CORRECT

Figure 4.15 The effects of font approximations.

mismatches between the font assumed by the creator and the one chosen by the printer, CORRECT distinguishes between two kinds of spacing correction (see Figure 4.16):

1. The white space between words is called *space correcting*. This space can safely be expanded a good deal without making the line too hard to read. However, it cannot be shrunk too much, or word spacings will not be evident. CORRECT will only shrink this space by the fraction *correctShrink* (an imager variable with index = 20) before it takes other steps. That is, a space of length s will never be shrunk to less than $s \times correctShrink$ (see Figure 4.17).

2. The spacing between two letterforms is called *mask correcting*. Expanding this space usually diminishes legibility, because the font was not designed to be used that way; CORRECT never expands this space. However, if a line must be shortened, and the maximum shrinkage of the space-correcting characters is insufficient to achieve the desired measure, letterforms will be moved closer together. This is clearly not good, but there is not much choice!

Every character in a font has associated with it a correction property that describes whether the character is of the mask-correcting, space-correcting, or no-correction type. Characters that are of the space-correcting type have an escapement metric that can be stretched or shrunk as required. In Western languages, only the space character has this property. In some Eastern character systems, typified by Japanese Kanji characters, every character is of this type.

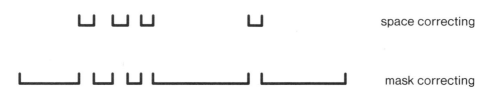

⊔ ⊔ ⊔ ⊔	space correcting
└─────┘ ⊔ ⊔ └─────┘ └─────┘	mask correcting

Figure 4.16 Space-correcting and mask-correcting characters.

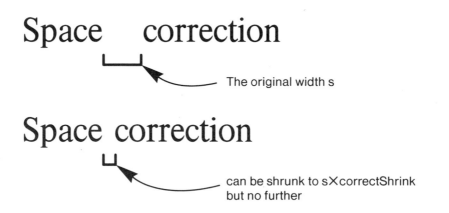

The original width s

can be shrunk to s✕correctShrink
but no further

Figure 4.17 The limit on space correction.

It is clear from this description that CORRECT may move characters around a little to correct the measure. This is one of the reasons why it is a good idea to use only relative positioning within a text line: if a character moves due to correction, you want the other objects related to it (for example, underlines, subscripts, superscripts, accents) to move with it. You even want the word to its right to move with it.

CORRECT can be used in many ways. We provide a template that will work in almost all cases for printing a line of text. The CORRECT operator takes a single body as its argument.

```
                        --CORRECT template: assume inside a page body--
tolerance 0 SETCORRECTTOLERANCE
correctShrinkValue 20 ISET
measure 0 SETCORRECTMEASURE
x y SETXY              --set starting position for text line--
CORRECT
{                      --start CORRECT body--
   --calls to SHOW, SETFONT, SPACE, SETXYREL, SETXREL, SETYREL, etc.--
   --are inserted here--
}                      --end CORRECT body, call CORRECT--
```

The first three lines of this template set various parameters. These lines can be omitted if the parameter already has been set to an appropriate value within the page body.

The imager variables *correctTX* and *correctTY* (indices 21 and 22) specify a tolerance parameter that tells CORRECT how accurate the line measures must be. These imager variables save the tolerance in device coordinates, but you should specify them in master coordinates using the SETCORRECTTOLERANCE operator:

$<$x:Number$>$ $<$y:Number$>$ SETCORRECTTOLERANCE $\rightarrow$ $<$ $>$

This operator converts the displacement x,y into device coordinates before saving it in the correctTX and correctTY imager variables.

The tolerance establishes the amount by which you are willing to permit the end point of the printed line to deviate from the end point of the justified line. One of these two values generally will be zero, but both may be nonzero for fonts with escapements that have nonzero values for both the x and y components. If the tolerance is large, CORRECT may need to do less work. For example, if the printer makes no font approximations, the text line should have almost exactly the right measure, but small round-off errors may prevent precision. If the line's measure is within the specified tolerance, a clever CORRECT implementation will not need to take any corrective action, and the interpretation of the master will be correspondingly faster. If, for example, a measure error of 0.5 points can be tolerated, the master should set the tolerance accordingly (for example, 5 0 SETCORRECTTOLERANCE when the MCS units are 1/10 of a point). The default value of tolerance, established at the beginning of each page body, is zero.

The *correctShrink* imager variable (index $=20$) limits the amount by which space-correcting characters will be shrunk when an entire line is shrunk. Its default value, established at the beginning of each page body, is 0.5, so a space never becomes smaller than one-half of its original size. There is no need to change this default if this value is acceptable.

The third parameter is the line's measure, the relative x and y displacements of the endpoint of the justified line from its beginning point, specified in persistent imager variables *correctMX* and *correctMY* (indices 2 and 3). Although it is saved in device coordinates, you should set the correct measure in master coordinates by using the SETCORRECTMEASURE operator:

<x:Number> <y:Number> SETCORRECTMEASURE → < >

Like the SETCORRECTTOLERANCE operator, this first converts the displacement to device coordinates and then saves it in the imager variables. The measure and tolerances parameters appear in Figure 4.18.

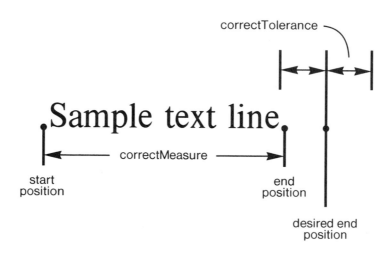

Figure 4.18 Correction parameters.

Generally, for languages in which printing is horizontal, correctMY will be zero; for languages in which printing is vertical, correctMX will be zero. Left-to-right, right-to-left, top-to-bottom, or bottom-to-top properties of languages are handled by the signs of these quantities. In some fonts, character escapements can have both x and y components; as a result, both values are nonzero. The measure may need to be changed more often than the other parameters, because different text lines on the page may have different measures. Sometimes, however, the previous measure value can be used; for example, all the lines in this paragraph, except the first and last ones, have the same measure.

The body following CORRECT invokes Interpress operators that print the text line. There are no restrictions on the operators contained in this body, but you should keep the following guidelines in mind:

- Use only relative positioning (SETXYREL, SETXREL, SETYREL, SPACE). The SPACE operator (described in a following section) should be used if the relative motion is generating white space that is to be treated as space correcting, such as space between words on a line. Use the other relative-positioning operators if the spacing is not to be altered by CORRECT.

- Do not use simple relative motions to move backward over characters already typeset within the line. If you need to use overstriking, or both super- and subscripts, somewhat more complex mechanisms are required: they are described later.

- Do not attempt persistent changes to the imager variables. Any nonpersistent imager variables changed within the CORRECT body will revert to their old values after CORRECT finishes. This behavior occurs when bodies are invoked with DOSAVE, which is used by CORRECT.

- The body passed to CORRECT will be interpreted either once or twice. Do not put operations in the body that depend on the number of times it will be executed. For example, if the body saves an object on the stack and leaves it there, one or two entries will be added to the stack, depending on whether the body is executed once or twice.

- Do not change the noImage variable to zero within a CORRECT body.

Example 4.9 demonstrates the use of the CORRECT template.

Example 4.9

```
Header "Interpress/Xerox/3.0 "      --header--
BEGIN                               --start of the master--
  { }                               --preamble--
  {                                 --start of the page--
    0.000035278 SCALE               --set MCS to 1/10-point units--
    CONCATT
    Identifier "xerox" Identifier "XC1-1-1" Identifier "times"
    3 MAKEVEC FINDFONT
    100 SCALE
    MODIFYFONT
    0 FSET                          --font 0 is 10-point Times Roman--
    Identifier "xerox" Identifier "XC1-1-1"
    Identifier "times-italic"
    3 MAKEVEC FINDFONT
    100 SCALE
```

```
MODIFYFONT
1 FSET                          --font 1 is 10-point Times Italic--
5 0 SETCORRECTTOLERANCE         --set tolerance to 0.5 points--
                                --leave correctShrink set at 0.5--
2281 0 SETCORRECTMEASURE        --set measure to 3.17 inches--
720 6480 SETXY                  --set starting position for line--
                                --x=1 inch, y=9 inches--
CORRECT
{                               --start CORRECT body--
   0 SETFONT                    --set current font to font 0--
   String "An example of the CORRECT operator in "
   SHOW                         --print text--
   1 SETFONT                    --set current font to font 1--
   String "Interpress."
   SHOW
}                               --end of CORRECT body--
}                               --end of the page body--
END                             --end of the master--
```

In Example 4.9, the measure is the computed width of the following text:

An example of the CORRECT operator in *Interpress*.

The width is computed using the escapements obtained from Table 4.1 and the MeasureX algorithm. If you want to check your work, here is a breakdown of the calculation:

MeasureX("An") = 131.2   MeasureX("example") = 359.6
MeasureX("of") = 87.5   MeasureX("the") = 134.7
MeasureX("CORRECT") = 503.3   MeasureX("operator") = 362.8
MeasureX("in") = 84.4   MeasureX("*Interpress.*") = 442.5

There are also 7 spaces in the line, each with measure 25
The total measure is 2281 units

Example 4.9 makes an important point: the purpose of CORRECT is not to achieve the appearance of a justified line of text, but rather to force a line of text to be its intended length even in the presence of font approximation. The key here is that "intended length" is the length of the line computed assuming perfect font matches. If you want to justify a line of text, use the techniques explained in the section on justifying text.

Now let us see just how the CORRECT operator works. The operator executes its body twice. The first time, CORRECT finds out how much error exists in the lines measured and learns how many mask-correcting operators and how much space-correcting distance it has to work with. The second time, it does the imaging, making the appropriate positioning adjustments (see Figure 4.19). At the start of the CORRECT operator, initialization is performed. Counters for the number of mask-correcting characters and amount of space-correcting distance are initialized to 0. The current position is stored so that it can be reset for the second pass. The noImage imager variable is set to 1 so that nothing will be drawn on the first pass, and the *correctPass* imager variable (index = 19) is set to 1. The body is then executed. As characters are executed by the SHOW operator, a check is made of the correctPass variable and, on pass 1, each mask-correcting character increments a counter, and each space-correcting character adds its width to the total space-correcting distance.

When the body has been executed, the current position is compared to a target position, which is where the line began, plus the correct measure (correctMX, correctMY). The difference between the target position and the actual position is the amount of correction needed. If the actual line measure is shorter than the target measure, the space-correcting characters will handle all the adjustment. If the actual line is too long, the compression needed may be more than the correctShrink imager variable allows. To find out whether it is, the CORRECT operator multiplies the total space-correcting distance by correctShrink, and compares the result to the position error. If the position error is less, the space-correcting characters can handle it. If not, the difference between the values must be handled by the mask-correcting characters.

The CORRECT operator computes the amount of distance to be adjusted by the space-correcting characters, and the amount, if any, to be adjusted by the mask-correcting characters. It then resets the current position, sets noImage to 0 so that the characters will be drawn, and changes correctPass to 2. It then executes the body a second time. This time, SHOW finds that correctPass is 2, and for each mask-correcting and space-correcting character, it performs the adjustment to the current position, which CORRECT has calculated. The characters are displayed in their corrected positions.

Finally, CORRECT changes correctPass to 0, which turns off the correction machinery. It checks that the result is now within tolerance, and sets the current position to be exactly the target position.

As we have described it, CORRECT always takes two passes and checks the tolerance only at the end. However, clever implementations may be able to process the body more efficiently if the line lies within tolerance. For example, CORRECT might image the body on the first pass and, if the line is within tolerance, skip the second pass. If the line exceeds tolerance, the imaging must be undone.

Interpress makes some of the machinery of the CORRECT operator available to you so that you can construct correctable objects. You may want to build

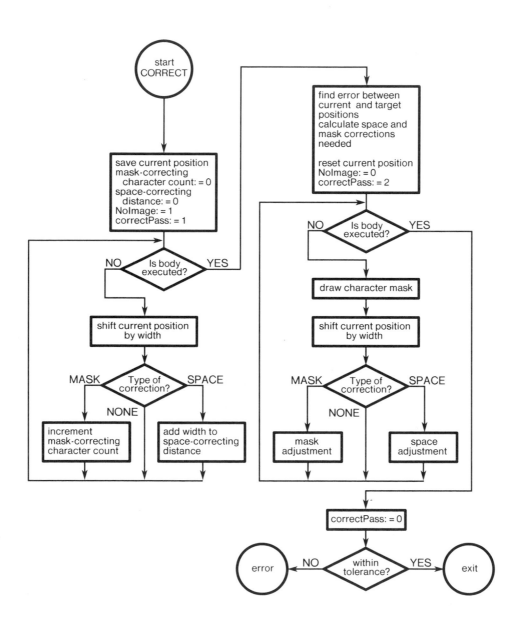

Figure 4.19 Outline of the correction process.

logos, special symbols, or other graphic objects that will be imaged along with a text string. Interpress lets you define these objects so that they can be space correcting or mask correcting. Thus, if the objects are included in a CORRECT body, any needed adjustment can be applied to your special symbols as well as to the characters. Suppose your correctable object is defined as a composed operator. To make this a mask-correcting operator, include in it a call to CORRECTMASK:

$$< > \text{ CORRECTMASK} \rightarrow < >$$

When SHOW images each mask-correcting character, it automatically calls CORRECTMASK; for your special symbol, however, your operator must make the call explicitly. The CORRECTMASK action depends on the correctPass imager variable. If correctPass is 1, CORRECTMASK increments a counter, to tell CORRECT how many mask-correcting objects are in its body. If correctPass is 2, CORRECTMASK makes an adjustment to the current position, indicating the amount of positioning error that CORRECT determines the mask-correcting objects must accommodate, divided by the number of mask-correcting objects. For any other value of correctPass, the CORRECTMASK operator does nothing at all.

To build a space-correcting operator, you should include a call to CORRECTSPACE:

$$<\text{x:Number}> \ <\text{y:Number}> \text{ CORRECTSPACE} \rightarrow < >$$

The operands x and y tell the operator the effective "width" of your object. Note that this does not make the object this width. You still need to use x y SETXYREL or an equivalent operation for your object to displace the current position. The operands simply report the amount of displacement that will take place to CORRECTSPACE. The actions of CORRECTSPACE also depend on the correctPass variable. If correctPass is 1, then CORRECTSPACE adds the x and y operands into a total for the amount of space-correcting distance in the CORRECT body. The CORRECT operator uses this total in determining how much of the error in the measure can be repaired by the space-correcting objects, and how much must be handled by the mask-correcting ones. If correctPass is 2, then CORRECTSPACE adjusts the current position by the amount that x and y should be changed. If correctPass is neither 1 nor 2, then CORRECTSPACE does nothing.

Underlining

Although underlining is frowned on in high-quality typography, the technique is often used in word-processing applications and other low-quality documents. In Interpress, an underline is actually a rectangle drawn under text. A special underlining method is offered for convenience. Text uses the current-position imager variables for positioning. So, if we wish to underline a text string, we should describe the underline running from the current position at the start of the string to the current position at the end of the string. We need a way to remember where the string starts. We can image the string with SHOW instructions, and then draw the underline from the stored initial position to a point governed by the current position of the end of the string.

The operator STARTUNDERLINE is used to remember where the string starts:

$$< > \text{STARTUNDERLINE} \rightarrow < >$$

This operator stores the starting position in the imager variable *underlineStart* (index = 17). It saves the x component of the current position in master coordinates, which is equivalent to GETCP POP 17 ISET. Because only the x coordinate is saved, this underline mechanism only works for lines that lie parallel to the master coordinate system's x axis (left-to-right text).

The underline is drawn by the MASKUNDERLINE operator:

$$< \text{dy:Number} > \ < \text{h:Number} > \ \text{MASKUNDERLINE} \rightarrow < >$$

This operator draws an underline of thickness h. The top of the underline is a distance dy below the baseline of the current character line (that is, dy below the y value of the current position in master coordinates). If x_s is the value saved in the underlineStart imager variable, and (x_{cp}, y_{cp}) is the current position in master coordinates, then the corners of the underline rectangle are:

$$(x_s, y_{cp} - dy - h), (x_s, y_{cp} - dy), (x_{cp}, y_{cp} - dy), (x_{cp}, y_{cp} - dy - h)$$

These are shown in Figure 4.20.

Figure 4.20 Definition of an underline.

Example 4.10 shows a typical application of the underline operator (see Figure 4.21).

Example 4.10

```
Header "Interpress/Xerox/3.0 "          --header--
BEGIN                                    --start of the master--
   { }                                   --preamble--
   {                                     --start of the page--
     Identifier "xerox" Identifier "XC1-1-1" Identifier "modern"
     3 MAKEVEC FINDFONT
     0.00706 SCALE
     MODIFYFONT
     0 FSET                              --define font 0--
     0 SETFONT                           --set current font--
     0.03 0.24 SETXY                     --start of text string--
     String "This is an "
     SHOW
     STARTUNDERLINE                      --underline words--
     String "underscore example"
     SHOW
     0.002 0.001 MASKUNDERLINE
     String " in Interpress"             --remainder of string--
     SHOW
   }                                     --end of the page--
END                                      --end of the master--
```

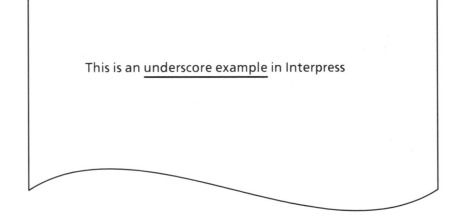

This is an <u>underscore example</u> in Interpress

Figure 4.21 The result of Example 4.10.

If, instead of underlining, we wanted to place a rule through the middle of the word–called a strikethrough–we use a negative value for dy so that the rule is placed above the baseline.

Because the starting position of an underline is stored in an imager variable, it can be saved and restored using the DOSAVE machinery. This means that you can nest underlines, as in an underlined word within an underlined string: you simply wrap the nested underlines with operator bodies, as in Example 4.11 (see Figure 4.22).

Example 4.11

```
Header "Interpress/Xerox/3.0 "              --header--
BEGIN                                       --start of the master--
  { }                                       --preamble--
  {                                         --start of the page--
    Identifier "xerox" Identifier "XC1-1-1" Identifier "modern"
    3 MAKEVEC FINDFONT
    0.00706 SCALE
    MODIFYFONT
    0 FSET                                  --define font 0--
    0 SETFONT                               --set current font--
    0.03 0.24 SETXY                         --start of text string--
    STARTUNDERLINE                          --start of string underline--
    String "Underlined "
    SHOW
    DOSAVESIMPLEBODY                        --save the underlineStart--
    {
      STARTUNDERLINE                        --start of word underline--
      String "word"
      SHOW
      0.001 0.001 MASKUNDERLINE             --underline the word--
    }                                       --restore underline start--
    String " in an underlined string"
    SHOW
    0.003 0.001 MASKUNDERLINE               --underline the string--
  }                                         --end of the page--
END                                         --end of the master--
```

Because the underline operators use the same current-position placement mechanism as text operators, they are fully compatible with CORRECT. An adjusted string will have a correspondingly adjusted underscore. However, you must be sure that the STARTUNDERLINE and MASKUNDERLINE are either both inside or both outside the CORRECT body.

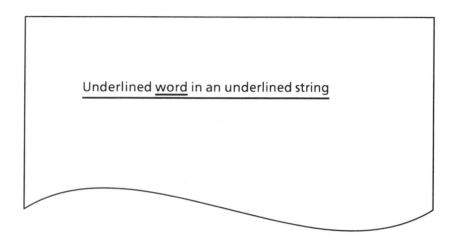

Figure 4.22 The result of Example 4.11.

Although it is intended for underlining text, the MASKUNDERLINE mechanism can be used all on its own for drawing horizontal lines, as shown in Example 4.12. (Actually, lines of any angle can be drawn with a properly rotated MCS.) This may be used as an alternative to MASKRECTANGLE, for example, in creating forms (see Figure 4.23).

Example 4.12

```
Header "Interpress/Xerox/3.0 "        --header--
BEGIN                                 --start of the master--
   { }                                --preamble--
   {                                  --start of the page--
      0.02 0.25 SETXY                 --upper-left corner--
      STARTUNDERLINE                  --remember the 0.02--
      0.16 SETXREL                    --set line length--
      0 0.003 MASKUNDERLINE           --draw a thick line--
      0.02 0.001 MASKUNDERLINE        --draw three thin lines--
      0.04 0.001 MASKUNDERLINE
      0.07 0.001 MASKUNDERLINE
   }                                  --end of the page--
END                                   --end of the master--
```

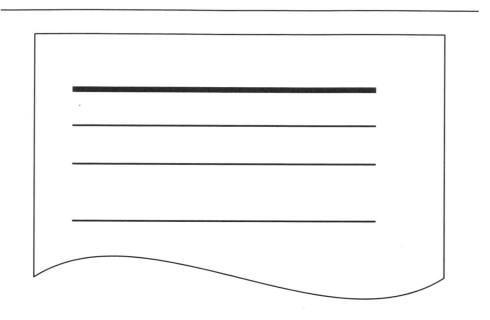

Figure 4.23 The result of Example 4.12.

Disabling Spacing Correction

Some times it is necessary to disable the effects of spacing correction in part, but not all, of the line of a text. If spacing correction is not required anywhere in a line, such as in computer listings, ragged-right text, or the last line of a justified paragraph, the CORRECT operator should not be used at all. However, if the line, as a whole, should have correct measure, but local regions of the line must not participate in the correction calculations, correction can be disabled locally.

The CORRECT mechanism is keyed to the correctPass imager variable (index = 19). The variable has the value 0 when correction is not taking place. You can temporarily disable correction by saving the current value of the variable and then changing it to 0. To reenable the CORRECT mechanism, you restore the variable's value. If you alter the correctPass variable, you should be very careful to restore it. Of course, both actions should occur within the body that follows a CORRECT operator.

We present two examples in which local disabling of CORRECT is useful. One is for superscript and subscripts and the other is for centered text.

Superscripts and Subscripts

Superscripts and subscripts are placed with relative positioning commands that shift the baseline to a new location, and shift it back again when the script is finished. To display the string "D_i," for example, we use SETYREL to move the current position down for the origin of the subscript, and then back up to continue with the rest of the string.

Example 4.13

```
0 SETFONT        --assume this is 10-point Times Roman--    --1--
String "D"                                                  --2--
SHOW             --show symbol--                            --3--
-40 SETYREL      --move baseline down 4 points--            --4--
3 SETFONT        --assume this is 8-point Times Roman--     --5--
String "i"                                                  --6--
SHOW             --show subscript--                         --7--
40 SETYREL       --restore baseline--                       --8--
0 SETFONT        --change back to 10-point Times Roman--    --9--
```

This code sequence could appear in a CORRECT body, or it could appear by itself. Superscripts are handled by using a positive displacement in line 4, and a corresponding negative displacement in line 8.

If a symbol has both subscripts and superscripts, the solution is a little more complicated. We need to remember the current position after the symbol has been printed and restore it for the second script. Thus, the procedure might be described as follows: (1) SHOW the symbol, (2) save the current position, (3) use SETYREL to establish the baseline for one of the scripts, (4) SHOW the script, (5) restore the current position, (6) use SETYREL to establish the baseline for the other script, (7) SHOW the script, (8) use SETYREL to return the baseline to its original position (see Figure 4.24). This procedure is illustrated in Example 4.14, which adds a superscript "3" to Example 4.13.

Example 4.14

```
0 SETFONT        --10-point Times Roman--
String "D"
SHOW             --show symbol--
0 IGET 1 IGET    --save current position on the stack--
-40 SETYREL      --move baseline down 4 points for subscript--
3 SETFONT        --8-point Times Roman--
String "i"
```

```
SHOW                --show subscript--
1 ISET 0 ISET       --restore current position--
45 SETYREL          --move baseline up 4.5 points for superscript--
String "3"
SHOW                --show superscript--
-45 SETYREL         --restore baseline--
```

Figure 4.24 The path of the current position when imaging two scripts.

The procedure outlined in Example 4.14 works in the absence of correction. However, when a symbol with both subscript and superscript appears within a justified line that is adjusted with CORRECT, a slightly different procedure is required. Correction is turned off in the shortest script, so as not to mislead CORRECT into thinking the line length can be changed by altering spacing within this script; the line length will not change because we will restore the current position that we saved, which will cancel any alterations CORRECT might have made (see Figure 4.25).

Thus, the recommended procedure is as follows: (1) SHOW the symbol, (2) save the current position and turn off correction, (3) use SETYREL to establish the baseline for the script with the shortest measure, (4) SHOW the shortest script, (5) restore the current position and correction information, (6) use SETYREL to establish the baseline for the longest script, (7) SHOW the longest script, (8) use SETYREL to return the baseline to its original position. Example 4.15 shows the modifications to Example 4.14 necessary in the presence of correction; the steps are shown in parentheses.

CORRECT believes it can change
the spacing by adjusting both scripts

Disable correction for one script

Figure 4.25 Disabling correction when imaging two scripts.

Example 4.15

```
0 SETFONT          --10-point Times Roman--
String "D"
SHOW               --(1) show symbol--
19 IGET            --(2) save correction state--
0 19 ISET          --(2) turn off correction--
0 IGET 1 IGET      --(2) save current position--
-40 SETYREL        --(3) move baseline down 4 points--
                   --for short script--
3 SETFONT          --8-point Times Roman--
String "i"
SHOW               --(4) show shortest script (subscript)--
1 ISET 0 ISET      --(5a) restore current position--
19 ISET            --(5b) restore correction state--
45 SETYREL         --(6) move baseline up 4.5 points--
                   --for long script--
String "3"
SHOW               --(7) show longest script (superscript)--
-45 SETYREL        --(8) restore baseline--
```

Another approach would be to turn off correction for both scripts, as shown in Example 4.16.

Example 4.16

```
0 SETFONT        --10-point Times Roman--
String "D"
SHOW             --(1) show symbol--
19 IGET          --(2) save correction state--
0 19 ISET        --(2) turn off correction--
0 IGET 1 IGET    --(2) save current position--
-40 SETYREL      --(3) move baseline down 4 points--
                 --for short script--
3 SETFONT        --8-point Times Roman--
String "i"
SHOW             --(4) show shortest script (subscript)--
1 ISET 0 ISET    --(5a) restore current position--
45 SETYREL       --(6) move baseline up 4.5 points--
                 --for long script--
String "3"
SHOW             --(7) show longest script (superscript)--
-45 SETYREL      --(8) restore baseline--
19 ISET          --(5b) restore correction state--
```

Centering

You can center text by computing its measure and positioning it accordingly. However, if font approximations are made, the text may not be centered correctly. Of course, you can use CORRECT with the measure set to the measure of the requested line. If you do this, CORRECT will change the character spacing to provide the requested length, and the text will be centered, but its appearance will be degraded (see Figure 4.26).

An alternative is to use the approximated font with its own escapements, but to alter the position of the start of the text so that it remains centered (see Figure 4.27). This technique can be employed by using CORRECT, preceding and following the string with generous and equal space, but turning correction off inside the text to be centered. In this way, CORRECT will adjust the space equally, and the text will remain centered.

For example, suppose the measure of the string "Interpress Sourcebook" is 980 units, including the space, in the master coordinate system, and that it is to be centered about the point $x = 3240$, $y = 7200$. We will put 1000 units of space on each end of the string, as shown in Example 4.17.

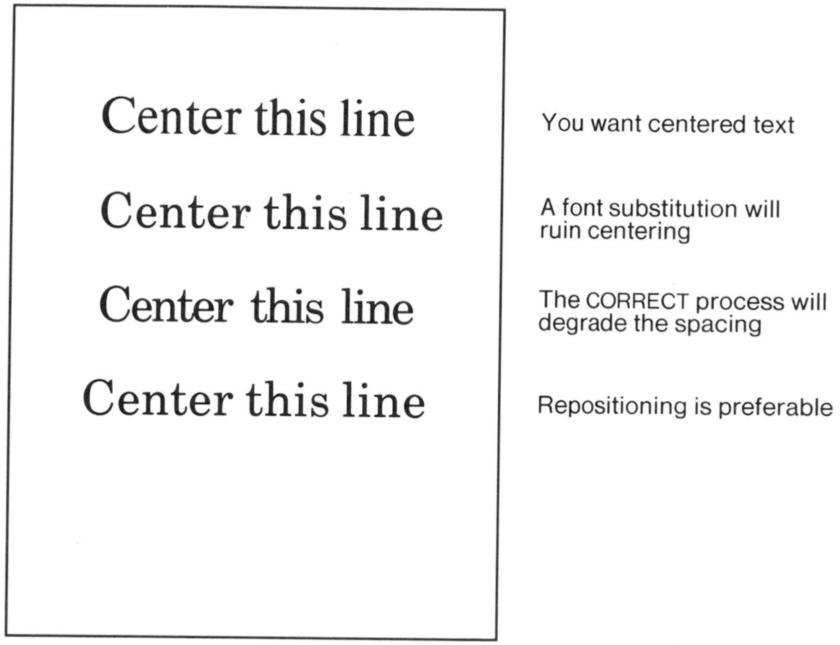

Center this line   You want centered text

Center this line   A font substitution will
ruin centering

Center this line   The CORRECT process will
degrade the spacing

Center this line   Repositioning is preferable

Figure 4.26 Techniques for line centering.

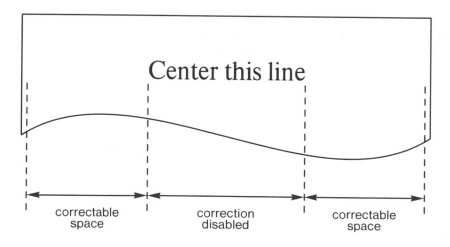

Center this line

correctable space   correction disabled   correctable space

Figure 4.27 Adjusting the space surrounding the text.

Example 4.17

```
Header "Interpress/Xerox/3.0 "        --header--
BEGIN                                 --start of the master--
  { }                                 --preamble--
  {                                   --start of the page--
    0.000035278 SCALE                 --set MCS to 1/10-point units--
    CONCATT
    Identifier "xerox" Identifier "XC1-1-1" Identifier "times"
    3 MAKEVEC FINDFONT
    100 SCALE
    MODIFYFONT
    0 FSET                            --font 0 is 10-point Times Roman--
    5 0 SETCORRECTTOLERANCE           --set tolerance to 0.5 points--
                                      --leave correctShrink set at 0.5--

    2980 0 SETCORRECTMEASURE          --set measure to--
                                      --1000+980+1000--

    1750 7200 SETXY                   --set starting position to--
                                      --x=3240-(2980/2), y=7200--

    CORRECT
    {                                 --start CORRECT body--
      1000 SPACE                      --first adjustable space--
      19 IGET                         --save correction state--
      0 19 ISET                       --turn off correction--
      0 SETFONT                       --set current font to font 0--
      String "Interpress Sourcebook"
      SHOW
      19 ISET                         --restore correction--
      1000 SPACE                      --second adjustable space--
    }                                 --end of the CORRECT body--
  }                                   --end of the page--
END                                   --end of the master--
```

Justifying Text

A number of techniques can typeset justified lines of text (see Figure 4.28). In all cases, the creator is concerned both with intercharacter spacing and with total line measure, so the CORRECT operator should be used to force the justified appearance even when font approximations must be made.

The first part of any justification mechanism determines where to break a line, such as at a space between words, at a hyphen in a hyphenated word, or at a hyphen inserted in a word. The details of this decision depend a great deal on the typographical rules and styles that the creator wants to uphold.

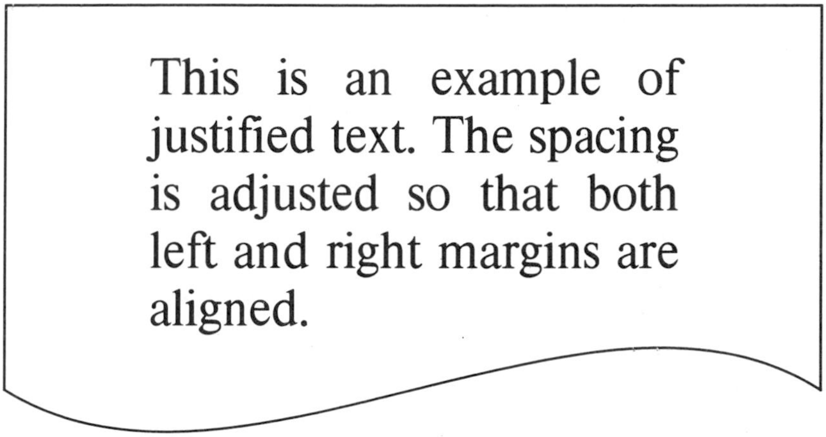

> This is an example of justified text. The spacing is adjusted so that both left and right margins are aligned.

Figure 4.28 Justified text.

However, a basic computation necessary to all rules is the determination of the measure of a word; that is, of the horizontal space that a word will occupy when printed in its prescribed font. This calculation is performed by the MeasureX algorithm from the section on Text Measuring.

The second part of a justification algorithm consists of computing the spacings between words that will achieve the proper total line length. Again, typographical styles differ. Simple justification algorithms will make all interword spaces equal, whereas more complex ones vary the widths slightly to avoid unpleasant visual effects such as *rivers* in blocks of justified text.

Justifying with the SPACE Operator. The most general way to typeset justified text in Interpress is to use relative positioning of the current position to specify the interword spacings. The SPACE operator is used for this purpose, because it both achieves relative motion and interacts with CORRECT to alter the space slightly if necessary to achieve the total line measure specified.

$$<x:\text{Number}> \text{SPACE} \rightarrow < >$$

The SPACE operator has an effect on the current position similar to that of x SETXREL, but the current position may be corrected slightly, if necessary, to account for font approximation. SPACE enables you to generate space-correcting interword spacings of any width you want.

Let's use as an example the line of text printed in Example 4.9. Suppose that the line of text is supposed to occupy 21 picas, or 3.5 inches, or 2520 units in the MCS we have chosen. We use the MeasureX algorithm to determine that the total width of the words in the text, not counting spaces, is 2106 units in the MCS. Thus, 2520 − 2106 or 414 units must be spread among the seven interword spaces. If each space is 59.14 units wide, the seven spaces will total 413.98 units, which is so close that the difference will not be apparent on the page. Or six of the seven spaces can be made 59 units wide and the remaining one made 60 units wide. Adopting this second approach, because it requires only integers to appear in the master, we obtain the master in Example 4.18.

Example 4.18

```
Header "Interpress/Xerox/3.0 "        --header--
BEGIN                                 --start of the master--
  { }                                 --preamble--
  {                                   --start of the page--
    0.000035278 SCALE                 --set MCS to 1/10-point units--
    CONCATT
    Identifier "xerox" Identifier "XC1-1-1" Identifier "times"
    3 MAKEVEC FINDFONT
    100 SCALE
    MODIFYFONT
    0 FSET                            --font 0 is 10-point Times Roman--
    Identifier "xerox" Identifier "XC1-1-1"
    Identifier "times-italic"
    3 MAKEVEC FINDFONT
    100 SCALE
    MODIFYFONT
    1 FSET                            --font 1 is 10-point Times Italic--
    5 0 SETCORRECTTOLERANCE           --set tolerance to 0.5 points--
                                      --leave correctShrink set at 0.5--
    2520 0 SETCORRECTMEASURE          --set measure to 3.5 inches--
    720 6480 SETXY                    --set starting position for line--
                                      --x=1 inch, y=9 inches--
    CORRECT
    {                                 --start CORRECT body--
      0 SETFONT                       --set current font to font 0--
      String "An" SHOW 59 SPACE       --first word and trailing space--
      String "example" SHOW 59 SPACE
      String "of" SHOW 59 SPACE
      String "the" SHOW 59 SPACE
      String "CORRECT" SHOW 59 SPACE
      String "operator" SHOW 59 SPACE
      String "in" SHOW 60 SPACE
      1 SETFONT                       --set current font to font 1--
```

```
        String "Interpress." SHOW
    }                                 --invoke CORRECT--
  }                                   --end of the page--
END                                   --end of the master--
```

Note, in Example 4.18, that the measure specified to CORRECT (2520 units) has been changed to reflect the length of the properly justified line.

This technique allows considerable flexibility in allocating space between words. Its only drawback is that the master gets rather bulky because each word is passed to SHOW individually. A more compact but less flexible technique is described in the next section.

Justifying with Amplified Spaces. It would seem that Example 4.18 could be shortened considerably if the master were able to instruct Interpress to alter the width of the "space" character while the line of text was printed. If the space character were altered to have a width of 59.14 units, just for this line, then words and spaces alike could be passed to SHOW and a justified line still could be obtained.

Interpress achieves this effect by using an *amplifying space*: a character operator in a font that is a space (prints no graphic symbol) but that has an adjustable escapement. Amplifying characters multiply their escapementX and escapementY values by the imager variable *amplifySpace* (index = 18) to determine the relative positioning to perform. So, by using amplifying spaces for interword spaces and by setting amplifySpace correctly, you can set the interword spaces so that the line is justified.

An element of the metrics for a character is a flag that tells whether the character is amplifying. This can be checked by the SHOW operator when imaging characters, and is available to you through the metric master for planning the appropriate amplifySpace values. If amplified = 0, the calculation that SHOW uses to change the current position is (escapementX escapementY SETXYREL). If amplified = 1, the calculation is (escapementX amplifySpace IGET MUL escapementY amplifySpace IGET MUL SETXYREL). If the amplified metric is not specified, it is assumed to have a value of 0.

To determine the value of amplifySpace that must be used to justify a line of text, it is necessary to measure the text such that the widths of amplified and normal characters are kept separate. The computation might be expressed as follows ($s[i]$ is the ith character of the string s and length(s) is the number of characters in the string):

```
var  m, ma:real; i:integer;
begin
m := 0;   ma := 0;
for i := 1 to length(s) do
```

```
if (amplified of s[i] from metric master) = 0 then
  m := m + (escapementX of s[i] from metric master)*(scale of s[i])
else
  ma := ma + (escapementX of s[i] from metric master)*(scale of s[i]);
```

The variable m is the sum of the widths of the normal characters and the variable ma is the sum of the widths of the amplified characters. Therefore, the width of the string would be $m + ma \times$ amplifySpace. If we know what the width of the line is supposed to be, we can easily solve for the value of amplifySpace that should be put in the master. In Example 4.18, the width of the line is 2520, m is 2106, and ma is 175 (note from Table 4.1 that the normal space character is amplifying). Thus, amplifySpace is (2520-2106)/175, which is the rational fraction 414/175 or 2.3657.

We can now rework Example 4.18 to use amplified spaces, as shown in Example 4.19.

Example 4.19

```
Header "Interpress/Xerox/3.0 "        --header--
BEGIN                                 --start of the master--
  { }                                 --preamble--
  {                                   --start of the page--
    0.000035278 SCALE
    CONCATT                           --set MCS to 1/10-point units--
    Identifier "xerox" Identifier "XC1-1-1" Identifier "times"
    3 MAKEVEC FINDFONT
    100 SCALE
    MODIFYFONT
    0 FSET                            --font 0 is 10-point Times Roman--
    Identifier "xerox" Identifier "XC1-1-1" Identifier "times-italic"
    3 MAKEVEC FINDFONT
    100 SCALE
    MODIFYFONT
    1 FSET                            --font 1 is 10-point Times Italic--
    5 0 SETCORRECTTOLERANCE           --set tolerance to 0.5 points--
                                      --leave correctShrink set at 0.5--
    2520 0 SETCORRECTMEASURE          --set measure to 3.5 inches--
    720 6480 SETXY                    --set starting position for line--
                                      --x=1 inch, y=9 inches--
    CORRECT
    {                                 --start CORRECT body--
      2.3657 18 ISET                  --set amplifySpace--
      0 SETFONT                       --set current font to font 0--
```

```
     String "An example of the CORRECT operator in "
     SHOW                        --print text--
     1 SETFONT                   --set current font to font 1--
     String "Interpress." SHOW
   }                             --end of CORRECT body--
 }                               --end of the page--
END                             --end of the master--
```

Note that the setting of amplifySpace will not persist beyond the execution of the CORRECT operator because, as we remarked earlier, nonpersistent imager variables changed inside the body argument of CORRECT revert to their former values when CORRECT terminates.

Example 4.19 shows how simple justification, such as might be suitable for word-processing output, can be achieved without appreciably lengthening the master or slowing its interpretation. For very high-quality typography or for more complex justification requirements, the SPACE operator, as illustrated in Example 4.18, is recommended.

The SHOW Operator

Now that we have seen fontDescriptions, character escapements, amplifySpace, and CORRECT, let us look once again at the SHOW operator and examine the work that it does (see Figure 4.29). SHOW must image each character referenced by the character indices in its vector operand. For each character index, it must first perform a TRANS to position the character's origin at the current position. It must get the fontDescription for the current font, and any transformations from MODIFYFONT. This transformation is concatenated onto the current transformation to shift to the character coordinate system. It also must extract the transformation property from the fontDescription and concatenate it onto T to yield the character-definition coordinates. This is the coordinate system that the character masks expect. SHOW must get the character masks from the fontDescription and find the particular mask operator for the desired character. The character-mask operator is executed with stack, frame, and imager variables protected from permanent change. SHOW arranges for the fontDescription to be on the top of the stack when the character mask is executed. We shall see at the end of this chapter how this feature is useful in defining characters as composites of other characters.

After the character is imaged, SHOW must displace the current position by the character's width. SHOW extracts the x and y escapements and the amplified property from the fontDescription. If the character is amplified, the escapements are multiplied by the current amplifySpace imager variable;

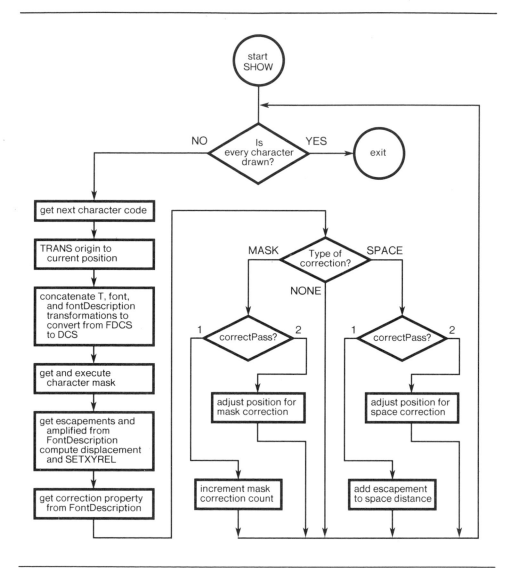

Figure 4.29 Outline of SHOW.

otherwise, they remain as defined. The (possibly amplified) escapements are then added to the current position.

Finally, the fontDescription is examined to find the character's correction properties. If the character is mask correcting, the CORRECTMASK operator is called. If it is space correcting, the (possibly amplified) escapements are used as operands in a call on the CORRECTSPACE operator.

SHOW uses DOSAVESIMPLEBODY for this operation, so only the persistent imager variables are changed.

Flush Left, Ragged Right

Flush-left, ragged-right text is handled simply in Interpress (see Figure 4.30). The starting position of the line is specified with SETXY, followed by commands to show the line. It usually is not necessary to use CORRECT for ragged-right text. If the right edge must not move too far in the presence of font approximations, though, CORRECT may be required. For example, if ragged text is fit inside a box with rules around it, CORRECT can ensure that text will never cross the rules.

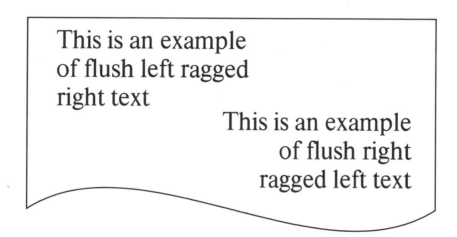

Figure 4.30 Flush-left, ragged-right and flush-right, ragged-left text.

Flush Right, Ragged Left

If lines of type are to align at their right sides, CORRECT must be used to ensure that font approximations do not cause the line length to vary (see Figure 4.30). The starting position of the line is specified with SETXY, and the line's total length (distance from starting position to right alignment point) is specified as the measure to CORRECT.

Kerning

Often the most pleasing spacing of a pair of characters is not the width associated with the first character. For example, if the two characters "A" and "V" are printed using normal spacing (the width of "A"), they will appear to be too far apart because the right side of the "A" and the left side of the "V" are parallel. Kerning is a technique for altering intercharacter spacing of pairs of characters for a better appearance (see Figure 4.31).

Normal placement   After kerning

Figure 4.31 Kerning to improve the placement of "A" and "V."

Kerning can be specified explicitly in the master by relative positioning. In this case, SETXREL is the best operator. To print the sequence "AV," we might use the following sequence:

string "A" SHOW −2 SETXREL string "V" SHOW

The call to SETXREL moves the current position to the left slightly so that the "V" is closer to the "A" than it would be otherwise. Do not forget that kerning adjustments alter the measure of a line, which needs to be taken into account by the MeasureX algorithm.

Relative positioning ensures that the master does not depend on highly-accurate correspondence between the character escapements known to the creator and those that will be used by the printer. If CORRECT alters the position of the "A" slightly, the position of the "V" will move as well. Note that we use SETXREL for kerning, rather than SPACE, because we do not want CORRECT to alter this relative motion at all.

The size of the kerning adjustment must be determined by the creator. Suggested kerning data may be available from the printer or may be derived by the creator from other information about the fonts in use. The Interpress conventions for character operators do not do kerning automatically for several reasons: current typographic practices discourage kerning except for occasional display type and very high-quality text; the amount of kerning adjustment is not always a unique property of a font, but changes with the application; and, if characters of different sizes or from different fonts are to be kerned, the number of different kerning adjustments that must be stored is too large for all Interpress imagers to save.

Letterspacing

In some cases, especially in headlines or display types, spacing between characters may be increased beyond the normal width spacing. Letterspacing can also be used to avoid "collisions" between characters: for example, "*f*)" rather than "*f*)." Letterspacing is just like kerning, except that the spacing corrections tend to be positive rather than negative. All our remarks about kerning in the previous section apply to letterspacing.

For letterspacing, you must provide positioning information for every character; SHOWANDXREL allows you to do this in a compact way:

$$< v:Vector > \text{SHOWANDXREL} \rightarrow < >$$

For each character, you need to specify a correction to its escapement. If you select an MCS such that coordinates and character escapements can be expressed as integers, then the necessary corrections to the escapements will be small integers. SHOWANDXREL lets you take advantage of this fact by interleaving correction values ranging between −128 and 127 with the character codes. You can make a single vector of mixed character codes and relative spacing adjustments. This vector can be compactly encoded as a series of bytes using a *sequenceString*. The odd elements of the vector are character codes, and are treated as they are by the SHOW operator; the even elements, modulo 256 and then minus 128, provide an additional relative spacing adjustment between the characters. SHOWANDXREL interprets the first, third, fifth, . . . elements of the vector as character codes and uses the second, fourth, sixth, . . . elements as the corresponding spacing adjustments. The actual adjustments in master coordinates are numbers, modulo 256 and biased by 128 (see Figure 4.32).

The SHOWANDXREL operator can also be useful for kerning. If kerning is used extensively, the Interpress master may become quite bulky because of the numerous calls to SHOW and SETXREL. The bulk can be reduced by encoding character indices and kern offsets alternately in a single vector and using the SHOWANDXREL operator. The previous example,

string "A" SHOW −2 SETXREL string "V" SHOW

could be encoded as

[65, 126, 86] SHOWANDXREL

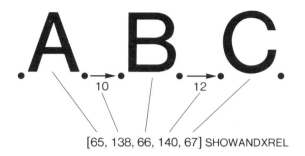

[65, 138, 66, 140, 67] SHOWANDXREL

Figure 4.32 SHOWANDXREL interprets odd elements as character indices and even elements as spacing adjustments.

Often, the letterspacing can be accomplished by a uniform adjustment to each character. For example, you may wish to print a headline such that the spacing between characters is uniformly expanded by a small amount. For this task, Interpress provides the SHOWANDFIXEDXREL operator. The operator takes a vector of character codes (just like SHOW) and a number:

$$< v:Vector > \ < x:Number > \ SHOWANDFIXEDXREL \rightarrow \ < \ >$$

The elements of the vector are character codes, which SHOWANDFIXEDXREL treats just as the SHOW operator would; an additional spacing adjustment x is included. Between imaging each character and spacing by its escapement, SHOWANDFIXEDXREL also performs a SETXREL by the value of the number operand. Therefore, this additional spacing adjustment is made between characters.

Accents

The handling of accents is controlled by designers of character sets and fonts. Three methods are common:

1. The character set contains a separate entry for each combination of character and accents. Thus, "é" would be represented as a single character in the character set.

2. The character set contains accent characters, which have escapements of zero. The accents are designed and positioned to have the correct relationship to a character placed next after the accent. Thus, to generate "é", the master would call string "´e" SHOW. (The accent mark "´" precedes the "e" in the string.) This technique is useful for modest-quality fonts, in which positioning accuracy is sufficiently poor that the detailed location of the accent mark over the character does not matter much.

3.   The font has individual accent characters, as described in (2), but the master must specify the accent's correct positioning.

For the third technique, positioning can be achieved with relative adjustments to the current position, but usually care must be taken to ensure that including the accent does not disrupt the spacing of characters in a word. That is, if a relative motion positions the accent properly, a compensating inverse relative motion returns the current position to its previous position. For example, to show the text "Bézier" and to position the acute accent carefully, we can use Example 4.20.

Example 4.20

```
String "B"
SHOW
2 3 SETXYREL              --adjust position for accent--
String "´"
SHOW                      --print accent--
-2 -3 SETXYREL            --return to position after showing "B"--
                          --assuming accent width=0--
String "ezier"
SHOW
```

An alternative is to save the current position on the Interpress operand stack and then restore it, as in Example 4.21.

Example 4.21

```
String "B"
SHOW
0 IGET 1 IGET             --save current position on the stack--
2 3 SETXYREL              --adjust position for accent--
String "´"
SHOW                      --print accent--
1 ISET 0 ISET             --restore current position--
String "ezier"
SHOW
```

As in kerning, the amount by which an accent is offset must be determined from external information about the font.

Besides the three methods listed earlier for dealing with accents, a fourth method is to use ligatures. For example, in ISO DP 6937 (see the Xerox Character Code Standard), a single graphic character "ä" is specified by two character codes in sequence: first one for "¨" and then one for "a." The graphic symbol "ä" is not just "a" overprinted with "¨" but rather a special graphic design. This approach allows other accented characters, such as "ü" or "ö," to be represented without requiring an explosion of character codes in the character set. This approach will not work in Interpress, however, because it is an automatic ligature. First, there is no easy way for the first character code to "remember" that an accent has been specified so that the second character code can select a different image. Second, the restriction on width calculations would require that all variants of the second character code have identical widths (for example, ä, ǎ, à, á, and so on would all have to have the same width).

Constructing a Font

To image characters in Interpress, you must first set the value of the font-imager variable to be the font you wish to use. There are two mechanisms for obtaining a font for this imager variable; you can find one in the printer's environment using FINDFONT, or you can make one. Finding a font is the typical mechanism. The resulting font is "made" for the printer and, in general, offers the greatest quality, efficiency, and support. Sometimes, you may wish to make your own font rather than finding one. You may need a font of special symbols that the printer does not provide or you may be creating a document that will be printed at different organizations that do not have a common font set. To help you to construct your own font, Interpress supplies the MAKEFONT operator.

$$< \text{fd:Vector} > \text{MAKEFONT} \rightarrow < \text{f:Font} >$$

MAKEFONT constructs a new font from a fontDescription fd, so you must first construct a fontDescription, then convert it into a font that the printer can use.

A fontDescription is a property vector that defines a font. You must supply four properties: transformation, characterMasks, characterMetrics, and substituteIndex. The transformation tells you what coordinate system to use in defining your characters; the characterMasks describe what each character looks like; the characterMetrics describe how to position the characters; and the substituteIndex tells the printer what to do if it encounters a character that you have not defined.

Consider first the transformation. To understand the size and orientation of the font, the printer must have the font expressed in the CCS. In this system, one unit is the nominal body size (roughly the distance between single-spaced lines of text in the font) and the origin is in the lower-left corner, with the x axis horizontal, and the y axis vertical. You do not have to define the font in the CCS coordinates, but you do have to provide a transformation from the font-definition coordinate system (FDCS) you use to the CCS. Suppose we are defining characters in the coordinate system shown

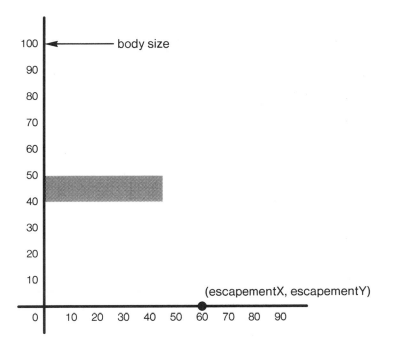

Figure 4.33 Definition of the dash.

in Figure 4.33, where the body size is 100 units. Then the transformation needed to convert this to the CCS would be

```
0.01  SCALE
```

The value of the characterMasks property is itself a property vector. Property vectors can use cardinals as the property names, and here we use the character indices as the names and composed operators as the values. The composed operators image the characters. You should construct them so that they call mask operators for the desired character shape. The SHOW operator performs a TRANS operation for each character. So, each time the composed operator is called, the origin of the CCS will be shifted to the spot closest to the current position. You should think of the origin of the CCS as the location the printer uses for the "position" of the character. You can use all the Interpress facilities in constructing the character masks, including strokes, outlines, and pixel arrays. As an example, let us construct an operator for the dash shown in Figure 4.33. We can construct this simple shape using MASKRECTANGLE (see Chapter 5 for a discussion of graphics operators):

```
MAKESIMPLECO
{
  0 40 45 10 MASKRECTANGLE          --use FDCS units--
}
```

As a second example, consider the "o" shape in Figure 4.34. Its mask could be constructed as follows:

```
MAKESIMPLECO
{
  10 15 ISET                   --set stroke width to 10--
  5 25 MOVETO
  45 25 5 25 ARCTO             --construct a circle in FDCS--
  MASKSTROKECLOSED             --image it--
}
```

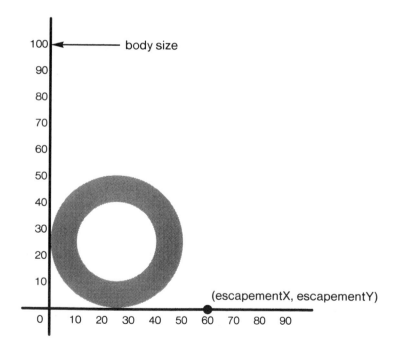

Figure 4.34 Definition of the "o."

The MOVETO, ARCTO and MASKSTROKECLOSED operators construct and image a circle, and are described in detail in Chapter 5. Suppose you need only these two character shapes in your font. Furthermore, suppose the character code for the dash is 45 and that for the "o" is 111. Then, your characterMasks' property vector would look like this:

```
45                                      --property name for the dash--
MAKESIMPLECO
{
   0 40 45 10 MASKRECTANGLE
}                                       --mask operator for the dash--
111                                     --property name for the "o"--
MAKESIMPLECO
{
   10 15 ISET
   5 25 MOVETO
   45 25 5 25 ARCTO
   MASKSTROKECLOSED
}                                       --mask operator for the "o"--
4 MAKEVEC                               --make the property vector--
```

The characterMasks vector supplies the character shapes, but you still have to define the character widths or escapements. This is done by the characterMetrics property vector. As in the characterMasks property vector, the characterMetrics property names are the character codes. The values are themselves property vectors containing the metrics properties for your characters. Suppose that, for both the dash and "o" characters in your font, you want an escapementX of 60 units and an escapementY of 0. That means that, on imaging a character, the current position shifts to the right by 0.6 of the body size (we are using coordinates where the body size is 100 units). Let us also suppose that the characters are nonamplifying and mask correcting. Then, a suitable property vector to use for their characterMetrics value is

```
Identifier "escapementX" 60     --width in x direction--
Identifier "escapementY" 0      --width in y direction--
4 MAKEVEC                        --make a vector of--
                                --the character properties--
```

Note that you do not have to include the amplified or correction properties in this case, because the desired behavior matches the defaults.

Now suppose you also wish to include a space in your font. You do not need a mask entry for a space because nothing is imaged, but you do need a metrics entry. Suppose you give the space a width of 60 units but allow it to be amplified and space correcting. Then, the properties for the space are:

```
Identifier "escapementX" 60        --describe its width--
Identifier "escapementY" 0
Identifier "amplified" 1           --it can be amplified--
Identifier "correction" 1          --it is space correcting--
8 MAKEVEC                          --bundle these properties--
                                   --in a vector--
```

Assuming the character code for the space is 32, the complete characterMetrics vector would look like this:

```
32                                 --code for space character--
  Identifier "escapementX" 60
  Identifier "escapementY" 0
  Identifier "amplified" 1
  Identifier "correction" 1
  8 MAKEVEC                        --metrics for space--
45                                 --code for dash--
  Identifier "escapementX" 60
  Identifier "escapementY" 0
  4 MAKEVEC                        --metrics for dash character--
111                                --code for "o"--
  Identifier "escapementX" 60
  Identifier "escapementY" 0
  4 MAKEVEC                        --metrics for "o"--
6 MAKEVEC                          --make characterMetrics--
                                   --property vector--
```

The only thing now required to complete the description of your font is the substituteIndex. You must pick a character with defined metrics that the printer can use as a substitute in the event you ask it to image a character that you have not defined. If you select the dash as your substitution character, then the substituteIndex value is 45.

To build a font, you must assemble all this to form a fontDescription, and then apply the MAKEFONT operator, as shown in Example 4.22.

Example 4.22

```
Identifier "transformation"        --transformation property--
  0.01 SCALE
Identifier "characterMasks"        --characterMasks property--
  45
  MAKESIMPLECO
  {
    0 40 45 10 MASKRECTANGLE
```

```
}
111
MAKESIMPLECO
{
   10 15 ISET
   5 25 MOVETO
   45 25 5 25 ARCTO
   MASKSTROKECLOSED
}
4 MAKEVEC
Identifier "characterMetrics"          --characterMetrics property--
   32
      Identifier "escapementX" 60
      Identifier "escapementY" 0
      Identifier "amplified" 1
      Identifier "correction" 1
      8 MAKEVEC
   45
      Identifier "escapementX" 60
      Identifier "escapementY" 0
      4 MAKEVEC
   111
      Identifier "escapementX" 60
      Identifier "escapementY" 0
      4 MAKEVEC
   6 MAKEVEC
Identifier "substituteIndex"           --substituteIndex property--
   45
8 MAKEVEC                              --construct FontDescription--
MAKEFONT                              --convert it to a font--
```

One more operator, MASKCHAR, is available to you for imaging characters:

$$<\text{fd:Vector}> \ <\text{i:Cardinal}> \ \text{MASKCHAR} \rightarrow \ <\text{fd}>$$

This operator takes a fontDescription fd and a character index i as its operands. The effect is to look up the mask operator for the character with index i in the fontDescription. The operator is then executed to form an image of the character. The frame, imager variables, and stack all are protected from changes made by the character-mask operator, so only the page image is affected. Note that this operator does *not* perform a TRANS to place the character's origin at the current position, nor does it shift the current position by the character's escapement after imaging. In fact, it does not even include the fontDescription's transformation so that characters are drawn using the character-definition coordinate values, regardless of the coordinate system that defines them. This can lead to strange size characters. MASKCHAR does only about half of the work needed for character imaging, and you may wonder whether it is useful for anything. It is—but not for imaging characters directly. It mainly allows you to use previously defined characters in the definition of new characters and to define accents and ligatures when you are building your own font. As an example, suppose we wanted a character that looked like an "o" with a bar over the top (a macron accent). We have already defined an "o" character and a bar character, so we shall use them in building our new character.

Notice that MASKCHAR takes a font description as an argument and leaves it as a result. This means that you can image a string of characters with a series of character-index and MASKCHAR operations, with the fontDescription available to each. To preserve the fontDescription, MASKCHAR duplicates it on the stack before extracting the character mask for imaging. This means that, when a character-mask operator is executed, a copy of the fontDescription that contains it will be on the top of the stack. The SHOW operator is defined in terms of MASKCHAR operations, so this behavior is true, in general. To reiterate, when a character-mask operator is executed, the stack contains the fontDescription from which it was extracted. This means that if, inside the character mask operator, there are further calls to MASKCHAR, there will be a fontDescription operand on the stack for them.

To draw the "o" part, we can invoke MASKCHAR on the "o" character (index 111). For the accent bar, we can use the dash character (index 45), but we must first position it above the "o." We can do this with a transformation that moves the origin over 2 units and up 15 units (see Figure 4.35). The entire character-mask operator for this accented character is shown in Example 4.23.

Example 4.23

```
MAKESIMPLECO                    --composed operator for--
{                               --drawing macron-accented "o"--
   111 MASKCHAR                 --draw the "o"--
   2 15 TRANSLATE CONCATT       --translate for the accent--
   45 MASKCHAR                  --draw the accent bar--
}
```

This composite character should be included in the fontDescription with the "o" and dash characters. Of course, you also will have to define metric properties specifically for this character and include them in the character-metrics component of the fontDescription.

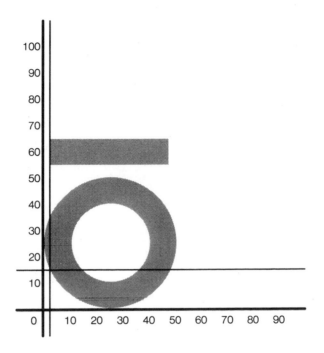

Figure 4.35 The "o" with accent.

We have illustrated how MASKCHAR can be used to build characters out of other characters. The composite character may be shown, and the processing may be more complex than simple duplication of the drawing operations of its components, but the representation is cleaner and more compact.

The ability to construct fonts in Interpress gives you some freedom from the restrictions of local printer environments. It also gives you a convenient way to express fonts for transfer between devices and installations. Further discussion and examples are presented in the Xerox Font Interchange Standard.

Summary

In this chapter, we have examined the Interpress facilities for fonts and text. We have seen how fonts can be located in the printer's environment, and how we can use fonts and the SHOW operator to image a string of characters. We noted that Interpress allows fonts with arbitrary character sets to be used and intermixed freely in a master. There is no such thing as a standard Interpress character set. Also, Interpress allows virtually arbitrary font names by naming fonts with vectors of identifiers. Subject only to a few restrictions that guarantee unique names, a font name may have an arbitrary number of identifiers with arbitrary meanings. We saw that the size, rotation, and position of character images are determined by the geometric transformations in force when the character operator is invoked. The size and rotation usually are controlled by both the transformation passed to MODIFYFONT and the current transformation at the time SHOW is called. Position is controlled by the current position when SHOW is called. The creation of fonts and character masks is summarized in Figure 4.36.

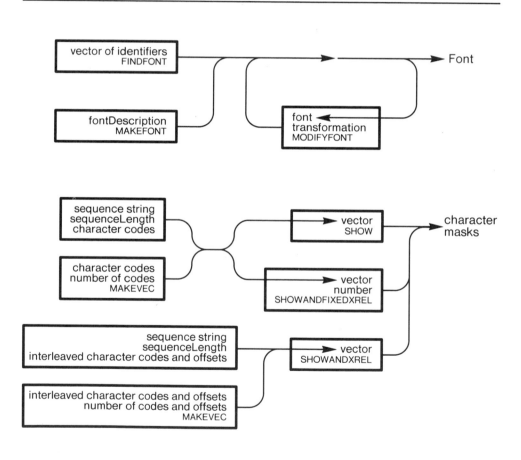

Figure 4.36 Building fonts and imaging characters.

We presented a number of techniques for achieving high-quality typography in Interpress. Interpress' basic facilities are quite simple: a master can place a character of arbitrary size and rotation at an arbitrary position on the page. Metric information, such as character widths, is supplied to the creator by a metric master. The creator usually reformats this information into a form more convenient to use.

The situation becomes more complex if we want to prepare masters that print acceptably, even when a printer must approximate the fonts requested by the master. The principal tools for legibility are:

- Relative positioning, so that, if a character's width changes when printed, other objects related to the character (such as subscripts, underlines, accents, and the succeeding character on a line) move to accept the new width. This technique preserves local relationships among objects.

- The CORRECT operator, which enforces a global relationship–the measure of a line of text. The operator will alter local relationships but tries to make most of its modifications in interword white space to preserve legibility.

Finally, we saw how to construct our own fonts with Interpress' graphics imaging facilities. In the next two chapters, we shall take a close look at these graphics facilities and learn how to construct images using both line-graphics and raster-graphics descriptions.

Chapter 5
LINE
GRAPHICS

"My name
means the shape
I am–and a
good handsome
shape it is, too.
With a name like
yours,
you might be any
shape, almost."

HUMPTY DUMPTY
*THROUGH THE LOOKING
GLASS*

T here are two approaches to describing graphical images. One uses geometrical constructs, such as lines, curves, and polygons, and synthesizes complex objects from these simple shapes. In traditional computer graphics, this approach models objects and generates images, and is sometimes called *synthetic graphics* or *line graphics*. The other approach describes the image as an array of dots where ink should be present. This approach is used by the image scanners and digitizers in facsimile machines, for example, and is often called *raster graphics*.

In this chapter, we describe the Interpress facilities for line graphics; in Chapter 6, we examine raster graphics.

Special Masks

We shall begin by looking at operators for imaging with special masks. We call these masks "special" because they each describe only a limited class of shapes.

Rectangles

We already introduced one such operator in the examples in Chapter 3; namely, MASKRECTANGLE (see Figure 5.1).

> $<$x:Number$>$ $<$y:Number$>$ $<$w:Number$>$ $<$h:Number$>$
> MASKRECTANGLE $\rightarrow$ $<$ $>$

This operator can create only rectangular shapes. Furthermore, the sides of the rectangles lie parallel to the x and y axes in the master coordinate system. The point (x, y) is the lower-left corner. The other corners are (x+w, y), (x, y+h), and (x+w, y+h); w specifies the width, and h the height. Notice that this operator actually has two functions: to construct the mask from the operands and to use this mask to add a shape to the page image. Remember

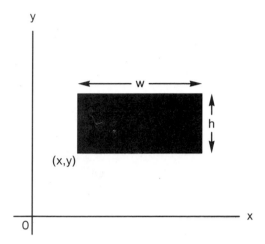

Figure 5.1 The shape created by MASKRECTANGLE.

that, in the Interpress model for imaging, the mask is transformed by the current transformation and then the current color is forced through the mask and onto the page.

Straight Lines

MASKVECTOR, a special Interpress operator, draws straight-line segments (see Figure 5.2). Here "vector" refers to a line segment in computer graphics (not the Interpress data type, nor the mathematical object). The line segment is specified by its endpoints (x_1, y_1) and (x_2, y_2).

> $<x_1$:Number$>$ $<y_1$:Number$>$ $<x_2$:Number$>$ $<y_2$:Number$>$
> MASKVECTOR $\rightarrow$ $<>$

For some display devices, such as simple pen plotters, this is all the information required. The pen is moved from one endpoint to the other, and the line is drawn. For other devices such as a high-resolution raster display, where you are setting dots rather than moving a pen, you also can control the thickness of the stroke. So Interpress offers a way for you to specify the width of the stroke. Because you are likely to draw several lines the same width, the width is stored in an imager variable called *strokeWidth* (index 15) (see Figure 5.3). You change the strokeWidth only when you want to change the thickness of your line. This avoids the bother of having to specify the width every time you draw a line. You do need to set the strokeWidth at least once, however, because it is initialized to zero and zero-width lines are difficult to see.

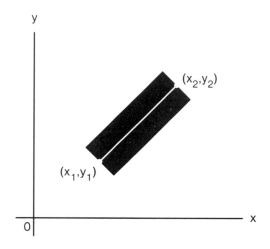

Figure 5.2 The shape defined by MASKVECTOR.

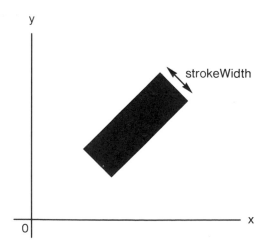

Figure 5.3 The strokeWidth parameter.

Example 5.1 demonstrates the use of MASKVECTOR. Figure 5.4 shows the scaled page output by Example 5.1.

Example 5.1

```
Header "Interpress/Xerox/3.0 "          --header--
BEGIN                                   --start of the master--
   { }                                  --preamble--
   {                                    --start of the page--
     0.003 15 ISET                      --set the strokeWidth--
     0.05 0.05 0.15 0.15 MASKVECTOR     --draw a line--
     0.002 15 ISET                      --change the strokeWidth--
     0.12 0.13 0.15 0.15 MASKVECTOR     --draw a second line--
     0.13 0.12 0.15 0.15 MASKVECTOR     --draw a third line--
   }                                    --end of the page--
END                                     --end of the master--
```

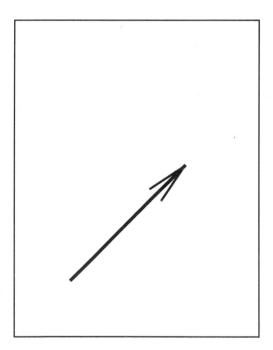

Figure 5.4 The result of Example 5.1.

Interpress also gives you control over the shape at the ends. You specify end caps using an imager variable called *strokeEnd* (index = 16). Three values are allowed for this variable, giving you a choice of three different end styles:

square, butt, and round (see Figure 5.5). A value of 0 indicates a square end; that is, the sides of the broadened line are extended at each end by one-half the line width. The ends as well as the sides are broadened. This is the default value for the line ends. A value of 1 indicates a butt end; that is, the line is squared off at the segment endpoints. A value of 2 indicates a round end. The line ends in a semicircle with a diameter equal to the strokeWidth and center located at the segment endpoint.

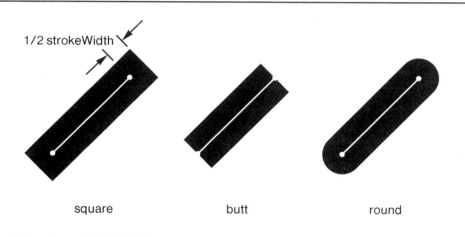

Figure 5.5 Stroke end styles.

Example 5.2 prints three thick lines with the three end-cap styles (see Figure 5.6).

Example 5.2

```
Header "Interpress/Xerox/3.0 "          --header--
BEGIN                                   --start of the master--
   { }                                  --preamble--
   {                                    --start of the page--
      0.02 15 ISET                      --set the strokeWidth--
      0 16 ISET                         --set strokeEnd to square--
      0.05 0.05 0.10 0.05 MASKVECTOR    --draw a line--
      1 16 ISET                         --set strokeEnd to butt--
      0.05 0.09 0.10 0.09 MASKVECTOR    --draw a line--
      2 16 ISET                         --set strokeEnd to round--
      0.05 0.13 0.10 0.13 MASKVECTOR    --draw a line--
   }                                    --end of the page--
END                                     --end of the master--
```

Figure 5.6 The result of Example 5.2.

It is possible to specify a zero-length line by using the same coordinates for both endpoints in MASKVECTOR. The effect of this depends on the strokeEnd value. For round ends, a circle is printed with a diameter equal to the strokeWidth. For butt ends, nothing is printed. For square ends, again, nothing is printed, but an appearance error is generated.

Trapezoids

Interpress has two special operators for drawing trapezoids because they match the imaging primitives of certain printers and can be executed efficiently in those cases. Trapezoids with parallel sides aligned with the scan direction are useful imaging primitives for two reasons: they are easy to implement (the printer just fills in scan-line segments between two lines, see Figure 5.7), and any polygon can be easily decomposed into them (see Figure 5.8). If you are using a printer with fast trapezoid processing, you may gen-

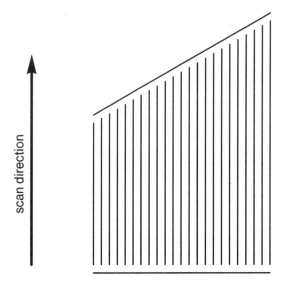

Figure 5.7 A trapezoid can be drawn by filling scan-line segments between two lines.

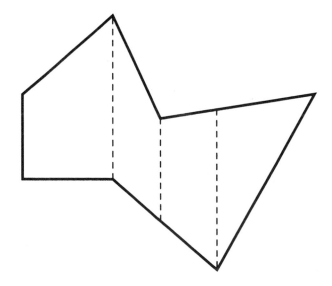

Figure 5.8 A polygon can be decomposed into trapezoids.

erate much more efficient Interpress programs by decomposing polygons into trapezoids, instead of using the more general constructs for specifying whole polygons that are presented in later sections of this chapter.

The two trapezoid operators are MASKTRAPEZOIDX and MASKTRAPEZOIDY (see Figure 5.9). They create trapezoids that have parallel sides aligned with the x and y axes, respectively.

$<x_1:Number> \; <y_1:Number> \; <x_2:Number>$
$<x_3:Number> \; <y_3:Number> \; <x_4:Number> \; \text{MASKTRAPEZOIDX} \to <>$
$<x_1:Number> \; <y_1:Number> \; <y_2:Number>$
$<x_3:Number> \; <y_3:Number> \; <y_4:Number> \; \text{MASKTRAPEZOIDY} \to <>$

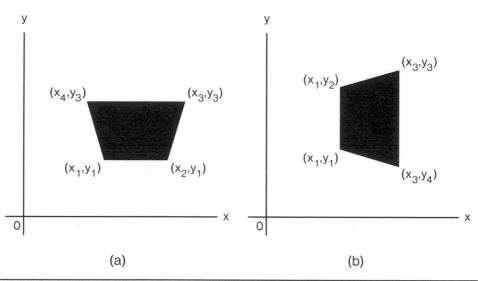

Figure 5.9 The shapes created by (a) MASKTRAPEZOIDX and (b) MASKTRAPEZOIDY.

The corner points for MASKTRAPEZOIDX are (x_1, y_1), (x_2, y_1), (x_3, y_3), and (x_4, y_3). Since the parallel sides are horizontal, this operator is best suited to printers with horizontal scan lines. The corner points for MASKTRAPEZOIDY are (x_1, y_1), (x_1, y_2), (x_3, y_3), and (x_3, y_4). This operator is the best choice for printers with vertical scan direction. Example 5.3 illustrates the use of these two operators (see Figure 5.10).

Example 5.3

```
Header "Interpress/Xerox/3.0 "           --header--
BEGIN                                    --start of the master--
   { }                                   --preamble--
   {                                     --start of the page--
                                         --draw the top trapezoid--
      0.07 0.14 0.17 0.19 0.23 0.11 MASKTRAPEZOIDX
                                         --draw the bottom trapezoid-
      0.03 0.08 0.10 0.18 0.12 0.04 MASKTRAPEZOIDY
   }                                     --end of the page--
END                                      --end of the master--
```

Figure 5.10 The result of Example 5.3.

Trajectories and Strokes

We shall now look at Interpress' more general drawing facilities. We showed how the MASKVECTOR operator lets you draw single line segments; now we shall see how you can draw connected sequences of segments, arcs, and curves. The technique is to specify the centerline for drawing and then to thicken it as we did for MASKVECTOR. You can think of the centerline as the path for a sequence of motions of an imaginary pen called a *trajectory*. The drawing made by the mask formed from the broadened trajectory is called a *stroke*. You can create a trajectory by specifying a starting point and then extending it with line segments. The operators you need to do this are MOVETO, which starts a trajectory, and LINETO, which adds a line segment to a trajectory.

<x:Number> <y:Number> MOVETO → <t:Trajectory>

The MOVETO command places a trajectory object on the stack. The first and last point of this trajectory is (x, y).

<t₁:Trajectory> <x:Number> <y:Number> LINETO → <t₂:Trajectory>

The LINETO operator extends trajectory t_1 with a line segment to form trajectory t_2. The line segment runs from the last point of t_1 to (x, y), which becomes the last point of t_2. Figure 5.11 shows how line segments extend trajectories.

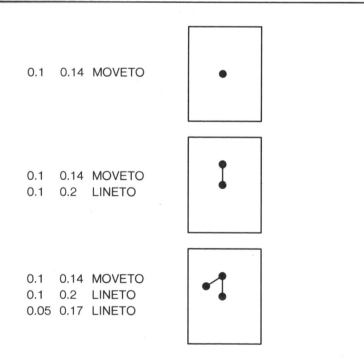

Figure 5.11 Trajectories.

Because trajectories are often composed of both horizontal and vertical lines, Interpress gives you convenience operators for extending the trajectory horizontally and vertically.

$$<t_1\text{:Trajectory}> \ <x\text{:Number}> \ \text{LINETOX} \rightarrow \ <t_2\text{:Trajectory}>$$

$$<t_1\text{:Trajectory}> \ <y\text{:Number}> \ \text{LINETOY} \rightarrow \ <t_2\text{:Trajectory}>$$

If the last point of trajectory t_1 is (x_0, y_0), then LINETOX extends it to (x, y_0) by adding a horizontal line segment from x_0 to x. The LINETOY operator adds a vertical line segment from (x_0, y_0) to (x_0, y).

The statements in Example 5.4 construct a trajectory for a 2-centimeter square with lower-left corner at the point $(0.09, 0.13)$ (see Figure 5.12).

Example 5.4

```
0.09 0.13 MOVETO        --start of square--
0.11 LINETOX            --line going right--
0.15 LINETOY            --line going up--
0.09 LINETOX            --line going left--
0.13 LINETOY            --line going down--
```

Building a trajectory does not draw anything; all it does is specify a path that can be used in the drawing operations. Note, however, that the trajectory is an object on the stack, so it can be copied or saved in a frame. Therefore, if you use a shape more than once in your document, you can build it once and save the results. The masks constructed from the trajectory undergo the transformations concatenated onto T. The transformation facility allows you to draw instances of the trajectory with different sizes, orientations, or positions.

We still need a way to turn the trajectory into a mask and to use that mask to construct an image on the page. This is done by the MASKSTROKE operator.

$$<t\text{:Trajectory}> \ \text{MASKSTROKE} \rightarrow \ < >$$

Like MASKVECTOR, MASKSTROKE broadens the line segments according to the strokeWidth imager variable. It uses the entire trajectory as the centerline for the broadening. Example 5.5 draws a resistor symbol using MASKSTROKE (see Figure 5.13).

Figure 5.12 A square trajectory.

Example 5.5

```
Header "Interpress/Xerox/3.0 "     --header--
BEGIN                              --start of the master--
  { }                              --preamble--
  {                                --start of the page--
    0.003 15 ISET                  --set the strokeWidth--
    0.05 0.14 MOVETO               --construct the symbol--
    0.065 LINETOX
    0.07 0.15 LINETO
    0.08 0.13 LINETO
    0.09 0.15 LINETO
    0.10 0.13 LINETO
    0.11 0.15 LINETO
    0.12 0.13 LINETO
```

```
      0.125 0.14 LINETO
      0.14 LINETOX
      MASKSTROKE                    --image the symbol--
   }                                --end of the page--
END                                 --end of the master--
```

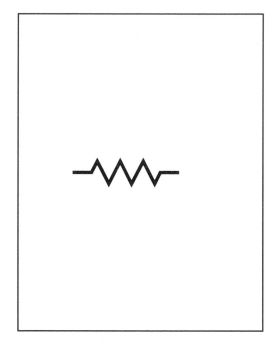

Figure 5.13 The result of Example 5.5.

In Example 5.6, we construct the trajectory for the resistor symbol and save it in the frame. Then, we mask three instances of it with different transformations to scale, rotate, and position the symbol. The result is a diagram with three resistors (see Figure 5.14).

Example 5.6

```
Header "Interpress/Xerox/3.0 "   --header--
BEGIN                            --start of the master--
   { }                           --preamble--
   {                             --start of the page--
      0.003 15 ISET              --set the strokeWidth--
```

```
     0.05 0.14 MOVETO            --construct the symbol--
     0.065 LINETOX
     0.07 0.15 LINETO
     0.08 0.13 LINETO
     0.09 0.15 LINETO
     0.10 0.13 LINETO
     0.11 0.15 LINETO
     0.12 0.13 LINETO
     0.125 0.14 LINETO
     0.14 LINETOX
     0 FSET                      --save it in the frame--
  DOSAVESIMPLEBODY               --save the current T--
  {
     -0.05 -0.14 TRANSLATE       --move an end to the origin--
     1 3 DIV SCALE               --reduce the size by 3--
     CONCAT
     0.05 0.16 TRANSLATE         --position the symbol--
     CONCAT
     CONCATT                     --include transformation in T--
     0 FGET                      --get the symbol--
     MASKSTROKE                  --image it--
  }                              --restore T--

  DOSAVESIMPLEBODY               --save T--
  {
     -0.05 -0.14 TRANSLATE       --move an end to the origin--
     1 3 DIV SCALE               --reduce the size by 3--
     CONCAT
     -90 ROTATE                  --rotate clockwise 90 degrees--
     CONCAT
     0.08 0.16 TRANSLATE         --position for the symbol--
     CONCAT
     CONCATT                     --include transformation in T--
     0 FGET                      --get the symbol--
     MASKSTROKE                  --image it--
  }                              --restore T--

  DOSAVESIMPLEBODY               --save T--
  {
     -0.05 -0.14 TRANSLATE
     1 3 DIV SCALE
     CONCAT
     0.08 0.16 TRANSLATE         --position for the symbol--
     CONCAT
     CONCATT
     0 FGET                      --get the third instance--
     MASKSTROKE                  --image it--
  }                              --end of body--
  }                              --end of the page--
END                              --end of the master--
```

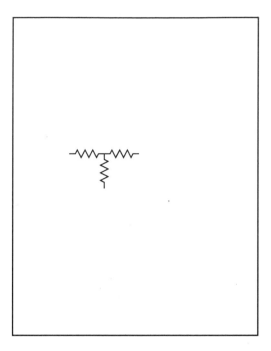

Figure 5.14 The result of Example 5.6.

Strokes have end caps that are controlled by the strokeEnd imager variable, just like the end caps you specify when you use MASKVECTOR. The ends can be square, butt, or round. Interpress also lets you specify what happens in the middle of a stroke at the joint between two line segments. The three possible joint styles are miter, bevel, and round (see Figure 5.15); their selection is governed by the *strokeJoint* imager variable (index = 23). A value of 0 indicates a mitered joint (the default), in which the sides of the broadened line segments are extended until they meet. A value of 1 means a beveled joint: the corners of the gap are joined by a straight line. A value of 2 means round joints: the ends of the gap are connected by a circular arc centered on the joint.

The nine possible joint and end combinations appear in Figure 5.16. The strokeJoint and strokeEnd specifications allow you to draw clean-looking strokes in most cases, but in one instance they fall short. Suppose you want to use a stroke to draw a closed curve, such as an object's boundary. Unless you use round joints and end caps, you will have a "funny" corner where the two ends of the stroke meet (see Figure 5.17).

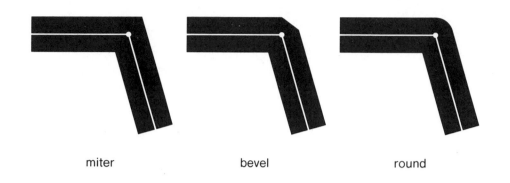

miter   bevel   round

Figure 5.15 Stroke joint styles.

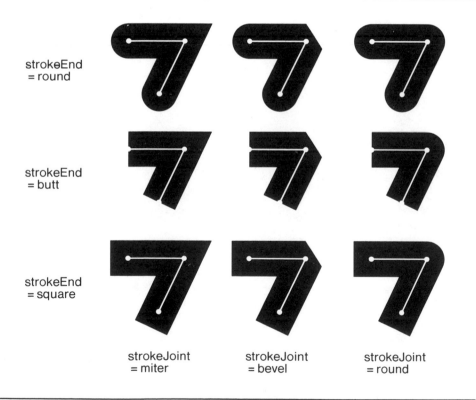

strokeEnd
= round

strokeEnd
= butt

strokeEnd
= square

strokeJoint   strokeJoint   strokeJoint
= miter   = bevel   = round

Figure 5.16 Stroke joint and end combinations.

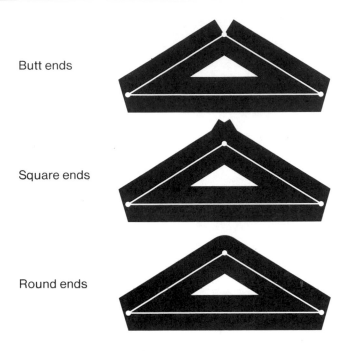

Butt ends

Square ends

Round ends

Figure 5.17 Corners where the ends of strokes meet.

You need a way to image a closed curve (a trajectory that ends where it starts) so that the point where the ends of the curve meet is treated as just another joint. Interpress' MASKSTROKECLOSED operator does this.

$$< t{:}Trajectory > \text{MASKSTROKECLOSED} \rightarrow < >$$

If you give this operator a trajectory that is not closed, it will first close the trajectory for you by adding a straight line from the last to the first point. It will broaden the trajectory to the stroke width and construct the requested stroke joint at every corner. Examples of MASKSTROKECLOSED appear in Figure 5.18.

Dashed Strokes

The other stroke-imaging operator is called MASKDASHEDSTROKE.

$$< t{:}Trajectory > \ < pattern{:}Vector\ of\ Number >$$
$$< offset{:}Number > \ < length{:}Number > \text{MASKDASHEDSTROKE} \rightarrow < >$$

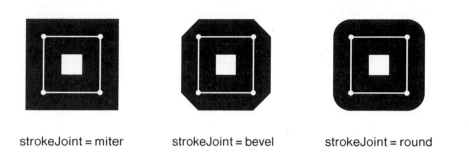

strokeJoint = miter   strokeJoint = bevel   strokeJoint = round

Figure 5.18 Examples of MASKSTROKECLOSED.

This powerful operator lets you draw the trajectory as a series of dashes, and with it, you can generate almost any dash pattern.

The operand t, the trajectory guiding the dashes, supplies the centerline for the dashes, each of which is broadened to the current strokeWidth. If a dash lies on top of a point where two line segments of the trajectory meet, then the dash will include a stroke joint (see Figure 5.19).

The dash pattern, controlled by the *pattern* vector, is a vector of numbers that gives the lengths of the dashes and the gaps in master coordinates. The first number in the vector is the length of the first dash, the second is the

Figure 5.19 A dashed trajectory with joints.

length of the first gap, the third is the length of the second dash, and so on (see Figure 5.20). At the end of the vector, you wrap back to its start, so the two-element vector [0.005, 0.01] acts like the vector [0.005, 0.01, 0.005, 0.01, 0.005, . . .], with as many elements as needed for the trajectory. This dash pattern has gaps twice as long as the dashes. If the dashes and gaps have the same length, your pattern vector only needs a single element—one that specifies that length. [0.01] acts like [0.01, 0.01, 0.01, . . .]. The three-element pattern [0.01, 0.005, 0.002] acts like [0.01, 0.005, 0.002, 0.01, 0.005, 0.002, . . .].

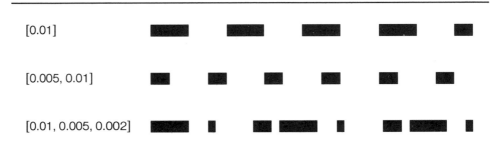

Figure 5.20 The effect of the pattern operand.

Each individual dash, which acts like a little stroke, is broadened to the strokeWidth. It has a stroke joint if it contains a point where two lines meet and is given end caps. If butt ends are selected, the dashes will have the lengths given by the pattern vector. If square or round stroke ends are in effect, then each dash will be lengthened by these stroke ends (see Figure 5.21).

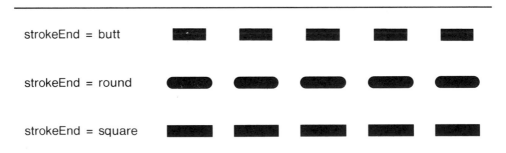

Figure 5.21 End caps on dashes.

So far, we have assumed that the start of the first dash coincides with the start of the trajectory, but suppose this is not what you want. You might want the start of the trajectory to be in the middle of a dash or at the start of a gap. The offset operand allows you to specify a distance into the dash pattern at which to start. For example, if the dash pattern is [0.01, 0.016], an offset of 0 will make the first dash 0.01 units long. An offset of 0.004 units, however, will start the dash pattern four-tenths into the first dash. Only the remaining six-tenths of the first dash (0.006 units) will be drawn. The partial dash will be followed by the 0.016-unit gap, then a full 0.01-unit dash, and so on. If an offset of 0.01 is used, the trajectory will begin with the first gap. An offset of 0.02 will begin the trajectory with a 0.006-unit gap (see Figure 5.22).

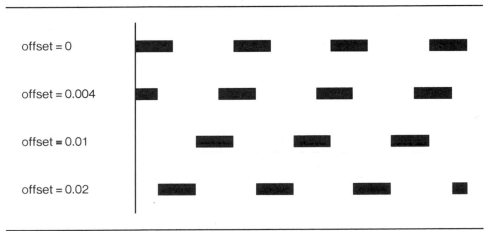

Figure 5.22　The effect of the offset operand.

The final operand for the MASKDASHEDSTROKE operator, length, stretches or shrinks the dash pattern. To see how you might use it, consider the problem of drawing dashes along the following trajectory:

```
0.01   0.01   MOVETO
0.09   0.09   LINETO
0.17   0.01   LINETO
```

You want dashes about 0.01 units in length, so you use [0.01] as the dash pattern. The difficulty is that, because the overall length of this trajectory is 0.2262742, you draw 11 dashes and 11 gaps and end with a dash 0.0062742 units in length. That is, the last dash on the trajectory is significantly shorter than the others. Your drawing would look much better if all the dashes were the same length. If the length of the trajectory had been 0.23 units, then you would have drawn 12 dashes separated by 11 gaps, all of exactly the same length. But because the trajectory length is shorter, you have to shorten the dash pattern lengths for the same effect of finishing at the end of a dash (see Figure 5.23).

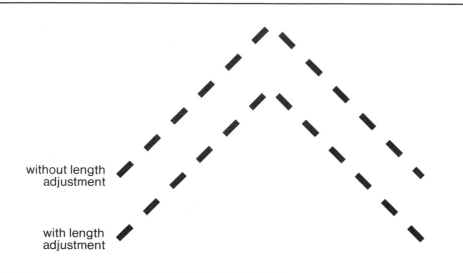

without length adjustment

with length adjustment

Figure 5.23 The effect of the length operand.

You can use the length operand to specify the scaling of the pattern. If you set the length operand to 0.23, it means "scale the dashes so that there are the same number of them as would be found on a trajectory of length 0.23." Another way to picture this is to imagine drawing the dashes for the specified length (0.23), then stretching or shrinking the pattern until the length matches the true length of the trajectory and, finally, placing the adjusted dashes on the trajectory (see Figure 5.24).

The length operand says "draw the dashed pattern as if the trajectory has this length." If zero or a negative number is used for the operand, it defaults to the actual length of the trajectory; so, if you do not need to use the length adjustment, just supply a zero.

When designing dash patterns, remember that a zero-length segment with round ends is printed as a dot. So you can make dot patterns as well as dash patterns. It is even possible to mix round dots with square-end dashes by drawing the trajectory twice, once for the dot patterns and once for the dash pattern, provided the patterns and offsets are arranged so that the dots lie in the gaps between dashes (see Figure 5.25).

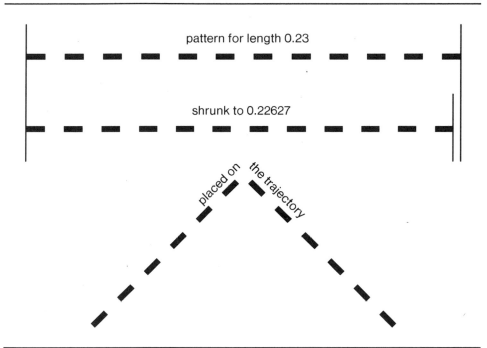

Figure 5.24 The length adjustment process.

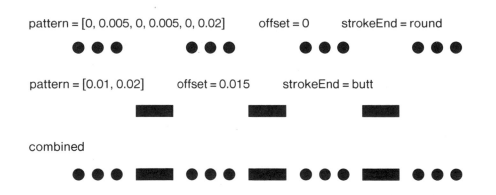

Figure 5.25 Combining dashed trajectories with round and butt ends.

The program in Example 5.7 demonstrates a dash-dot stroke that requires only a single drawing because all dashes have round ends (see Figure 5.26).

Example 5.7

```
Header "Interpress/Xerox/3.0 "   --header--
BEGIN                            --start of the master--
   { }                           --preamble--
   {                             --start of the page--
      0.002 15 ISET              --set the strokeWidth--
      2 16 ISET                  --set round ends--
      1 23 ISET                  --set beveled joints--
      0.04 0.12 MOVETO
      0.11 0.155 LINETO
      0.11 0.135 LINETO
      0.18 0.17 LINETO           --trajectory to be dashed--
      0.01 0.005 0 0.005         --dash-dot pattern--
      4 MAKEVEC
      0                          --no offset--
      0.19                       --make so it look like the pattern--
                                 --for a 0.19-meter-long trajectory--
      MASKDASHEDSTROKE           --draw it--
   }                             --end of the page--
END                              --end of the master--
```

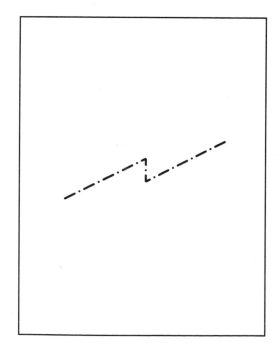

Figure 5.26 The result of Example 5.7.

Curves

We have seen how to draw lines and how to construct trajectories made out of lines. Now suppose you want to draw circles, elliptical arcs, or cubic curves. In Interpress, you specify these shapes with an extension of a trajectory, which can contain circular arcs, conic curves, and cubic curves, as well as straight-line segments. In this section, we discuss the operators that allow you to incorporate these curves in a trajectory.

Arcs

Let's begin with a circular arc. The operator that appends an arc to a trajectory is ARCTO.

$$<t_1:\text{Trajectory}> \; <x_1:\text{Number}> \; <y_1:\text{Number}>$$
$$<x_2:\text{Number}> \; <y_2:\text{Number}> \; \text{ARCTO} \to \; <t_2:\text{Trajectory}>$$

The operator appends the arc, which starts at the last point of trajectory t_1, (x_0, y_0), passes through the point (x_1, y_1), and ends at the point (x_2, y_2) (see Figure 5.27). The arc is circular in the master coordinates, but could deform into an elliptical arc in the Interpress coordinate system if you use nonuniform scaling (SCALE2).

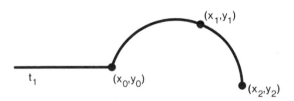

Figure 5.27 An ARCTO trajectory segment.

To see how ARCTO is used, consider drawing a figure eight, as shown in Example 5.8 (see Figure 5.28).

Example 5.8

```
Header "Interpress/Xerox/3.0 "     --header--
BEGIN                              --start of the master--
   { }                             --preamble--
   {                               --start of the page--
      0.005 15 ISET                --set the strokeWidth--
      0.08 0.12 MOVETO             --build the trajectory--
      0.12 0.16 LINETO
```

```
        0.08 0.20 0.08 0.16 ARCTO        --top arc--
        0.12 0.12 LINETO
        0.08 0.08 0.08 0.12 ARCTO        --bottom arc--
        MASKSTROKECLOSED                 --draw it--
      }                                  --end of the page--
    END                                  --end of the master--
```

Figure 5.28 The result of Example 5.8.

There are a couple of special cases for the ARCTO operator. If the start and endpoints (x_0, y_0) and (x_2, y_2) are exactly the same, then ARCTO constructs a full circle, drawn counterclockwise with the middle point (x_1, y_1) diametrically opposed to the start and endpoints. If the three points all lie on the same line, and the start point is different from the endpoint, then ARCTO acts in the same way as the two straight-line segments x_1 y_1 LINETO x_2 y_2 LINETO (see Figure 5.29).

Note that this method of describing arcs has some instabilities. Small changes in the point positions (like those arising from round-off errors) can cause large changes in the arc's shape. One case in which this occurs is when

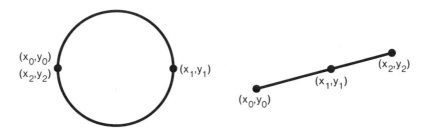

Figure 5.29 Special cases for ARCTO.

two of the three points are close together (see Figure 5.30). Another is when the three points are almost colinear and (x_2, y_2) lies between (x_0, y_0) and (x_1, y_1) or (x_0, y_0) lies between (x_1, y_1) and (x_2, y_2) (see Figure 5.31). ARCTO works best when the three points are widely distributed.

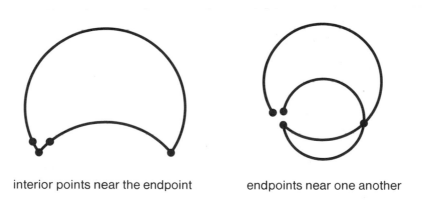

interior points near the endpoint   endpoints near one another

Figure 5.30 Instabilities when two points are close together.

In Example 5.9, we use ARCTO to create a composed operator for drawing circles with designated center and radius parameters. This composed operator relies on ARCTO's property of drawing circles when the first and last points are the same. The operator expects the circle's center point (x, y) and radius r on the stack (see Figure 5.32).

$$<\text{x:Number}> \ <\text{y:Number}> \ <\text{r:Number}>$$
$$\text{CircleComposedOperator} \to \ < \ >$$

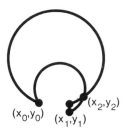

Figure 5.31 Instabilities when two points are almost colinear.

Example 5.9

```
Header "Interpress/Xerox/3.0 "        --header--
BEGIN                                 --start of the master--
  { }                                 --preamble--
  {                                   --start of the page--
    MAKESIMPLECO                      --start of circle operator--
    {
      0 FSET                          --save r--
      1 FSET                          --save y--
      2 FSET                          --save x--
      2 FGET                          --x--
      1 FGET                          --y--
      0 FGET                          --r--
      ADD                             --y+r--
      DUP 4 FSET                      --save y+r--
      MOVETO                          --(x, y+r)--
      2 FGET
      1 FGET
      0 FGET
      SUB                             --(x, y-r)--
      2 FGET
      4 FGET                          --(x, y+r)--
      ARCTO                           --make circle--
      MASKSTROKECLOSED                --draw it--
    }                                 --end of the operator--
    10 FSET                           --save it--
    0.003 15 ISET                     --set strokeWidth--
    0.1 0.14                          --center point, (x, y)--
    0.05                              --radius, r--
    10 FGET DO                        --test the operator--
  }                                   --end of the page--
END                                   --end of the master--
```

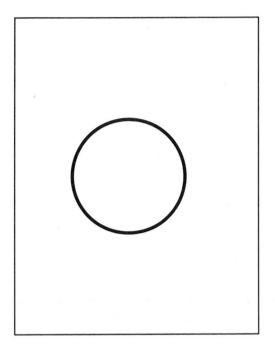

Figure 5.32 The result of Example 5.9.

Conics

Another shape that can be added to a trajectory is a conic curve segment. The conic curve can be an ellipse, parabola, or hyperbola, depending on the operands. The curve is specified by three points and a shape parameter (see Figure 5.33). The curve starts at the point (x_0, y_0) and ends at (x_2, y_2). The shape parameter s tells where the curve intersects the line segment connecting (x_1, y_1) and the midpoint between (x_0, y_0) and (x_2, y_2). The s value is the ratio of the distance p between the intersection point and the midpoint to the distance q between (x_1, y_1) and the midpoint.

The s parameter can have values between 0 and 1 and tells how strongly the curve is pulled toward the peak of the triangle, (x_1, y_1). For s near 1, the curve lies near the (x_0, y_0) to (x_1, y_1) and the (x_1, y_1) to (x_2, y_2) sides of the triangle, with a sharp bend near (x_1, y_1). For s near 0, the curve lies near the (x_0, y_0) to (x_2, y_2) line and is mostly flat, with sharp turns at the endpoints.

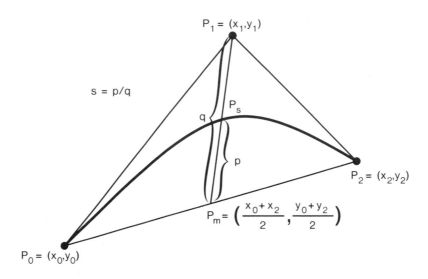

Figure 5.33 The definition of a conic segment.

For s less than 0.5, the curve is a piece of an ellipse. It is a piece of a parabola for s equal to 0.5, and a piece of a hyperbola for s greater than 0.5 (see Figure 5.34).

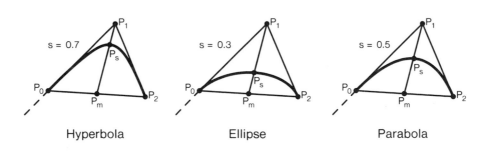

Figure 5.34 Examples of conic curve segments.

This representation of a curve has several nice properties. You know where the curve starts and ends, and the curve will be fully contained within the (x_0, y_0), (x_1, y_1), (x_2, y_2) triangle. The curve will be constructed so that it is tangent to the line through (x_0, y_0), (x_1, y_1) at the point (x_0, y_0) and also tangent to the line through (x_1, y_1), (x_2, y_2) at the point (x_2, y_2)–so you know the slope of the curve at the endpoints. This is helpful in matching the slopes of the curves in a trajectory to get a smooth path (see Figure 5.35). The curve can be transformed by simply transforming the three control points (the shape parameter does not change), which is a helpful property for the printer software writer. One problem with this representation is that it takes at least three curve segments to construct a closed curve (such as a circle).

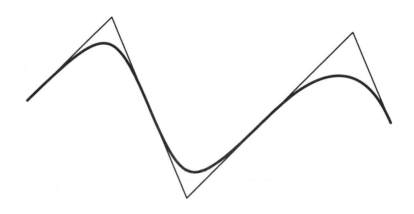

Figure 5.35 Conic segments in a trajectory can be constructed so that their slopes match at the joints.

The operator that extends a trajectory with conic curve segments is CONICTO.

$$<t_1\text{:Trajectory}> \ <x_1\text{:Number}> \ <y_1\text{:Number}> \ <x_2\text{:Number}>$$
$$<y_2\text{:Number}> \ <s\text{:Number}> \ \text{CONICTO} \rightarrow \ <t_2\text{:Trajectory}>$$

The point (x_0, y_0) is the last point of trajectory t_1. The points (x_1, y_1) and (x_2, y_2), and the shape parameter s, are specified as operands. The last point of the resulting trajectory t_2 is (x_2, y_2).

As an example of using the CONICTO operator, let's reexamine the problem of creating a composed operator that draws circles. This time, we will build the circle from four conic segments, instead of using ARCTO. We will still use the center point and radius as operands. We shall construct the circle from four quarters, as shown in Figure 5.36. The s value for a quarter circle is

$$s = \frac{r - (\sqrt{2r^2})/2}{(\sqrt{2r^2})/2} = \sqrt{2} - 1 = 0.4142136$$

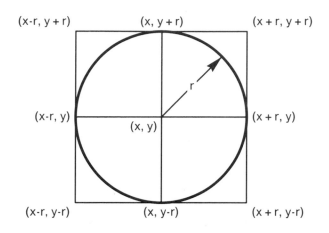

Figure 5.36 A circle constructed from four conics.

The output from Example 5.10 is shown in Figure 5.37.

Example 5.10

```
Header "Interpress/Xerox/3.0 "     --header--
BEGIN                              --start of the master--
   { }                             --preamble--
   {                               --start of the page--
     MAKESIMPLECO                  --make a circle operator--
     {
       0 FSET                      --save r--
       1 FSET                      --save y--
       2 FSET                      --save x--
       2 FGET 0 FGET ADD 3 FSET    --save x+r--
       2 FGET 0 FGET SUB 4 FSET    --save x-r--
       1 FGET 0 FGET ADD 5 FSET    --save y+r--
       1 FGET 0 FGET SUB 6 FSET    --save y-r--
       3 FGET 1 FGET MOVETO        --start trajectory at (x+r, y)--
                                   --construct the circle--
       3 FGET 5 FGET 2 FGET 5 FGET 0.4142136 CONICTO
       4 FGET 5 FGET 4 FGET 1 FGET 0.4142136 CONICTO
       4 FGET 6 FGET 2 FGET 6 FGET 0.4142136 CONICTO
       3 FGET 6 FGET 3 FGET 1 FGET 0.4142136 CONICTO
       MASKSTROKECLOSED            --draw it--
     }                             --end of the operator--
     10 FSET                       --save it--
                                   --now test it--
```

```
        0.003 15 ISET            --set strokeWidth--
        0.1 0.14                 --center point--
        0.05                     --radius--
        10 FGET DO               --test the operator--
      }                          --end of the page--
END                              --end of the master--
```

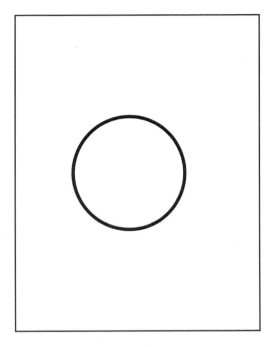

Figure 5.37 The result of Example 5.10.

Cubic Curves

Another curve often used in computer graphics is a cubic curve. Interpress supports cubic curves described by Bézier control points–four points that define the shape of the curve (see Figure 5.38). The curve begins at (x_0, y_0) and is tangent to the line containing (x_0, y_0) and (x_1, y_1). It moves toward (x_1, y_1), then toward (x_2, y_2), and finally ends at (x_3, y_3). The end of the curve is tangent to the line containing (x_2, y_2) and (x_3, y_3). As is true of conic curves, it is easy to connect several cubic curves smoothly because you know and can control the slopes at the endpoints.

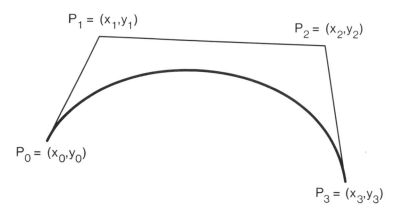

Figure 5.38 The definition of a Bézier cubic curve.

The Bézier curve also has properties useful to the printer software implementor. The transform of the Bézier curve is just the curve defined by the transformed control points. Also, the curve is completely contained within the quadrilateral formed by its four control points. This aids in clipping because, if the quadrilateral does not intersect a clipping boundary, then neither will the curve within it. Using cubics, you can construct curve segments that have inflection points, and even curves that cross themselves (see Figure 5.39).

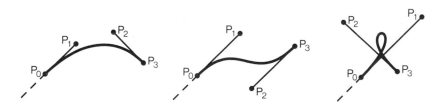

Figure 5.39 Examples of cubic curves.

The operator for appending these shapes to a trajectory is CURVETO.

$<t_1$:Trajectory$>$ $<x_1$:Number$>$ $<y_1$:Number$>$
$<x_2$:Number$>$ $<y_2$:Number$>$ $<x_3$:Number$>$ $<y_3$:Number$>$
CURVETO → $<t_2$:Trajectory$>$

The last point of trajectory t_1 is used as (x_0, y_0). The point (x_3, y_3) becomes the last point of trajectory t_2.

Example 5.11 uses CURVETO to construct a "D" shape (see Figure 5.40).

Example 5.11

```
Header "Interpress/Xerox/3.0 "          --header--
BEGIN                                    --start of the master--
   { }                                   --preamble--
   {                                     --start of the page--
      0.005 15 ISET                      --set the strokeWidth--
      0.07 0.1 MOVETO                    --starting point--
      0.07 0.2 LINETO                    --vertical bar--
      0.2 0.2 0.2 0.1 0.07 0.1 CURVETO   --curved part--
      MASKSTROKECLOSED                   --draw it--
   }                                     --end of the page--
END                                      --end of the master--
```

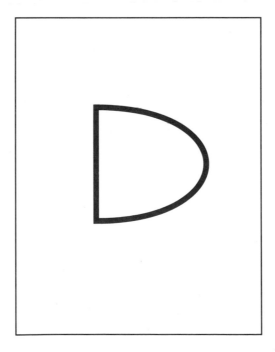

Figure 5.40 The result of Example 5.11.

The CURVETO operator is great provided that you know the Bézier control points, but there are many other possible ways to describe cubic curves. If your system uses one of these other descriptions, you may be faced with the problem of calculating the control points so that you can give them to CURVETO. The following discussion may help a little.

One of the other ways of describing the cubic curve segment is with the parametic equations.

$$x = a_x t^3 + b_x t^2 + c_x t + d_x$$
$$y = a_y t^3 + b_y t^2 + c_y t + d_y$$

As t takes on values from 0 to 1, the point (x, y) moves along the curve segment. The coefficients a_x, b_x, c_x, d_x, a_y, b_y, c_y, d_y govern the shape of the curve.

For each curve defined by Bézier control points, a corresponding set of coefficients define the same shape using the parametric description. The relation between the control points and coefficients is the following:

$$a_x = x_3 - 3x_2 + 3x_1 - x_0 \qquad a_y = y_3 - 3y_2 + 3y_1 - y_0$$
$$b_x = 3x_2 - 6x_1 + 3x_0 \qquad b_y = 3y_2 - 6y_1 + 3y_0$$
$$c_x = 3x_1 - 3x_0 \qquad c_y = 3y_1 - 3y_0$$
$$d_x = x_0 \qquad d_y = y_0$$

These equations tell us how to find the parametric form if we know the Bézier control points. We can invert them to solve the reciprocal problem: given the parametric form, find the corresponding Bézier control points. The result is as follows:

$$x_0 = d_x \qquad y_0 = d_y$$
$$x_1 = c_x/3 + d_x \qquad y_1 = c_y/3 + d_y$$
$$x_2 = b_x/3 + 2c_x/3 + d_x \qquad y_2 = b_y/3 + 2c_y/3 + d_y$$
$$x_3 = a_x + b_x + c_x + d_x \qquad y_3 = a_y + b_y + c_y + d_y$$

If you can express your cubic curve in the parametric form, then you can use these equations to find the Bézier control points needed to draw it.

To illustrate this, let's say that your graphics editor uses B-splines to draw cubic curves. The parametric equations for the B-spline form use the coefficients:

$$a_x = (\tilde{x}_3 - 3\tilde{x}_2 + 3\tilde{x}_1 - \tilde{x}_0)/6 \qquad a_y = (\tilde{y}_3 - 3\tilde{y}_2 + 3\tilde{y}_1 - \tilde{y}_0)/6$$
$$b_x = (3\tilde{x}_2 - 6\tilde{x}_1 + 3\tilde{x}_0)/6 \qquad b_y = (3\tilde{y}_2 - 6\tilde{y}_1 + 3\tilde{y}_0)/6$$

$$c_x = (3\tilde{x}_2 - 3\tilde{x}_0)/6 \qquad\qquad c_y = (3\tilde{y}_2 - 3\tilde{y}_0)/6$$
$$d_x = (\tilde{x}_2 + 4\tilde{x}_1 + \tilde{x}_0)/6 \qquad d_y = (\tilde{y}_2 + 4\tilde{y}_1 + \tilde{y}_0)/6$$

To convert to the Bézier form, you substitute these expressions into those given previously for the Bézier control points. The result is the transformation from the B-spline control points $(\tilde{x}, \tilde{y})$ specified by your editor to the Bézier control points (x, y) required by an Interpress master to describe the same curve.

$$x_0 = (\tilde{x}_2 + 4\tilde{x}_1 + \tilde{x}_0)/6 \qquad y_0 = (\tilde{y}_2 + 4\tilde{y}_1 + \tilde{y}_0)/6$$
$$x_1 = (\tilde{x}_2 + 2\tilde{x}_1)/3 \qquad\qquad y_1 = (\tilde{y}_2 + 2\tilde{y}_1)/3$$
$$x_2 = (2\tilde{x}_2 + \tilde{x}_1)/3 \qquad\qquad y_2 = (2\tilde{y}_2 + \tilde{y}_1)/3$$
$$x_3 = (\tilde{x}_3 + 4\tilde{x}_2 + \tilde{x}_1)/6 \qquad y_3 = (\tilde{y}_3 + 4\tilde{y}_2 + \tilde{y}_1)/6$$

Filled Outlines

We have seen how to construct and draw strokes like those that might be made with a pen. Remember, however, that one of the virtues of a raster device is its ability to display solid areas. It can show filled shapes such as polygons and circles, not just their outlines. This section describes how filled shapes are drawn using Interpress.

The basic way to describe a shape is to use a trajectory. Instead of broadening the trajectory, we use it as the boundary of the area to be filled. You might think that filling a trajectory is all that is needed, but that is not quite true, because we also want the method to describe objects with holes in them. An object with a hole requires two trajectories: one for the outer boundary and one for the hole (see Figure 5.41).

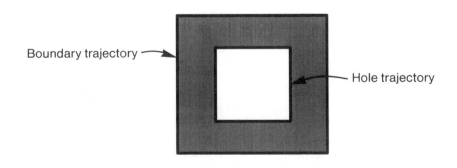

Figure 5.41 Objects with holes are defined by multiple trajectories.

In general, an object can have any number of holes, so we need a list of trajectories to describe it. In Interpress, this list is called an *outline*; it is constructed by the MAKEOUTLINE operator.

$<$t$_1$:Trajectory$>$ $<$t$_2$:Trajectory$>$...$<$t$_n$:Trajectory$>$ $<$n:Cardinal$>$
MAKEOUTLINE $\rightarrow$ $<$o:Outline$>$

This operator will group any number of trajectories to form an outline. It requires a number n on the top of the stack to decide how many trajectories to collect. Each trajectory is closed by a line segment if its first and last points differ.

If we are drawing an object with a hole, our trajectory for the hole is completely enclosed by the trajectory for the object. This is not a requirement of the MAKEOUTLINE operator, however. MAKEOUTLINE happily collects trajectories that are completely separate, as in Figure 5.42. Thus, a filled object in Interpress need not be a connected object.

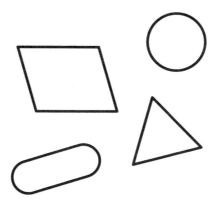

Figure 5.42 These trajectories can be made into a single outline using MAKEOUTLINE.

Because we can specify trajectories within trajectories, trajectories that cross one another and even trajectories that cross themselves, we must be very clear as to what we mean by the "inside" of an outline; that is, what areas are to be filled. The inside is defined in terms of a *winding number* or *wrap number* that counts the number of times a point is surrounded by an outline. The winding number of a point, with respect to an outline, is the net number of times a point traversing the trajectories that form the outline wraps around the given point in a counterclockwise direction. Figure 5.43 shows the winding numbers for several points.

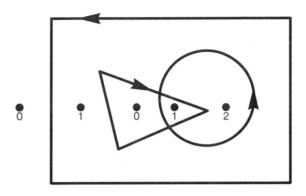

Figure 5.43 Winding numbers for several points.

Interpress allows you to use the winding number to fill objects in two ways. One is to fill all areas with odd winding numbers. With this scheme, every time you cross a trajectory, you flip between outside and inside (unfilled and filled). The second scheme interprets areas with zero winding numbers as outside and everything else as inside. When you use a nonzero winding number for filling, you must consider not only the number of trajectories crossed, but also the direction in which the trajectory is drawn. Figure 5.44 shows examples of trajectories and illustrates how each of the two schemes would fill them.

The nonzero-winding-number scheme is assumed when you use MAKEOUTLINE. If you prefer to use the odd-winding-number definition, you should construct the outline with the MAKEOUTLINEODD operator.

$<t_1\text{:Trajectory}> <t_2\text{:Trajectory}>...<t_n\text{:Trajectory}> <n\text{:Cardinal}>$
MAKEOUTLINEODD → $<o\text{:Outline}>$

MAKEOUTLINEODD acts exactly like the MAKEOUTLINE procedure, except that the inside of the resulting outline is defined by an odd winding number instead of by a nonzero winding number.

Each outline remembers the winding-number rule used to create it. The rule is selected by which operator you use to construct the outline. The outline fully defines the filled shape to be drawn, but it does not do the drawing. For that, you need the MASKFILL operator.

$<o\text{:Outline}>$ MASKFILL → $< >$

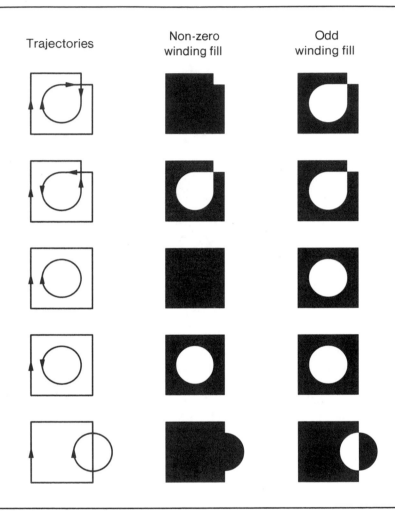

Figure 5.44 Winding number conventions.

This operator forms a mask from the outline, defining the interior points of the mask according to the winding rule accompanying the outline, and uses that mask to place an image on the page.

The nested triangles of Example 5.12 demonstrate the use of outlines and MASKFILL (see Figure 5.45).

Example 5.12

```
Header "Interpress/Xerox/3.0 "     --header--
BEGIN                              --start of the master--
   { }                             --preamble--
   {                               --start of the page--
      0.04 0.08 MOVETO             --one triangle--
      0.16 LINETOX
      0.1 0.2 LINETO               --MAKEOUTLINE will close it--
      0.07 0.1 MOVETO              --hole in the triangle--
      0.1 0.16 LINETO
      0.13 0.1 LINETO              --MAKEOUTLINE will close it--
      0.09 0.12 MOVETO             --a triangle inside the hole--
      0.11 LINETOX
      0.1 0.14 LINETO              --MAKEOUTLINE will close it--
      3 MAKEOUTLINE                --outline has three trajectories--
      MASKFILL                     --draw it--
   }                               --end of the page--
END                                --end of the master--
```

Figure 5.45 The result of Example 5.12.

You can draw filled outlines with borders. The technique you use is to duplicate the defining trajectory. Use one copy for the filled outline, and the other copy for the border stroke. You have to use different colors for the filled outline and the stroke to distinguish them. The method is illustrated in Example 5.13, which draws a simple house shape. Trajectories for the front, side, and roof are constructed and duplicated. Each is converted to an outline and filled with a different color. The trajectory copies remain on the stack. The color is then changed to black, and the borders are drawn using the saved trajectories (see Figure 5.46).

Example 5.13

```
Header "Interpress/Xerox/3.0 "    --header--
BEGIN                             --start of the master--
   { }                            --preamble--
   {                              --start of the page--
      1 5 ISET                    --set priorityImportant--
                                  --image objects in the order shown--
      0.05 0.1 MOVETO             --construct the front--
      0.1 LINETOX
      0.15 LINETOY
      0.075 0.18 LINETO
      0.05 0.15 LINETO
      DUP                         --save copy to use for border--
      1 MAKEOUTLINE               --make an outline for filling--
      0.5 SETGRAY                 --set the color--
      MASKFILL                    --draw the front--
      0.1 0.1 MOVETO              --construct the side--
      0.15 0.13 LINETO
      0.18 LINETOY
      0.1 0.15 LINETO
      DUP                         --save copy to use for border--
      1 MAKEOUTLINE               --make an outline for filling--
      0.8 SETGRAY                 --set the color--
      MASKFILL                    --draw the side--
      0.1 0.15 MOVETO             --construct the roof--
      0.15 0.18 LINETO
      0.125 0.21 LINETO
      0.075 0.18 LINETO
      DUP                         --save copy to use for border--
      1 MAKEOUTLINE               --make an outline for filling--
      0.3 SETGRAY                 --set the color--
      MASKFILL                    --draw the roof--
      1 SETGRAY                   --set color to black for borders--
      0.003 15 ISET               --set the strokeWidth--
      2 23 ISET                   --set joints to round--
      MASKSTROKECLOSED            --draw border around the roof--
```

```
        MASKSTROKECLOSED              --draw border around the side--
        MASKSTROKECLOSED              --draw border around the front--
    }                                 --end of the page--
END                                   --end of the master--
```

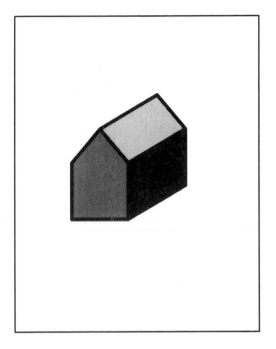

Figure 5.46 The result of Example 5.13.

Clipping

In Chapter 3, we introduced the idea of a clipping region–the area of the page in which imaging can take place. You can think of it as an additional stencil through which the ink must pass before reaching the page. Initially, this region is the size of the printable field for the page, but Interpress lets you change it. The two operators for creating the clipping stencils are CLIPRECTANGLE and CLIPOUTLINE.

<x:Number> <y:Number> <w:Number> <h:Number>
CLIPRECTANGLE → < >

<o:Outline> CLIPOUTLINE → < >

The CLIPRECTANGLE operator builds a rectangular clipping region in exactly the same way as MASKRECTANGLE constructs a rectangular mask. The point (x, y) is the lower-left corner of the region, w is its width, and h is its height. The region is specified in the current master coordinates.

The CLIPOUTLINE operator produces a clipping stencil from an outline. The stencil has the same shape as the mask that would be produced by MASKFILL.

Both CLIPRECTANGLE and CLIPOUTLINE not only build the clipping stencil but also install it as the current clipping region. Recall, however, that the effect of installing a new clipping region is to *intersect* it with the previous clipping region. An image prints only if it survives both the previous clipper and the new clipping outline; the image must pass through your new clipping stencil and also the previous clipping stencils. This lets you clip composed operators that also employ clipping.

Let's look at an example that would stress the abilities of most printers. We shall construct a squiggly outline, install it as a clipping region, and print some text through it (see Example 5.1 and Figure 5.47).

Example 5.14

```
Header "Interpress/Xerox/3.0 "      --header--
BEGIN                               --start of the master--
  { }                               --preamble--
  {                                 --start of the page--
    Identifier "xerox" Identifier "XC1-1-1" Identifier "modern"
    3 MAKEVEC FINDFONT
    0.0353 SCALE
    MODIFYFONT                      --100-point Modern font--
    12 ISET                         --set the current font--
    0.08 0.13 MOVETO                --make the clipping trajectory--
    0.11 0.16 0.14 0.12 0.17 0.15 CURVETO
    0.17 0.17 0.15 0.17 ARCTO
    0.12 0.14 0.09 0.18 0.06 0.15 CURVETO
    0.06 0.13 0.08 0.13 ARCTO
    1 MAKEOUTLINE                   --make it into an outline--
    CLIPOUTLINE                     --install as the clipping region--
    0.015 0.14 SETXY
    String "INTERPRESS"
    SHOW                            --the second line--
  }                                 --end of the page--
END                                 --end of the master--
```

Some interesting effects can be produced using the Interpress imaging functions, clipping, color, and priority. In Example 5.15, we draw a gray rectangle and then write the word "INTERPRESS" on top of it in black. We

Figure 5.47 The result of Example 5.14.

next define a curved outline (the same one we used in Example 5.14) and fill it with black. Finally, we use the curved outline as the clipping region and write the word "INTERPRESS" again in white. Because of the clipping, the white letters appear only within the outline. They exactly replace the letters that were covered when the outline was filled (see Figure 5.48).

Example 5.15

```
Header "Interpress/Xerox/3.0 "  --header--
BEGIN                           --start of the master--
  { }                           --preamble--
  {                             --start of the page--
    Identifier "xerox" Identifier "XC1-1-1" Identifier "modern"
    3 MAKEVEC FINDFONT
    0.0353 SCALE MODIFYFONT      --100-point Modern font--
    12 ISET                      --set the current font--
    1 5 ISET                     --set priorityImportant--
```

```
      0.5 SETGRAY                 --draw gray background rectangle--
      0.01 0.11 0.2 0.08 MASKRECTANGLE
      1 SETGRAY                   --print "INTERPRESS" in black--
      0.015 0.14 SETXY
      String "INTERPRESS"
      SHOW
      0.08 0.13 MOVETO            --make the clipping trajectory--
      0.11 0.16 0.14 0.12 0.17 0.15 CURVETO
      0.17 0.17 0.15 0.17 ARCTO
      0.12 0.14 0.09 0.18 0.06 0.15 CURVETO
      0.06 0.13 0.08 0.13 ARCTO
      1 MAKEOUTLINE DUP           --make it into an outline--
      MASKFILL                    --fill the outline with black--
      CLIPOUTLINE                 --install it as the clipping region--
      0 SETGRAY                   --print "INTERPRESS" again in white--
      0.015 0.14 SETXY
      String "INTERPRESS"
      SHOW
   }                              --end of the page--
 END                             --end of the master--
```

Figure 5.48 The result of Example 5.15.

Summary

In this chapter, we have seen how to draw synthetic or line graphics in Interpress. We have seen the special operators for drawing rectangles and trapezoids, which are included for efficiency, and also the general mechanisms for drawing strokes and filled outlines. Strokes rely on imager variables for their width, joint, and end specifications. They can be open, closed, or dashed. The dash mechanism allows you to construct almost any pattern and to shift or stretch it along the trajectory. The trajectories are composed of segments, which can be straight lines, circular arcs, conic curves, or cubic curves. You can collect the trajectories into outlines to represent filled shapes, even those containing holes. You can define the filling by using either nonzero or odd winding numbers. Finally, we saw how you can use outlines to define complex clipping regions. Figure 5.49 summarizes the mask operators for line graphics.

In the next chapter, we shall look at raster graphics. You will learn how outlines can be filled with patterns and how photographic images can be included in your master.

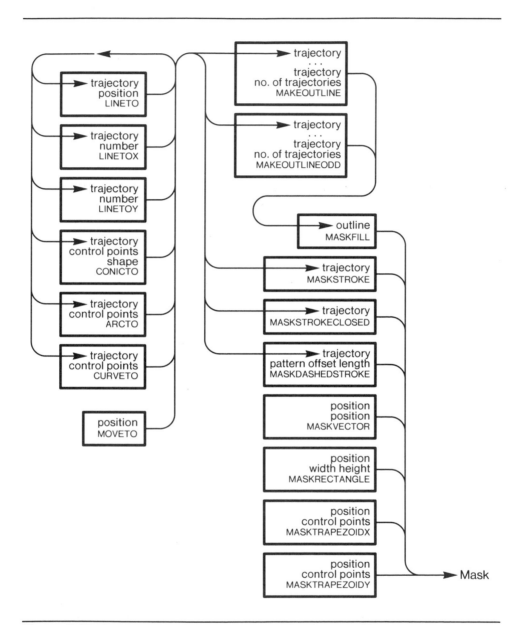

Figure 5.49 A summary of mask operators for line graphics.

Chapter 6
RASTER
GRAPHICS

*"I never could
make out
what those
damned dots
meant."*

LORD RANDOLPH
CHURCHILL

Besides text, lines, and geometric shapes, an Interpress master can contain scanned images or bitmaps. A scanned image is an array of image samples defined on a *raster* or rectangular grid. In this chapter, we will describe how Interpress constructs pixel arrays from binary scanned images, where the sample values are either 0 or 1. Although we usually refer to them as if they came from a document scanner, scanned images can come from a computer program or bitmap editor as well and can represent graphics, line copy, and halftones. Interpress uses an object known as a pixel array to represent the samples of a scanned image. Interpress masters can use binary pixel arrays either as a mask, specifying where ink goes on the page, or as a sampled black-and-white ink. Using a binary pixel array to specify an ink or color is a special case of the more general use of gray and full-color scanned images as sampled colors, which we will consider in Chapter 7. In this chapter, we will describe how to construct and image binary pixel arrays and efficiently encode them in a master.

Scanned Images

A scanned image is obtained by sampling an image in a regular pattern or raster. A raster is a set of evenly-spaced parallel lines or scan lines, along which the scanning device samples the image content at regular intervals to produce a rectangular array of pixels (Figure 6.1). A pixel can have a single one-bit sample, as it does in the case of a binary image; a single sample with multiple bits, as in the case of a gray scale image; or multiple samples with multiple bits, as for a color image. The single bit of a binary image shows where there is ink in the scanned image and where there is none. How you scan an image to obtain pixels will not be our concern here; we will examine only how Interpress uses the results.

Creating Binary Pixel Arrays

To describe a scanned image or bitmap to a printer, an Interpress master constructs an object known as a *pixel array* from a vector of binary image samples and two additional pieces of information—the format of the scanned

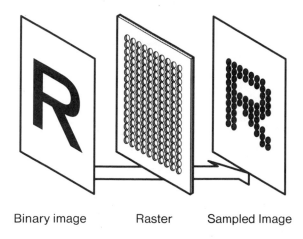

Binary image   Raster   Sampled Image

Figure 6.1 Image scanning model.

image and a transformation. The format includes the scanned image dimensions, measured in pixels, which enable the printer to reconstruct the two-dimensional scanned image from the sample vector and represent it in the scanner coordinate system. The printer then uses the transformation to orient and, if desired, scale and position the scanned image. How the scanned image finally appears depends on the transformations applied to it.

The samples are stored in the vector in the same order that they were scanned. Scanning the binary image in Figure 6.2 with a raster that has 5 scan lines, with successive scan lines ordered left to right, and 7 pixels per scan line, with successive pixels in a scan line running from bottom to top, produces the sample sequence

1 1 1 1 1 1 0 0 0 1 0 0 1 0 0 1 1 0 0 1 0 1 0 1 0 0 1 1 0 0 0 1 1 0

You would make this into a binary sample vector by appending the statement 35 MAKEVEC.

The first piece of information that the master passes to the printer, along with the binary sample vector, is the number of scan lines and the number of pixels per scan line. With this information, the printer separates the sample vector into scan lines so that it can reconstruct the scanned image. Pixel arrays, like characters, have their own coordinate system as a framework for reconstructing the image and describing its transformation. Interpress uses a *scanner coordinate system* (SCS). The first pixel in the sample vector is placed at the origin of this coordinate system, and successive pixels in the first scan

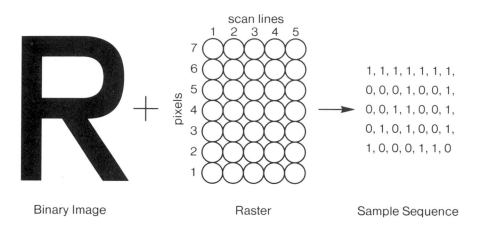

scan lines

pixels

Binary Image   Raster   Sample Sequence

Figure 6.2 Scanning an image to obtain a sample sequence.

line are placed upward along the y axis. The first pixels of successive scan lines are placed along the x axis of the scanner coordinate system in the direction of increasing x, with pixels in each scan line running upward in the direction of increasing y. The scanned image dimensions in the scanner coordinate system are xPixels scan lines and yPixels pixels per scan line. A unit in this coordinate system equals the size of a pixel.

In Figure 6.3, the first 7 elements of the sample sequence are the 7 pixels of the first scan line, the next 7 elements are the pixels of the second scan line, and so on. We use the Interpress convention and place the start of the sampling raster (the first pixel) at the origin of the scanner coordinate system, with y increasing along a scan line and x increasing with successive scan lines. Therefore, the height of the scanned image is the number of pixels per scan line and its width is the number of scan lines.

The second piece of information that the printer requires to create a pixel array is a transformation from scanner to master coordinates (see Figure 6.3). This transformation takes into account other scanning orders than the standard order (bottom to top, left to right) and scales, orients, and positions the pixel array as desired in the master coordinate system.

The MAKEPIXELARRAY Operator

The creation of a binary pixel array is a special case of the more general capabilities of MAKEPIXELARRAY. The definition of MAKEPIXELARRAY is

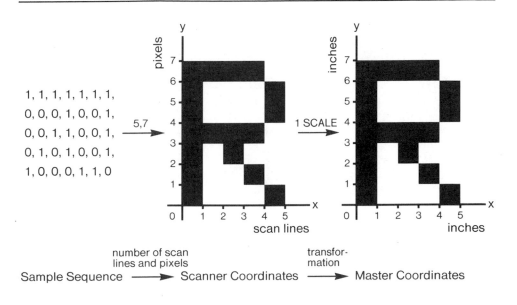

Figure 6.3 Building a pixel array.

<xPixels: Cardinal> <yPixels: Cardinal>
<samplesPerPixel: Cardinal>
<maxSampleValue: Cardinal or Vector of Cardinal>
<samplesInterleaved: Cardinal>
<m: Transformation>
<samples: Vector of Cardinal>
MAKEPIXELARRAY → <pa: PixelArray>

Because of the Interpress convention that orients the scanner coordinate system with respect to the raster, the number of pixels per scan line is yPixels and the number of scan lines is xPixels. For a binary image, the other format arguments–samplesPerPixel, maxSampleValue, and samplesInterleaved–all are 1. (When we use MAKEPIXELARRAY to represent gray-scale and color scanned images, these arguments can have other values; this will be discussed in Chapter 7.) The definition of a pixel array specifies a transformation m that we can use to orient, scale, and position the scanned image in master coordinates.

The Interpress master in Example 6.1 uses the primitive operator MAKEPIXELARRAY to construct the pixel array of Figure 6.3 from a binary sample vector, the raster dimensions, and the transformation from scanner to master coordinates.

Example 6.1

```
Header "Interpress/Xerox/3.0 "   --header--
BEGIN                            --start of the master--
  { }                            --preamble--
  {                              --start of the page--
    0.0254 SCALE CONCATT         --inches for master coordinates--
    5                            --5 scan lines--
    7                            --7 pixels per scan line--
    1 1 1                        --indicates a binary scanned image--
    1 SCALE                      --transform to master coordinates--
    1 1 1 1 1 1 1                --first scan line--
    0 0 0 1 0 0 1
    0 0 1 1 0 0 1
    0 1 0 1 0 0 1
    1 0 0 0 1 1 0                --last scan line--
    35 MAKEVEC                   --make sample vector--
    MAKEPIXELARRAY               --construct pixel array--
  }                              --end of the page--
END                              --end of the master--
```

This master constructs a pixel array from a sample vector that contains 35 pixels, produced by a raster with 5 scan lines and 7 pixels per scan line. The line "1 1 1" in the master indicates a binary pixel array, where each pixel consists of a single binary sample with a value of either 0 or 1. The transformation converts from the scanner coordinate system to the master coordinate system. For this example, a value of 1 SCALE would mean the pixel array is 5 inches wide and 7 inches high. Although this is a legal Interpress master, it performs no imaging operations.

Sampled Masks

Scanning an image is the complement of imaging an object on the page in Interpress: scanning converts a physical image into an array of intensity values, while imaging converts a pattern of numbers into a page image. The binary pixel array plays the same role in scanning that the mask does in imaging: both indicate where there is ink. Therefore, you can place a scanned binary image on a page by using its pixel array as the mask through which you apply ink.

The MASKPIXEL Operator

In Chapter 5, you saw how an Interpress master took a collection of trajectories, made them into an outline using MAKEOUTLINE, and then created a mask from the outline and deposited ink onto the page through it using MASKFILL. In an analogous way, an Interpress master can take a collection of binary image samples, make them into a pixel array using MAKEPIXELARRAY, and then use MASKPIXEL to image the pixel array in the same way that MASKFILL images the filled outline.

The definition of MASKPIXEL is

$$< \text{pa: PixelArray} > \text{MASKPIXEL} \rightarrow \; < \; >$$

MASKPIXEL takes a single argument, a binary pixel array pa, and creates from it a mask through which the printer applies the current color or ink to the page. The masked region of the page is the xPixels by yPixels rectangle with its lower-left corner at the origin of the scanner coordinate system, transformed to master coordinates by the transformation m, which is part of the pixel array definition, and then transformed to device coordinates by the current transformation T. Therefore, the overall transformation applied to the pixel array is m T CONCAT. These transformations are discussed in detail in the next section. The printer deposits ink on the page where the sample values in the transformed array are 1; no ink is deposited where the sample values are 0.

We can use MASKPIXEL to image the pixel array formed in Example 6.1, as shown in Example 6.2. The result is shown in Figure 6.4.

Example 6.2

```
Header "Interpress/Xerox/3.0 "    --header--
BEGIN                             --start of the master--
  { }                             --preamble--
  {                               --start of the page--
    0.0254 SCALE CONCATT          --inches for master coordinates--
    1 SETGRAY                     --set current ink to black--
    5                             --5 scan lines--
    7                             --7 pixels per scan line--
    1 1 1                         --binary scanned image--
    1 SCALE                       --transformation to MCS--
    1 1 1 1 1 1 1                 --first scan line--
    0 0 0 1 0 0 1
    0 0 1 1 0 0 1
    0 1 0 1 0 0 1
    1 0 0 0 1 1 0                 --last scan line--
    35 MAKEVEC                    --make sample vector--
    MAKEPIXELARRAY                --construct pixel array--
```

```
        MASKPIXEL                      --draw using pixel array as a mask--
      }                                --end of the page--
  END                                  --end of the master--
```

Figure 6.4 The result of Example 6.2.

The Interpress master in Example 6.3 uses MASKPIXEL to image a scanned pen-and-ink drawing and produce the result shown in Figure 6.5.

Example 6.3

```
Header "Interpress/Xerox/3.0 "      --header--
BEGIN                               --start of the master--
  { }                               --preamble--
  {                                 --start of the page--
    0.0254 SCALE CONCATT            --inches for master coordinates--
    1 SETGRAY                       --set current ink to black--
    2400 1800                       --pixel-array size--
    1 1 1                           --binary scanned image--
```

```
    1/600 SCALE                    --transformation--
    2 1.5 TRANSLATE CONCAT         --to master coordinates--
    . . .                          --sample vector--
    MAKEPIXELARRAY                 --construct pixel array--
    MASKPIXEL                      --construct mask and apply color--
  }                                --end of the page--
END                                --end of the master--
```

Figure 6.5 The result of Example 6.3.

The drawing was scanned in the standard order (bottom to top, left to right) and cropped to 2400 scan lines and 1800 pixels per scan line. Because of the many samples in this image, it is usually impractical or impossible to encode them as 2400×1800 numbers followed by 4,320,000 MAKEVEC. Later in the chapter, we describe how to include large sample vectors in a master.

The transformation m that is an argument of the MAKEPIXELARRAY operator is (1/600 SCALE 2 1.5 TRANSLATE CONCAT). In two stages, it maps the 2400×1800 rectangle with its lower-left corner at the origin of the scanner coordinate system to a 4- by 3-inch rectangle with its lower-left corner at the point (2,1.5) in the master coordinate system (see Figure 6.6).[†]

[†] A third stage was added when this page was composed: it translated the output of Example 6.3 to its final position on the page.

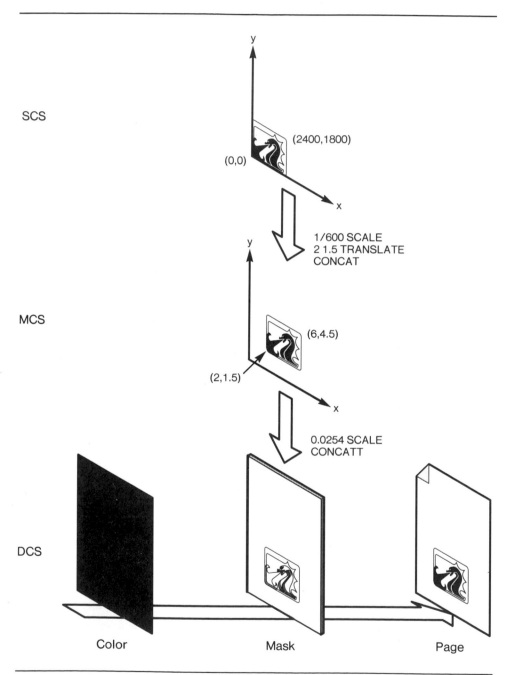

Figure 6.6 Converting a binary pixel array to a mask.

The first stage is the transformation 1/600 SCALE. It scales the scanned image so that its size in the master coordinate system is 4- by 3-inches but leaves the lower-left corner of the image at the origin of the coordinate system. You can think of the scale transformation as equating 1 unit in the scanner coordinate system with 1/600 of a unit in the master coordinate system. It effectively says that the image was scanned at 600 pixels per inch, so that each pixel will be a 1/600 inch square on the page. The overall image height then is 1800/600 or 3 inches.

Once the scanned image has the desired size, the second stage of the transformation 2 1.5 TRANSLATE moves the origin of the scanner coordinate system up 2 inches and right 1.5 inches. This is the pixel array that is passed to the MASKPIXEL operator. MASKPIXEL transforms the array to device coordinates using the current transformation T and then places black ink on the page wherever the sample values of the transformed array are 1.

Image Transformations

Some objects in an Interpress master, such as rectangular masks, can be defined directly in master coordinates, as you saw in Chapter 5. However, scanned images and pixel arrays, like characters, have their own coordinate system, and you must explicitly transform them to master coordinates before you can use them.

For MASKPIXEL, we defined m as the transformation from scanner to master coordinates and T as the transformation from master to device coordinates. In fact, these two transformations combine many transformation stages. You have some choice as to which of these stages are placed in m and which are placed in T. However you choose to define m and T, the important thing is that the overall result is the desired transformation T_{SD} from scanner to device coordinates.

The various stages that make up T_{SD} (see Table 6.1) are concatenated as follows:

$$T_{SD} = T_{SP} \times T_{PM} \times T_{MM} \times T_{MI} \times T_{ID}$$

Table 6.1 Scanned image coordinate transformations.

Transformation	Action
T_{SP}	compensate for mismatched scanning orders
T_{PM}	convert from pixel-array to master coordinates
T_{MM}	orient, scale, and position the image
T_{MI}	convert from master to Interpress coordinates
T_{ID}	convert from Interpress to device coordinates

Figure 6.7 shows the effect these transformations have on a scanned image (compare with Figure 3.28). First we shall consider T$_{SP}$, which transforms the scanner coordinate system (SCS) to the *pixel-array coordinate system* (PCS) and orients images that are not scanned in the standard order.

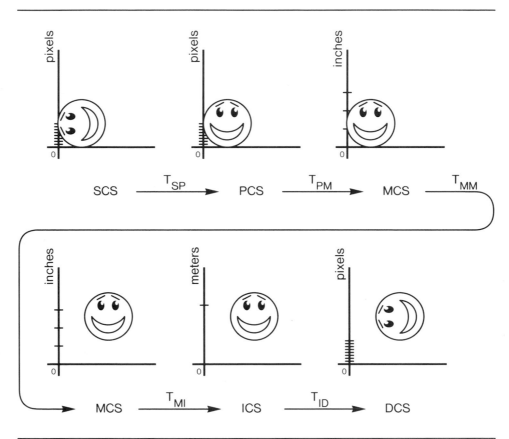

Figure 6.7 Transforming from scanner to device coordinates.

Scanning Order

In all our examples up until now, we assume that images were scanned in the standard order, with pixels in a scan line ordered from bottom to top and successive scan lines ordered from left to right. You would encounter this scan order, for example, on a drum scanner with a traversing sensor (see Figure 6.8a). Although this is a common way to scan an image, you are likely to encounter other scanning orders as well, such as left to right, top to bottom on a facsimile scanner with an internal CCD array (see Figure 6.8b).

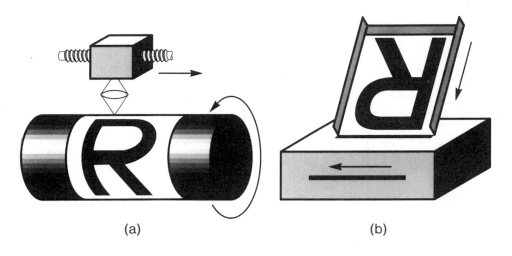

(a)   (b)

Figure 6.8 Scanning order examples.

The scanning order determines the orientation of the scanner coordinate system: Interpress places the origin at the start of the sampling raster, with pixels in a scan line laid down in the direction of increasing y and scan lines laid down in the direction of increasing x. This guarantees that an image scanned in the standard order (bottom to top, left to right, with the first scan line at the left edge of the image and successive scan lines starting along the bottom of the image) is right way up in the scanner coordinate system. "Right way up" means that the left edge of the image lies along the y axis of the coordinate system and the bottom edge along the x axis. However, no matter how you scan an image, yPixels is the number of pixels per scan line and xPixels is the number of scan lines.

The Interpress standard defines a pixel-array coordinate system in which the scanned image is right way up, independent of the scanning order. The transformation T_{SP} converts from the scanner coordinate system to the pixel-array coordinate system. For the standard scanning order, the transformation T_{SP} from scanner to pixel-array coordinates is simply the identity transformation 1 SCALE.

What happens if you take an image that was scanned in some nonstandard order and display it using the standard scanning order to interpret its samples? The image will look reflected or rotated or both. For example, if the image were scanned top to bottom but displayed bottom to top, the top and bottom will appear flipped about the horizontal midline.

The master in Example 6.4 takes an image that was scanned in a nonstandard order (left to right, top to bottom) and images it on the page using MASKPIXEL. The result is shown in Figure 6.9.

Example 6.4

```
Header "Interpress/Xerox/3.0 "    --header--
BEGIN                             --start of the master--
   { }                            --preamble--
   {                              --start of the page--
     0.0254 SCALE CONCATT         --inches for master coordinates--
     1 SETGRAY                    --set current ink to black--
     1200 1200                    --pixel-array size--
     1 1 1                        --binary scanned image--
     1/600 SCALE                  --transformation m--
     3 1.5 TRANSLATE CONCAT       --to master coordinates--
     . . .                        --sample vector--
     MAKEPIXELARRAY               --construct pixel array--
     MASKPIXEL                    --construct mask and apply color--
   }                              --end of the page--
END                               --end of the master--
```

Figure 6.9 The result of Example 6.4.

The transformation m converts a 1200 by 1200 rectangle with its lower-left corner at the origin of the scanner coordinate system to a 2 by 2 rectangle with its lower-left corner at the point (3,1.5) in the master coordinate system. The scan lines, which run from left to right, top to bottom in the image, run from bottom to top, left to right in the scanner and master coordinate systems. As a result, the image in Figure 6.9 appears rotated counterclockwise 90 degrees.

The error in appearance owing to mismatched scanning orders can be corrected by the compensating transformation T_{SP}. The purpose of the transformation is to orient the image so that it is right way up with respect to the x-y axes in the pixel-array and master coordinate systems.

As is usual with transformations, there are two ways to look at what happens. One view is that the original image, when displayed in the scanner coordinate system, comes out wrong and must be transformed to be oriented correctly. In this view, the coordinate system is fixed, and the image is transformed. The alternative view is that the image is always upright, but the coordinate system used to scan the image is different from the coordinate system used to display it. In this view, the transformation converts from the scanner coordinates to the pixel-array coordinates. The two views are equivalent, and you can choose the one with which you feel most comfortable. The compensating transformation can be thought of as either changing the image within the pixel-array coordinates or converting from the scanner to the pixel-array coordinates.

To re-orient an image scanned left to right, top to bottom, we will take the approach of converting from the scanner coordinate system (see Figure 6.10a) to the pixel-array coordinate system (see Figure 6.10c). (If for some reason you want the image to appear on its side on the page, then the image is already "right way up" with respect to the axes of Figure 6.10a and the transformation from scanner to pixel-array coordinates would be 1 SCALE.) The instruction -90 ROTATE transforms the axes of Figure 6.10a to those of Figure 6.10b, which have the desired orientation, but the desired origin is now at $(0, -\text{xPixels})$. The transformation 0 xPixels TRANSLATE maps $(0, -\text{xPixels})$ to $(0,0)$. Therefore, for the left-to-right, top-to-bottom scanning order, the transformation T_{SP} is

```
-90 ROTATE                --orient coordinate axes--
0 xPixels TRANSLATE       --define origin--
CONCAT
```

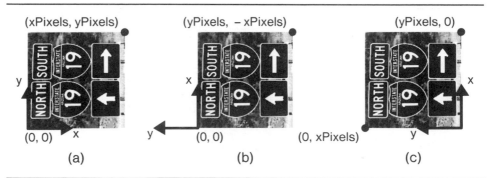

Figure 6.10 Converting from scanner to pixel array coordinates.

Combining this result with Example 6.4 gives the master in Example 6.5, which produces an upright image (see Figure 6.11).

Example 6.5

```
Header "Interpress/Xerox/3.0 "    --header--
BEGIN                             --start of the master--
  { }                             --preamble--
  {                               --start of the page--
    0.0254 SCALE CONCATT          --inches for master coordinates--
    1 SETGRAY                     --set current ink to black--
    1200 1200                     --pixel-array size--
    1 1 1                         --binary scanned image--
    -90 ROTATE                    --to orient image in--
    0 1200 TRANSLATE CONCAT       --pixel-array coordinates--
    1/600 SCALE CONCAT            --transformation from pixel-array--
    3 1.5 TRANSLATE CONCAT        --to master coordinates--
    . . .                         --sample vector--
    MAKEPIXELARRAY                --construct pixel array--
    MASKPIXEL                     --construct mask and apply color--
  }                               --end of the page--
END                               --end of the master--
```

Figure 6.11 The result of Example 6.5.

Figure 6.12 shows the results of the eight possible scanning orders, along with the transformations T$_{SP}$ that will orient each upright in the pixel-array coordinate system. The Interpress master should include, as part of the transformation m, the transformation that corresponds to the order in which the samples were scanned.

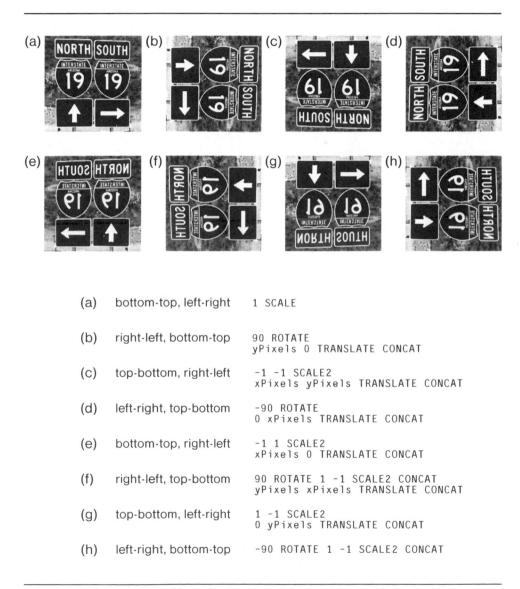

(a)	bottom-top, left-right	`1 SCALE`
(b)	right-left, bottom-top	`90 ROTATE` `yPixels 0 TRANSLATE CONCAT`
(c)	top-bottom, right-left	`-1 -1 SCALE2` `xPixels yPixels TRANSLATE CONCAT`
(d)	left-right, top-bottom	`-90 ROTATE` `0 xPixels TRANSLATE CONCAT`
(e)	bottom-top, right-left	`-1 1 SCALE2` `xPixels 0 TRANSLATE CONCAT`
(f)	right-left, top-bottom	`90 ROTATE 1 -1 SCALE2 CONCAT` `yPixels xPixels TRANSLATE CONCAT`
(g)	top-bottom, left-right	`1 -1 SCALE2` `0 yPixels TRANSLATE CONCAT`
(h)	left-right, bottom-top	`-90 ROTATE 1 -1 SCALE2 CONCAT`

Figure 6.12 Transformations for nonstandard scanning orders.

Conversion to Master Coordinates

Pixel arrays have a natural unit of length–the size of a pixel–that is used in the pixel-array coordinate system. To fit this image onto our page, however, we want to know its size in our master coordinates. To relate the two, we need to know the size of a pixel in terms of meters, inches, or whatever master coordinates we are using. By converting the image from the pixel-array coordinates to the master coordinates, we express its size and shape in the same terms as our other drawing instructions. We can then determine scales to make the image the desired size and translations to place it at the desired position. Therefore, we need a transformation, T_{PM}, to convert from the *pixel-array coordinate system* (PCS) to the *master coordinate system* (MCS). This is often just a scale. For example, if our MCS is the same as the default *Interpress coordinate system* (ICS), then the transformation is just a scale by the size of a pixel in meters. If our MCS uses inches, the T_{PM} will be a scale by the size of a pixel in inches. If, however, we have inverted, or rotated, or translated the MCS, then the corresponding adjustments convert the PCS (which has the same position and orientation as the ICS) to the MCS.

We saw in Example 6.5 how a (1/600 SCALE) transformation was used to convert to master coordinate units. This is the scaling needed to convert from pixels to inches.

Consider again the image of Figure 6.11. It resulted from generating a 2-by 2-inch area of a halftoned photograph from left to right, top to bottom, at 600 pixels per inch, so that xPixels is 1200 and yPixels is 1200. When the MCS units are inches, then the scaling transformation T_{PM} is

```
1/600  SCALE        --pixel is 1/600-inch square--
```

This transformation defines the pixel array over a rectangle with its lower-left corner at the origin and its upper-right corner at (2, 2) in the MCS.

Interpress does not require that the sampling resolution be the same in both directions. If there are rx pixels per inch and ry scan lines per inch, then T_{PM} is

```
1/rx       --scan line spacing is 1/rx inches--
1/ry       --pixel spacing on scan line is 1/ry inches--
SCALE2
```

If the scaling transformations follow the transformation from scanner to pixel-array coordinates, then the x and y scanning resolutions are stated with respect to the x and y axes of the pixel-array (rather than the scanner) coordinate system.

Image Size, Orientation, and Position

Correcting for scan directions and converting to master coordinates results in an image equivalent to the scanned original, but this may not be what you want. You might prefer to display the image at half the original size, or you might want to rotate it. You will almost always want to position it on the page. This can be done with the now familiar rotate, scale, and translate transformations. They may be used for pixel arrays as they were for rectangles in Chapter 3. For this set of transformations, you can imagine keeping the coordinates fixed and transforming the image. Think of transforming the object within the context of master coordinates. We have labeled this transformation T_{MM}. It may actually be the concatenation of scaling, rotating, and translating transformations.

We see an example of the T_{MM} component in Example 6.5 in the 3 1.5 TRANSLATE instructions. This is a transformation to position the image.

Some form of translation is almost always present, since this is the only mechanism provided in Interpress to position pixel arrays. However, you do have a choice as to whether the translation is folded into m or T. A revised version of Example 6.5, where the translation is carried out in T, is shown in Example 6.6.

Example 6.6

```
Header "Interpress/Xerox/3.0 "      --header--
BEGIN                                --start of the master--
   { }                               --preamble--
   {                                 --start of the page--
      0.0254 SCALE CONCATT           --inches for master coordinates--
      1 SETGRAY                      --set current ink to black--
      1200 1200                      --pixel-array size--
      1 1 1                          --binary scanned image--
      -90 ROTATE                     --transformation from scanner--
      0 1200 TRANSLATE CONCAT        --to pixel array coordinates--
      1/600 SCALE CONCAT             --to master coordinates--
      . . .                          --sample vector--
      MAKEPIXELARRAY                 --construct pixel array--
      3 1.5 TRANSLATE CONCATT        --position the image--
      MASKPIXEL                      --construct mask and apply color--
   }                                 --end of the page--
END                                  --end of the master--
```

A variation on this technique, shown in Example 6.7, sets the current position to the desired position for the image and then use either the MOVE or TRANS operator to construct and concatenate the translation transformation. The TRANS operator has the advantage of aligning the pixels in the image with the spots produced by the printer.

Example 6.7

```
Header "Interpress/Xerox/3.0 "        --header--
BEGIN                                 --start of the master--
  { }                                 --preamble--
  {                                   --start of the page--
    0.0254 SCALE CONCATT              --inches for master coordinates--
    1 SETGRAY                         --set current ink to black--
    1200 1200                         --pixel-array size--
    1 1 1                             --binary scanned image--
    -90 ROTATE                        --transformation from scanner--
    0 1200 TRANSLATE CONCAT           --to pixel array coordinates--
    1/600 SCALE CONCAT                --to master coordinates--
    . . .                             --sample vector--
    MAKEPIXELARRAY                    --construct pixel array--
    3 1.5 SETXY TRANS                 --position the image--
    MASKPIXEL                         --construct mask and apply color--
  }                                   --end of the page--
END                                   --end of the master--
```

In placing the pixel array on the page using MASKPIXEL, the important thing is the overall effect of m T CONCAT. This means that you can use alternate definitions for m and T, as long as the overall transformation m T CONCAT is the same.

You can also use different models for building the transformation, as long as it leads to the proper size and orientation. The scheme we have just presented is first to convert to master coordinates, and then to scale and rotate the object within the MCS. At the risk of causing confusion, we shall present an alternative scheme for arriving at the correct size and orientation in master coordinates. This approach is analogous to the method we used for fonts. In the case of a font, we started with characters 1 unit high and then scaled and rotated them to the proper size and orientation in master coordinates. This was done by the MODIFYFONT operator. To take the same approach for a pixel array, you can first scale it to be 1 unit high and then scale and rotate it to the proper size and orientation. Instead of using T_{PM} to convert from pixel array to master coordinates, we would use T_{PN} to convert from pixel-array to *normalized pixel-array coordinates* (NPCS). This transformation is an easy one; it is just a scale by the reciprocal of the pixel-array height in pixels. If the image is Y pixels high, then scaling by 1/Y will make it 1 unit high. To get the proper size and orientation in master coordinates, you use T_{NM}, instead of T_{PM}, to transform from normalized pixel-array to master coordinates. The T_{NM} transformation takes a unit-high object and scales it to the desired height in master coordinates. It works in exactly the same way as the transformation given to MODIFYFONT to scale characters. The alternative to T_{PM} for simple scaling then looks like

```
1/Y SCALE               --normalize image height--
size SCALE CONCAT       --scale image to desired size--
```

Of course, you will still need to include a translation for positioning the image. Example 6.8 demonstrates this approach, in which we place the normalizing transformation T_{PN} in m and all the other transformations in T. It has the same effect as the master of Example 6.5 and produces Figure 6.11.

Example 6.8

```
Header "Interpress/Xerox/3.0 "  --header--
BEGIN                           --start of the master--
  { }                           --preamble--
  {                             --start of the page--
    2 SCALE                     --scale image to desired size--
    3 1.5 TRANSLATE CONCAT      --position image--
    0.0254 SCALE CONCAT         --scale to Interpress coordinates--
    CONCATT                     --convert to device coordinates--
    1 SETGRAY                   --set current ink to black--
    1200 1200                   --pixel-array size--
    1 1 1                       --binary scanned image--
    -90 ROTATE                  --transformation from scanner--
    0 1200 TRANSLATE CONCAT     --to pixel-array coordinates--
    1/1200 SCALE CONCAT         --normalize image height--
    . . .                       --sample vector--
    MAKEPIXELARRAY              --construct pixel array--
    MASKPIXEL                   --construct mask and apply color--
  }                             --end of the page--
END                             --end of the master--
```

If you compare the masters of Example 6.5 and Example 6.8, you will see that the transformation m T CONCAT is the same in both cases.

```
-90 ROTATE                  --transformation from scanner--
0 1200 TRANSLATE CONCAT     --to pixel-array coordinates--
1/1200 SCALE CONCAT         --normalize image height--
2 SCALE CONCAT              --scale to desired size--
3 1.5 TRANSLATE CONCAT      --position in inches--
0.0254 SCALE CONCAT         --scale to Interpress coordinates--
T_ID CONCAT                 --transform to device coordinates--
```

Net Transformation

Interpress defines the *net transformation* T_{net} as the transformation from the standard coordinates used to represent an object to Interpress coordinates. In the case of a scanned image, the net transformation is

$$T_{net} = T_{SP} \times T_{PM} \times T_{MM} \times T_{MI}$$

It can include scales, rotations, and translations, so that the scanned image has the desired size, orientation, and position in the ICS. Because it is assumed that a printer can handle arbitrary translations, we will consider scales and rotations only as part of the net transformation. Therefore, the net transformation describes the size and orientation of the image in Interpress coordinates. For the scanned image used with MASKPIXEL in Example 6.8, the net transformation is

```
-90 ROTATE                --compensate for scanning order--
1/1200 SCALE CONCAT       --normalize image height--
2 SCALE CONCAT            --scale to desired size--
0.0254 SCALE CONCAT       --scale to Interpress coordinates--
```

which reduces to

```
-90 ROTATE 0.00004233 SCALE CONCAT
```

An Interpress printer specifies a set of *easy* net transformations that it can handle efficiently. For net transformations other than those in the easy set, such as arbitrary scalings and rotations, the printer performance may be severely degraded, or the printer may decline to perform the transformations. For example, image rotations to compensate for a mismatch in scanning orders are computationally expensive operations, and a particular raster printer may exclude them from its set of easy net transformations. To produce a scanned image on the page, this printer would expect the scan lines in the scanned image to be oriented the same way as the scan lines in the printer raster. If they were not, it would ignore the image and generate an appearance error.

When your Interpress printer is a raster device, then the page image created by MASKPIXEL eventually ends up as a pixel array at the printer's resolution. You can think of the transformation m T CONCAT as converting from scanner or pixel-array coordinates at the input scanned image resolution to pixel-array coordinates at the output printer resolution.

The printer sets the current transformation T at the start of each page to T_{ID}, so that it converts from the Interpress coordinate system to the device coordinate system. In the printer that was used to produce this book, T_{ID} is essentially

```
90 ROTATE 0.2347 0 TRANSLATE CONCAT 47244 SCALE CONCAT
```

This means the printer scans the page left to right, top to bottom, and the printer resolution is 47244 dots per meter or 1200 dots per inch (see Figure 6.7). If you insert this value for T_{ID} in the expression for the overall transformation m T CONCAT given previously, then the scale transformation from pixel array to device coordinates is 2 SCALE. The printer resolution is twice the scanned image resolution. Where there is a single pixel in the scanned image, there is a 2 by 2 block of printer dots. The printer must fill in all four dots by some algorithm. The obvious approach is to give all four the same black or white color as the pixel in the scanned image. The solution is not as obvious when the printer resolution is not a multiple of the scanner resolution. If the overall scale factor had not been an integer, then the printer would have either rendered scanned image pixels with varying number of printer dots or subsampled the scanned image by using a subset of the pixels from the pixel array. Some printers may exclude scale transformations from their set of easy net transformations if they lead to noninteger scale factors in the overall transformation T_{SD} from scanner to device coordinates. Although Interpress allows you to specify arbitrary scaling and rotations for scanned images, it does not require that all printers implement them efficiently, if they implement them at all.

Sampled Inks

To produce Figure 6.5, we used a binary pixel array as a sampled mask to specify where the printer applied black ink to the page. Or we can use the same binary pixel array to specify a sampled black-and-white ink that the printer applies to the page through a rectangular mask to achieve the same result.

The MAKESAMPLEDBLACK Operator

The Interpress operator MAKESAMPLEDBLACK creates a sampled ink from a binary pixel array.

<pa: PixelArray> <um: Transformation> <clear: Cardinal>
MAKESAMPLEDBLACK → <color: Color>

The argument pa specifies a binary pixel array created by MAKEPIXELARRAY. The xPixels×yPixels rectangle with its lower-left corner at the origin of the pixel-array coordinate system is transformed to device coordinates by the transformation m um CONCAT. m is the transformation that is part of the pixel-array definition, while um has the same role as T for the MASKPIXEL case. In fact, we usually just use the current transformation T as um.

MAKESAMPLEDBLACK returns on the stack an object of type color that the master can store in the imager variable called color. This variable specifies the ink used in masking operations. The sampled ink created by MAKESAMPLEDBLACK is black where the sample values of the transformed pixel array are 1. The argument clear specifies the effect of the ink when the sample values are 0. If clear is 0, then a zero sample value is treated as an opaque white ink; when it is applied to the page through a mask, it replaces whatever ink was already there. If clear is 1, then a zero sample value is transparent; applying it through a mask has no effect on the color already on the page.

The Interpress master in Example 6.9 uses the MAKESAMPLEDBLACK operator to produce Figure 6.5.

Example 6.9

```
Header "Interpress/Xerox/3.0 "    --header--
BEGIN                             --start of the master--
  { }                             --preamble--
  {                               --start of the page--
    0.0254 SCALE CONCATT          --convert inches to meters--
    2400 1800                     --pixel-array size--
    1 1 1                         --binary scanned image--
    1/600 SCALE                   --transformation from pixel array--
    2 1.5 TRANSLATE CONCAT        --position in master coordinates--
    . . .                         --sample vector--
    MAKEPIXELARRAY                --construct pixel array--
    4 IGET                        --um is current transformation T--
    0                             --use opaque white ink--
    MAKESAMPLEDBLACK              --construct sampled ink--
    13 ISET                       --save sampled ink in imager--
    2 1.5 4 3 MASKRECTANGLE       --apply through rectangular mask--
  }                               --end of the page--
END                               --end of the master--
```

In this example, MAKESAMPLEDBLACK uses the pixel array that was created in Example 6.3. The pixel array defines a 4- by 3-inch scanned image with its lower-left corner at (2,1.5) in the MCS. MAKESAMPLEDBLACK transforms it to device coordinates using the current transformation as um. The current transformation is stored in imager variable 4, and the master has already defined it as the transformation from master to device coordinates.

MAKESAMPLEDBLACK then converts the transformed pixel array into a printer-dependent representation for a sampled ink and stores it in the imager variable *color* (index 13) using the instruction 13 ISET. Samples in the transformed array with value 1 are interpreted as black ink, and samples with value 0 as white ink, because the argument clear has value 0. The printer extends the ink definition beyond the region specified by the pixel array through tiling; that is, stepping and repeating the pixel array so that it covers the entire page (see Figure 6.13). This does not mean that the printer stores multiple copies of the array. Tiling is invoked only when ink is needed to fill a masked region not covered by the transformed pixel array. The effect

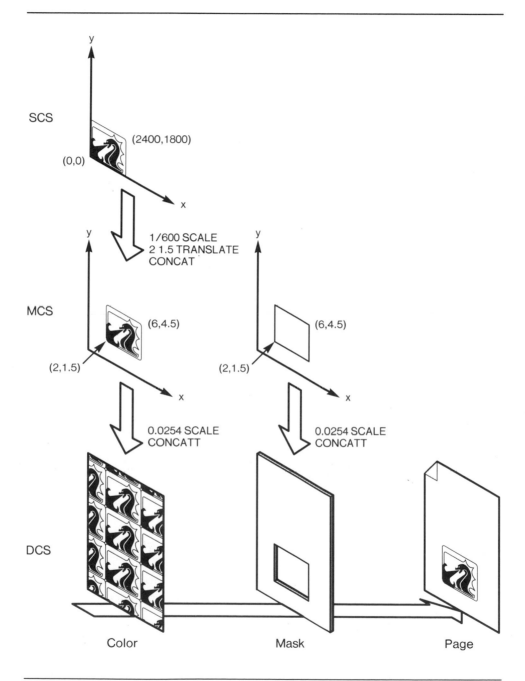

Figure 6.13 Converting a pixel array to a sampled color.

of replicating the pixel array can be achieved at the printer by mapping the coordinates of the mask region into the corresponding coordinates of the original pixel array.

MASKRECTANGLE creates a rectangular mask with the same size, position, and orientation in the master coordinate system as the pixel array from which the sampled ink was created. It then applies the current color, created by MAKESAMPLEDBLACK, to the page through the mask.

Interpress offers a convenience operator, SETSAMPLEDBLACK, that reduces the number of steps it takes to define a sampled ink from a binary pixel array. The definition of SETSAMPLEDBLACK is

<pa:PixelArray> <vm:Transformation> <clear:Cardinal>
SETSAMPLEDBLACK → < >

This operator differs from MAKESAMPLEDBLACK in two ways. First, the transformation applied to the binary image to convert it from pixel-array coordinates to device coordinates is m vm CONCAT T CONCAT, instead of m um CONCAT. The use of the current transformation T is implicit in SETSAMPLEDBLACK, whereas it was explicit in MAKESAMPLEDBLACK. Second, SETSAMPLEDBLACK automatically stores the sampled ink it creates in the color imager variable, so that 13 ISET is not needed. Therefore, the effect of

```
pa                      --binary pixel array--
vm                      --transformation to master coordinates--
clear                   --opaque or transparent white ink--
SETSAMPLEDBLACK         --create and store sampled ink--
```

is identical to the longer sequence

```
pa                      --binary pixel array--
vm                      --transformation to master coordinates--
4 IGET CONCAT           --transformation to device coordinates--
clear                   --opaque or transparent white ink--
MAKESAMPLEDBLACK        --create sampled ink--
13 ISET                 --store sampled ink--
```

Rewriting the Interpress master of Example 6.9 so that it uses SETSAMPLEDBLACK gives the master in Example 6.10.

Example 6.10

```
Header "Interpress/Xerox/3.0 "    --header--
BEGIN                             --start of the master--
  { }                             --preamble--
  {                               --start of the page--
    0.0254 SCALE CONCATT          --convert inches to meters--
```

```
      2400 1800                        --pixel-array size--
      1 1 1                            --binary scanned image--
      1/600 SCALE                      --transform from pixel-array--
      2 1.5 TRANSLATE CONCAT           --to master coordinates--
         . . .                         --sample vector--
      MAKEPIXELARRAY                   --construct pixel array--
      1 SCALE                          --use identity transform as vm--
      0                                --use opaque white ink--
      SETSAMPLEDBLACK                  --construct and save sampled ink--
      2 1.5 4 3 MASKRECTANGLE          --apply through rectangular mask--
   }                                   --end of the page--
END                                    --end of the master--
```

Image Transformations Revisited

We have considered three Interpress operators for imaging pixel arrays; each concatenates a different series of transformations to convert a binary scanned image from scanner coordinates to device coordinates.

$$m \times T \qquad \text{for MASKPIXEL}$$
$$m \times um \qquad \text{for MAKESAMPLEDBLACK}$$
$$m \times vm \times T \qquad \text{for SETSAMPLEDBLACK}$$

All these transformation sequences serve the same function; namely, to convert from the scanner coordinates to the printing device coordinates. We have seen how this overall transformation can be thought of as a series of steps or component transformations. We have some freedom as to how to divide the components between m and the other transformations, but a basic model for MASKPIXEL is that m converts from the scanner to the master coordinates and T from the master to the device coordinates. Sizing, rotating, and positioning of the image can take place in either m or T. You can use the same model for MAKESAMPLEDBLACK and SETSAMPLEDBLACK. You can construct the pixel array in the same manner, using the same m. For MAKESAMPLEDBLACK, you use the instructions 4 IGET to get T for use as um. For SETSAMPLEDBLACK, you can use 1 SCALE for vm.

The fact that you have the third transformation vm available in SETSAMPLEDBLACK means that you also have the option of placing some of the component transformations (such as those for sizing or positioning) in vm, rather than in m or T.

Because it offers the opportunity to avoid T, MAKESAMPLEBLACK is perhaps the most interesting of the three operators. Although you would typically set um to be the current transformation T, you are not required to do so. Failure to use T results in a file that is device-dependent–the ink's pattern frequency depends on the printer's resolution. The file will also be insensitive to overall transformations of the file. If you scale or rotate the page, the ink pattern will not scale or rotate. You may find this to be rather strange in a language with a goal of device independence and wonder why you would ever use it. It is intended to support certain high-quality images on particular devices.

Suppose you want to draw a gray box on a particular printer. Suppose further that you are very particular about the halftone dot pattern that forms the gray. You can carefully construct the gray pattern with MAKESAMPLEDBLACK. Because you know the particular device, you can supply the master-to-device coordinate transformations in um without reference to T.

Now consider what happens if the page which contains your gray box is rotated or scaled. In this case, the box is changed, but the ink is not. The scaled or rotated box is still filled with your carefully designed gray pattern. If you define your ink in terms of the current transformation (the usual technique), then when T is changed to rotate or scale the box, the ink will be rotated or scaled as well; your carefully created pattern will be altered or corrupted. Remember, however, that the price of a transformation-independent ink pattern is a device-dependent master.

Patterned Inks

MAKESAMPLEDBLACK is the special case, specifically designed for binary scanned images, of the more general operator MAKESAMPLEDCOLOR (see the discussion of this operator in Chapter 7). Although MAKESAMPLEDCOLOR is the only Interpress mechanism for placing gray and color scanned images on a page, you can use either MASKPIXEL or MAKESAMPLEDBLACK to place binary images on a page. The advantage of the MAKESAMPLEDBLACK operator over the MASKPIXEL operator is that it can easily create patterned inks and inks with a limited amount of transparency.

An Interpress printer extends the ink definition beyond the region covered by the transformed pixel array by tiling. It uses the pixel array as if it were a mosaic tile or piece of wallpaper; you give the printer one piece of the pattern and it replicates that pattern over the entire page. Thus, if you want to fill a mask region with some repeated pattern or texture, you need to describe only the basic or periodic pattern element, and the printer repeats it until it covers the mask. Tiling, a property of sampled inks, applies whether the ink is created from binary or color image samples. Figure 6.14 shows two examples of texture patterns.

Pattern A is based on a houndstooth weaving pattern. The Interpress master in Example 6.11 creates a sampled ink from the Pattern A and applies it to the page through a character mask.

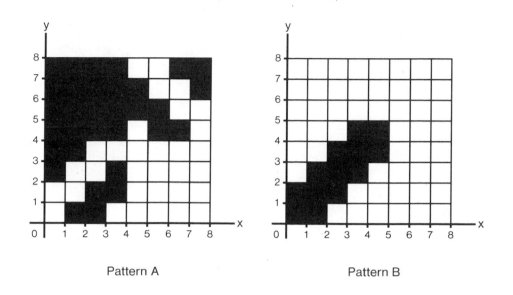

Pattern A   Pattern B

Figure 6.14 Texture patterns.

Example 6.11

```
Header "Interpress/Xerox/3.0 "   --header--
BEGIN                            --start of the master--
  { }                            --preamble--
  {                              --start of the page--
    0.0254 SCALE CONCATT         --convert inches to meters--
    Identifier "xerox" Identifier "XC1-1-1" Identifier "modern"
    3 MAKEVEC FINDFONT
    1.5 MODIFYFONT               --font size is 1.5 inches--
    0 FSET                       --font 0 is 108-point Modern--
    8 8                          --pattern dimensions--
    1 1 1                        --binary scanned image--
    1/8 SCALE                    --normalize tile size--
    0 0 1 1 1 1 1 1              --samples--
    1 0 0 1 1 1 1 1
    1 1 0 0 1 1 1 1
    0 1 1 0 1 1 1 1
    0 0 0 0 0 1 1 0
    0 0 0 0 1 1 0 0
    0 0 0 0 1 0 0 1
    0 0 0 0 0 0 1 1
    64 MAKEVEC                   --make sample vector--
    MAKEPIXELARRAY               --construct pixel-array--
```

```
      1/16 SCALE                --set tile size to 1/16"--
      0                         --opaque white--
      SETSAMPLEDBLACK           --construct and save sampled ink--
      0 SETFONT                 --set current font to font 0--
      0 0 SETXY                 --set current position--
      String "Pattern" SHOW     --apply ink through character mask--
    }                           --end of the page--
  END                           --end of the master--
```

The sampled ink is created from a 1/16-inch-square "tile" with its lower-left corner at origin of the MCS. Figure 6.15 shows the image created by this master. (An additional translation moved it to the position shown.)

Figure 6.15 The result of Example 6.11.

Transparent Inks

The ink created by MAKESAMPLEDBLACK and SETSAMPLEDBLACK differs from the ink created by other Interpress operators in that it can be transparent. According to the Interpress imaging model, when an ink is applied to the page through a mask, it replaces whatever was there before. An exception to the Interpress rule of opaque ink is the sampled ink you create using MAKESAMPLEDBLACK with the value of the argument clear set to 1. In this case, the samples of the transformed pixel array that have value 1 still behave as an opaque black ink. However, the samples with value 0 are interpreted as a clear or transparent ink that has no effect on the page beneath them; whatever ink was previously laid down will still be visible. The effect is analogous to what an animator achieves by overlaying multiple images written on clear acetate sheets.

This means that you can create composite patterns and images by successively imaging primitive patterns. Figure 6.16 is an example of the effect you can obtain: it fills a rectangular mask with sampled inks created from Pattern B of Figure 6.14. The master that created it is shown in Example 6.12.

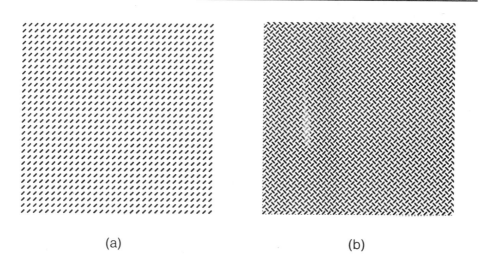

(a)   (b)

Figure 6.16 The result of Example 6.12.

Example 6.12

```
Header "Interpress/Xerox/3.0 "   --header--
BEGIN                            --start of the master--
  { }                            --preamble--
  {                              --start of the page--
    1 5 ISET                     --set priority important--
    0.0254 SCALE CONCATT         --convert inches to meters--
    8 8                          --pattern dimensions--
    1 1 1                        --binary scanned image--
    1 SCALE                      --tile size is 8 units--
    1 1 0 0 0 0 0 0              --samples for Pattern B--
    1 1 1 0 0 0 0 0
    0 1 1 1 0 0 0 0
    0 0 1 1 1 0 0 0
    0 0 0 1 1 0 0 0
    0 0 0 0 0 0 0 0
    0 0 0 0 0 0 0 0
    0 0 0 0 0 0 0 0
    64 MAKEVEC                   --make sample vector--
    MAKEPIXELARRAY               --construct pixel array--
    0 FSET 0 FGET                --save in frame[0]--
    1/128 SCALE                  --set tile size to 8/128=1/16 inch--
    0                            --opaque white--
    SETSAMPLEDBLACK              --construct and save sampled ink--
    1.5 1.5 2 2 MASKRECTANGLE    --see Figure 6.16a--
```

```
          4.0 1.5 2 2 MASKRECTANGLE    --start Figure 6.16b--
          0 FGET                       --retrieve Pattern B pixel array--
          -90 ROTATE                   --transform--
          4 9 TRANSLATE CONCAT
          1/128 SCALE CONCAT           --set tile size to 1/16 inch--
          1                            --transparent white--
          SETSAMPLEDBLACK              --construct and save sampled ink--
          4.0 1.5 2 2 MASKRECTANGLE    --see Figure 6.16b--
        }                              --end of the page--
  END                                  --end of the master--
```

In this master, the imager variable priorityImportant is set to 1, so that objects are imaged in the order in which they occur in the master. The master first makes a pixel array from the samples of Pattern B, creates a sampled ink from the array, and then applies the ink to the page through the rectangular mask; the intermediate result is shown in Figure 6.16a. The master then creates a sampled ink from a transformed version of Pattern B, with clear set to 1, and applies it through a mask with the same position on the page (Figure 6.16b). When you use an ink created by either MAKESAMPLEDBLACK or SETSAMPLEDBLACK when clear is set to 1, it is as if the ink acts as its own mask, besides the mask that you directly invoke to add ink to the page. Therefore, in Example 6.12, ink is only added to the page where the sampled ink itself is black and lies within the region defined by the MASKRECTANGLE operator.

Encoding Binary Sample Vectors

We have so far described how you create and use binary pixel arrays in an Interpress master. We now turn our attention to the sample vector from which you construct the pixel array. Most of the cost associated with storing and transmitting masters that contain pixel arrays results from the large amount of data required to represent even the lowest-resolution scanned images. For example, scanning an A4-size page (210 by 297 millimeters) at 300 pixels per inch on CCITT[†] Group 4 facsimile equipment would produce over 8.7 million image samples. Although the resolution and size of your scanned images may differ, how you encode the sample vector in a master can have a significant effect on the cost and performance of your system.

Standard Encodings

The sample vector of a binary pixel array contains xPixels×yPixels samples. Each sample is a cardinal or nonnegative integer. You could include a sample

---

[†]CCITT are the initials in French for the International Telegraph and Telephone Consultative Committee.

vector in a master in the obvious way as a sequence of xPixels×yPixels integers, followed by MAKEVEC.

> sample(0) . . . sample(xPixels×yPixels−1) xPixels×yPixels MAKEVEC

The amount of storage the vector requires depends on how you represent integers. While you are free to use any encoding you wish with Interpress, Xerox offers a standard encoding in which integers between −4000 and 28,767 are represented as a 2-byte Short Number token. This is adequate for most of the operand values that you will use in an Interpress master, but is unusually inefficient for binary samples: two bytes only contain one bit of information. Moreover, attempts to construct a large sample vector on the stack can quickly lead to stack overflow, since printer implementations are required to support only 1000 values.

The need to represent large data vectors occurs often enough that the Xerox standard encoding has a special sequence format to handle them. The sequence encoding for a vector is

> sequenceLargeVector sequenceLength bytesPerElement
> sample(0) . . . sample(xPixels×yPixels−1)

SequenceLargeVector is a byte token with hexadecimal value E8. For a Long Sequence type, the sequenceLength is a 3-byte token that specifies the number of bytes in the following sequence (see Appendix B). The first byte in the sequence is bytesPerElement, which says how many bytes are used to encode each sample. Following it are xPixels×yPixels×bytesPerElement bytes. When the printer encounters this sequence in a master, the effect is equivalent to executing

> sample(0) . . . sample(xPixels×yPixels−1)
> (sequenceLength−1)/bytesPerElement MAKEVEC

where individual samples are encoded as two's-complement bytePerElement-byte tokens.

We will represent this and other encodings for large vectors by

> LargeVector "bytesPerElement sample(0) . . .
>   sample(xPixels×yPixels−1)"

The notation "LargeVector" represents a byte token that signifies a long sequence of type sequenceLargeVector and 3 bytes indicating the sequence length. With this encoding, the printer knows the size of the vector before it sees any sample values and does not need to push values onto the stack, waiting for a MAKEVEC operator or a possible stack overflow.

If you scan an A4-size page at 300 samples per inch using the CCITT scanning format (left to right, top to bottom), the number of pixels per scanline on the page is 2480, and the number of scan lines is 3508 (Figure 6.17).

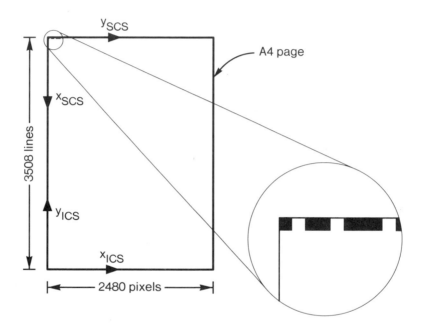

Figure 6.17 Scanning an image using CCITT Group 4 format.

The encoding for the resulting sample vector in the master is shown in Example 6.13.

Example 6.13

```
LargeVector "01 01 00 01 01 00 01 01 01 . . ."
```

The sequence is $2480 \times 3508 + 1$ bytes long: the first byte "01" says each sample is encoded as a single byte. It is followed by 2480×3508 sample values; in this example, the first eight sample values are "01 00 01 01 00 01 01 01." Although this would be a compact encoding for byte image samples, using a byte to store a bit is still inefficient. Reducing the size of the sample vector any further requires explicitly compressing the scanned image data.

Data Compression

For a binary sample vector, packing eight samples into a single byte is a simple example of data compression. Where the first eight samples were encoded before as 8 separate bytes, they would now be encoded as single byte "10110111" with hexadecimal value B7. Even a compression scheme this simple reduces the amount of space required to store the binary samples by a factor of 8.

Interpress does not have a primitive operator for decoding or decompressing samples not encoded in the standard way. You have to supply an operator decompress to do this.

$$<\text{v:Vector}> \text{decompress DO} \rightarrow <\text{samples:Vector}>$$

The operator decompress takes a vector that contains compressed sample data and other information needed to decode the data. When executed by the DO operator, decompress returns on the stack a sample vector in the standard encoding.

The use of a packing algorithm can best be explained by showing you, in Example 6.14, the compressed data vector that it produces and that it would pass to the operator decompress.

Example 6.14

```
LargeVector "02 00 01 09 C0 B7 34 . . ."
```

The length of the sequence is 1,094,501 bytes: the first byte is "02," which says that each element of the vector is encoded as a 2-byte token. Following it are the 1,094,500 bytes that define the elements of the vector passed as an argument to the operator decompress:

```
0001 09C0 B734 . . .
```

The algorithm interprets the first 2 bytes "0001" as the number of bits per sample; in this case, 1. The next 2 bytes "09C0" give the line length (2496: 2480 scanned samples, padded with 16 zeros to make the line length a multiple of 32). Following that are 1,094,496 ($2496 \times 3508/8$) bytes of packed data, which the decompress operator unpacks 2 bytes at a time. The first eight samples are obtained by unpacking the byte with hexadecimal value B7.

Because Interpress is a programming language, albeit one specifically designed for imaging, you could write your own Interpress program for decoding a packed data vector and include it in the master as a composed operator. Although Interpress allows you this option, the resulting performance is likely to be unacceptably slow. Best performance is obtained when the master obtains a decompression operator from the environment of the printer using FINDDECOMPRESSOR.

$$< v:\text{Vector of Identifiers} > \text{FINDDECOMPRESSOR} \rightarrow \ < \text{decompress:Operator} >$$

FINDDECOMPRESSOR takes a vector of identifiers v that is the universal name of the decompression operator, looks it up in the printer's environment, and returns the operator decompress in printer-dependent form on the stack. For example, the operator may be a routine written in the printer's native code, or it may use custom hardware in the printer.

To decode sample vectors compressed using this packing algorithm, we would devise a decompression operator, give it the name [Xerox, Packed] and register it in the printer environment. The encoding for the packed sample vector is shown in Example 6.15.

Example 6.15

```
                                  --compressed sample vector--
LargeVector "02 00 01 09 C0 B7 34 . . ."
Identifier "Xerox"
Identifier "Packed"
2 MAKEVEC                         --name of decompression operator--
FINDDECOMPRESSOR                  --retrieve from printer environment--
DO                                --execute decompression operator--
```

The Xerox Raster Encoding Standard defines the [Xerox, Packed] decompression operator, along with three other standard operators for compressed binary data: [Xerox, Compressed], [Xerox, Adaptive], and [Xerox, CCITT-4]. Interpress defines a sequence type for use with each. For example, the encoding shown in Example 6.15 for a packed sample vector compressed using the [Xerox, Packed] algorithm can be replaced by the instruction given in Example 6.16.

Example 6.16

```
PackedPixelVector "00 01 09 C0 B7 34 . . ."
```

If you use the Xerox encoding for Interpress, you would replace the PackedPixelVector token with the byte token sequencePackedPixelVector, which has hexadecimal value E9, and three bytes indicating the length of the following sequence. PackedPixelVector assumes that each element of the sequence uses 2 bytes, so that we do not need to start the sequence with "02," as we did in Example 6.15. The length of the sequence is thus reduced by one byte.

When the printer encounters PackedPixelVector in a master, it pushes the compressed sample vector onto the stack and executes

```
Identifier "Xerox" Identifier "Packed" 2 MAKEVEC FINDDECOMPRESSOR DO
```

The result of Example 6.16 is equivalent to executing the instruction

```
01 00 01 01 00 01 01 01 . . . 8755968 MAKEVEC
```

on a printer with a stack almost 9,000,000 elements deep.

An Interpress printer will usually not decompress the encoded data and build this vector of samples on the stack but instead will simply mark the compressed vector as requiring decompression before it can be used. The printer will perform the decompression only when the image is needed. Therefore, you should not assume that executing decompression operators is unacceptably slow or requires large amounts of storage.

Although the printer invokes the standard decompression operators [Xerox, Compressed], [Xerox, Adaptive], and [Xerox, CCITT-4] in the same way as unpacking operators such as [Xerox, Packed], the internal computations are much more complex. These operators decode sample vectors that are compressed on the basis of statistical redundancies in the binary image data to achieve storage efficiencies as much as an order of magnitude or more greater than simple packing.

The [Xerox, CCITT-4] operator decodes the compression algorithm defined in the international standard for Group 4 facsimile equipment. An Interpress master would encode a CCITT Group 4 compressed sample vector as shown in Example 6.17.

Example 6.17

```
                                --compressed sample vector--
LargeVector "02 scanLength reverseBits . . . compressed data"
Identifier "Xerox"
Identifier "CCITT-4"
2 MAKEVEC                       --name of decompression operator--
FINDDECOMPRESSOR                --retrieve from printer environment--
DO                              --execute decompression operator--
```

The compression parameters are scanLength and reverseBits. (See the Raster Encoding Standard for a full description of the algorithm.) Since the Xerox standard encoding provides a sequence type for CCITT compressed data, just as it did for packed data, the instructions in Example 6.17 can be replaced by the instruction in Example 6.18.

Example 6.18

```
CCITT-4PixelVector "scanLength reverseBits . . . compressedData"
```

The Xerox encoding represents the token CCITT-4PixelVector with the byte token sequenceCCITT-4PixelVector, which has hexadecimal value ED and three bytes specifying the sequence length. The effect of the instruction in Example 6.18 is analogous to that of PackedPixelVector: when the printer encounters CCITT-4PixelVector in a master, it pushes the compressed sample vector onto the stack and executes

```
Identifier "Xerox" Identifier "CCITT-4" 2 MAKEVEC FINDDECOMPRESSOR DO
```

For a series of representative documents, the CCITT algorithm compresses scanned binary image data by a factor between 2 and 25. Since hardware is available for decompressing CCITT Group 4 compressed images, it is an excellent candidate for encoding sample vectors in Interpress masters. The following Interpress master reproduces an A4-size page scanned and encoded using the CCITT Group 4 standard at 300 pixels per inch.

Example 6.19

```
Header "Interpress/Xerox/3.0 "   --header--
BEGIN                            --start of the master--
  { }                            --preamble--
  {                              --start of the page--
    0.0254 SCALE CONCATT         --use inches for master coordinates--
    1 SETGRAY                    --set current ink to black--
    3508 2480                    --pixel-array size--
    1 1 1                        --binary scanned image--
    -90 ROTATE                   --transform from scanner--
    0 3508 TRANSLATE CONCAT      --to pixel-array coordinates--
    1/300 SCALE CONCAT           --and then to master coordinates--
                                 --compressed sample vector--
    CCITT-4PixelVector "09B0 0000 . . . compressedData "
                                 --scanLength=09B0 hex=2480--
                                 --reverseBits=0--
    MAKEPIXELARRAY               --construct pixel array--
    MASKPIXEL                    --construct mask and apply color--
  }                              --end of the page--
END                              --end of the master--
```

Summary

In this chapter, we have seen how Interpress allows you to represent and display binary raster images. We have seen how such images can be used as a mask through which a color is pressed, or as the color or ink that is pressed through other masks, causing shapes to be filled with images or patterns. We paid particular attention to the transformations required to prepare the image. Transformations are needed to compensate for mismatched scanning orders, to convert to master coordinates, and to size, orient, and position the image. We also discussed the encodings used by Interpress to represent the potentially huge vectors of pixel samples, and some of the compression schemes that reduce the size of this data (see Figure 6.18).

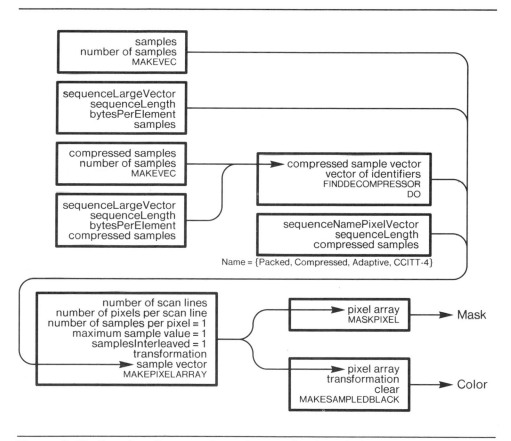

Figure 6.18 Constructing sample vectors and using pixel arrays.

In Chapter 7, we shall continue our discussion of inks by generalizing them to full color, and we shall describe how Interpress handles both constant colors and full-color images.

Chapter 7
COLOR

"Well, I'll be hanged
if I can describe this
red–it's not Turkish
and it's not Roman
and it's not Indian,
but it seems to partake
of the two last, and yet
it can't be either of
them...anyway, with
what brains you have
left choose me and
send some–many–
patterns of this
exact shade."

ROBERT LOUIS STEVENSON

By now, you are familiar with the Interpress model for producing a page: an ink is pushed through a mask onto the page. Where the ink goes on the page is defined by a mask operator in the Interpress master; what it looks like is determined by the Interpress imager variable *color*. Previous chapters have shown you the Interpress facilities for creating masks from characters, geometric shapes, and scanned binary images. We will now turn our attention to how you specify and create inks in an Interpress master.

In Interpress, color or ink (the two are used interchangeably) can be black and white or gray, as well as full color, and can be either constant or sampled. When the color is constant, then the printer fills the area on the page defined by the mask with a uniform ink or flat color. When the color is sampled, the printer uses an ink created from a pixel array or scanned image: the overall ink is a pixel-by-pixel color specification. In Chapter 6, you saw how the MAKESAMPLEDBLACK operator created a patterned black-and-white ink from a binary pixel array. In this chapter, we will describe how you specify gray and full-color inks in an Interpress master, create the ink or color that makes objects visible on a page, and produce color images on an Interpress printer.

Color Representations

There are several ways of describing the color content of a page: how it was specified in the design, how it looks to a human observer, how it would be analyzed by an instrument, or how it would be physically produced by a printer. Each description is appropriate at a different point in the production cycle of a document, from its design at a workstation through its specification in an Interpress master to its physical realization on an Interpress printer. Interpress does not limit the descriptions that you can use. You are free to use the color models or ink descriptions in your Interpress master that are most convenient for your application, provided that your printer supports or understands them.

The way that you specify ink in a master and the way you specify shapes differ significantly. You can define a geometric shape only in terms of straight lines, arcs, conics, and Bézier splines, because Interpress supplies primitive operators only for these cases. For ink, Interpress offers a primitive operator only for shades of gray so that a master is self-contained only when it specifies gray ink. To obtain full-color inks, you use operators that work in cooperation with the printer; the master accesses ink descriptions that are part of the printer's environment, rather than part of the language. You have already seen this in Chapter 4 in connection with fonts that are obtained from the printer's environment using the FINDFONT operator. The Interpress mechanisms for specifying ink in the general case are similar: you either find inks or find the operators that produce them in the printer's environment.

As a result, a document creator and a printer have to agree beforehand on the color representations the master will use. This agreement usually takes the form of a standard description to which both the creator and the printer subscribe. The standard color descriptions that the creator uses in the master are part of the printer's environment. Providing an Interpress master with mechanisms for accessing standard color representations, rather than making the representations part of the language itself, is a powerful feature of Interpress, as we shall see.

Interpress describes an ideal image, which the printer attempts to produce. The image should be specified in a device-independent manner and not in terms of a particular printer's capabilities. Just as you typically use device-independent spatial coordinates to describe the position, size, and orientation of an object in an Interpress master, you use device-independent color descriptions of the visual appearance of an object. And just as a particular Interpress printer converts the device-independent spatial description into an equivalent printer-specific description, the printer converts the color described by the master into a visually equivalent or matching color that could be obtained with its physical inks. For example, if the master uses the instruction 0.5 MAKEGRAY to specify a medium-gray ink, then a black-and-white binary printer converts that instruction to one that results in a halftone dot pattern on the page whenever the ink is applied (see Figure 7.1). A CRT display that can produce intensity levels of gray, on the other hand, would image the object with medium-gray phosphor intensity.

An Interpress master indicates the color to be used by placing a color specification in the imager variable *color* (index 13). This imager variable requires an object of type color. Interpress does not define a standard encoding for the type color, as it does for integers, for example. This allows the printer to use a device-dependent encoding when it constructs an object of type color from the device-independent specification contained in the master. As a result, you can perform only a limited number of operations with an object of type color. You can neither open it up and look inside nor alter it. You cannot obtain a third color by adding two objects of type color together. You can, however, move an object of type color around on the stack using any of the

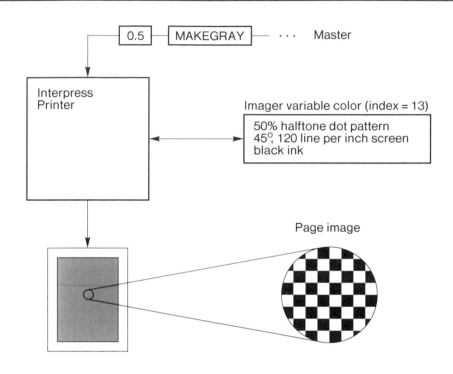

Figure 7.1 Color representations.

stack operators, you can store it in a frame with FSET, and you can combine it with other elements in a vector using MAKEVEC.

The most useful thing you can do with an object of type color is to store it in imager variable 13, which is where the printer looks for ink when it executes a mask operator. In effect, the imager variable color is the inkwell into which a mask operator dips its pen before writing on the page. The ink applied through the mask replaces or modifies whatever was previously laid down at the same position on the page. (As we saw in Chapter 6, the ink that you create with MAKESAMPLEDBLACK can modify rather than replace the ink already on the page). At the beginning of each page body, the printer sets the value of the imager variable color to black.

The Interpress instructions in Example 7.1 illustrate some of the legal operations you can perform on inks. It assumes an object of unknown type on top of the stack, and it checks to see whether that object's type is Color. If so, then the object is stored in the imager variable color; if not, the instructions within the IF body replace the object on the stack with black ink (1 MAKEGRAY) and generate an appearance error.

Example 7.1

```
    . . .                              --check object on top of stack--
    DUP                                --copy it for the test--
    TYPE                               --get its type--
    7 EQ                               --is it type color?--
    NOT IF                             --if not--
    {
       POP                             --discard object--
       1 MAKEGRAY                      --make a black ink--
       66 65 68 32 67 79 76 79 82      --BAD COLOR--
       9 MAKEVEC                       --error message--
       50 ERROR                        --appearance error--
    }
    13 ISET                            --save in imager--
```

Interpress provides several ways of creating ink, such as 1 MAKEGRAY, that are specifically designed to generate objects of type color.

Constant Color

A *constant color* is an ink that has the same value at every point. Therefore, no matter where you position a mask, the ink applied through it looks the same. Interpress has several mechanisms with which you can specify constant color. You can request a color by referencing its name or by executing a color-generating operator. The need for generating gray or neutral colors occurs often enough that Interpress has a primitive operator specifically for grays. The MAKEGRAY operator that builds constant-colored inks from gray-intensity values is described next.

Gray Intensity

The Interpress operator MAKEGRAY allows you to specify directly shades of gray on a scale from black to white.

$$<f:Number> \text{ MAKEGRAY} \rightarrow <col:Constant\ Color>$$

It takes as its argument a number f between 0 and 1 and returns on the stack a constant color col with absorptance (the fraction of light absorbed) proportional to f. Absorptance is the complement of intensity; the more light an ink absorbs, the lower its intensity.

Absorptance is maximum (f=1) for black and minimum (f=0) for white. Intermediate values describe intensities along a linear scale between these two extremes. If the intensity of white is I_w and the intensity of black is I_b, then the intensity of the constant ink f MAKEGRAY is $I_w - f(I_w - I_b)$.

If the constant color created by MAKEGRAY is destined for the imager variable color, then the convenience operator SETGRAY can be used instead. SETGRAY takes the same argument as MAKEGRAY and creates the same constant color but transfers it to the imager variable color rather than leaving it on the stack.

$$< \text{f:Number} > \text{SETGRAY} \rightarrow < >$$

Therefore, the sequence f SETGRAY in an Interpress master is equivalent to f MAKEGRAY 13 ISET.

Absorptance is not the only way of scaling gray intensities. Work with transparent materials has led to the idea of optical density. The material absorbs some of the light shining through it; the thicker the material, the more light absorbed. So, instead of specifying the light absorbed, we can specify the thickness of the material needed to absorb the light, or the optical density. The relation between the absorptance, f, and density, d, is

$$f = 1 - 10^{-d}$$

Suppose we want to see uniform steps in a density scale. We can do this by selecting a set of density values (say 0, 0.3, 0.6, 0.9, and 1.2), converting them to absorptance values using the above equation, and displaying them using rectangular masks and SETGRAY.

The Interpress master in Example 7.2 uses SETGRAY to create a neutral scale with uniform increments in density (see Figure 7.2).

Example 7.2

```
Header "Interpress/Xerox/3.0 "   --header--
BEGIN                            --start of the master--
  { }                            --preamble--
  {                              --start of the page--
    0.0254 SCALE CONCATT         --inches for master coordinates--
    1 1 TRANSLATE CONCATT        --include offset as part of T--
    0.94 SETGRAY                 --set density to 1.2--
    0 0 1 1 MASKRECTANGLE
    0.87 SETGRAY                 --set density to 0.9--
    1 0 1 1 MASKRECTANGLE
    0.75 SETGRAY                 --set density to 0.6--
    2 0 1 1 MASKRECTANGLE
    0.50 SETGRAY                 --set density to 0.3--
    3 0 1 1 MASKRECTANGLE
    0 SETGRAY                    --set density to 0--
    4 0 1 1 MASKRECTANGLE
```

```
        }                        --end of the page--
       END                       --end of the master--
```

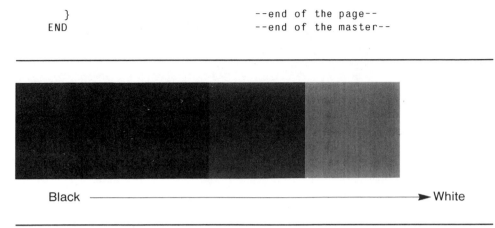

Black ───────────────────────────────────────▶ White

Figure 7.2 The result of Example 7.2.

MAKEGRAY is the only primitive operator in Interpress for generating color–that is, gray ink is the only color that comes for free with the Interpress language. The other ways of obtaining color in an Interpress master use either composed operators or operators that rely on the printer environment. In addition, MAKEGRAY is the only Interpress operator designed to create gray or neutral inks. None of the ways of obtaining ink that we shall discuss next make a distinction between gray and full color–they can be applied with equal fluency to both.

Color Names

Common, everyday uses of color occur in simple business graphics (see Plate 1), maps, cartoons, and engineering drawings. These documents typically need only a few colors that can be easily recognized and distinguished. The important thing about these colors is not their form, but their function and the improved clarity and appearance they bring to the document. When a document uses few colors, the simplest way of specifying them is by name.

Finding a Color

We used five colors in Plate 1: red, green, blue, light gray, and black. If standard names are defined for these colors, then a document creator would use the FINDCOLOR operator in a master to instruct the printer to look up the specified color by name in its environment and to return the color on the stack. The formal definition of FINDCOLOR is

$$< v{:}\text{Vector of Identifiers} > \text{FINDCOLOR} \rightarrow\ < col{:}\text{constantColor} >$$

The vector of identifiers v is the universal name of the color. If we use the name [IPBook, Red] to describe the red ink that we used in Plate 1, then the statements in Example 7.3 will create and save the specified ink.

Example 7.3

```
Identifier "IPBook"
Identifier "Red"
2 MAKEVEC                    --color name--
FINDCOLOR                    --look up ink--
13 ISET                      --save in imager--
```

Identifier "IPBook" Identifier "Red" 2 MAKEVEC is the name that FINDCOLOR uses to look up the specified ink in the printer's environment. If the printer cannot find the ink, then it substitutes another color and generates an appearance error. The color substituted for the unknown one is chosen by the printer. The printer could, for example, select the color that has the name most closely resembling the name of the color it could not find.

Named colors in an Interpress master offer an efficient interface to simple color printers and pen plotters. Typically, you would define a named color and assign it a tolerance or range of acceptable values that gives the printer the greatest possible latitude in creating the ink when it is specified in the master. For example, you might define [IPBook, Red] with a large tolerance and then use it when you want an ink that unambiguously looks red. You are not particular about the precise appearance of the red, as long as it is not confused with magenta, orange, or pink. The way that a printer implements [IPBook, Red] reflects the tolerance. A color printer might simply overprint solid areas of magenta and yellow ink to obtain red. Different printers use different inks (physical or printer inks, not Interpress inks) so that no two reds will look exactly the same. As long as they are within tolerance, however, they are valid representations of [IPBook, Red]. If you want to specify red more precisely, then you can use a color name with tighter tolerance, such as [nbs, cns, strongRed], which is the color "Strong Red" in the National Bureau of Standards color naming scheme (a standard of names and associated colors). You can use this name in a master if your printer supports this standard. The resulting ink will be specified within the tolerances of this standard.

Interpress gives you a great deal of freedom in defining what is meant by a color name. It provides the look-up mechanism, but the definition of actual colors is left to whatever standard the creator and printer agree on. Standards for color names that will be used by Xerox Corporation are, at the time of this writing, being developed as part of the Xerox Color Encoding Standard.

Two examples will show you the power and flexibility of the Interpress named-color mechanism. The first is the named color [Xerox, Highlight], used by Xerox printers. In a text document, you could use it to highlight important words or figures. On a black-and-white printer, the instructions that find the named color [Xerox, Highlight] produce the same ink as 0.3 MAKEGRAY. However, on a two-color printer, where the two colors are black and "other" (such as red or blue), a reference to [Xerox, Highlight] would produce the "other" color. On a full-color printer, you could define the highlight color as red, magenta, or whatever other color you wish. As a second example, you can invent a named color [IPBook, TransparentRed]. As the name suggests, you can define it on your printer in such a way that it mixes with rather than replaces whatever ink was previously laid down on the page. Although this might seem to contradict the Interpress imaging model, it is the printer rather than Interpress that specifies the effect of an ink. When you know how the printer defines an ink, then you can specify that ink in your Interpress master and obtain very predictable results.

Color Maps

When you are dealing with a large number of colors, you may wish to arrange them in an orderly way. You can do this by placing the colors in vectors and accessing them by their vector indices. For example, you could generate a table of colors from all possible combinations of M amounts of N printer inks. If the inks are cyan, magenta, and yellow and are combined in an all or none fashion, then $N=3$, $M=2$ and $M^N=8$ colors would result. You would easily recognize the eight colors as cyan, magenta, yellow, red, green blue, black, and white. When the set of colors is this small, names work just as well as numbers, but when M is large, say 10, then the sample set would consist of 1000 colors, and it would be awkward to identify each by name. The alternative is to number them and then refer to individual colors by number.

To illustrate how this works, we can take the colors we used in Plate 1, add a few more and form the 3 by 3 color matrix or map shown in Plate 2. We could store the colors in this matrix as a three-element vector, where each element of the vector is itself a vector made from the three colors in a column of the matrix.

Example 7.4

```
Identifier "IPBook" 4 FSET    --save universal identifier for reuse--
4 FGET Identifier "Blue"      --name is IPBook/Blue--
2 MAKEVEC FINDCOLOR           --retrieve the color IPBook/Blue--
4 FGET Identifier "Cyan"
2 MAKEVEC FINDCOLOR           --IPBook/cyan--
```

```
4 FGET Identifier "Green"
2 MAKEVEC FINDCOLOR          --IPBook/green--
3 MAKEVEC                    --make vector of inks in column 0--
1 MAKEGRAY                   --black--
0 MAKEGRAY                   --white--
0.5 MAKEGRAY                 --medium gray--
3 MAKEVEC                    --make vector of inks in column 1--
4 FGET Identifier "Magenta"
2 MAKEVEC FINDCOLOR          --IPBook/magenta-
4 FGET Identifier "Red"
2 MAKEVEC FINDCOLOR          --IPBook/red-
4 FGET Identifier "Yellow"
2 MAKEVEC FINDCOLOR          --IPBook/yellow-
3 MAKEVEC                    --make vector of inks in column 2--
3 MAKEVEC                    --make matrix--
0 FSET                       --save in frame[0]--
```

We can then build a composed operator that takes a vector containing the column and row number of the desired ink and execute it to retrieve the ink from the matrix. The statements in Example 7.5 retrieve the color [IPBook, Red] in column 2, row 1 of the matrix.

Example 7.5

```
MAKESIMPLECO
{
    2 FSET                   --save column and row number--
    0 FGET                   --retrieve color matrix--
    2 FGET 0 GET             --get column number--
    GET                      --extract column from matrix--
    2 FGET 1 GET             --get row number--
    GET                      --extract row from column--
}
1 FSET                       --save composed operator--
. . .
2 1 2 MAKEVEC                --column 2, row 1--
1 FGET DO                    --get and execute the operator--
13 ISET                      --save the color--
```

Placing the colors in a vector establishes a correspondence between numbers (the vector indices) and colors (the vector elements). Such a correspondence is called a *color map*. One of the virtues of a color map is that it makes it easy to change colors throughout a page (or document). Suppose you create a color map at the start of a page, and that throughout the page you always access colors indirectly via the map. When you want red, you look in the color map under the index of the red entry. The color obtained from the color map is then stored in the imager variable color. Now suppose you decide orange would look better than red on the page. You have to change only the entry in the color map. You reconstruct the vector so that the element that formerly contained red now contains orange. Since the rest of the page references the color-map entry by its index, all attempts to get the red entry will now yield orange. So with this single change, all red objects become orange.

Color Operators

A color map is only one example of the many schemes that have been devised for mapping full colors onto numbers. MAKEGRAY is another: it maps 0 to white, 1 to black and numbers in between to shades of gray. As we shall see in the section on color models, an ordered triple of numbers is often used to specify a color. To use the general approach of specifying color by number, we need an operator that takes a numeric specification of a color and converts it to an ink or object of type Color. Interpress defines a *color operator* to do this. You use a color operator whenever you specify color by number rather than by name.

An Interpress color operator takes a vector of numbers as an operand and returns a constant color.

<v:Vector of Numbers> <colorOp:Operator> DO → <col:ConstantColor>

The operand v is a vector, so that color operators that use one, two, three, or more numbers to specify a color can all use the same format. The composed operator stored in frame variable 1 of Example 7.5 is a simple example of a color operator.

Finding a Color Operator

As you have seen, including a color map and a composed color operator in your master lets you build and use custom color tables. You can replace or add colors to the table as the need arises. If the map grows very large, however, the master becomes unwieldy and printer performance suffers. When this happens, you might want to move both the map and operator into your printer's environment. You can still reference colors in the same way, but now your master, rather than defining the operator itself, obtains the color operator from the printer's environment using FINDCOLOROPERATOR.

<v:Vector of Identifiers> FINDCOLOROPERATOR → <colorOp:Operator>

The universal name of the desired color operator is v. The printer uses it to look up the operator in the environment and return it on the stack. If the named color operator cannot be found, then a master error occurs.

If we transferred the color operator from Example 7.5 to the printer's environment and named it [IPBook, ColorMapOp], then we could use the statements in Example 7.6 to specify color in the master. The statements assume that the color map that the color operator uses also exists in the printer's environment.

Example 7.6

```
. . .
2 1 2 MAKEVEC                    --column 2, row 1--
Identifier "IPBook"
Identifier "ColorMapOp"
2 MAKEVEC                        --name of color operator--
FINDCOLOROPERATOR               --retrieve the operator--
DO                               --execute it to get the color--
13 ISET                          --save the color--
```

Besides leading to the efficient implementation of color operators, FINDCOLOROPERATOR also lets you include standard color maps in your printer where a master can access them. For example, if you want to use the Pantone color set, you build a table that maps the Pantone color numbers to printer inks and install the table on your printer with the named color operator [YourName, PantoneOp]. You can then use this named operator in your Interpress masters.

Placing a color operator in the printer's environment frees us from some of the limitations of the Interpress language while at the same time allowing an Interpress master access to all capabilities of the printer. When you use a composed color operator, you are restricted to manipulating color or ink with the Interpress primitive operators. Example 7.1 showed us some of these limitations. However, when you use color operators found in the printer's environment, you can use the full repertoire of the printer commands to manipulate and modify the ink.

Color operators do not necessarily require a color map to make the correspondence between numbers and colors. Color operators may instead generate the printer's color representation directly from the numbers passed to it in the operand vector. This can be done when there is a simple function or model describing the relationship between a number and a color. If the color operator is based on such a function instead of a table, it might allow the numbers that specify colors to be fractions, as in the case of MAKEGRAY.

Color Models

The practical limit to the size of a set of named or mapped colors falls far short of all the colors you can perceive and conceivably use in a document. Even a conservative estimate puts the number of perceptible colors at over 1 million; some estimates are as high as 10 million. Some applications, such as graphic design and computer-aided engineering, are satisfied with anywhere from a dozen to several hundred judiciously selected colors. Other applications, such as computer image generation and color picture processing, need continuously variable color to obtain precise color control and smooth shading. Applications that require continuous or finely quantized digital colors use color coordinates or scales to specify the colors that they use.

We use various *color models* or spaces to help us organize how we think about and control color. For example, we could conceive of a color that we would describe as a dark grayish red. This description illustrates the three variables of subjective color appearance: hue (red), saturation or chroma (grayish), and lightness (dark). In Figure 7.3, hue is the attribute with a circular scale, labeled with the names blue, green, yellow, red, purple, and so on. Lightness is the intensity of the color on a scale from dark through light. Gray or neutral colors have no hue but can range in lightness from black to white. Chroma is the difference between a color and a gray with the same lightness. Hue, chroma, and lightness define a cylindrical coordinate system for color space. Many people have attempted to devise numeric scales for these variables; the Munsell Color System is one of the earliest and most popular. To define it, subjects were asked to select painted samples that they judged under controlled viewing conditions to be uniformly distributed along the dimensions of hue, chroma, and lightness.

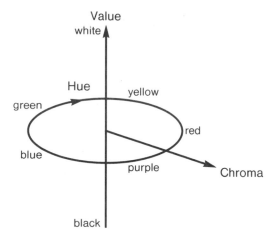

Figure 7.3 Hue, Value, Chroma color coordinate system.

Besides subjective measures of color appearance, we can also use objective measures that ultimately rely on instrument standards. Objective color coordinate systems are based on *trichromacy*, an experimental law of human color vision that states that most human observers can match any color by adding suitable amounts of light from three fixed primary colors. The amounts of the primaries used to match a given color are called its tristimulus values. They specify the visual appearance of a color in the sense that two colors that have the same tristimulus values will look the same. Trichromacy explains why color output devices need only three inks or phosphors; to reproduce tristimulus values, they need only three degrees of freedom.

You can use tristimulus values based on any three primaries. To standardize the determination of tristimulus values, the International Commission on Illumination[†] has defined an ideal or standard observer, so that instruments rather than human subjects can measure and specify tristimulus values. The tristimulus values of the standard observer are labeled X, Y, and Z. The description of a color *C* in terms of XYZ values is

$$C = X\,\boldsymbol{X} + Y\,\boldsymbol{Y} + Z\,\boldsymbol{Z}$$

The "=" signifies that the color *C* is matched by the sum of X units of light from primary *X*, Y units from *Y*, and Z units from *Z*. The standard system was designed so that the Y value is the luminance, the correlate of intensity; two different colors with the same luminance have the same intensity or lightness.

Although we could define a color operator that expected XYZ tristimulus values, it makes sense in practical systems to use tristimulus values based on a set of primaries that are close to those used by color output devices. In particular, if the primaries are red, green, and blue, then their tristimulus values R, G, and B would represent the red, green, and blue content of a color. Since the color-matching equation is linear, RGB values are related to XYZ values by a linear transformation. Most color scanners, many computer-graphics programs, and all color monitors use RGB values; as a result, the latter are an excellent choice for representing color in an Interpress master.

In the same way that we used x,y spatial coordinates in previous chapters to specify the position of a mask on a page, we can use RGB tristimulus values to specify the location of an ink in color space. Black is at the origin of the coordinate system. The red, green, and blue primaries usually are calibrated so that equal amounts give grays along a scale from black to white. The amounts of the primaries that are added to give white usually are normalized such that they have value 1. Therefore, the white point is at (1,1,1) in the

---

[†]This organization usually is referred to by the initials for its French name, Commission Internationale de l'Éclairage: CIE.

coordinate system. The line joining the black and white points in color space is the neutral or gray axis. The point (1,1,0), for example, represents the additive mixture of the red and green primaries, or yellow (see Figure 7.4 and Plate 3).

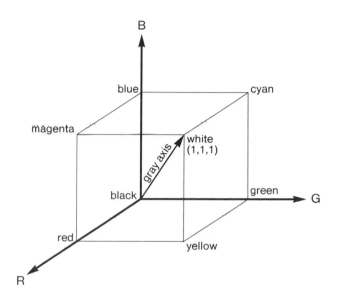

Figure 7.4 RGB color coordinate system.

To use RGB values in a master, we will invent a color operator [IPBook, RGBOp] and register it in the environment of our printer. [IPBook, RGBOp] converts the color specification R G B 3 MAKEVEC into a constant ink. We use our operator in the master in Example 7.7 to create the color chart shown in Plate 2.

Example 7.7

```
Header "Interpress/Xerox/3.0 "   --header--
BEGIN                             --start of the master--
  { }                             --preamble--
  {                               --start of the page--
    0.0254 SCALE CONCATT          --use inches for master coordinates--
    1 1 TRANSLATE CONCATT         --include offset in T--
    0 0 1 3 MAKEVEC               --R,G,B values for blue--
    Identifier "IPBook"
```

```
Identifier "RGBOp"
2 MAKEVEC                        --color-operator name--
FINDCOLOROPERATOR                --retrieve from environment--
0 FSET                           --save in frame--
0 FGET DO                        --retrieve and execute operator--
13 ISET                          --save color--
0 0 1 1 MASKRECTANGLE            --apply ink to page--

0 1 1 3 MAKEVEC 0 FGET DO 13 ISET            --set color to cyan--
0 1 1 1 MASKRECTANGLE
0 1 0 3 MAKEVEC 0 FGET DO 13 ISET            --green--
0 2 1 1 MASKRECTANGLE
0 0 0 3 MAKEVEC 0 FGET DO 13 ISET            --black--
1 0 1 1 MASKRECTANGLE
1 1 1 3 MAKEVEC 0 FGET DO 13 ISET            --white--
1 1 1 1 MASKRECTANGLE
0.5 0.5 0.5 3 MAKEVEC 0 FGET DO 13 ISET      --medium gray--
1 2 1 1 MASKRECTANGLE
1 0 1 3 MAKEVEC 0 FGET DO 13 ISET            --magenta--
2 0 1 1 MASKRECTANGLE
1 0 0 3 MAKEVEC 0 FGET DO 13 ISET            --red--
2 1 1 1 MASKRECTANGLE
1 1 0 3 MAKEVEC 0 FGET DO 13 ISET            --yellow--
2 2 1 1 MASKRECTANGLE
}                                --end of the page--
END                              --end of the master--
```

The sequence Identifier "IPBook" Identifier "RGBOp" 2 MAKEVEC is the name that FINDCOLOROPERATOR uses to retrieve the color operator from the printer's environment. The master saves the operator in the frame, so it does not have to look up the operator every time it converts an RGB vector to an ink. Since Interpress itself does not define standard color operators other than MAKEGRAY, there is no primitive operator to make a color from an RGB specification. However, the sequence 0 FGET DO in this master fetches and executes such an operator that originated in the printer's environment.

The printer that rendered Plate 2 substituted its notion of red, green, and blue for the primaries we used to specify the ink. When it is important to use RGB values to define a color precisely, then the exact nature of the red, green, and blue primaries and the white used to normalize them must be specified (usually in terms of CIE Standard tristimulus values, X,Y,Z) and made part of the color operator.

The color operator [IPBook, RGBOp] behaves analogously to the current transformation T in Chapter 3. Just as T converts master coordinates to device coordinates, a color operator converts the master's color representation of an ink to the device-dependent version of the ink (see Figure 7.5).

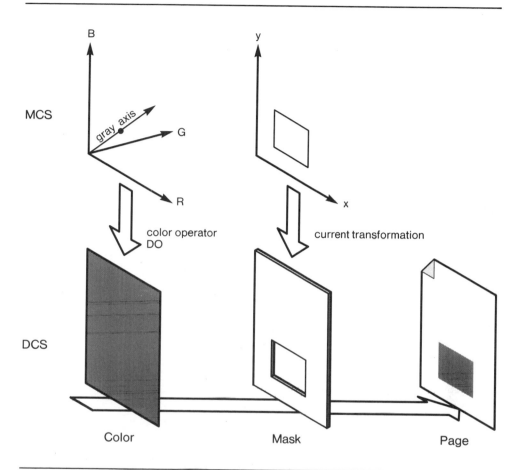

Figure 7.5 Specifying a constant ink by color coordinates.

The use of named color operators allows each printer to retrieve from its environment an operator that produces a color that is the best interpretation of what the document creator specified in the master. On a color printer, the [IPBook, RGBOp] operator would create an ink using all three color coordinates. On the other hand, the [IPBook, RGBOp] operator on a black-and-white or gray-scale printer would create a gray ink that is the printer's best effort at producing the ink specified by the master. The printer might, for instance, use a gray ink based on the maximum value of the RGB values. Or it might do what black-and-white film or a black-and-white television receiver does when presented with a color scene: reproduce the intensity of the colors in the scene but ignore their hue and chroma.

As a programmer, you can ease the burden that full-color specifications place on black-and-white printers by using black-and-white-compatible color coordinate systems to describe full-color inks. A black-and-white compatible color system aligns one of its three coordinate axes with the neutral or gray axis. Therefore, one of the coordinates records the gray intensity or achromatic content of the color, whereas the other two record the hue and chroma or chromatic content of the specified color. As an example of a black-and-white-compatible system, we will define a new coordinate system called YES. YES coordinates are related to RGB coordinates by the following linear transformation:

$$Y = a_1 R + a_2 G + (1 - a_1 - a_2) B$$
$$E = \tfrac{1}{2}(R - G)$$
$$S = \tfrac{1}{4}(R + G) - \tfrac{1}{2} B$$

Y is the luminance; a_1 and a_2 are constants that depend on the red, green, and blue primaries and white that define the RGB tristimulus values. We will use the values $a_1 = 0.68$ and $a_2 = 0.25$, which are based on the red, green and blue phosphors used in broadcast studio monitors and the standard white illumination used in the graphic arts. For white, $Y = 1$. E and S are opponent-color values: E is red minus green and S is yellow minus blue. For gray, R, G, and B are all equal; so E and S are zero. (See Figure 7.6 and Plate 4).

To use YES coordinates in a master, we invent a color operator, call it [IPBook, YESOp], and install it in the environment of our color and black-and-white printers. On a color printer, the operator is defined so that it created a full-color ink, much as if you had used an RGB representation in the master. When a black-and-white printer encounters an ink specified in terms of YES values, it uses its version of the [IPBook, YESOp] to ignore the E and S values and thus to create a gray ink based on the luminance value Y. The effect of executing the color operator [IPBook, YESOp] on a black-and-white printer with the argument Y E S 3 MAKEVEC is equivalent to the statements in Example 7.8.

Example 7.8

```
Y E S 3 MAKEVEC        --YES values--
0 GET                  --get Y, ignore E and S--
NEG 1 ADD              --f=1-Y--
MAKEGRAY               --make gray ink--
```

The master in Example 7.9 encodes color using YES coordinates. It produces Plate 2 when executed on a color printer, and Figure 7.7 when run on a black-and-white printer.

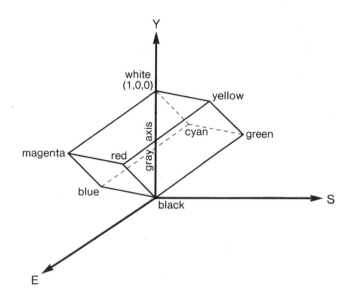

Figure 7.6 YES color coordinate system.

Example 7.9

```
Header "Interpress/Xerox/3.0 "   --header--
BEGIN                            --start of the master--
  { }                            --preamble--
  {                              --start of the page--
    0.0254 SCALE CONCATT         --use inches for master coordinates--
    1 1 TRANSLATE CONCATT        --include offset in T--
    0.07 0 -0.5 3 MAKEVEC        --YES values for blue--
    Identifier "IPBook"
    Identifier "YESOp"
    2 MAKEVEC                    --color operator name--
    FINDCOLOROPERATOR            --retrieve from environment--
    0 FSET                       --save in frame--
    0 FGET DO                    --retrieve and execute operator--
    13 ISET                      --save color--
    0 0 1 1 MASKRECTANGLE        --apply ink to page--

    0.75 -0.5 -0.25 3 MAKEVEC 0 FGET DO 13 ISET    --cyan--
    0 1 1 1 MASKRECTANGLE
    0.68 -0.5 0.25 3 MAKEVEC 0 FGET DO 13 ISET     --green--
    0 2 1 1 MASKRECTANGLE
    0 0 0 3 MAKEVEC 0 FGET DO 13 ISET                  --black--
```

```
1 0 1 1 MASKRECTANGLE
1 0 0 3 MAKEVEC 0 FGET DO 13 ISET              --white--
0 0 1 1 MASKRECTANGLE
0.5 0 0 3 MAKEVEC 0 FGET DO 13 ISET            --gray--
1 2 1 1 MASKRECTANGLE
0.32 0.5 -0.25 3 MAKEVEC 0 FGET DO 13 ISET     --magenta--
2 0 1 1 MASKRECTANGLE
0.25 0.5 0.25 3 MAKEVEC 0 FGET DO 13 ISET      --red--
2 1 1 1 MASKRECTANGLE
0.93 0 0.5 3 MAKEVEC 0 FGET DO 13 ISET         --yellow--
2 2 1 1 MASKRECTANGLE
}                             --end of the page--
END                           --end of the master--
```

Figure 7.7 The result of Example 7.9 on a black-and-white printer.

Color Model Operators

The YES color encoding used by the operator [IPBook, YESOp] assumes that
the Y value is 0 for black and 1 for white. However, you could encode
luminance in a digital master using 6, 8, 10, or however many bits of precision

you need. When Y is represented by 8 bits, it has 256 levels, with black at 0 and white at 255. You could invent a new color operator for this encoding, but supplying a different color operator for every conceivable encoding would be inefficient and also would be a wasteful use of printer storage.

Interpress allows you to group different color operators that share the same general characteristics and to treat them as a single color model. An example of a color model is the group of color operators for all possible encodings of YES values. A master uses a *color model operator* to extract one particular operator from the model.

$$< \text{parameters:Vector} > \quad < \text{colorModelOp:Operator} >$$
$$\text{DO} \rightarrow \; < \text{colorOp:Operator} >$$

The operator colorModelOp returns on the stack the color operator colorOp, specified by the vector argument parameters.

You have the option of composing your own color model operator and including it in a master. For 8-bit Y values, it would return a composed color operator that scaled the 8-bit YES values by 1/255 and then invoked the color operator [IPBook, YESOp]. However, as with color operators, obtaining color model operators from the printer's environment almost always leads to more efficient implementations. You can do this with FINDCOLORMODELOPERATOR.

$$< \text{v:Vector of Identifiers} >$$
$$\text{FINDCOLORMODELOPERATOR} \rightarrow \; < \text{colorModelOp:Operator} >$$

The universal name of the color model operator is v. If the master cannot find the named operator in the environment, then a master error occurs.

To handle different YES encodings in a master, we will invent a color model operator, call it [IPBook, YESModel], and define it to take the argument vector (s_{white} s_{black} $s_{neutral}$ s_{range} 4 MAKEVEC). Executing this color model operator returns a color operator that first scales the encoded YES values so that Y lies between 0 and 1 and E and S lie between -0.5 and 0.5. It then executes the [IPBook, YESOp] color operator to convert the normalized YES values to a constant ink. The mappings of the encoded YES values are determined by the elements of the color model operator's argument vector parameters.

$$Y = (Y_{encoded} - s_{black})/(s_{white} - s_{black})$$
$$E = (E_{encoded} - s_{neutral})/s_{range}$$
$$S = (S_{encoded} - s_{neutral})/s_{range}$$

This mapping lets you encode E and S, which can both have negative values, as positive integers in a master. The YES specification for magenta is 0.41 0.5 -0.25 3 MAKEVEC. Let's assume that the YES values are each encoded with 8 bits and that an offset is added to E and S so that their encoded values are positive. In this case, the parameters vector containing s_{white}, s_{black}, $s_{neutral}$, s_{range} is 255 0 128 255 4 MAKEVEC and magenta is encoded as 105 255 64 3 MAKEVEC; and the mapping of the encoded YES values for magenta is

$$Y = (105 - 0) / (255 - 0) = 0.41$$
$$E = (255 - 128) / 255 = 0.50$$
$$S = (64 - 128) / 255 = -0.25$$

The statements in Example 7.10 create a constant ink from the YES specification for magenta using this encoding.

Example 7.10

```
105 255 64 3 MAKEVEC        --encoded YES values for magenta--
255 0 128 255 4 MAKEVEC     --argument for color model operator--
Identifier "IPBook"
Identifier "YESModel"
2 MAKEVEC                   --color model operator name--
FINDCOLORMODELOPERATOR      --retrieve it--
DO                          --execute it to get color operator--
DO                          --execute color operator to get color--
```

Standard Color Models

The progression from FINDCOLOR through FINDCOLOROPERATOR to FINDCOLORMODELOPERATOR allows increasing degrees of abstraction in specifying color or ink color in an Interpress master. Using them permits you to specify color in a way that is most suited to your application, while allowing the printer to implement the color representation in the most efficient way.

The named colors, operators, and color models that creator software uses in a master and a printer stores in its environment are not part of the Interpress standard, but they are defined in companion standards. Interpress is only one part of a distributed document-processing system, and color descriptions must apply to all elements of the system, not just to the link between a document creator and a printer. By obtaining colors and color models from its environment, a printer can use the same color descriptions as the other system elements. Xerox printers, for example, follow the Xerox Raster Encoding Standard, which defines color models for gray or neutral colors. It includes color models for gray values sampled in luminance, density, and lightness, as well as models for both mapped color and gray values. The Xerox models for full-color representation are under development. They have been described in the literature, but they have not yet been issued as standard. They will take the form that has been described here.

As an example of a color model operator defined in the Xerox Raster Encoding Standard, we shall look at the [Xerox, GrayDensity] operator. We saw in Example 7.2 how optical density can be used to specify grays. In that example, we took density values and converted them by hand to absorptance values, which we then gave to SETGRAY. Now we shall see how we can replace SETGRAY with a color operator that can use encoded density values directly. This operator will be generated by the [Xerox, GrayDensity] color model operator.

The GrayDensity color model operator takes a vector of the form [s_{white}, s_{black}, D_{black}, pixelMap] as its operand. The mapping from the encoded density value $d_{encoded}$ to the density value d proceeds in two steps. In the first step, the printer looks to see if pixelMap is a number with value 0 or a vector. If pixelMap is a vector, then the printer uses pixelMap as a lookup table with $d_{encoded}$ as the index to provide an extra level of mapping. If pixelMap is 0, then $d_{encoded}$ is used directly in the second step of the mapping, which is

$$d = [\,(d_{encoded} - s_{white})\,/\,(s_{black} - s_{white})\,] \times D_{black}$$

For the simple case of $d = d_{encoded}$ we will create a color model operator with $s_{white} = 0$, $s_{black} = 1$, $D_{black} = 1$, pixelMap = 0. To show how this works, we can redo Example 7.2, making and using the density color operator (see Example 7.11).

Example 7.11

```
Header "Interpress/Xerox/3.0 "   --header--
BEGIN                            --start of the master--
  { }                            --preamble--
  {                              --start of the page--
    0.0254 SCALE CONCATT         --inches for master coordinates--
    1 1 TRANSLATE CONCATT        --include offset as part of T--
    0 1 1 0 4 MAKEVEC            --color model operator parameters--
    Identifier "Xerox"
    Identifier "GrayDensity"
    2 MAKEVEC                    --color model operator name--
    FINDCOLORMODELOPERATOR       --find the color model operator--
    DO                           --create the color operator--
    0 FSET                       --save it in frame[0]--
    1.2 1 MAKEVEC                --density 1.2--
    0 FGET DO                    --execute the color operator--
    13 ISET                      --install result as current color--
    0 0 1 1 MASKRECTANGLE        --show it--

    0.9 1 MAKEVEC 0 FGET DO 13 ISET      --set density to 0.9--
```

```
1 0 1 1 MASKRECTANGLE
0.6 1 MAKEVEC 0 FGET DO 13 ISET        --set density to 0.6--
2 0 1 1 MASKRECTANGLE
0.3 1 MAKEVEC 0 FGET DO 13 ISET        --set density to 0.3--
3 0 1 1 MASKRECTANGLE
0 1 MAKEVEC 0 FGET DO 13 ISET          --set density to 0--
4 0 1 1 MASKRECTANGLE
}                                --end of the page--
END                              --end of the master--
```

This produces the same output as Example 7.2. When we use the printer's GrayDensity color model operator in the master, a change in color is a little more work for the printer and a little less work for the creator.

Sampled Color

We saw in Chapter 6 how black-and-white spots can be represented as a vector of binary sample values. We created pixel arrays from the samples, and used them to print pictures and patterns. Now we have also seen how to specify colors in Interpress. We can combine these two techniques to image colored pictures and patterns. We can construct samples vectors for which each sample specifies the color of a pixel. Each pixel can have its own color, and the combined raster will form the colored ink. We call this *sampled color*. Sampled color places black-and-white, gray, or full-color raster images on a page. The images can come from a document scanner or from a computer program; they can be scanned photographs, computer-generated scenes, or graphic designs. They are all represented as pixel arrays in which each pixel consists of a color specification. For example, each pixel could have red, green, and blue intensity values. This means that there might be more than one sample value per pixel. We would need a sample value for each coordinate, so a single pixel in our example would need three samples (one for the red intensity, one for the green, and a third for the blue).

It is also possible to use named colors in the specification of pixels if we first make a table of all the named colors we wish to use. We can then make a samples vector from the indices into the table. In this case, each pixel will have a single sample value, which is a table index. The corresponding entry in the table is the color of the pixel.

Multisample Pixel Arrays

We construct a colored pixel array in the same way as we built a binary pixel array in Chapter 6, using the MAKEPIXELARRAY operator. The difference is that now we need all the arguments to the operator; before, three of them–samplesPerPixel, maxSampleValue, samplesInterleaved–were always set to 1. MAKEPIXELARRAY acts somewhat like the array declaration and initialization statements found in most computer languages. You construct an object known as a pixel array from a vector of image samples, the parameters that describe their format, and the raster that produced them. Once again, the formal description of MAKEPIXELARRAY is

$$< \text{xPixels: Cardinal} > \quad < \text{yPixels: Cardinal} >$$
$$< \text{samplesPerPixel: Cardinal} >$$
$$< \text{maxSampleValue: Cardinal or Vector of Cardinal} >$$
$$< \text{samplesInterleaved: Cardinal} >$$
$$< \text{m: Transformation} >$$
$$< \text{samples: Vector of Cardinal} >$$
$$\text{MAKEPIXELARRAY} \rightarrow \; < \text{pa:PixelArray} >$$

As we saw in the previous chapter, the convention that Interpress uses to orient the pixel-array coordinate system with the sampling raster defines the number of pixels per scan line as yPixels and the number of scan lines in the raster as xPixels. The definition of the sampling raster also includes samplesPerPixel, because a pixel can require more than one sample to specify its color. A color image might have three samples per pixel, specifying, for example, the red, green, and blue content at each point in the image. Each sample is a separate element in the samples vector; therefore, the number of elements in the vector is

$$\text{xPixels} \times \text{yPixels} \times \text{samplesPerPixel}$$

An image sample is a cardinal (a nonnegative integer) that can have a value between 0 and a maximum specified in the pixel-array declaration. This limit allows mapping between a normalized range of samples used by the printer and the ranges natural to packed encoding of the samples. For example, the printer may use 1 for black and 0 for white. This is a good match for binary images, but for a gray scale image the scanner may supply 256 gray levels. These could be packed as 1 byte per sample, so each sample value can be an integer between 0 and 255, inclusive. The maxSampleValue indicates the largest possible number that can occur as a sample value, which indicates the minimum number of bits required to store an arbitrary sample. The printer can use this information if it attempts to pack the samples vector into a compact internal representation.

When there is only one sample per pixel, then its value lies between 0 and the argument maxSampleValue. For 1-bit samples, the maximum sample value is 1; for 8-bit samples, it is 255. When there is more than one sample per pixel, then we must know the maximum value for each component in the color specification. If they are all the same (say 255 for each), then we need to specify only the single maxSampleValue number.

Interpress, however, allows us to set different limits for each of the maxSampleValue components. Suppose that we allow 3 bits for each red sample, 3 bits for each green sample, but only 2 bits for each blue sample. The red and green samples can have values between 0 and 7, but the blue samples can range only between 0 and 3. To make this known to the printer, we use a vector of cardinals as maxSampleValue, rather than a single cardinal. In this case, maxSampleValue is 7 7 3 3 MAKEVEC.

When maxSampleValue is a vector, the ith sample of a pixel has a value that lies between 0 and (maxSampleValue i GET), which is the ith element of maxSampleValue. Since the maxSampleValue vector uses zero-based indexing, $0 \leq i \leq$ samplesPerPixel-1. Although Interpress does not allow negative sample values, this is not a serious limitation because, as we have seen, color operators with a built-in offset can be constructed from color model operators.

The scanned data for multiple-sample pixels are ordered in the samples vector in the same way that they were scanned or generated. Although the vector samples containing the image samples is a one-dimensional vector of length xPixels $\times$ yPixels $\times$ samplesPerPixel, it can also can be considered to be a three-dimensional array sample(x,y,i), where the three indices select the scan line x, the pixel on the scan line y, and sample of the pixel i. There are six permutations of three indices, which reduce to three combinations, since pixels (y index) have to be nested within scan lines (x index). To show the three ways of ordering samples, pixels, and scan lines, we use the following three Pascal array-type definitions:

```
(* 1 - samples interleaved *)
  array [0..xPixels-1] of
    array[0..yPixels-1] of
      array [0..samplesPerPixel-1] of sample;

(* 2 - sample lines interleaved *)
  array [0..xPixels-1] of
    array [0..samplesPerPixel-1] of
      array [0..yPixels-1] of sample;

(* 3 - sample arrays interleaved *)
  array [0..samplesPerPixel-1] of
    array [0..xPixels-1] of
      array[0..yPixels-1] of sample;
```

These array-type definitions nest arrays from bottom to top, with the index of the bottommost array looping fastest. Each of these type definitions implies a different ordering of the image samples in the sample vector argument to MAKEPIXELARRAY.

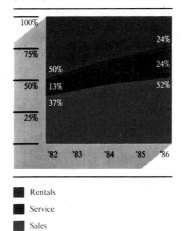

Sales, Service, Rentals as Percent of Business Products and Systems Revenues

(Percent)

100%

24%

75%

24%

50%

50%

13%

52%

37%

25%

'82   '83   '84   '85   '86

Rentals

Service

Sales

Plate 1. An example of color in business graphics.

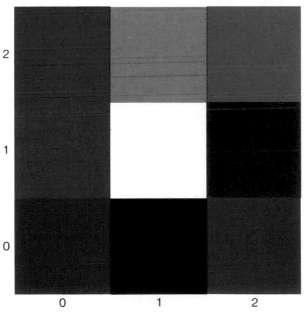

Plate 2. The result of Example 7.9

Plate 3. Color solid obtained by assigning colors to RGB coordinates.

Plate 4. Color solid obtained by assigning colors to YES coordinates.

Plate 5. Color graphic using constant and sampled colors.

Plate 6. The result of Example 7.17

The first ordering interleaves samples so that the different samples of a single pixel are successive elements in the vector. You can think of the vector as xPixels×yPixels successive sequences of samplesPerPixel elements. Imagine a scanner that examines each pixel and determines that pixel's complete color specification (for example, red, green, and blue components) before moving on to the next pixel. This ordering is also natural to computer-generated sample images, for which the computer determines the complete color specification of each pixel. The sample sequence is

R G B R G B R G B ... R G B

The third ordering divides the sample vector into samplesPerPixel successive sequences of xPixels×yPixels elements. The first sequence contains the first color component for all the pixels, the second sequence contains all the sample values for the second component, and so on. A samples vector with this ordering would be produced by a scanner that first samples an entire image through a red filter to obtain the red color component of every pixel. Next it samples the entire image through a green filter to obtain the green components. Finally, the scanner samples the image through a blue filter. The result is three consecutive "images," as seen through the red, green, and blue filters. Putting these three images together yields the full-color image. The sample sequence is

R R R ... R G G G ... G B B B ... B

Because the first and third orderings are common, they are directly supported by MAKEPIXELARRAY. Your samples can be in either of these two orders, and all you need to do is to specify which order you are using with the *samplesInterleaved* parameter. If its value is nonzero, the first ordering is assumed and the samples for the various color components are said to be *interleaved*. If samplesInterleaved is zero, then the third ordering is assumed.

The statements in Example 7.12 construct a pixel array from the red, green, and blue samples values of the color matrix shown in Plate 2. The samples occur in the standard order: the first pixel of the array is located at the lower-left corner of the matrix, and the pixels are read bottom to top and left to right. In this example, the samples are not interleaved, and the samplesInterleaved argument is set to 0.

Example 7.12

```
3                              --3 scan lines--
3                              --3 pixels per scan line--
3                              --3 samples per pixel--
255                            --same maximum value for all--
0                              --samples not interleaved--
```

```
1 SCALE                          --standard scanning order--
0 0 0 0 255 128 255 255 255      --red samples--
0 255 255 0 255 128 0 0 255      --green samples--
255 255 0 0 255 128 255 0 0      --blue samples--
27 MAKEVEC                       --make samples vector--
MAKEPIXELARRAY                   --construct pixel array--
8 FSET                           --save in frame for next example--
```

When there is only one sample per pixel, then there is no difference between interleaved and noninterleaved sample vectors, and the value of samplesInterleaved can be either zero or nonzero.

The second ordering of the three corresponds to interleaved sample lines. Because this ordering is not as common as the other two, it is not directly supported by Interpress. Although you can construct a sample vector in this form, you cannot use it as an argument for MAKEPIXELARRAY; instead, you have to reorder the sample values such that they have one of the two forms that MAKEPIXELARRAY accepts. This reordering can be accomplished by means of a decompression operator. As the name suggests, these operators are intended for decompressing image data, but they can be used for any reordering of sampled image data. As we saw in Chapter 6, a decompression operator takes as its argument a vector that contains the pixel data and any other parameters that it needs, and returns a vector with either interleaved or noninterleaved samples.

Once you have constructed a pixel array, you can no longer access individual sample values. You can form a new pixel array, however, by selecting a subset of the samples for all the pixels in the array. Your source file may have three color components per sample, but you may wish to image only one of them. Perhaps you intend to send the image to a black-and-white printer; instead of relying on the printer's best effort to print the colored image, you prefer to select and print one of the color components. Or perhaps you have a full-color printer, but wish to image only one or two of the components for proofing purposes. Interpress provides the primitive operator EXTRACTPIXELARRAY to do this:

$$<\text{pa:PixelArray}> \quad <\text{select:Vector of Cardinal}>$$
$$\text{EXTRACTPIXELARRAY} \rightarrow \quad <\text{p:PixelArray}>$$

EXTRACTPIXELARRAY creates a pixel array p from the samples of the original array pa, the indices of which are given in the vector select. For example, to form a pixel array that contains the first (red) and third (blue) color components of the pixel array that Example 7.12 stored in frame variable 8, you would write Example 7.13.

Example 7.13

```
8 FGET                  --retrieve pixel array of Example 7.12--
0 2                     --select samples with indices 0 and 2--
2 MAKEVEC                --make it into a vector--
EXTRACTPIXELARRAY       --construct pixel array from selected samples--
```

The pixel array p created by EXTRACTPIXELARRAY has the same values for xPixels, yPixels, samplesInterleaved, and the transformation m as does the original pixel array pa. SamplesPerPixel is equal to the number of elements in the vector select. Just as EXTRACTPIXELARRAY extracts the indicated samples from each pixel in the original array, it also extracts their maximum sample values from the original maxSampleValue vector to form a new maxSampleValue vector.

The MAKESAMPLEDCOLOR Operator

The pixel arrays that we created from binary samples in Chapter 6 could be made into masks or black-and-white inks. The pixel arrays that we now know how to make from color samples cannot be made into masks, but they can be made into inks. An Interpress master places scanned color images on the page by making them into sampled inks and applying them through a mask.

To create a sampled ink from a pixel array, you have to supply two pieces of information. One is a coordinate transformation, so that the printer can map the pixel array to device coordinates. The other is a color operator that tells the printer how to interpret the sample values of the pixel array. The Interpress operator MAKESAMPLEDCOLOR uses both of these to create a sampled ink from a pixel array:

<pa:PixelArray> <um:Transformation> <colorOp:Operator>
MAKESAMPLEDCOLOR → <col: Color>

The argument pa is the array of pixels: each pixel consists of samplesPerPixel samples, which the color operator colorOp uses as coordinates of the color specified by each pixel in a color space or a color map. You have to match the color operator to the contents of the pixel array. If the pixel array contains RGB values encoded with 8 bits, for example, then you must specify the color operator that converts that encoding to ink values.

The xPixels by yPixels scanned image is transformed to device coordinates by the transformation m um CONCAT. The transformation m is part of the pixel-array definition; you can use it to size, orient, and position the pixel array in the master coordinate system. You then use um to transform the pixel array from master to device coordinates; um is usually the same as the current transformation. In Chapter 6, we described the use of the m and um transformations in imaging binary pixel arrays. We use them in the same way when dealing with gray or color pixel arrays.

MAKESAMPLEDCOLOR combines the transformation, color operator, and pixel array to create an object of type Color, which it leaves on the stack. To show the ink created by MAKESAMPLEDCOLOR, you would store it in the imager variable color using the statement 13 ISET, and then you would use a mask operator to apply it to the page.

We defined a color operator as taking a vector of numbers and using them to produce a constant ink. In the case of MAKESAMPLEDCOLOR, the samples of a pixel are the arguments to the color operator. Therefore, the color operator converts an array of pixels into an array of constant inks or a sampled ink. This ink can be tiled in the same way that the sampled ink we created by using MAKESAMPLEDBLACK in Chapter 6 could be tiled. MAKESAMPLEDBLACK can, in fact, be considered a special case of MAKESAMPLEDCOLOR. Instead of a color operator, MAKESAMPLEDBLACK used the variable clear, since there were only two possible interpretations for the binary sample values of the array (0 is white ink or transparent ink, 1 is black ink).

To convert the pixel array that we created in Example 7.12 to a sampled ink, we need a color operator for 8-bit R,G,B values. Although we could define a color model operator for R,G,B samples and use it to produce a color operator for 8-bit values, we will instead create a color operator [IPBook, RGBOp8] specifically for this encoding. This color operator is obtained by executing the statements in Example 7.14.

Example 7.14

```
Identifier "IPBook"
Identifier "RGBOp8"
2 MAKEVEC                    --color operator name--
FINDCOLOROPERATOR            --look up color operator---
```

The Interpress master in Example 7.15 uses the result of Example 7.14 to produce the color image shown in Plate 2.

Example 7.15

```
Header "Interpress/Xerox/3.0 "   --header--
BEGIN                            --start of the master--
  { }                            --preamble--
  {                              --start of the page--
    0.0254 SCALE CONCATT         --use inches for MCS--
    1 1 TRANSLATE CONCATT        --include offset in T--
    3                            --3 scan lines--
```

```
3                                        --3 pixels per scan line--
3                                        --3 samples per pixel--
255                                      --same maximum value for all--
0                                        --samples not interleaved--
1 SCALE                                  --image is 3 inches square--
0 0 0 0 255 128 255 255 255              --red samples--
0 255 255 0 255 128 0 0 255              --green samples--
255 255 0 0 255 128 255 0 0              --blue samples--
27 MAKEVEC                               --make samples vector--
MAKEPIXELARRAY                           --construct pixel array--
4 IGET                                   --um is current transformation--
Identifier "IPBook"
Identifier "RGBOp8"
2 MAKEVEC                                --color operator name--
FINDCOLOROPERATOR                        --look up color operator--
MAKESAMPLEDCOLOR                         --create sampled ink--
13 ISET                                  --save in imager--
0 0 3 3 MASKRECTANGLE                    --apply ink to page--
     }                                   --end of the page--
 END                                     --end of the master--
```

The transformation 1 SCALE produces a 3-inch-square pixel array in the master coordinate system, with its lower-left corner at the origin. Um is the transformation (1 1 TRANSLATE 0.0254 SCALE CONCAT T_{ID} CONCAT). It first translates the pixel array in master coordinates to the desired location on the page using 1 1 TRANSLATE. It then transforms the array to device coordinates using 0.0254 SCALE T_{ID} CONCAT. MAKESAMPLEDCOLOR converts the transformed pixel array to a sampled ink using the color operator for 8-bit RGB values. To image the pixel array on the page, we store the sampled ink created in the color imager variable and then call the MASKRECTANGLE operator to apply the ink to the page (see Figure 7.8).

When we use constant inks that by definition have the same value over the entire page, the object that we want to make visible on the page is defined by the mask. With a sampled ink created from a scanned image, however, the object we want to make visible is defined by the ink, so we must pay particular attention to how it is transformed. We position the pixel array (and hence the sampled ink) as required and make sure that the rectangular mask has the same position. The pixel array and mask start with the same position and size in the master coordinate system. The pixel array is transformed to device coordinates by the transformation um. Since um and T have the same value in this example, the sampled ink and the mask end up with the same size and position in the device coordinate system.

Interpress has the convenience operator SETSAMPLEDCOLOR for creating sampled inks:

<pa: PixelArray> <vm:Transformation> <colorOp:Operator>
SETSAMPLEDCOLOR → < >

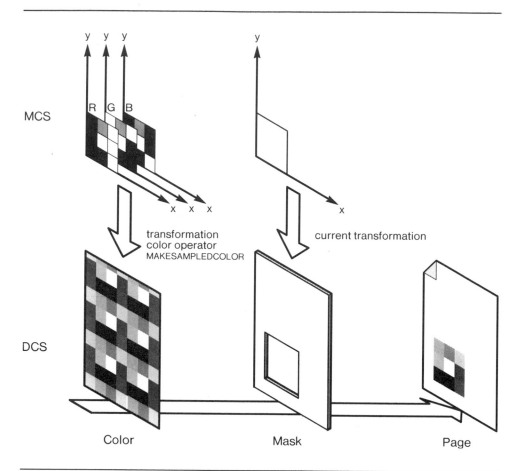

MCS

R G B

transformation
color operator
MAKESAMPLEDCOLOR

current transformation

DCS

Color   Mask   Page

Figure 7.8 Specifying a sampled ink by a pixel array.

SETSAMPLEDCOLOR differs from MAKESAMPLEDCOLOR in two ways. First, it does not leave the sample ink on the stack; instead, it transfers the ink to the imager and there is no need to use 13 ISET. Second, SETSAMPLEDCOLOR applies the transformation m vm CONCAT T CONCAT to the pixel-array to map it from pixel-array to device coordinates. With MAKESAMPLEDCOLOR, you had to transform the ink to device coordinates explicitly, but you do not have to be too concerned about device coordinates when you use SETSAMPLEDCOLOR. You can include the translation required for positioning in the current transformation, as we did for MAKESAMPLEDCOLOR. In this case, vm is the identity 1 SCALE.

Or, you can use vm to specify the positioning transformation. You define vm so that the transformation m vm CONCAT positions the ink where you want it in the master coordinate system. SETSAMPLEDCOLOR then automatically applies the current transformation T to map the ink to device coordinates. Unless you need direct control over the placement of sampled ink in device coordinates, you would normally use SETSAMPLEDCOLOR to create sampled inks in master coordinates and then let the current transformation take care of their placement in the device coordinate system. (See the section on Image Transformations Revisited in Chapter 6; the differences between the use of transformations with MAKESAMPLEDBLACK and SETSAMPLEDBLACK apply to MAKESAMPLEDCOLOR and SETSAMPLEDCOLOR as well.)

We can rewrite Example 7.15 using SETSAMPLEDCOLOR, as shown in the master in Example 7.16.

Example 7.16

```
Header "Interpress/Xerox/3.0 "      --header--
BEGIN                               --start of the master--
  { }                               --preamble--
  {                                 --start of the page--
    0.0254 SCALE CONCATT            --inches for master coordinates--
    1 1 TRANSLATE CONCATT           --include offset in T--
    3                               --3 scan lines--
    3                               --3 pixels per scan line--
    3                               --3 samples per pixel--
    255                             --same maximum value for all--
    0                               --samples not interleaved--
    1 SCALE                         --image is 3 inches square--
    0 0 0 0 255 128 255 255 255     --red samples--
    0 255 255 0 255 128 0 0 255     --green samples--
    255 255 0 0 255 128 255 0 0     --blue samples--
    27 MAKEVEC                      --make samples vector--
    MAKEPIXELARRAY                  --construct pixel-array--
    1 SCALE                         --already positioned and sized--
    Identifier "IPBook"
    Identifier "RGBOp8"
    2 MAKEVEC                       --color operator name--
    FINDCOLOROPERATOR               --retrieve color operator--
    SETSAMPLEDCOLOR                 --create and store sampled ink--
    0 0 3 3 MASKRECTANGLE           --apply ink to page--
  }                                 --end of the page--
END                                 --end of the master--
```

In Example 7.16, we placed the origin of the master coordinate system at the lower-left corner of the image. The rectangular mask has the same size and position in master coordinates as the pixel array. We defined the current transformation T so that it would translate both the mask and array together to the desired page location, expressed in master coordinates, and then transform them to device coordinates.

Although our examples created only simple sampled inks, the principles they demonstrate apply equally well to imaging larger and more complicated pixel arrays. Plate 5 and Plate 6 show some of the documents you can produce with Interpress. The image in Plate 5 was created by first laying down a sampled color background. The master used about 80 Bézier spline segments, grouped into 5 trajectories and made into an outline, to define the small figure used in the foreground. The master then used a composed operator to successively image the figure by pushing a constant color (or a sampled color in one case) through a mask made from the outline. As daunting as this may sound, the master that produced Plate 5 was, of course, generated by a computer program that converted the graphic designer's user-friendly commands to printer-friendly Interpress instructions.

The masters that generated Plate 5 and Plate 6 both used sampled color in the same way. To illustrate this, we will examine the master that produced Plate 6. It takes a 4- by 5-inch color photograph, scanned by an RGB input scanner in the standard order (bottom to top, left to right) at 200 pixels per inch in both directions. Executing this master produces the illustration shown in Plate 6.

Example 7.17

```
Header "Interpress/Xerox/3.0 "    --header--
BEGIN                             --start of the master--
  { }                             --preamble--
  {                               --start of the page--
    0.0254 SCALE CONCATT          --use inches for master coordinates--
    1 1 TRANSLATE CONCATT         --include offset in T--
    1000                          --1000 scan lines--
    800                           --800 pixels per line--
    3                             --3 samples per pixel--
    255                           --same maximum value for all--
    1                             --samples interleaved--
    1/200 SCALE                   --scale to 4- by 5-inches--
    LargeVector "01 . . . "       --long sequence encoding of sample--
                                  --vector, 1 byte per sample--
                                  --800x1000x3 samples--
    MAKEPIXELARRAY                --construct pixel array--
    1 SCALE                       --vm is identity transformation--
    Identifier "IPBook"
    Identifier "RGBOp8"
    2 MAKEVEC                     --color operator name--
    FINDCOLOROPERATOR             --look up color operator--
    SETSAMPLEDCOLOR               --create and save sampled ink--
    0 0 5 4 MASKRECTANGLE
```

```
        }                           --end of the page--
     END                            --end of the master--
```

The master in Example 7.17 uses the LargeVector encoding (described in Chapter 6) to encode the sample vector as a sequence of 2,400,001 bytes.[†] The first byte in the sequence is "01"; it means that each of the samples is stored in a single byte. The master scales the pixel array by 1/200, so that its size is 4-by 5-inches. The ink created by SETSAMPLEDCOLOR and the rectangular mask through which it will be applied to the page have the same position and size in the master coordinate system. The printer applies the current transformation to transform them both to device coordinates.

Color Operators Revisited

The scanned image in Example 7.18 has 800,000 pixels: you would not casually send the master that contains it to your local printer. We sent this master to a process color printer that used four halftoned inks (cyan, magenta, yellow, and black or C,M,Y,K) to produce Plate 6. In processing the master, the printer applied the [IPBook, RGBOp8] color operator 800,000 times. The effect that this could have on printer performance is so important that we will consider again what it means to apply a color operator.

The color operator [IPBook, RGBOp8] converts the RGB specification of the sampled ink in the master to a halftoned CMYK specification that the printer uses to render the image. In practice, this conversion is done in two steps. The first step transforms R,G,B values to C,M,Y,K values (color correction with undercolor removal).[††] The second converts C,M,Y,K values to binary images at the resolution of the printer (halftoning).

Although you could include a composed color operator in the master to do the color correction and halftoning, you would not want to constrain the printer to use it because the resulting performance probably would be intolerable. Any constraints on printer performance should come from the printer, not from the master. A color operator retrieved from the printer's environment almost always gives superior performance, because its implementation is printer specific and can take advantage of special features

---

[†]Besides defining standard color model operators, the Raster Encoding Standard defines a standard interface that uses the sequenceInsertFile instead of the sequenceLargeVector encoding to insert scanned images in an Interpress master. The use of sequenceInsertFile is described in Chapter 8.

[††]Color correction converts red, green, and blue values to the cyan, magenta, and yellow ink amounts that give the same color; undercolor removal is the process of replacing the black produced by overprinting the three colored inks with an equivalent amount of black ink.

that the printer has for dealing with certain color encodings. For example, the printer may have hardware for both color correction and halftoning. In this case, applying the color operator would require simply marking or tagging the pixel array for hardware processing. On less capable printers, the color operator may have to do the actual processing, using whatever software it has at its disposal.

Or, the document creator could assume some of the burden of preparing printer-ready (printer-dependent) samples. The document creator could include in a master CMYK images that are already color corrected, along with a color operator that halftones them, or else could include printer-dependent halftoned CMYK images or bitmaps in the form of binary pixel arrays in the master. (We saw in Chapter 6 how we can use black-and-white halftoned images in a master.) Nothing in Interpress prevents you from using either of these alternatives. Whether you use CMYK or RGB files in the master (as we did in Example 7.17) Interpress can handle the task, given the proper color operators and printer environment. Which you use is determined by the standards and procedures for representing color images on your network. Since Interpress was designed for the device-independent representation of printable pages and documents, it encourages the use of device-independent color representations as well by providing powerful facilities in the form of color operators to support them.

Summary

In this chapter, we considered color and the ink component of the Interpress imaging model. We saw how to produce constant gray shades with the primitive MAKEGRAY and SETGRAY operators. We described how any constant color can be specified either by name, or by means of a color operator from the printer's environment. We learned how color operators can be generated by color model operators. Finally, we saw how full-color patterns and images can be represented as arrays of samples in cases where more than one sample per pixel may be needed. The images can be derived from the samples vectors by the MAKESAMPLEDCOLOR and SETSAMPLEDCOLOR (see Figure 7.9).

This chapter concludes our discussion of the Interpress facilities for describing page images. In Chapter 8, we consider how Interpress deals with entire documents. It is these capabilities that make Interpress a document-description language.

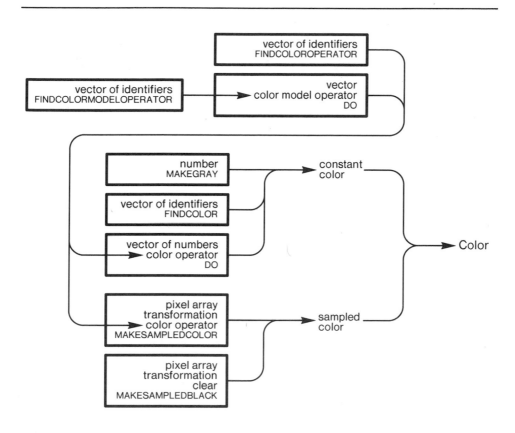

Figure 7.9 Constructing a color.

Chapter 8
DOCUMENT
PRINTING

*"Till wak'd
and kindled
by the master's
spell..."*

SAMUEL ROGERS

In previous chapters, we described how Interpress creates page images. In this chapter, we describe how to organize page images into documents and how to construct documents from pages or from other documents. Interpress also offers a way to specify control over document printing and administrative information about the document; as a result, Interpress is particularly well suited to publishing applications.

We shall introduce the Interpress skeleton structure and show how it is used to construct documents. The skeleton structure also allows you to find and extract the individual pages for merging and overlaying selected pages. We shall also examine techniques for specifying document information, and operations that apply to the entire document.

We shall see how to combine portions of different documents into a new document, and how to generate new, content-independent layouts, including two-up, head-to-toe, and signature printing. We shall show how to create a master document from which subset copies can be generated, each subset copy having different page-content information, and including different sets of pages. We shall learn how to select different media for the pages and how to print pages in simplex or duplex format. We shall describe how to specify binding offsets and binding operations (for example, stapling or gluing). We shall learn how to construct documents from other documents by means of file references, and we shall tell how to declare resource requirements, such as the language-capability level, and the fonts, files, colors, and decompressors required. We shall also learn how to include administrative information, such as the author, date, and copies to be printed.

The Interpress Skeleton

The Interpress skeleton provides a framework for organizing and identifying pages within a document; it is the skeleton that makes Interpress a document-description language. The skeleton also allows additional instructions to be associated with pages, blocks of pages, and the entire document.

The simplest Interpress master is shown in Example 8.1.

Example 8.1

```
Header "Interpress/Xerox/3.0 "   --version and encoding--
BEGIN                            --start of the master--
  { }                            --empty preamble--
END                              --end of the master--
```

The master begins with a header, which is a string of characters that terminates with a space. The header identifies a file as an Interpress master and also shows the Interpress version and the encoding used. The Interpress language can be encoded many different ways. For example, it can be expressed in compact machine-readable binary codes or as text strings that humans can read. When you create a master with Interpress, you must use an encoding that your target printer understands. The Interpress standard does not limit the encodings that you can use, but it does offer a standard encoding that all Xerox printers support. The header for the encoding in Example 8.1 is the text string "Interpress/Xerox/3.0 "; note that the string ends with a terminating space.[†]

Preambles and Page Bodies

In the simplest master, the header is followed by a BEGIN token, which indicates the start of a block. The END token indicates the end of a block. Within the block, there is a series of bodies or other blocks. A body is a collection of Interpress literals enclosed in brace tokens { }. The first body in each block is called a *preamble*, and must be present. It does no imaging but rather establishes a global *page initial frame* of data values or operators, which are used by the page bodies contained in the block. Page bodies follow the preamble, and each describes the image for a page. In the simplest master (Example 8.1), there are no page bodies, so this master prints no pages. Furthermore, there are no Interpress literals in the preamble (there is only an empty body), so this master does not even establish any global information. It is simple but not very useful.

The master in Example 8.2 produces three page images.

The preamble in Example 8.2 is empty, and page 1, page 2, and page 3 represent the Interpress operations and the data that image their respective pages. The sequence of page bodies specifies the page order for the finished

---

[†]This string is limited to the character codes in the ISO 646 seven-bit coded character set for information-processing interchange.

Example 8.2

```
Header "Interpress/Xerox/3.0 "     --header--
BEGIN                              --start of the master--
   { }                             --empty preamble--
   {page 1}                        --first page--
   {page 2}                        --second page--
   {page 3}                        --third page--
END                                --end of the master--
```

document, regardless of how the printing device operates. Some printers, for example, print from back to front; they image page 3, then page 2, and finally page 1. The final document, however, presents the pages in order: 1, 2, 3. To support variations in printing sequence, Interpress strictly enforces *page independence*. Actions that occur within a page body can have no effect outside that body. Page 2 cannot affect page 3, so it does not matter in what order the pages are imaged, as long as the final document is correctly assembled.

Page independence also allows you to use page-level editing functions, such as extracting pages, combining documents, and creating overlays. These operations are discussed in later sections of this chapter. A master with a nonempty preamble is shown in Example 8.3.

Example 8.3

```
Header "Interpress/Xerox/3.0 "     --header--
BEGIN                              --start of the master--
   {preamble}                      --nonempty preamble--
   {page 1}                        --first page--
   {page 2}                        --second page--
   {page 3}                        --third page--
END                                --end of the master--
```

In Example 8.3, the Interpress instructions represented by "preamble" are executed before any of the page bodies. At the end of the preamble, the contents of the frame are saved in what we call the *page initial frame*. These data initialize the Interpress frame for each page so that, at the start of each page body, the frame is identical to the frame at the end of the preamble. Values or operators that are saved in the frame during the preamble execution are available to each page, but actions occurring within the page execution never carry forward to other pages. Each page can modify its copy of the frame, but these changes cannot be detected by other page bodies. The preamble, therefore, supplies a means for document-level processing. Actions that apply to an entire document can be carried out in the document's preamble.

Printing Instructions

To print a document, you must supply more information than just descriptions of images for the pages. You may also want to select paper type, to specify the number of copies and to print on one or both sides of the paper, as well as to indicate finishing actions such as stapling. Some of this information may be supplied with the document itself. For example, you may intend to image a page of the document on a preprinted form. Without the form, the page may not make sense, so you would like the document to call out the form as the proper medium for the page. Interpress provides a general mechanism, called *printing instructions*, that you can use to incorporate such information in a document. Printing instructions can supply information such as the document name, creator, and creation date. They can also describe information that can be used to route the document to the most appropriate printer or to aid the printer in scheduling the job.

Printing instructions are contained in the master's *instructions body*, which is optional; if present, it is found between the header and the first BEGIN token, as shown in Example 8.4.

Example 8.4

```
Header "Interpress/Xerox/3.0 "    --header--
{instructions}                    --document instructions body--
BEGIN                             --start of the master--
   {preamble}                     --preamble--
   {page 1}                       --first page--
   {page 2}                       --second page--
END                               --end of the master--
```

An instructions body contains Interpress commands for building a property vector of instruction names and data values. The instructions property vector is a general mechanism for holding information either for control of the printing process or for administrative purposes. The instructions property vector can control the document printing by selecting pages or indicating number of copies. It can select finishing options and provide supplemental information about the document, such as when it was created and by whom and what resources it requires.

The instructions body of the document is not the only source of printing instructions; the instructions also can be given from some printer-dependent external source. Such instructions arrive with the document, but are not part of it. They are part of the protocol used to deliver the document to the printer. For example, they could specify the number of copies to print.

We can imagine instructions being found in both the master's instructions body and the external instructions. The printer must resolve any conflicts between the instructions arriving from the two sources, usually by giving precedence to one of the sources for the instruction. For example, if the instructions body contained the instruction to print three copies, but the external source gave an instruction to print two copies, precedence would be given to the external instruction, and two copies would be printed. In this case, we interpret the instruction in the master as providing a default value for the number of copies (three). You will get this default number of copies unless you specifically ask for a different number by means of the external instructions.

The printer goes through several steps in determining the instructions it will use. First, unlike the preamble and page bodies, the stack is not empty at the start of the document instructions body. Instead, it is initialized to a property vector that is created from the external instructions. The instructions body in your master can examine this vector to learn which external instructions are present. You can conditionally create instructions for the document, based on the values found for the external instructions. The instructions body specifies the document's instructions by creating one or more property vectors containing instruction names and values. At the end of the instructions body, all property vectors left on the stack are merged to form one property vector that contains the document's instructions.

In the next step, the printer compares the document's instructions and the external instructions and resolves any conflicts between them. The method of resolution depends on the instruction, but it usually gives precedence to one of the two sources.

The printer then checks to see whether any necessary instructions are missing; if they are, it supplies a default value. For example, if neither the document's instructions body nor the external instructions specifies how many copies to print, the printer defaults this parameter to one copy.

Finally, the printer may have to override a requested instruction. For example, you can request that printing occur on both sides of the paper (duplex). If the printer does not support this capability, however, it overrides the instruction, replacing it with simplex.

Content Instructions

Besides the master's instructions body, you can use instructions bodies associated with each page. These are called *content-instructions bodies*, and immediately precede the page to which they apply. Example 8.5 shows their use.

Example 8.5

```
Header "Interpress/Xerox/3.0 "              --header--
BEGIN                                        --start of the master--
  { }                                        --empty preamble--
  CONTENTINSTRUCTIONS {inst 1} {page 1}     --first page and--
                                             --its instructions--
  {page 2}                                   --second page--
  CONTENTINSTRUCTIONS {inst 3} {page 3}     --third page and--
                                             --its instructions--
END                                          --end of the master--
```

Example 8.5 shows content instructions for pages 1 and 3. To distinguish content-instructions bodies from page bodies, a CONTENTINSTRUCTIONS token is used. Like the document instructions body, the content-instructions body creates a property vector. The vector contains the instruction names and values that apply to the following page (or block of pages). For example, they can indicate whether the page should be printed or what medium should be used.

Some content instructions can conflict with the instructions for the entire document. The printer must resolve such conflicts, and the rules used depend on the particular instructions. In general, the content instructions are given precedence over the document instructions.

Nested Blocks

The skeleton has one more level of complexity: any page body may be replaced by a *block* of pages. A block is a BEGIN token, a preamble, a list of nodes, and an END token, where each node can be either a body or another block. Therefore, a nested block of page bodies is legal anywhere you can have a page body. Blocks also can replace the pages within a nested block, so multiple nesting is allowed, and rather complex skeletons can be created. We will find this nesting of blocks useful in constructing large Interpress documents out of smaller ones.

Example 8.6 shows a master with a nested block.

Example 8.6

```
Header "Interpress/Xerox/3.0 "       --header--
BEGIN                                 --top-level block--
  { }                                 --top-level preamble--
```

```
{page 1}                    --first page--
BEGIN                       --nested block--
  { }                       --nested block's preamble--
  {page 2}                  --second page--
  {page 3}                  --third page--
END                         --end of nested block--
{page 4}                    --fourth page--
END                         --end of the master--
```

In Example 8.6, instead of three page bodies, the outermost block contains a page body (page 1), a block (with pages 2 and 3), and a page body (page 4). The order of pages in the final document is 1, 2, 3, 4. The ordering rule is that the pages in the nested block come after the pages that precede the block (page 1), and before the pages that follow the block (page 4).

Example 8.7 shows a more complex skeleton structure (see Figure 8.1).

Example 8.7

```
Header "Interpress/Xerox/3.0 "  --header--
BEGIN                           --start of outer block--
  {preamble 0}                  --outermost preamble--
  {page 1}                      --first page--
  BEGIN                         --start of a nested block--
    {preamble 2.0}              --preamble for the nested block--
    {page 2.1}                  --second page, initialized by--
                                --both preamble 0 and preamble 2.0--
    BEGIN                       --start of a block--
                                --in a block in a block--
      {preamble 2.2.0}          --preamble for innermost block--
      {page 2.2.1}              --third page, initialized by--
                                --all three preambles--
    END                         --end of the deepest block--
  END                           --end of the first nested block--
  CONTENTINSTRUCTIONS {inst 3}  --instructions for a nested block--
  BEGIN                         --start of another nested block--
    {preamble 3.0}              --preamble for the block--
    {page 3.1}                  --fourth page, initialized by--
                                --preambles 0 and 3.0--
    {page 3.2}                  --fifth page--
  END                           --end of the nested block--
END                             --end of the master--
```

In Example 8.7, the outermost block contains a page and two blocks. The first nested block contains a preamble (preamble 2.0), a page (page 2.1), and a further nested block containing a preamble and page 2.2.1. The order of pages for this skeleton is 1, 2.1, 2.2.1, 3.1, 3.2.

Notice that each block has a preamble. Preamble 0 for the outermost block determines the initial frame to be used with page 1. This also is the initial

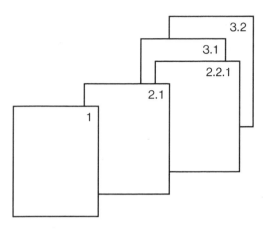

Figure 8.1 The result of Example 8.7.

frame for the execution of preamble 2.0; so a nested preamble can inherit initial frame values from its surrounding block. Preamble 2.0 can replace some or all of the inherited values, and set new frame values of its own. The result of both preamble 0 and preamble 2.0 is the initial frame for page 2.1. Likewise, the result of preamble 0, followed by preamble 2.0, followed by preamble 2.2.0, initializes page 2.2.1. The initial frame for pages 3.1 and 3.2 is the result of preamble 0 followed by preamble 3.0.

In Example 8.7, the final nested block is preceded by a content-instructions body. Content instructions can be used with either page bodies or blocks. The content instructions for a block apply to all of the pages within the block and apply only to their corresponding page or block and not to other parts of the master.

It is possible for each of several levels of nested blocks to have its own content instructions. Once again, this leads to potential conflict between instructions. The printer must resolve instructions from all the surrounding contents. The rules can be tailored to each instruction, but generally the innermost content takes precedence over the instructions from surrounding blocks for the page or block to which it applies.

Specifications for the Entire Document

You have seen how the Interpress skeleton offers two bodies that contain information that applies to the entire document: the document's instruction body and the outermost preamble. We shall now discuss how to use these bodies.

First consider the document preamble. It determines the initial frame for each of the following page bodies. Since values stored in the page initial frame are available to every page body, the preamble can help make the document more efficient or more compact. If a complex or costly operation is performed in the preamble and the result passed to each page, then the operation need be performed only once. Operators that cause imaging cannot be executed in the preamble, but they can be defined there, avoiding redefinition on each page.

The preamble also can aid in establishing a uniform style or format for the document. If each page uses style parameters defined in the preamble, instead of defining them individually, then inconsistencies are eliminated. Furthermore, the style of the document can be changed by altering the single definition in the preamble, rather than by locating and altering the definitions in each page. We shall discuss examples of how you can use the document preamble.

Establishing Fonts and Colors

Fonts in the printer's environment are located by the FINDFONT operator, then scaled and rotated using MODIFYFONT. These may not be particularly efficient operations, so that you should perform them only once for each font and store the result in the frame. These operations should be done in the preamble. This results in fewer font lookups, and stored fonts are guaranteed to be the same on each page. You could, for example, establish the convention that the font in frame variable 2 is used for subscripts and be assured that all subscripts will look alike. The Interpress master in Example 8.8 has a preamble that stores modern and modern-italic fonts in frame variables 0 and 1 (see Figure 8.2).

Example 8.8

```
Header "Interpress/Xerox/3.0 "    --header--
BEGIN                             --start of the master--
  {                               --start of the preamble--
    Identifier "xerox"
    Identifier "XC1-1-1"
    Identifier "modern"
    3 MAKEVEC FINDFONT
    0.00635 SCALE                 --get an 18-point modern font--
    MODIFYFONT
    0 FSET                        --put it in frame[0]--
    Identifier "xerox"
    Identifier "XC1-1-1"
```

```
        Identifier "modern-italic"
        3 MAKEVEC FINDFONT
        0.00635 SCALE                --get an 18-point italic font--
        MODIFYFONT
        1 FSET                       --put it in frame[1]--
    }                                --end of preamble--
                                     --frame is saved--
    {                                --start of the page--
                                     --frame is initialized--
        0 SETFONT                    --normal font is used--
        0.05 0.25 SETXY
        String "Printing "           --to print a string--
        SHOW
        1 SETFONT                    --now the italic font--
        String "Italics"
        SHOW                         --is used for a word--
    }                                --end of the page--
END                                  --end of the master--
```

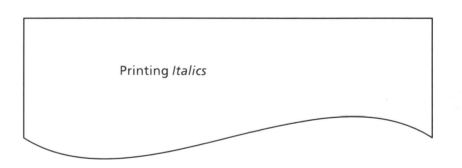

Printing *Italics*

Figure 8.2 The result of Example 8.8.

Colors can be established in a similar manner. Colors can be either constructed (MAKEGRAY), or located in the environment (FINDCOLOR). They also can be constructed by finding an operator in the printer's environment, and then applying it (FINDCOLOROPERATOR and FINDCOLORMODELOPERATOR). As is true when you are finding fonts, it is best to minimize these operations by executing them in the preamble, and saving their results in the frame. Example 8.9 uses the preamble to establish a font and two colors (see Figure 8.3).

Example 8.9

```
Header "Interpress/Xerox/3.0 "  --header--
BEGIN                            --start of the master--
  {                              --start of the preamble--
    Identifier "xerox"
    Identifier "XC1-1-1"
    Identifier "modern"
    3 MAKEVEC FINDFONT
    0.00635 SCALE
    MODIFYFONT                   --get a font--
    0 FSET                       --place it in frame[0]--
    1 MAKEGRAY                   --create black color--
    1 FSET                       --place it in frame[1]--
    Identifier "xerox"
    Identifier "highlight"
    2 MAKEVEC FINDCOLOR          --find highlight color--
    2 FSET                       --place it in frame[2]--
  }                              --end of preamble--
                                 --remember the frame--

  {                              --start of the page--
                                 --initialize the frame--
    0 SETFONT                    --set the current font--
    1 FGET                       --take black color from the frame--
    13 ISET                      --set the color to black--
    0.05 0.25 SETXY
    String "Change color for "
    SHOW                         --print string in black--
    2 FGET                       --get the highlight color and--
    13 ISET                      --make it the current color--
    String "highlights"
    SHOW                         --highlight this string--
  }                              --end of the page--
END                              --end of the master--
```

Figure 8.3 The result of Example 8.9.

Establishing Headings

Suppose you wish to put a logo or heading at the top of each page. With the preamble, you can define a composed operator that images the heading and invoke it at the start of each page. The composed operator can be defined but cannot be executed in the preamble since the preamble does no imaging. In fact, it is an error to try to execute an imaging operator (operators with MASK in their name) in the preamble. Example 8.10 shows how a heading operator works (see Figure 8.4).

Example 8.10

```
Header "Interpress/Xerox/3.0 "  --header--
BEGIN                                --start of the master--
  {                                  --start of the preamble--
    Identifier "xerox" Identifier "XC1-1-1" Identifier "modern"
    3 MAKEVEC FINDFONT
    0.00635 SCALE
    MODIFYFONT
    0 FSET                   --make and save a font--
    MAKESIMPLECO             --make a composed operator--
      {                      --heading operator definition--
        0 SETFONT            --install the desired font--
        0.03 0.26 SETXY      --position for the string--
        String "My Heading"
        SHOW                 --print the heading--
                             --print a rule--
        0.025 0.257 0.17 0.002 MASKRECTANGLE
      }                      --end of the heading operator--
    1 FSET                   --save the operator in frame[1]--
  }
  {                          --start of the page, initial frame--
                             --has font and heading operator--
    1 FGET DOSAVEALL         --get and execute heading operator--
  }                          --end of the page--
END                          --end of the master--
```

In this example, a composed operator is saved in frame variable 1. When called, this operator prints the words "My Heading" and draws a rule below them. At the start of the page body, the command 1 FGET DOSAVEALL executes a copy of this composed operator.

One subtlety about composed operators is that, while executing, they use the frame that existed when they were defined. The frame values present when the operator is called are temporarily replaced. In this example, the composed operator accesses frame variable 0 with the SETFONT operator. This is valid because a font was placed in this frame variable before defining the operator. When the operator is defined, there is a font in frame variable 0. If

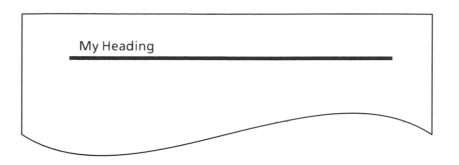

Figure 8.4 The result of Example 8.10.

you reverse the order of the font location and the operator definition in the preamble, the program will not work. The preamble still sets up an initial frame with a font in frame variable 0 and an operator in frame variable 1, but, when the operator is executed, it imposes a copy of the frame that existed when that operator was defined. This frame does not yet have a font in frame variable 0, and the SETFONT command fails.

Establishing Document Attributes

Interpress data structures include an operand stack, a collection of imager variables, and a frame. At the start of each page body, the stack is cleared, the imager variables are set to default values (defined by the Interpress standard), and the frame is set to the page initial frame (defined by the preamble). The imager variables describe aspects of the document's format or style, such as stroke thickness, joint style, stroke end-cap style, and the initial font and color. Sometimes you will want to establish values for the imager variables other than the standard defaults. For example, the default current transformation uses meters as the coordinate units, but you may prefer to use inches, points, or some other unit. The default stroke-width value is 0, but you probably want some positive value so that you can see the lines. You can generate Interpress instructions within each page body to set the imager variables directly, or you can store those values in the initial frame, and then copy the values into the imager variables at the start of each page. The reason for the two-step process is to achieve consistency across pages by giving a single point at which style parameters are declared.

For example, if you wish to make the strokes slightly thicker, with the preamble, you can define the value to be assigned to the stroke width. You can cause every page to copy this value into the stroke-width imager variable, so that the strokes in every page will be thickened in the same manner. Example 8.11 shows an Interpress master that establishes centimeters as the master coordinate units, stroke widths of 1 millimeter, and round joints and end caps.

Example 8.11

```
Header "Interpress/Xerox/3.0 "     --header--
BEGIN                               --start of the master--
  {                                 --start of the preamble--
    Identifier "xerox" Identifier "XC1-1-1" Identifier "modern"
    3 MAKEVEC FINDFONT
    0.353 SCALE
    MODIFYFONT
    0 FSET                          --declare the font to be used--
    0.01 SCALE 1 FSET               --declare the coordinate scale--
    0.1 2 FSET                      --strokeWidth is 1 millimeter--
    2 3 FSET                        --strokeEnd is round--
    2 4 FSET                        --strokeJoint is round--
  }
  {                                 --start of a page--
                                    --install the imaging style--
                                    --in imager variables--
    1 FGET CONCATT                  --set current transformation--
    0 SETFONT                       --set current font--
    2 FGET 15 ISET                  --set strokeWidth--
    3 FGET 16 ISET                  --set strokeEnd--
    4 FGET 23 ISET                  --set strokeJoint--
  }                                 --end of the page--
END                                 --end of the master--
```

Example 8.11 places each initial imager-variable value in the frame and then copies them into imager variables at the start of every page. A more compact method for this initialization defines a composed operator in the preamble, which establishes the imager-variable values. Then you simply execute this operator at the start of each page (see Example 8.12).

Example 8.12

```
Header "Interpress/Xerox/3.0 "     --header--
BEGIN                               --start of the master--
  {                                 --start of the preamble--
    Identifier "xerox" Identifier "XC1-1-1" Identifier "modern"
    3 MAKEVEC FINDFONT
    0.353 SCALE                     --10-point font if MCS is cm--
    MODIFYFONT
```

```
        0 FSET                          --save the font--
        MAKESIMPLECO
        {                               --begin the initialization--
                                        --composed operator definition--
            0 SETFONT
            0.01 SCALE CONCATT          --set T for MCS in cm--
            0.1 15 ISET                 --set strokeWidth to 1 millimeter--
            2 16 ISET                   --set strokeEnd to round--
            2 23 ISET                   --set strokeJoint to round--
        }                               --end of the definition--
        1 FSET                          --save operator in frame[1]--
    }                                   --end of the preamble--
    {                                   --start of a page--
        1 FGET DO                       --execute composed operator--
                                        --to initialize imager variables --
    }                                   --end of the page--
END                                     --end of the master--
```

The notion of establishing imaging style characteristics in the preamble is not limited to the imager variables. Any value that governs style can be saved in the page initial frame and accessed as needed. For example, the dash-pattern vector used in the calls to MASKDASHEDSTROKE can be constructed in the preamble. When you want to image the dashed stroke, you can use a copy of this vector from the frame as the pattern operand.

Structuring Copies

In this section, we shall discuss the instructions body and show how you can construct and select copies of a document. Interpress allows you to build documents so that not all copies are exactly alike. This is useful when variations of the document are needed, as for form letters or forms with different supplemental information on each copy or reports that include different sections for different recipients or catalogs tailored to the customer. With the pageSelect instruction, you can select which page bodies are included on a copy-by-copy basis. You can also change the content of individual pages by using the copyName instruction and IFCOPY operator. You can specify which copies should be printed with the copySelect instruction.

Printing instructions such as copySelect and pageSelect, in general, are found in the master's instructions body and also in the printing protocol that sends the master to the printer. When instructions come from both sources, the printer gives priority to the protocol. The master's instructions body gives default values, which can be overridden by the document printing request.

For example, suppose that your document is a letter and that you usually print two copies, one to be sent and one for the files. When you create a master for this letter, you include a copySelect instruction specifying two copies, so that a simple print request results in two copies being printed. You can still get exactly one copy, or three, or 20, by an explicit request that overrides the default in the master.

Now let us see how you can build the copySelect instruction. Note that, because "copies" can be different, you need a specification that considers each copy and decides whether it should be printed. One way to do this is to associate a 0 or 1 with each copy: 1 means to print the copy, and 0 means to skip it. You could make a vector of these numbers in copy order, so that [1,1,1,0,0,1,0,0, . . .] means print copies one, two, and three, skip copies four and five, print six, and so on. The problem with this notation is that it takes a lot of numbers. If you want to print a thousand copies you have to list a thousand 1s. To get around this, a *run-length* notation is used. Numbers are considered in pairs, where the first number tells how many instances of the second number are needed. For example, [3,1,2,0,1,1,2,0 . . .] specifies three 1s, followed by two 0s, followed by a single 1, followed by two 0s, and so on. This encoding allows you to select any pattern of copies, but you can specify printing the first 1000 copies simply by writing [1000,1].

To make a complete copySelect instruction, you must collect the copy selection specification into an Interpress vector. A copySelect identifier and this vector are then included in the property vector constructed by the instructions body. Example 8.13 shows an instructions body that selects copies 1 through 5 and 7 through 9 (see Figure 8.5).

Example 8.13

```
{                       --start of instructions body--
   Identifier "copySelect"
   5 1 1 0 3 1          --run of five 1s, one 0, three 1s--
   6 MAKEVEC            --select copies 1 through 5 and 7 through 9--
   2 MAKEVEC            --property vector with name and value--
}                       --end of instructions body--
```

If neither the instructions body nor the printing protocol specify a copySelect printing instruction, then a default value of [1,1], which is a single copy, is assumed.

The various copies of a document have been identified by number (first, second, third, and so on), but it also is possible to associate names with copies

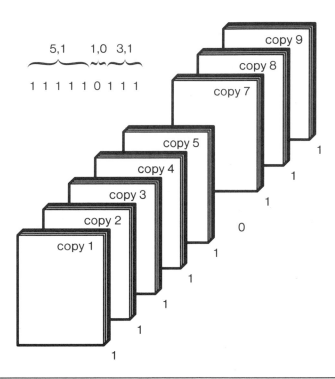

Figure 8.5 Run encoding of copySelect values in Example 8.13.

or groups of copies. The copy name (as well as the copy number) can be used in the IFCOPY operator's test, described in the following paragraphs.

The copyName instruction associates names with individual copies. A run-length encoding scheme also is used for copy names, which are specified by number-name pairs, where the number indicates how many times the particular name is applied. For example, [3, "NormalCopy," 1, "FileCopy"] indicates that copies 1, 2, and 3 have the name "NormalCopy," whereas copy 4 is named "FileCopy." If you print more copies than are covered by the copyName instruction, then the name mapping wraps back to the start of the specification. So, copies 5, 6, and 7 are named "NormalCopy," copy 8 is named "FileCopy," and so on (see Figure 8.6).

Example 8.14 shows an instructions body that sets the default number of copies to three, and names them "ForSmith," "ForJones," and "ForBrown" (see Figure 8.7).

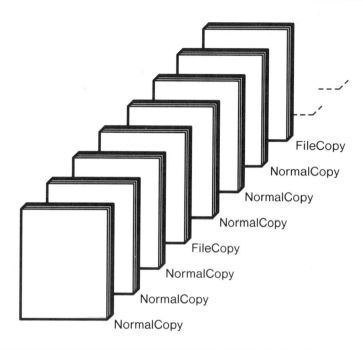

FileCopy
NormalCopy
NormalCopy
NormalCopy
FileCopy
NormalCopy
NormalCopy
NormalCopy

Figure 8.6 Assigning names to copies.

Example 8.14

```
{                              --start of instructions body--
    Identifier "copySelect"
    3 1 2 MAKEVEC              --three 1s mean copies 1 through 3--
    Identifier "copyName"     --instruction to give names to copies--
    1 Identifier "ForSmith"   --value is run of the names--
    1 Identifier "ForJones"   --each name is used only once--
    1 Identifier "ForBrown"
    6 MAKEVEC                  --three run-length value pairs--
    4 MAKEVEC                  --two property pairs in the vector--
}                              --end of instructions body--
```

The IFCOPY operator allows you to alter the appearance of a page on different copies. IFCOPY has two arguments: a test operator and a body, which may be executed, depending on which copy is being printed. For example, you might want two versions of a price list, one for regular customers and a second for preferred customers. You can place the pricing information within two IFCOPY bodies. One body executes only for regular copies, the other executes on preferred copies. The decision whether the body should be executed

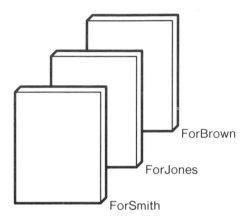

ForBrown

ForJones

ForSmith

Figure 8.7 The result of Example 8.14.

involves the test operator argument. IFCOPY places the current copy number and copy name on the stack and executes this operator. Your operator must remove the copy name and copy number from the stack, and return a single number that is tested to determine whether the body should be executed. If your test operator returns 0, the body is skipped; otherwise, it is executed. The Interpress master in Example 8.15 uses IFCOPY operators to select between two price values. It also uses a copyName instruction to give names to the copies (see Figure 8.8).

Example 8.15

```
Header "Interpress/Xerox/3.0 "    --header--
{                                 --start of the instructions body--
   Identifier "copyName"
   1 Identifier "regular"
   1 Identifier "preferred"       --copyName value has two names --
   4 MAKEVEC                      --each is used once--
   2 MAKEVEC                      --make the instructions vector--
}                                 --end of instructions body--
BEGIN                             --start of the main block--
   {                              --start of the preamble--
      Identifier "xerox" Identifier "XC1-1-1" Identifier "modern"
      3 MAKEVEC FINDFONT
      0.00706 SCALE
      MODIFYFONT
      0 FSET                      --save font in frame[0]--
   }                              --end of the preamble--
   {                              --start of the page--
```

```
0 SETFONT                       --set the current font--
0.03 0.25 SETXY
String "The current price is "
SHOW                            --print a string--
MAKESIMPLECO
{                               --test operator for the IFCOPY--
   Identifier "regular"         --test for "regular" copyName--
   EQ EXCH POP                  --and remove the copyNumber--
}
IFCOPY
{                               --body to print regular price--
   String "$12.95"
   SHOW
}
MAKESIMPLECO
{                               --test operator for the IFCOPY--
   Identifier "preferred"       --test for "preferred" copyName--
   EQ EXCH POP                  --and remove the copyNumber--
}
IFCOPY
{                               --body to print preferred price--
   String "$10.95"
   SHOW
}
   }                            --end of the page--
END                             --end of the master--
```

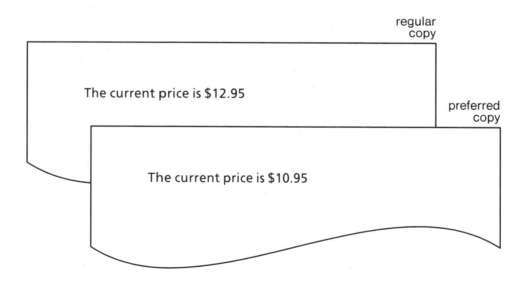

Figure 8.8 The result of Example 8.15.

The MAKESIMPLECOs define test operators, which compare an identifier against the name of the current copy, producing a 0 or 1. They then exchange this result with the copy number so that the copy number can be removed. The result of the EQ test is then left on the stack. If there is a match (1), then the IFCOPY operator executes the body, which images the appropriate price.

There are restrictions on IFCOPY and on the test operator. The test operator must remove only the copy name and number and can place only a single number on the stack. Because it can contain only base-language operators, it can do no imaging. In effect, it is executed by a DOSAVEALL so that any changes to the frame or imager variables are cleared. The body of the IFCOPY cannot access the stack beyond what it itself pushes onto it and it must, on completion, leave the stack undisturbed. It also is effectively executed by a DOSAVEALL command, so IFCOPY cannot produce any side effects other than to change the actual image.

As a second example of the use of IFCOPY, consider a master that prints mailing addresses (possibly the address that will show through the transparent portion of an envelope). Using IFCOPY, you can construct a page body that contains the full mailing list, but prints only a single address on each copy, as shown in Example 8.16 (see Figure 8.9).

Example 8.16

```
Header "Interpress/Xerox/3.0 "    --header--
BEGIN                             --start of the master--
  {                               --start of the preamble--
    Identifier "xerox" Identifier "XC1-1-1" Identifier "modern"
    3 MAKEVEC FINDFONT
    0.00706 SCALE
    MODIFYFONT
    0 FSET                        --save a font--
  }                               --end of the preamble--
  {                               --start of the page--
    0 SETFONT
    0.05 0.26 SETXY
    String "To: "                 --print "To: "--
    SHOW
    MAKESIMPLECO
    {
      POP 1 EQ                    --test operator removes copyName --
    }                             --and compares 1 to copyNumber--
    IFCOPY
    {
      String "John Smith"         --print "John Smith"--
      SHOW                        --if copyNumber is 1--
    }
    MAKESIMPLECO
```

```
{
    POP 2 EQ                    --test operator for copy 2--
}
IFCOPY
{
    String "Mary Jones"         --print "Mary Jones"--
    SHOW                        --if copyNumber is 2--
}
MAKESIMPLECO
{
    POP 3 EQ                    --test for copy 3--
}
IFCOPY
{
    String "Chris Brown"        --print "Chris Brown"--
    SHOW                        --if copyNumber is 3--
}
 . . .
}                               --end of the page--
END                             --end of the master--
```

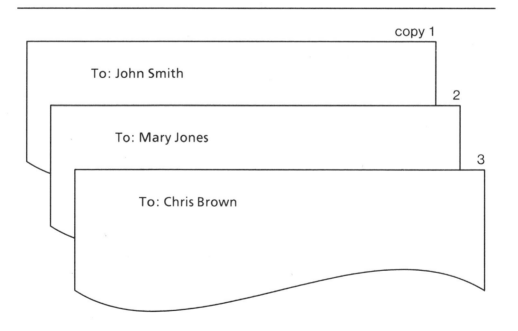

Figure 8.9 The result of Example 8.16.

In this example, copies are identified by their numbers rather than their names, so instructions to establish names are not needed. The test operator pops the default name, "Null," for each copy and tests the copy number.

You could code this example more cleverly by creating a composed operator in the preamble that pops a number and name from the stack, uses IFCOPY to compare the number against the current copy count, and shows the name if it matches. With this operator in the page initial frame (say, frame variable 20), the page body looks like

```
1 String "John Smith" 20 FGET DO
2 String "Mary Jones" 20 FGET DO
3 String "Chris Brown" 20 FGET DO
```

These commands place the copy number and corresponding name on the stack for use by the operator, then get the operator from the frame and execute it. To construct such an operator, you must have it move the operands from the stack to the frame so that they can be communicated to the test operator and the IFCOPY body. The operator looks like Example 8.17.

Example 8.17

```
MAKESIMPLECO          --make an operator to move data to the frame--
                      --then use it in an IFCOPY test--
{                     --begin the operator--
  21 FSET             --save name in frame[21]--
  22 FSET             --save copy number in frame[22]--
  MAKESIMPLECO        --test operator gets number and compares--
  {
    POP 22 FGET EQ
  }
  IFCOPY              --IFCOPY body gets string and images it--
  {
    21 FGET SHOW
  }
} 20 FSET             --save in frame[20]--
```

You also can control the structure of copies by selecting which pages should be included on a copy-by-copy basis. For example, suppose your document is a 30-page report, and the first page contains a summary or abstract. You might wish to print five copies of the full report and fifteen copies of just the summary. You can do this with the *pageSelect* instruction. Like the copySelect instruction, pageSelect can occur either in the master's instruction body or in the printing protocol, with the printing protocol taking precedence and the instructions body supplying a default. The pageSelect instruction uses the run-length encoding scheme twice; first, to describe which pages should be included in a copy and second, to tell how many copies should have that page pattern. In the report master of Example 8.18, [30,1] selects the entire document. The vector [1,1,29,0] selects only the summary page: it prints the summary on page 1 and skips the remaining 29 pages. The vector [5,[30,1],15,[1,1,29,0]] creates five copies of the full document, followed by 15 copies of the summary page. The example shows an instructions body to print the entire job (see Figure 8.10).

Example 8.18

```
{                                   --start of the instructions body--
    Identifier "copySelect"         --a copySelect instruction--
    20 1 2 MAKEVEC                   --selects 20 copies--
    Identifier "pageSelect"         --pageSelect instruction--
    5                               --for first five copies--
    30 1 2 MAKEVEC                   --select 30 pages--
    15                              --for 15 copies--
    1 1 29 0 4 MAKEVEC              --select only the first page--
    4 MAKEVEC                        --vector for pageSelect value--
    4 MAKEVEC                        --instructions vector--
}                                   --end of the instruction body--
```

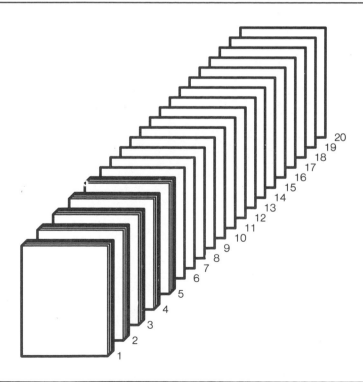

Figure 8.10 The result of Example 8.18.

The pageSelect instruction offers a powerful mechanism for constructing individualized documents from a pool of page images.

Document-Finishing Specifications

Interpress instructions allow you to specify how the images are placed on the print medium, what print medium is used, whether the document is stapled, and how the printed copies are stacked. However, your printer may not support every feature. You can request that each copy be stapled, but this will be done only if the printer has a stapler. The printer ignores instructions that it cannot carry out.

The *plex* instruction tells the printer whether to print the document *simplex* or *duplex* (see Figure 8.11), and the instruction's value is a simple identifier, either "simplex" or "duplex." Simplex printing places a single page body image on each piece of paper. Duplex printing uses both sides of the paper so that two page-body images are printed on each sheet.

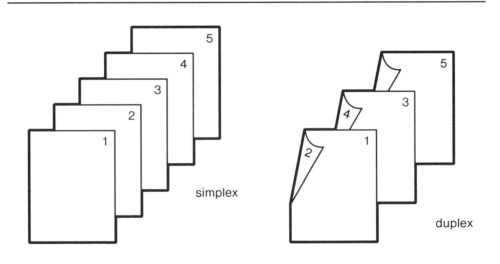

Figure 8.11 Simplex and duplex printing.

When constructing a master for duplex printing, you may want blank pages to force certain images (such as the start of a chapter) to occur on odd-numbered pages (righthand pages in a bound book). Blank pages might also be inserted to arrange for two pages to face each other, making a two-page spread. However, if the document is printed on a simplex device, or if you explicitly request a simplex copy, then the blank pages become extraneous. Interpress provides the *onSimplex* instruction as a way to skip such pages. This instruction is a run-encoded list of 1s and 0s, where 1 means print the page body, and 0 means skip the page body when printing in simplex mode (see Figure 8.12). If you print duplex, this instruction is ignored. For example, suppose that there are seven pages in Chapter 1, five pages in Chapter 2, and

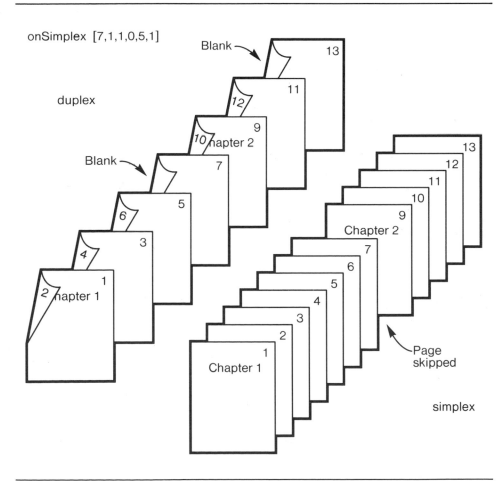

Figure 8.12 The onSimplex instruction lets you skip pages when printing simplex.

a blank page (page 8) between the chapters. This causes Chapter 2 to begin on the odd page 9 when printing duplex. You want to skip printing page 8 when in simplex mode so that you include an onSimplex instruction with value [7,1,1,0,5,1]. This shows that, when printing simplex, the printer should image the first seven page bodies, skip the eighth, and image the next five.

You can select the medium for each page of your document–that is, you can use different sizes or weights of paper, colored paper, preprinted forms, and so on. Your document may have a cover sheet on yellow paper, three pages on the default medium, and the last page on a special preprinted form (see Figure 8.13). Interpress allows you to give these specifications in two steps. The first step gives the printer a list of media that your document requires. The list of required media is specified by the *media* instruction, which is a vector of property vectors called *mediumDescriptions*. Each mediumDescription contains properties that identify the desired medium, using characteristics such as its name, dimension, and a message that can be sent to the printer operator.

The second step, which tells which medium to use with each page, is specified by the *mediaSelect* instruction. Like the pageSelect instruction, its value is a run-encoded vector of run-encoded vectors for handling both copies and pages. It assigns a number to each page in each copy. The number is the index into the media-instruction vector.

Consider again the example of the document with three media: the yellow cover, the default pages, and a preprinted form on the last page. Suppose the media instruction lists the default medium first, then the yellow paper medium, and the special form third. To print four copies of this document, you would construct a mediaSelect instruction with value [4,[1,2,3,1,1,3]]. This says that for the first four copies use one page of the second medium, three pages of the first medium, and one page of the third medium.

You can specify a binding offset for the document with the *xImageShift* instruction. This shifts the image on the page left or right. For simplex printing, it shifts every page to the right if the value is positive, and to the left if the value is negative. For duplex printing, a positive value shifts odd page images to the right and even page images to the left (see Figure 8.14).

You can specify the sorting or stacking of the printed copies with the *outputPosition* instruction. This instruction's value is a run of numbers that give an "output bin" for each copy. For example, [1,1,3,2] puts the first copy in the first output bin, and the next three copies in the second output bin. If it can, the printer separates the first copy from the next three. If more copies are requested than are covered by the output position instruction, the positions are repeated. So [1,1,1,2] alternates copies in the first and second output positions, no matter how many copies are made.

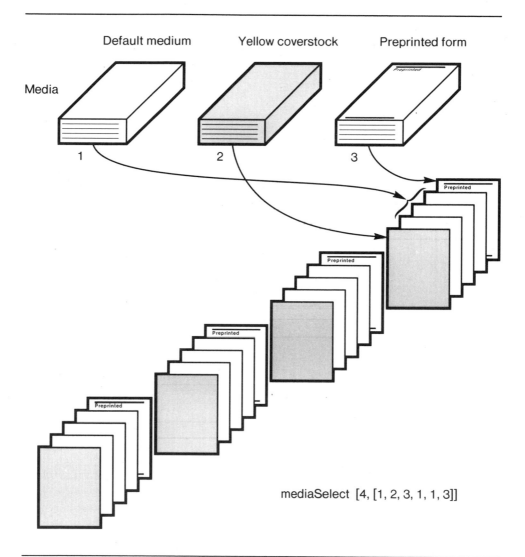

Figure 8.13 The media and mediaSelect instructions let you select the medium used on each page of each copy.

The *finishing* instruction controls the handling of a document. It specifies finishing options such as stapling.

Example 8.19, which shows an instructions body for the instructions discussed in this section, prints a document with the first page on coverstock

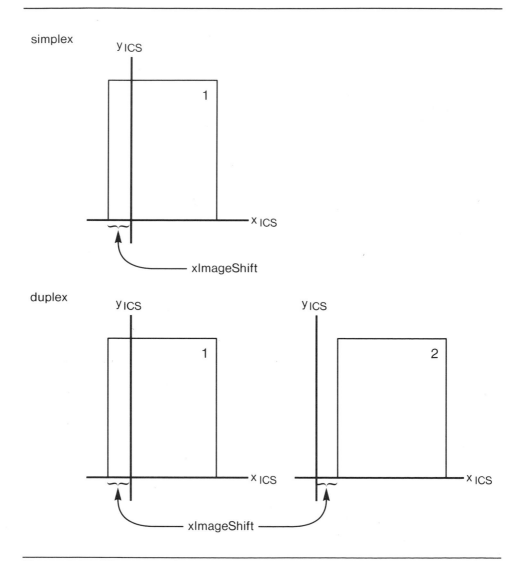

Figure 8.14 The xImageShift instruction shifts the position of the ICS on the page to provide a binding offset.

It usually prints duplex but, if it must be printed simplex, then the back of the cover page is skipped. The onSimplex and mediaSelect instructions account for a document of 10,000 pages, but the document can be smaller. The document is stapled, and successive copies alternate between output positions 1 and 2. The binding offset is 1 centimeter.

Example 8.19

```
{                                      --begin the instructions body--
    Identifier "plex"                  --plex instruction--
    Identifier "duplex"                --print duplex--
    Identifier "onSimplex"             --onSimplex instruction--
    1 1 1 0 10000 1 6 MAKEVEC          --second page not printed simplex--
    Identifier "media"                 --media instruction--
    Identifier "mediumName"            --describe a media by name--
    Identifier "Xerox"
    Identifier "CoverStock"
    2 MAKEVEC                          --and this is the name--
    2 MAKEVEC                          --total description of a medium--
    Identifier "mediumName"            --describe a second medium by name--
    Identifier "DefaultMedium"         --which is the default--
    2 MAKEVEC                          --total description of a medium--
    2 MAKEVEC                          --vector of all media (two of them)--
    Identifier "mediaSelect"           --mediaSelect instruction--
    1                                  --one copy--
    2 1 10000 2 4 MAKEVEC              --cover stock--
                                       --for both sides, pages 1 and 2--
    2 MAKEVEC                          --vector for run of copies--
    Identifier "outputPosition"        --outputPosition instruction--
    1 1 1 2 4 MAKEVEC                  --alternate positions 1 and 2--
    Identifier "finishing"             --finishing instruction--
    Identifier "CornerStaple"
    Identifier "xImageShift"           --xImageShift instruction--
    0.01                               --binding offset of 0.01 meter--
    14 MAKEVEC                         --total instructions vector--
}                                      --end of the instructions body--
```

Storing Information About the Document

Besides controlling document makeup and finishing, the instructions body provides a convenient place to store document information. The instructions body builds a property vector so that you can add new properties if you wish to store information about the document. The printer looks for the properties it can deal with and ignores all others. However, if you do add a "private" property, you should use a universal name as the property name to avoid confusion with other private properties or Interpress extensions.

The instructions that hold information about the document can be grouped into two classes: instructions that hold information for the break page (a page that separates and identifies print jobs) and instructions that specify what resources the document requires. The *docCreationDate*, *docCreator*, and *docName* instructions allow you to save identifying information in the document. This information also might be used by the printer for display on the document's break page.

The *docComment* instruction provides a comment to be printed on the break page. Because this information is intended for the break page, there are limits on its font. With the *breakPageFont* instruction, you can specify one to be used on the break page. This allows you to print the break-page information in a specific language. If, for example, the document is in Arabic, you can arrange to have the break-page information printed in an Arabic font as well.

Four instructions indicate what the document contains: *insertFileNames, environmentNames, pixelArrayTransformationUses,* and *set.* Some printers use these instructions to improve their performance. This information also might be used to route the document to the best printer for the job. The set instruction tells which Interpress types and primitives are required to print the document. A document requiring only the Commercial Set might be routed to a faster printer than one requiring the Professional Graphics Set.

The insertFileNames instruction lists the files that your document references, so that the printer can acquire these files before printing.

The environmentNames instruction lists the printer resources (fonts, colors, decompressors) that are needed to print the document perfectly. The document might be routed to a printer that has the necessary resources, or the printer might acquire the needed resources before printing your document.

The pixelArrayTransformationUses instruction indicates the resolution and orientation of the pixel arrays in the document. It can be used to route the document to a matching printer.

Line-Printer Printing

The document structure model we have used thus far considers each print job as a separate document. This model may not always be appropriate. For example, a line printer may see only a sequence of pages, rather than individual jobs. An Interpress printer can support this model by giving the printer a single, very long document. When the printer is initialized, an initial BEGIN token is generated, and each page is sent as an Interpress page body. The printer can be given an overall instructions body with a media instruction that lists the supported media, although the instructions body does not contain job information. However, content instructions can supply control information to the printer on a page-by-page basis. The instructions that can be used in a content-instructions body are different from those in the document's instructions body, but they cover many of the same functions. For example, consider the problem of selecting page media. Suppose a page in the sequence requires a special preprinted form. The *pageMediaSelect* instruction, which corresponds to the mediaSelect instruction, tells the printer what medium to use on the following page, or block of pages.

Page-Level Editing

Interpress strictly enforces page independence. Furthermore, the skeleton structure makes it fairly easy to locate the page bodies within Interpress masters. This makes it simple to do content-independent page-level editing, such as extraction, merging, and overlaying of pages in documents. These actions treat the page body as the basic unit; that is, you never look to see what is inside the page body. This and following sections consider how to construct programs that extract pages from Interpress masters and combine them to form new masters.

A prerequisite for page-level editing is finding the pages. The pages in an Interpress master using the Xerox encoding are located by top-level parsing of the master, with attention paid to only the skeleton tokens. The Pascal program in Example 8.20 does this. The work is done in the *findpages* procedure, which skims over the header and then parses the master. This program ignores preambles and instructions bodies, but could be modified to note them as well. The *bodylevel* counter distinguishes the top-level bodies in the skeleton from other nested bodies. The *blocklevel* counter keeps track of nested blocks, so that you can tell whether an END token means the end of the master or just a nested block. The program uses the procedures *getbyte* and *skipbytes* to access the tokens in the file. The internals of these procedures are system dependent and are not shown. The *findpages* procedure stores the starting and ending byte positions for each page body in the *pagedirectory* array.

Example 8.20

```
program findpagesprog (ipmaster, output);
const
   maxpages = 100;
   begintoken = 102;
   endtoken = 103;
   contentinstructionstoken = 105;
   leftbracetoken = 106;
   rightbracetoken = 107;
   spacecharacter = 32;
   shortopcodes = 128;
   longopcodes = 160;
   shortsequencecodes = 192;
   longsequencecodes = 224;
type
```

```
      pageposition = (startofpage, endofpage);
      byte = 0..255;
var
   ipmaster: file of byte;
   pagedirectory: array [pageposition, 1..maxpages] of integer;
   bytecount: integer;
   pagecount: integer;
   i: integer;
   savebytepair: integer;
function getbyte: integer;
begin
(* extract the next byte from the ipmaster file *)
   bytecount := bytecount + 1;
end;
procedure skipbytes(howmany: integer);
begin
(* skip the next howmany bytes in the ipmaster file *)
   bytecount := bytecount + howmany;
end;
procedure findpages;
var
   ininstructions: Boolean;
   inpreamble: Boolean;
   foundend: Boolean;
   bodylevel: integer;
   blocklevel: Integer;
   token: integer;
begin
   ininstructions := true;
   inpreamble := false;
   foundend := false;
   bodylevel := 0;
   blocklevel := 0;
   (* skip past header *)
   repeat token := getbyte
   until token = spacecharacter;
   while not (foundend or eof (ipmaster)) do
      begin (* main parsing loop *)
         token := getbyte;
         if token < shortopcodes
         then token := getbyte (* skip rest of number *)
         else if token < longopcodes
         then (* skip short op *)
         else if token < shortsequencecodes
         then begin (* check the long op *)
            (* get operator *)
            token := (token - longopcode) * 256 + getbyte;
               if token = begintoken
               then begin (* note start of a block *)
                  ininstructions := false;
                  inpreamble := true;
```

```
                           blocklevel := blocklevel + 1;
                           end
                     else if token = endtoken
                     then begin (* check for end of master *)
                        blocklevel := blocklevel - 1;
                        if blocklevel = 0 then foundend := true;
                        end
                     else if token = contentinstructionstoken
                     then ininstructions := true
                     else if token = leftbrace token
                     then begin (* start of a body *)
                        bodylevel := bodylevel + 1;
                        if (bodylevel = 1)
                           and not ininstructions
                           and not inpreamble
                        then begin (* it is a page body *)
                           pagecount := pagecount + 1;
                           (* save starting position of the page *)
                           pagedirectory[startofpage, pagecount] := bytecount
                           end
                        end
                     else if token = rightbracetoken
                     then begin (* end of a body *)
                        bodylevel := bodylevel - 1;
                        (* if it is a page body, save its ending position *)
                        if ininstructions
                        then ininstructions := false
                        else if inpreamble
                        then inpreamble := false
                        else if bodylevel = 0
                        then pagedirectory[endofpage, pagecount] := bytecount
                        end
                  end
               else if token < longsequencecodes
               then skipbytes(getbyte) (*skip past short sequence *)
               else begin (* skip past long sequence *)
                  token := getbyte;
                  token := 256 * token + getbyte;
                  token := 256 * token + getbyte:
                  skipbytes(token)
                  end
            end
   end;
begin (* program which locates the page bodies in ipmaster *)
   reset (ipmaster):
   bytecount := 0;
   pagecount := 0;
   findpages;
   (* at this point page count contains the number of pages
      and pagedirectory contains their boundary positions *)
end
```

Procedures such as this enable you to locate preambles and page bodies. Now we shall consider some of the tasks that might be done with these procedures.

Page Selection

Perhaps the simplest page-level operation is page selection; that is, creating a new master containing a subset of the pages in the original master (see Figure 8.15).

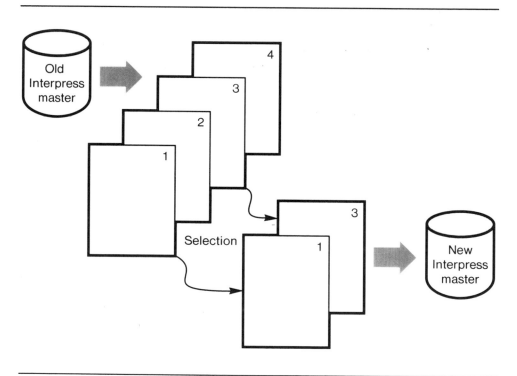

Figure 8.15 Selecting pages.

This is similar to the pageSelect instruction, except that the editing function permanently removes the page bodies; they no longer occupy space in the Interpress master file, and there is no danger of their reappearance. The new master has the same preamble as the original and the selected page bodies. Consider an original document of the form shown in Example 8.21.

Example 8.21

```
BEGIN
   {preamble 0}
   {page 1}
   {page 2}
   {page 3}
   {page 4}
END
```

If you select just the odd-numbered pages, the result is Example 8.22.

Example 8.22

```
BEGIN
   {preamble 0}
   {page 1}
   {page 3}
END
```

If the document has a nested block structure, then the result document should preserve that structure, so that each page body gets the proper page initial frame.

Consider the original document shown in Example 8.23.

Example 8.23

```
BEGIN
   {preamble 0}
   {page 1}
   BEGIN
      {preamble 2.0}
      {page 2.1}
   END
   BEGIN
      {preamble 3.0}
      {page 3.1}
      {page 3.2}
   END
END
```

The result of selecting the odd pages is shown in Example 8.24.

Example 8.24

```
BEGIN
  {preamble 0}
  {page 1}
  BEGIN
    {preamble 2.0}     --empty--
  END
  BEGIN
    {preamble 3.0}
    {page 3.1}
  END
END
```

Of course, there are no page bodies included for the first nested block, and it contributes nothing to the master. So a better result is that shown in Example 8.25.

Example 8.25

```
BEGIN
  {preamble 0}
  {page 1}
  BEGIN
    {preamble 3.0}
    {page 3.1}
  END
END
```

If there are content instructions in the original document, then those corresponding to selected pages or blocks with selected pages can be included in the result document. In general, copying content instructions is no problem because they apply to the entire block or page. They do not refer to the structure within a block that may be altered by your selection. This is not true of the document instructions body; in general, a new document instructions body must be built for the page-level editing functions that alter the master's structure.

Merging Documents

Another Interpress editing function constructs a new master from pages selected from two or more given masters (see Figure 8.16). The simplest case has no nested blocks and identical preambles, as would occur if you had created the original masters using a "standard" preamble. For this simple case, the new master's preamble is a copy of the preamble in the source masters, and its page bodies correspond to the selected pages. For example,

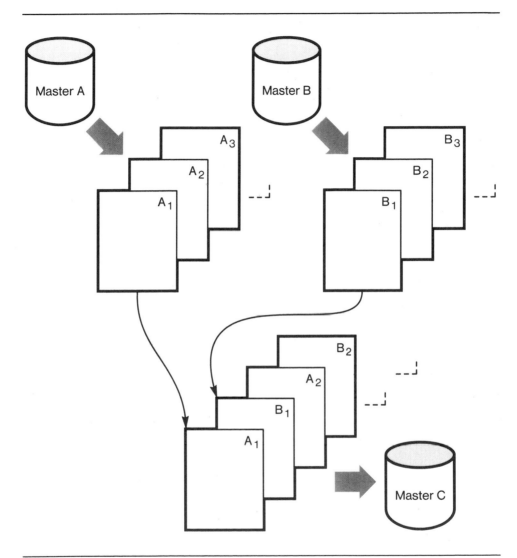

Figure 8.16 Merging documents.

suppose Interpress master A contains a cover page followed by captions and descriptions of a set of pictures, and master B contains the pictorial images. You require the odd pages to come from master A, and the even pages from master B so that pictures and captions are on facing pages.

Example 8.26

```
BEGIN              --Master A--
   {preamble}
   {page A1}
   {page A2}
      . . .
END

BEGIN              --Master B--
   {preamble}
   {page B1}
   {page B2}
      . . .
END
```

The merged document looks like Example 8.27.

Example 8.27

```
BEGIN              --Master C--
   {preamble}
   {page A1}
   {page B1}
   {page A2}
   (page B2}
      . . .
END
```

The merging of documents with different preambles is a little more complicated because you must ensure that each page gets the same initial frame its source master generates. The easiest technique uses nested blocks. Consider again the example of merging pictures and captions. The given masters are shown in Example 8.28.

Example 8.28

```
BEGIN              --Master A--
   {preamble A}
   {page A1}
   {page A2}
      . . .
END

BEGIN              --Master B--
   {preamble B}
   {page B1}
   {page B2}
      . . .
END
```

The resulting master is shown in Example 8.29.

Example 8.29

```
BEGIN              --Master C--
  {preamble A}
  {page A1}
  BEGIN
    {preamble B}
    {page B1}
  END
  {page A2}
  BEGIN
    {preamble B}
    (page B2}
  END
  .  .  .
END
```

Or, you could use preamble B in the outermost block and wrap the pages from master A in blocks with preamble A. You could also leave the outermost preamble empty and wrap all pages in blocks for a symmetric but somewhat larger and less efficient master, as shown in Example 8.30.

Example 8.30

```
BEGIN              --Master C--
  { }
  BEGIN {preamble A} {page A1} END
  BEGIN {preamble B} {page B1} END
  BEGIN {preamble A} {page A2} END
  BEGIN {preamble B} (page B2} END
  .  .  .
END
```

Page bodies from complex masters containing nested blocks can be extracted and merged. You simply wrap each page body in a sequence of blocks that copy the block structure and preambles for the page body in its original master.

Geometric Transformations of Pages

Another page-level action you can perform is applying a page transformation. For example, you can translate the page to center it or to impose a binding offset, scale it to fit a larger or smaller medium, or rotate it for landscape or portrait orientation. You can do transformations easily, provided that the document uses only CONCATT to change the current transformation. If your documents follow this rule, then you can transform a page by concatenating a new outer transformation to the current transformation just before executing the page body. If the document concatenates new transformations, your initial transformation is always included, resulting in the desired behavior. Say we want to prefix each page of the master in Example 8.31 with a transformation.

Example 8.31

```
BEGIN
  {preamble}
  {page 1}
  {page 2}
    . . .
END
```

The resulting master is shown in Example 8.32.

Example 8.32

```
BEGIN
  {preamble}
  {transformation CONCATT page 1}
  {transformation CONCATT page 2}
    . . .
END
```

For example, suppose your document will be bound at the top (head-to-toe printing), and you want a vertical binding offset. All pages should be shifted down 1 centimeter, and even pages should be rotated 180 degrees and translated back onto the medium. The resulting master is shown in Example 8.33 (see Figure 8.17).

Example 8.33

```
BEGIN
  {preamble}
  {0 -0.01 TRANSLATE CONCATT page 1}
  {180 ROTATE 0.2159 0.2694 TRANSLATE CONCATT CONCATT page 2}
    . . .
END
```

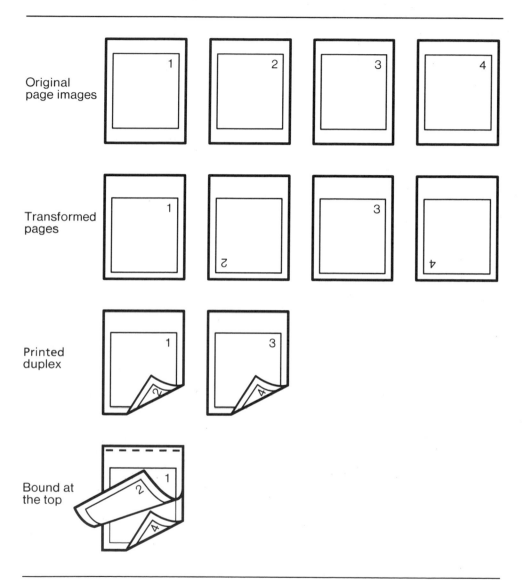

Figure 8.17 Transforming pages for head-to-toe printing.

As a second example, consider converting from portrait to landscape orientation (see Figure 8.18). You should rotate each page 90 degrees, scale it by three-quarters so that an 11-inch page fits in 8.5 inches, and translate and center the image. The resulting master is shown in Example 8.34.

Example 8.34

```
BEGIN
  {preamble}
  {
     90 ROTATE
     0.75 SCALE
     0.212725 0.0587375 TRANSLATE
     CONCATT CONCATT CONCATT
     page 1
  }
  . . .
END
```

Original
image

Rotate and
scale

Rotate
paper

Figure 8.18 Transformations to print a portrait image in landscape orientation.

You can clip pages in a similar manner. Since Interpress clipping regions restrict the visible area, you can clip a page by setting the clipper imager variable. For example, suppose you wish to extract the first page and the top 14 centimeters of the second page from a document. The resulting master is shown in Example 8.35.

Example 8.35

```
BEGIN
  {preamble}
  {page 1}
  {0.0 0.1394 0.2159 0.14 CLIPRECTANGLE page 2}
END
```

Overlays, Signatures, Forms, and Pictures

You may wish to combine several page images into a single page. An example is combining a picture from one master with text from a second master (see Figure 8.19). Another example is signature printing, which involves placing several page images on each sheet of paper such that the paper can be folded and stitched to make a booklet (see Figure 8.20). A third example combines a form with the text that fills it.

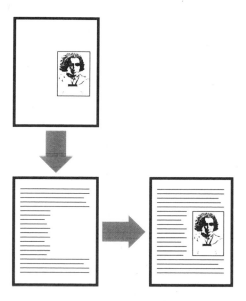

Figure 8.19 A page overlay to combine text with an image.

In general terms, you start with two page bodies {page A} and {page B}, and wish to combine them into a single page body {page AB}. As a first attempt, you might just append the two page bodies {page A page B}. What is wrong with this? First, you must require both pages to expect similar preambles so that they have consistent initial frames. Further, page A must leave the Interpress state (the stack, the frame, and the imager variables) in a clean condition for page B. Because there is no guarantee that these conditions hold, a better approach protects page B from damage by page A. Assume for the moment that the preambles are identical and concentrate on protecting stack, frame, and imager variables.

There is an Interpress mechanism for protecting frame and imager variables; namely, the save and restore operations that occur with DOSAVE,

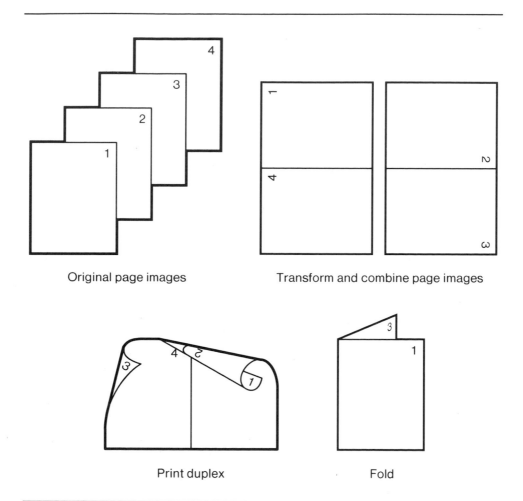

Figure 8.20 Arranging several images on a page to form a simple signature.

DOSAVESIMPLEBODY, and DOSAVEALL. Although DOSAVEALL gives the most protection, its use entails turning all of page A into a composed operator, which the printer would have to store in case it is called. This can be done, but a more efficient approach uses DOSAVESIMPLEBODY to protect the frame and nonpersistent imager variables.

```
{DOSAVESIMPLEBODY {page A} page B}
```

If you want total protection, the persistent imager variables must be reset to their default values between page A and page B. The default values are all

0 for these four variables and can easily be reset explicitly, as shown in Example 8.36.

Example 8.36

```
{
    DOSAVESIMPLEBODY {page A}   --page A, protecting frame and--
                               --nonpersistent imager variables--
    0  0  ISET                 --reset persistent imager variables--
    0  1  ISET
    0  2  ISET
    0  3  ISET
    page B
}
```

The DOSAVESIMPLEBODY and ISETs take care of the frame and imager variables but you might still wish to guarantee an empty stack. To clear the stack, count its elements, combine them into a vector, and pop the vector, as shown in Example 8.37.

Example 8.37

```
{
    0 MARK                       --mark the stack--
    DOSAVESIMPLEBODY {page A}    --page A, protecting frame and--
                                 --and nonpersistent imager variables--
    0 0 ISET 0 1 ISET            --reset persistent imager variables--
    0 2 ISET 0 3 ISET
    COUNT MAKEVEC POP UNMARK0    --clear the stack--
    page B
}
```

This technique safely combines two pages with identical preambles and places page B directly on top of page A.

Often, you want to insert a transformation before each page so that the pages can be shifted or aligned in some way. An example is two-up printing, where two page images are reduced, rotated, and placed side by side on one piece of paper. Here you might rotate both pages by 90 degrees, scale them by two-thirds, and place page A at the bottom (left in landscape orientation), page B at the top (right in landscape). Example 8.38 prints a two-up page.

Example 8.38

```
{                              --start of the combined page--
    90 ROTATE                  --rotate 90 degrees--
    2 3 DIV SCALE              --scale to two-thirds--
```

```
    0.201 0 TRANSLATE              --origin at bottom right--
    CONCATT CONCATT CONCATT
    0 MARK
    DOSAVESIMPLEBODY {page A}      --image page A--
    0 0 ISET 0 1 ISET             --reset everything--
    0 2 ISET 0 3 ISET
    COUNT MAKEVEC POP UNMARKO
    0.21 0 TRANSLATE               --move origin to middle right--
    CONCATT
    page B                         --image page B--
}                                  --end of the combined page--
```

Now consider what you do when the preambles differ. You might use preamble B as the preamble for the combined page, but you still need to create the appropriate initial frame for page A. You cannot use nested blocks, but you can copy the preamble for page A into its body. If the preamble just sets up an initial frame, and does not dirty the stack or imager variables, then this is all that is needed, as shown in Example 8.39.

Example 8.39

```
BEGIN
    {preamble B}
    {
        0 MARK
        DOSAVESIMPLEBODY {preamble A page A}
        0 0 ISET 0 1 ISET 0 2 ISET 0 3 ISET
        COUNT MAKEVEC POP UNMARKO
        Page B
    }
END
```

If there is a danger of preamble A altering the image variables or leaving elements on the stack, you can protect page A by inserting commands to set the relevant imager variables explicitly to their default values and to clear the stack.

Forms can be handled as a one-page Interpress master that is overlaid on pages. You can develop the form as a separate master and print it to validate its correctness. When you wish to include the form on a page of a document, you can extract its page body and combine it with the document page. To make the combination easy, you should construct the form master with an empty preamble, and take care that it leaves the stack and imager variables in their original state.

For the following form master:

```
BEGIN { } {form} END
```

the combined page is simply

```
{DOSAVESIMPLEBODY {form} page}
```

The sequenceInsertFile feature of the Xerox encoding of Interpress is particularly useful for forms (see Figure 8.21). This encoding places the name of a file in the Interpress master. The effect is to replace the file name by the contents of the file. The details of how this is done depend on the format of the file, to allow for precompiled forms on some printers. All printers, however, should accept the *Interpress fragment* format. An Interpress fragment is identified by a header of the form "Interpress/Xerox/3.0/filetype/N.M " where the character string "filetype/N.M" names the fragment type and version number. You might place the header "Interpress/Xerox/3.0/myform/1.0 " in your forms, for example. (The printer treats any file with a header in this format as an Interpress fragment, no matter what characters are present for "filetype" and "N.M" so that this portion of the header is solely for your use.)

An Interpress fragment file contains a series of Interpress tokens between BEGIN and END tokens. On insertion, the header and everything up to and including the BEGIN token are skipped, the tokens between the BEGIN and END are inserted and replace the sequenceInsertFile reference, and the END token is skipped. If you construct an Interpress master for a form that looks like

```
"Interpress/Xerox/3.0 " BEGIN { } {form} END
```

then you can convert it into the following fragment:

```
"Interpress/Xerox/3.0/myform/1.0 " BEGIN {form} END
```

This fragment is suitable for use with sequenceInsertFile.

The form can be given a name "formfile," and then inserted into a file by simply referencing its file name. A page body that includes the form looks like

```
{DOSAVESIMPLEBODY sequenceInsertFile "formfile" rest-of-page}
```

The sequenceInsertFile encoding also is used to include sampled images in a document. You can place the sampled image in a separate file and insert it in the document. This technique is preferable to placing the image directly in the page body, because sampled images tend to be resolution dependent. If you place a 300-spot-per-inch (spi) image in a master and then send it to a printer with 1000-spi resolution or perform some scaling transformation on the page (such as in printing it two-up), the image probably will not look very good.

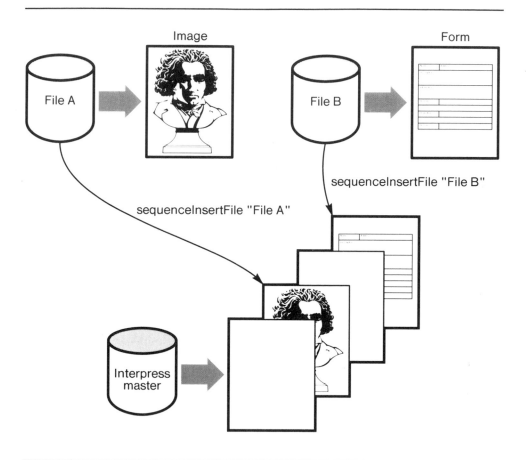

Figure 8.21 SequenceInsertFile lets you insert images into a page body of an Interpress master.

You need a version of the image designed for the actual display size and resolution. Even for printers at the same resolution, you may want versions of the image that match halftone patterns to the display or printer technology. So you may have a 300-spi version of the image for your proof printer and a 1000-spi version for your film printer. You do not want separate copies of the document master, however, because they may be inconsistent (and will double storage requirements). The solution is to make a single master that references the image by means of the sequenceInsertFile. Along with the Interpress master for the document, you send the 300-spi version of the image to the proof printer and you send the 1000-spi version to the film printer.

An Interpress fragment for inserting images is described in the Xerox Raster Encoding Standard. The header for this fragment is

```
"Interpress/Xerox/3.0/RasterEncoding/1.0 "
```

Executing the tokens in the fragment places eight elements on the stack. The first is a vector that contains the x and y scale factors (in meters per pixel) at which the image is expected to be printed. The second and third are the width and height in pixels of the image's rectangular bounding box. The fourth element is either a pixel array to be used as an image mask or zero. If zero, the mask is assumed to be the rectangular bounding box. The fifth element is either a pixel array to be used as an ink (sampled color) or zero, implying the image has no sampled color. The sixth element is a color operator used with the sampled color. The seventh is a property vector containing information about the image that is not needed for printing. The eighth is the signature number 13086, which identifies the result as indeed coming from a raster-encoding fragment.

If your document includes a sequenceInsertFile of a raster-encoding fragment, the inserted file places these eight elements on the stack. You can then use the elements to draw the image with MASKPIXEL, or with MASKRECTANGLE and MAKESAMPLEDBLACK or MAKESAMPLEDCOLOR.

If you use sequenceInsertFile to reference multiple versions of an image, confusion still can occur because the versions use the same file name. Interpress has the *insertFileMapping* printing instruction to avoid this confusion (see Figure 8.22). As a printing instruction, it may arrive either in the instructions body or from the printing protocol (with the printing protocol taking precedence). The instruction is a vector of pairs of file names. Each pair maps between a name in a sequenceInsertFile construct, and an actual name used for the insertion. Thus, you can use an alias file name within the master, and then bind the file you actually want to use just before printing. For example, you can include

```
sequenceInsertFile "myPicture"
```

in the document, but, when you send that document to your proof printer, include in the printing protocol an insertFileMapping instruction for

```
myPicture, myPicture300
```

The file myPicture300 is used by the proof printer. If you send the document to your film printer, include the insertFileMapping instruction for

```
myPicture, myPicture1000
```

The printer will then insert the file myPicture1000 into the document.

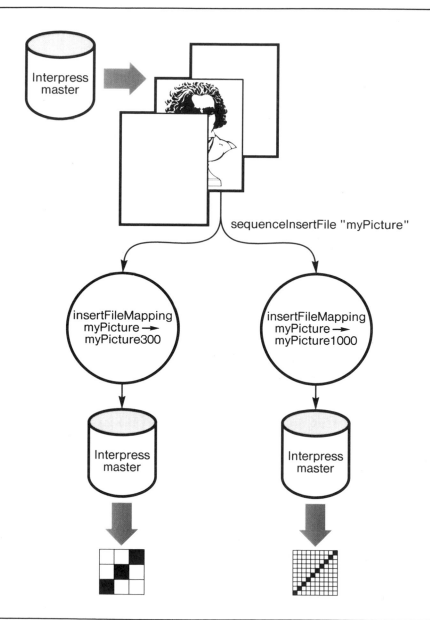

Figure 8.22 InsertFileMapping maps the file named in the master to the appropriate real file for the particular printer.

Protecting Against Errors

Whenever you insert files into a master, something could go wrong: the wrong file may be used; or the file may be corrupted, incorrect, or unavailable. Here's how to guard against these problems. Processing of an insertion can be divided into two stages: the actual file insertion, and the processing of the insertion. If the printer uses a bad or nonexistent file, an error is generated in the insertion stage. If the wrong file is used, the results of the insertion will be different from what you expect. You might check for appropriate results with the Interpress IF operator. This is why the raster-encoding fragment leaves a special integer on the top of the stack. After inserting a raster-encoding fragment, you can check for this integer; if it is not there, you know something has gone wrong. If you discover a problem, you can call the Interpress ERROR operator. Errors may also be discovered by the printer–for example, missing arguments or arguments with incorrect type.

When a master error occurs, the printer performs a *mark recovery* to reach a clean state so that execution can continue. On a mark recovery, the stack is popped until a mark is found; composed operators are exited until the operator which placed the mark is found; and operators in the input stream are skipped until an UNMARK0 is reached. This means that you can use the placement of MARK and UNMARK0 commands to limit the effects of error conditions. Suppose you wish to perform an imaging function that involves an inserted file. Often, the effects of the function are localized in that you start with a clean state, prepare for the insertion, perform the insertion, complete the imaging operation, and return to the starting state. Marks can be used to reach the clean state in the event of an error. Consider the Interpress instructions in Example 8.40.

Example 8.40

```
0 MARK
DOSAVESIMPLEBODY
{
    . . .                           --prepare for image insertion--
    sequenceInsertFile "filename"
    . . .                           --complete the image--
}
UNMARK0
```

In the event of an error within the body, a mark recovery returns the stack, frame, and nonpersistent imager variables to the state they were in just before the body was executed. Further instructions are executed following the UNMARK0. This is the same state as is present when the body executes normally, so the remainder of the master is protected from the error.

The protection scheme just described works for processing that has no long-term effects on the imager variables or frame. It also can be extended to situations in which you want a permanent change by providing default values in case of errors. This may best be seen with an example. Suppose you are to read in a raster-encoding-format Interpress fragment and extract the second pixel array, turn it into a sampled color, store it in frame variable 10, and also give it to the color imager variable for use in the rest of the page body. You will use a 50-percent gray constant color as the default color in the event of an error. The Interpress master that does this is shown in Example 8.41.

Example 8.41

```
MARK                                --mark the stack in case of error--
0.5 MAKEGRAY
10 FSET                             --50-percent gray in frame[10]--
DOSAVESIMPLEBODY
{                                   --insert the RES file--
   sequenceInsertFile "ResColorFile"
   13086 EQ NOT                     --check file's signature--
                                    --to see if it is RES--
   IF                               --if not--
   {
      String "Not an RES file"
      0 ERROR
   }                                --generate an error--
                                    --and skip to UNMARK0--
   POP                              --remove editing parameters--
                                    --make PCS-to-DCS transform--
   6 1 ROLL DUP 0 GET EXCH 1 GET SCALE2 CONCATT
   4 IGET EXCH MAKESAMPLEDCOLOR     --make the sampled color--
   4 3 ROLL POP POP POP             --remove other stack elements--
}
10 FSET                             --place sampled color in frame[10]--
UNMARK0                             --skip to here if an error occurs--
10 FGET 13 ISET                     --set color to value in frame[10]--
```

After placing a mark on the stack, a default value for the color is created and stored in frame variable 10. Then the DOSAVESIMPLEBODY creates the new color. The raster-encoding file is inserted, and a check sees whether the file performed as expected. Next the property vector is popped, the vector of scale factors rolled to the top of the stack, the scales extracted, and a transformation made. This transformation is concatenated to the current transformation and this net transformation, along with the pixel array and color operator from the file, are used to create a sampled color. The remaining three arguments are removed, and the body is finished. If all has been successful, the constructed color is left on the stack, and may be copied into frame variable 10 to replace the default value. If any master error occurs—whether in insertion of the file, in our check for the special integer, or in the subsequent calculation—the printer skips to the UNMARK0 instruction, clears the stack, and restores the frame and imager variables to their values before the DOSAVESIMPLEBODY. In particular, frame variable 10 is restored to 50-percent gray. Thus, if any error occurs, the default value is copied from the frame to the color imager variable. If all goes well, the value calculated from the file is used.

A similar technique determines whether an error occurs without sacrificing protection. You can mark the stack and set a frame variable to true, then execute the dangerous code. Next you reset the frame variable to false and UNMARK0. If an error occurs, the reset of the frame variable is skipped, and its value remains true. If there are no errors, normal processing resets it to false.

Block-Level Editing

In publishing applications, large documents often are constructed from small documents or document fragments. This allows several people to work simultaneously, writing, editing, and revising separate components. Small sections are faster and easier to work on than large documents, and documents often have a natural structure (chapters, sections, pages) that promote this division of labor. As various components are completed, they can be encoded as Interpress files to be printed and proofed. At the end of this process, you are faced with assembling the components into the full document. It would be handy if you could easily combine the component Interpress files: page independence and the nested-block structure of the Interpress skeleton make this easy to do.

As an example, consider the problem of concatenating two documents. You want to append document B to document A. Suppose their Interpress masters are as shown in Example 8.42.

Example 8.42

```
    BEGIN {preamble A} {page A1} {page A2} . . . END  --document A--
and
    BEGIN {preamble B} {page B1} {page B2} . . . END  --document B--
```

One way to combine the documents is to construct a new master that includes the two original masters as nested blocks, as shown in Example 8.43.

Example 8.43

```
    BEGIN
      { }
```

```
        BEGIN {preamble A} {page A1} {page A2} . . . END
        BEGIN {preamble B} {page B1} {page B2} . . . END
END
```

You can also add new pages. Example 8.44 adds a new cover page to the document, which includes documents A and B as components.

Example 8.44

```
BEGIN
   {cover preamble} {cover page}
   BEGIN {preamble A} {page A1} {page A2} . . . END
   BEGIN {preamble B} {page B1} {page B2} . . . END
END
```

Note that the result of combining two or more Interpress documents also is an Interpress document. These can be further combined with other Interpress files to make an even larger master. Thus, sections can be built by combining groups of pages, chapters made by combining sections, books or reports constructed by combining chapters, and so on.

In Example 8.44, a new master is formed by copying the blocks from the component masters directly, the only alteration being removing the header and any instructions.

An alternate way of combining masters, called sequenceInsertMaster, avoids copying component masters by simply referencing the component Interpress file. It is an encoding construct that gives the file name of an Interpress master to be inserted. For example, using sequenceInsertMaster in our last problem of combining two masters with a cover yields Example 8.45 (see Figure 8.23).

Example 8.45

```
BEGIN
   {cover preamble} {cover page}
   sequenceInsertMaster "Master A"
   sequenceInsertMaster "Master B"
END
```

Combining masters in this way is quick and easy. The resulting master is small because it includes references only to the component files and not to their contents. Furthermore, if a component is revised, the overall document automatically contains the revision. There is no danger of inconsistency between the component and the combined masters.

SequenceInsertMaster acts much like sequenceInsertFile, but there are some differences. SequenceInsertMaster is used only at the skeleton level

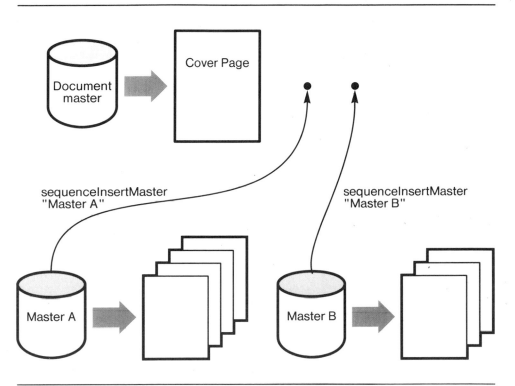

Figure 8.23 Building a document with sequenceInsertMaster.

between page bodies, whereas sequenceInsertFile can only occur within a page body. SequenceInsertFile inserts a sequence of Interpress tokens between, but not including, the BEGIN and END tokens. SequenceInsertMaster inserts an entire block–everything between and including the BEGIN and END tokens. It also includes blocks nested within the block being inserted.

When a master is used as a component in an overall master, only the block is used, and not its instructions body; the instructions are discarded. This is because the instructions for the component document may not make sense in the context of the combined document. You can still specify instructions for the component block by means of a content-instructions body. Content instructions apply to entire blocks and not to selected pages within the block. The contentPageSelect instruction includes the block in various copies, but this includes or excludes all the pages within the block. There is also a content plex instruction, which switches between simplex and duplex for the block. As an example, consider a document of three parts–a table of contents, a main report, and an appendix–each constructed as a separate Interpress master.

The problem is to construct an overall master that prints the table of contents in simplex mode and the remainder of the document in duplex. Three copies of the full document should be printed, followed by two copies that exclude the appendix (see Example 8.46 and Figure 8.24).

Example 8.46

```
Header "Interpress/Xerox/3.0 " --header--
{                                 --start of the instructions body--
   Identifier "copySelect"        --copy select instruction--
   5 1 2 MAKEVEC                   --select first five copies--
   Identifier "plex"              --plex instructions--
   Identifier "duplex"            --request duplex--
   4 MAKEVEC                       --make instructions property vector--
}                                 --end of the instructions body--
BEGIN                             --start of the top-level block--
   CONTENTINSTRUCTIONS            --content instructions--
                                  --for a nested block--
   {                              --start of content instructions body--
      Identifier "contentplex"
      Identifier "simplex"        --use simplex for this block--
      2 MAKEVEC                    --make content instructions vector--
   }                              --end of content instructions body--
                                  --insert the nested block with TOC--
   sequenceInsertMaster "TableOfContents"
                                  --insert another nested block--
                                  --(document instructions apply)--
   sequenceInsertMaster "MainReport"
   CONTENTINSTRUCTIONS            --content instructions--
                                  --for the third nested block--
   {                              --start of content instructions body--
      Identifier "contentPageSelect"   --page-selection instruction--
      3 1 2 0 4 MAKEVEC           --include this block--
                                  --on first three copies--
      2 MAKEVEC                    --make content instructions vector--
   }                              --end of content instructions body--
   sequenceInsertMaster "Appendix" --insert the nested block--
END                               --end of the master--
```

In Example 8.46, an instructions body requests five duplex copies. A content-instructions body temporarily changes the plex value to simplex for the block containing the table of contents, which is inserted by a sequenceInsertMaster. Next, the block containing the main report is inserted. Then, another content instructions body that contains a contentPageSelect instruction says to print pages from the following block on the first three copies, but to skip them on the next two copies. This applies to the final block, containing the appendix.

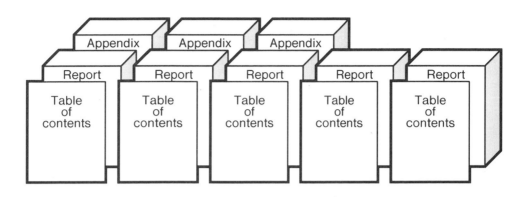

Figure 8.24 The result of Example 8.46.

Content instructions can precede either blocks or page bodies. So the pageMediaSelect and pageOnSimplex instructions, described earlier in this chapter, can apply to entire blocks of pages. For example, you can change the medium for a block. You also can use an instruction such as contentPageSelect with individual pages.

Some content instructions perform the same functions as master instructions, and each nested block can have its own content instructions. This means that a page can have several layers of instructions dictating its behavior. When instructions are inconsistent, you should understand which specification takes priority (for most instructions, the innermost one wins). In Example 8.46, the outer instructions body specifies duplex, but for the table of contents there is an inner content-instructions body that specifies simplex. So, for this block, the inner simplex specification is used.

An exception to the "innermost wins" rule is the behavior of the two instructions, insertFileMapping and contentInsertFileMapping. Recall that insertFileMapping maps a file name alias in a sequenceInsertFile encoding to the actual file name. The contentInsertFileMapping is similar but applies only to the following block or page body. When these instructions are nested, the mappings accumulate rather than replace one another. A file name undergoes the innermost mapping, then that result undergoes the next mapping layer, and so on. For example, suppose the document has blocks for Chapters 1 and 2, and that in Chapter 1 there is a sequenceInsertFile insertion of Figure1. A content instruction can map the file name Figure1 to the name Chap1Fig1, and a document instruction can then map Chap1Fig1 to Chap1Fig1at300, as shown in Example 8.47.

Example 8.47

```
Header "Interpress/Xerox/3.0 "  --header--
{                                --document instructions body--
   Identifier "InsertFileMapping"
   String "Chap1Fig1"            --alias name at document level--
   String "Chap1Fig1at300"       --actual file name--
   2 MAKEVEC                      --mapping--
   1 MAKEVEC                      --vector of mapping--
   2 MAKEVEC                      --instructions vector--
}
BEGIN                            --start of top-level block--
   { }                           --preamble--
   CONTENTINSTRUCTIONS
   {
      Identifier "contentInsertFileMapping"
      String "Figure1"           --alias name at chapter level--
      String "Chap1Fig1"         --alias name at document level--
      2 MAKEVEC                   --mapping--
      1 MAKEVEC                   --vector of mapping--
      2 MAKEVEC                   --content instructions--
                                 --property vector--
   }
   BEGIN          ,              --block for Chapter 1--
      {Chapter 1 preamble}
      {  . . .
         sequenceInsertFile "Figure1"
                                 --the file name gets mapped--
                                 --from Figure1 to Chap1Fig1 to--
      }                          --Chap1Fig1at300 before inserting--
      . . .
   END
   BEGIN
      {Chapter 2 preamble}
      {page} . . .
   END
END
```

You may wonder why you must bother with additional mapping in the content instructions, instead of just using a single overall mapping in the document instructions. One reason is that the contentInsertFileMapping instruction can resolve name conflicts that can occur when you build large documents out of smaller ones. Suppose there are two authors working on a document. One author creates Chapter 1, the second creates Chapter 2, and both authors include "Figure1" in their chapters. When individual proofs are printed, "Figure1" is mapped to the appropriate file for the chapter being printed. When they finish, you are given both masters and asked to combine them. You have a problem: a single mapping lets you map "Figure1" into either the file for Chapter 1 or the file for Chapter 2, but not both. The contentInsertFileMapping instruction solves this problem by providing an additional level of mapping. You map the name "Figure1" into the name "Chap1Fig1" for the block containing Chapter 1, and map it into the name "Chap2Fig1" for the block containing Chapter 2. Now, when you need to map the internal file names to actual files you have distinct names to work with. Your results might look like Example 8.48 (see Figure 8.25).

Example 8.48

```
Header "Interpress/Xerox/3.0 "        --header--
{
   Identifier "InsertFileMapping"
   String "Chap1Fig1"                 --document-level name--
   String "Chap1Fig1at300"            --actual file name--
   2 MAKEVEC                          --mapping--
   String "Chap2Fig1"                 --another name pair--
   String "Chap2Fig1at300"
   2 MAKEVEC                          --made into a mapping--
   2 MAKEVEC                          --vector of mapping--
   2 MAKEVEC                          --instructions property vector--
}
BEGIN
   { }
   CONTENTINSTRUCTIONS
   {
      Identifier "contentInsertFileMapping"
      String "Figure1"                --chapter-level name--
      String "Chap1Fig1"              --document-level name--
      2 MAKEVEC
      1 MAKEVEC
      2 MAKEVEC
   }
   sequenceInsertMaster "Chapter1"    --includes a reference --
                                      --to Figure1, which becomes--
                                      --Chap1Fig1at300--
   CONTENTINSTRUCTIONS
   {
      Identifier "contentInsertFileMapping"
      String "Figure1"                --chapter-level name--
      String "Chap2Fig1"              --document-level name--
      2 MAKEVEC
      1 MAKEVEC
      2 MAKEVEC
   }
   sequenceInsertMaster "Chapter2"    --includes a reference--
                                      --to Figure1, which becomes--
                                      --Chap2Fig1at300--
   END
```

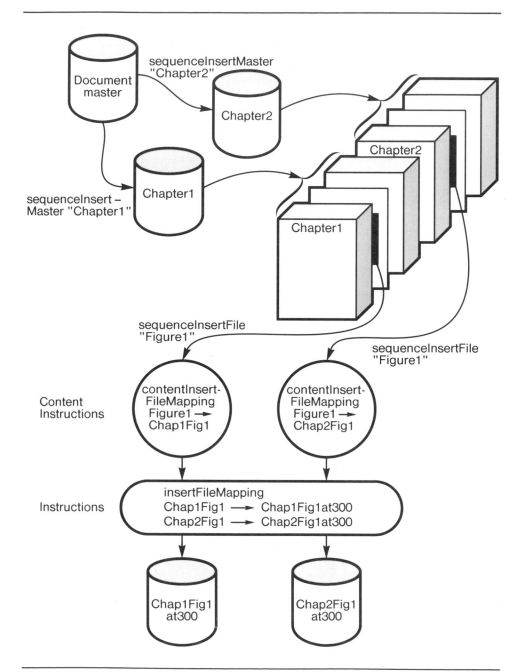

Figure 8.25 Mapping file names to avoid collisions and accommodate dependencies.

Summary

Interpress is a document-description language that operates on both documents and pages. Its concepts of page independence and the skeleton supply a framework for constructing documents from pages or other documents and allow you to reference pages within a document. This chapter began with a discussion of the skeleton structure and the organization of Interpress masters. It next looked at operations and specifications that apply to entire documents. You saw how the document preamble and instructions body can be used. The preamble sets up an initial frame, which can aid in establishing a uniform style for the document. It also offers a place to perform costly operations and to set up operators to be used throughout the document. The instructions body can specify the page structure of copies. This, along with the IFCOPY operator, allows you to print different versions of one document. You also can specify the medium for each page, select simplex or duplex mode, set the binding offset, and indicate finishing options. The instructions body also has a place to store information about the document.

You next saw how the individual pages within a document can be located easily. Because of page independence, pages can be extracted from documents and used to form new documents. You saw how to select pages, merge documents, and overlay pages. Page overlays are useful for printing signatures, and for inserting images and forms. The sequenceInsertFile encoding and Interpress fragments can be used to assemble pages from file references. You also learned ways to handle errors that may occur when a file is inserted.

Finally, you saw how to combine several documents to form new documents. The Interpress block structure makes this easy, and the sequenceInsertMaster encoding allows it to be done with simple file references. You saw that Interpress not only allows you to create images, but also supports the construction and maintenance of entire documents, as is appropriate and necessary for publishing applications.

This completes our description of the Interpress language. In the next chapter, we will focus our attention on some of the practical issues involved in actually developing software to generate Interpress masters.

Chapter 9
PRACTICAL
ISSUES

"From shadows and types to the reality."

CARDINAL NEWMAN

Developing software to generate Interpress programs is not difficult. Often, you use only a small subset of Interpress' capabilities. Typically, you have an image-creation program, and your problem is to convert from the format used by this program to the Interpress description of the image. You will not be writing Interpress programs but rather programs that generate Interpress programs. It's not as hard as it sounds and offers the advantage of only having to debug once. After you remove the bugs from your generator program, all the Interpress programs that it creates will be correct.

Writing the software for the execution of Interpress at the printer proves a harder task, because all components of the language should be implemented, in case someone decides to use them. To ease the task, a printer's software may implement only a subset of the full Interpress language. Printer software may also take shortcuts to improve performance, resulting in reduced functionality.

The Interpress standard attempts to introduce order to this selective implementation by defining three Interpress sets. The printer software should commit to implementing at least all operators in a set. Your Interpress creator can then restrict the operators used to those in a set, and you will know that printers supporting the set will print the document. The sets are described in Appendix A.

In this chapter, we shall discuss some of the practical issues involved in generating Interpress masters that will perform efficiently on printers of different capabilities. We shall also summarize mechanisms for tailoring Interpress to your particular needs and techniques for troubleshooting.

Performance Guidelines

Besides working within the boundaries of one of the three sets, you (as a writer of Interpress masters) may wish to follow further guidelines to generate efficient masters.

The Interpress document-description language is rich in primitive operators that allow you to specify a wide variety of printed pages. Nevertheless, as an Interpress creator dedicated to producing efficient

Interpress masters, you should use the complex Interpress facilities only when absolutely necessary. Using the simplest operators suitable for the task will streamline the Interpress master. Although an Interpress printer is required to handle all Interpress operators in a set, most will optimize for text strings and simple graphics. The SHOW and MASKRECTANGLE operators will be structured for fast execution. Operators such as CORRECT and MASKSTROKE probably will cause performance degradation during Interpress interpretation. Once the printing instructions and preamble have been executed, the ideal Interpress master contains mainly nonredundant instances of SETXY and SHOW, or MASKRECTANGLE.

Efficiency in the Interpress master can be viewed as having two components—size and execution speed—both of which contribute to the performance of the printer. Some decisions you will face require a tradeoff between the size of the master and the time required to decompose and image specific operators. Where appropriate, these tradeoffs are noted.

The following are guidelines for creating efficient Interpress masters. These rules are structured for a generic Interpress printer. If the output device is known, more detailed optimizations can be made.

1. Avoid redundancy. Avoid any redundancy in the setting of imager variables. The current position should be reset only if a position change has occurred. If a sequence of lines share a common length, the correctMeasure imager variables (correctMX and correctMY) should be set only once at the start of the sequence. If a single font is used for a series of strings, the font imager variable should be set only once. Similarly, the color, strokeWidth, strokeJoint, and strokeEnd variables should be set only when a change has occurred. Concatenations of the identity transformation to the current transformation should be eliminated.

Never duplicate the storage of a frame variable. Storing frame variables that are never retrieved should be avoided. Although storage of nonreferenced frame variables is not strictly speaking a redundancy, eliminating this practice gives a more streamlined master.

2. Never use a variable when a constant will do. Whenever possible, you should precalculate values and simply give the constant in the Interpress master. This approach saves the printer computation, storage and retrieval time.

If you do not have enough information to perform the calculations, the printer can perform the computations once, store the results, and retrieve the constant as needed. Or, the printer can compute the constant each time it is needed. The operational overhead that occurs each time an Interpress frame variable is stored or retrieved must be weighed against the cost for the printer to compute the variable each time it is used. Some imager variables are relatively inexpensive to compute; others, notably the current transformation and font imager variables, are generally more expensive to generate than to store.

Although Interpress printers can execute the control, test, stack and arithmetic operators, the execution speed of these operators depends on the computing power of the printer and the operator implementation. Generally, the printer will not optimize these operators.

3. Use the most specific or most efficient operator. Whenever possible, use SETXREL or SETYREL rather than SETXYREL, use LINETOX or LINETOY rather than LINETO, and use MAKEVEC rather than MAKEVECLU. The more specific operators cost the printer fewer arithmetic operations, decrease the size of the Interpress master, and reduce the number of stack operations.

The mask operators can be ordered by increasing degree of difficulty:

MASKRECTANGLE, MASKUNDERLINE
MASKTRAPEZOIDX, MASKTRAPEZOIDY
MASKVECTOR
MASKFILL
MASKSTROKE

Use the most efficient mask operator equal to the task. In particular, use MASKRECTANGLE and MASKTRAPEZOIDX or MASKTRAPEZOIDY instead of MASKSTROKE or MASKFILL whenever possible.

The scale for page coordinates should be tuned so that a master can use integers, rather than rational numbers, for coordinates. (A suggested scale is 1/1200 inch.) This reduces the size of the master and may improve its speed.

Concatenation of transformations, which requires work at the printer, can sometimes be avoided. When possible, work with one coordinate system.

In general, SCALE2 should be avoided. Although setting up an alternative page coordinate system may seem the perfect solution to some situations, the results of a nonuniform coordinate system are tricky to understand and may have unexpected ramifications for font selection and pixel arrays. The font problems can be solved with the proper MODIFYFONT operator. Graphic images and pixel arrays require compensating transformations. However, to achieve the expected results from the SCALE2 operator, you should be certain of the proper MODIFYFONT operator and compensating transformations for pictures. (Typically, this operator moves the origin to the upper-left corner of the page.)

4. Create line length text strings whenever possible. Most printers are optimized to SHOW text strings. Overhead is incurred whenever a new string is started. Therefore, unless a font change occurs, pieces of text should not be broken at character or word boundaries. On the other hand, a buildup of round-off error occurs as characters are relatively placed within a single string, so string length should be less than 250 characters.

Absolute positioning at the beginning of each line may enhance parallel processing in some systems.

5. **Minimize the use of vectors and vector operations.** An Interpress printer can represent a vector internally as a single entity, duplicating and moving the entire vector as an operator demands. Or, the vector can be stored once, and pointers to the vector can be generated as operators demand. A highly intelligent printer may treat the first instance of the vector as an entity, satisfying subsequent references with a pointer. You usually do not know the printer's approach to vectors, however, so scrutinize your use of vector operations carefully. Before using a vector and its accompanying operators, you should assume the worst possible vector representation in the printer for the particular scenario, and then weigh the performance costs accordingly.

Minimize the use of property vectors. Even if the printer is optimized in its vector implementation, searching long vectors for properties can be a time-intensive operation. Unless there is no alternative, you should avoid the repeated use of large property vectors when performance is important.

Never use a vector operation on a sample vector. For the sake of efficiency, a printer's representation of a sample vector may be different from an ordinary vector, resulting in such operations either being costly or not being implemented at all.

Because most printers are optimized for strings, use a sequenceString encoding rather than MAKEVEC to encode a vector of character codes.

6. **Avoid composed operators and user-defined fonts.** Each composed operator carries an overhead for storage. Even if the printer executes the body of the composed operator directly from the input stream, the frame used by the operator requires storage. When the composed operator is executed, a new set of frame variables is made current. Depending on the form of the DO operator that invokes the composed operator, a portion or all of the imager variables may have to be stored. The composed operator is then executed. After the execution, the frame variables, and perhaps the imager variables, are reset.

The compensating tradeoff for the overhead of storing and using composed operators is a shorter Interpress master. Since the composed operator body is only fully defined once, the master does not contain repeated iterations of the body. Also, preservation of the frame and imager variables is done automatically at the time the composed operator is invoked, thus eliminating specific FSET and ISET commands. Weigh the storage and usage overhead of a composed operator against the cost of a larger Interpress master and possible IGET-ISET operations.

You may want to use a composed operator for a large, repeated group of operators that contain references to frame and imager variables. However, you should expand short composed operators that do not change the frame variables or imager variables.

Most printers are optimized for standard fonts, and poor performance or unimplemented features may result from defining your own font in the master.

7. Use CORRECT only when font substitution will seriously degrade output. Most printers require two passes over a corrected body; one pass to determine the amount of correction needed, and a second pass to perform the imaging with the proper correction. Two passes rather than one will cause performance degradation that parallels the frequency of usage of the CORRECT operator. The CORRECT operator also suffers from the overhead of saving state information so that a second pass can be performed. Recognize that the use of CORRECT definitely affects the printer's performance, and avoid it whenever possible.

If CORRECT must be used, correctTolerance (correctTX and correctTY) should be initialized to the largest number, n, that produces visually acceptable output. Clever implementations of CORRECT can avoid the second pass if the string's image is within the tolerance. The number n is clearly not the default value (0), which could easily produce correction owing to the printer's round-off buildup rather than because of font substitution.

Lines should be justified with the amplifySpace imager variable. Do not use a CORRECT body for justification.

8. Use care in setting imager variables. To maintain device independence, imager variables measured in device coordinates should be set with the suitable Interpress primitive rather than with ISET. Use current-position operators to set values of the positional imager variables. Use CONCATT to modify the current transformation, except when restoring a previously stored transformation. Likewise, avoid the use of IGET.

9. Minimize references to the printer's environment and state. In general, referencing the printer's environment and state make preprocessing of the Interpress master awkward. GETCP, for example, should be avoided, since both the current position and the current transformation must be known to execute this operator.

10. Use only easy transformations on pixel arrays. Make the net transformation an "easy" transformation on pixel arrays, thus ensuring that the printer can execute the master. Some printers can handle only easy transformations; on other printers, a difficult transformation is time-consuming. The best guess for an easy transformation for any printer is the identity transformation.

11. Use the instructions for predeclarations. InsertFiles should be declared in the printing instructions, allowing the printer to obtain external resources needed for the master before it executes the page bodies. Take advantage of the environmentUses printing instruction to ensure routing of the master to a properly equipped printer.

12. Make priority important only when absolutely necessary. Preserving the priority of imaging operators may require more computations at the printer than arbitrary reordering of the images. Therefore, unless there is a specific reason not to do so (such as needing to have overlapping objects painted in different colors), the priorityImportant imager variable should be left set to the default value, 0, indicating that priority is unimportant.

Printer Capabilities

Not all Interpress printers will interpret all the complexities of Interpress. Some printers may have image-producing hardware unsuited to handling complex images; other printers may have software that can handle only some parts of Interpress. Although the Interpress standard can encompass printers with few or many capabilities, as a creator you can choose to limit the Interpress masters you generate to be able to print on as wide a variety of devices as possible.

You must anticipate limitations on a printer's capabilities when the master is generated. There are several dimensions along which a printer may be limited:

- The printer may interpret only a subset of the Interpress facilities—that is, a subset of the operators and data types defined by the standard. Interpress defines three application sets to help standardize the selection.

- The printer's environment contains only a limited collection of fonts, forms, and so on. Moreover, the printer may not have elaborate font-approximation facilities.

- A printer may not be able to handle certain printing instructions. Interpress does not require the implementation of all printing instructions, and it has no way for a printer to indicate which instructions it can handle.

- A printer's hardware and software may impose limits on the total *complexity* of an image it can print.

You need to know a good deal of information about a printer to prepare masters for it effectively. Printer information comes from two sources. Because some of the information is determined by the printer hardware and software, it is specified by the printer manufacturer. Other information may be specific to a particular printer installation and so must be determined by the organization responsible for installing and operating the printer.

Manufacturer's Information

The following information is generally supplied by the manufacturer of an Interpress printer:

- *Set*. What is the set of Interpress master that the printer can accept? In addition to the set names, this information should include any prose required to specify the capabilities of the printer. For example, if only certain pixel arrays can be handled, easy net transformations should be listed. If a printer offers the Commercial Set, but also can draw diagonal (45-degree) lines, this additional function must be specified explicitly. Any special performance hints, especially any that are counterintuitive, should be explained.

- *Limits*. What are the minimum sizes and precisions of various important objects that the master uses? Interpress mandates the minimum requirements listed in Table 9.1; additional information is needed for further resource limitations. For example, a printer may limit the maximum size of an Interpress encoding because the disk storage available for buffering the master is limited. Or a printer may limit the maximum number of pages in a master or in a printing job in order to cope with various operational problems, such as clogging the printing queue with long jobs.

  The printer also may exceed the limits of Table 9.1. For example, a printer might offer more than 50 elements in its top frame, reasoning that more frame elements are needed to hold fonts for complex printing jobs. In this case, the printer's capabilities might be phrased as "*Commercial Set* with *topFrameSize* limit of 100."

Table 9.1 Minimum values for size limits.

Name	Miminum Limit
maxCardinal	$2^{24}-1$
maxIdLength	100 characters
maxBodyLength	10,000 literals
maxStackLength	1,000 values
maxVecSize	1,000 elements
maxFileNesting	8 files
topFrameSize	50 elements

- *Image complexity*. Is the printer limited or unlimited? Perhaps the most difficult problem in describing a printer's capabilities is that of overall image complexity. Can the printer produce an image of 1 million "A" characters? Or 1000 strokes? Can it print more strokes if the strokes are only horizontal and vertical, and not diagonal? What if 100 characters are all overprinted directly on top of one another? The answers to these questions depend on details of printing hardware. Often, it is impossible to express the capability of the printer with a formula that would be useful to the creator.

Some so-called unlimited printers can handle imagery of arbitrary complexity. These printers operate by storing, usually on a disk, a raster representation of the page to be printed. High-speed printers avoid storing the raster image of the entire page by generating it on the fly, as the printing hardware consumes it. Although this technique has impressive performance advantages, it may limit the image complexity. Some printing hardware makes unlimited complexity easier to attain by allowing the printing to stop if the data-generation process has been slowed down by complexity. If the maximum page complexity is limited, the limitations should be characterized.

- *Image fidelity.* How precisely can the printer render the image specified in the Interpress master? In most cases, the resolution of the printing hardware will determine the answer to this question.

- *Font and color approximations.* How are approximations made? The approximation rule used by the printer software should be described. In some cases, printers may adopt conventions about the interpretation of hierarchical names, and these should be described.

- *SequenceInsertMaster and sequenceInsertFile.* What is the format for file names? What are the syntax and semantics of sequenceInsertFile?

- *Printing instructions.* What printing instructions are available and how are they specified?

- *Communications.* How does the creator communicate with the printer? This includes information about transmitting masters to the printer, determining the status of a print request, and obtaining the metric master. It is especially important to describe the kinds of errors that can occur and how they are reported.

- *Environment.* What are the fixed elements in the environment of the printer? Decompression operators usually are built into the printer hardware, even though they are expressed as an environment object in Interpress. The function of these operators must be described precisely so that creators can compress pixel data accordingly. Some printers also may have a few fonts permanently resident in the environment, and these should be given. Color model operators may be built in, and the printer may have a permanent set of named colors.

Still more information about the printer will be provided by the manufacturer, such as how to operate the printer, how to install forms on it, how to update fonts, and so on. This information is vital to the operator of the printer but is not required by the creator software.

Installation Information

Each printer installation may configure a printer differently. If printers have different fonts, the creator is informed through the metric master. However, other differences are important to the creator as well:

- *Environment.* What forms are available on the printer to be used with sequenceInsertFile? What are the hierarchical naming conventions used in the organization, and are there any guidelines about generating masters with maximum device independence on all the printers in the organization?
- *Printing instructions.* An installation may restrict some of the printer's capabilities. For example, it may stock only certain paper sizes; it may not allow stapling; or it may use special cost-accounting practices.
- *Operational restrictions.* For various reasons, the operator of a printer may restrict the printer's use. The maximum number of pages in a print job might be restricted at all times or during certain peak hours to keep the printer queue flowing smoothly. Programmers might be able to work around a length restriction; they need to know about it.

Tailoring and Extending Interpress

Interpress gives you not only the constructs for creating almost any image but also the mechanisms to extend or tailor the language to your imaging needs. In this section, we shall review such mechanisms.

Interpress Encoding

Although a particular encoding is given in the standard, Interpress is not limited to it. You can construct printers that accept other encodings. For example, you may wish to use a textual encoding, either to make it readable by humans, or to ensure its transmission over most communication channels; or you may design an encoding in which page bodies may be found in a table rather than by scanning the master. Such an encoding would require more work by the creator but might improve printer performance on random pages.

The Interpress header is intended to provide encoding and version information about the master. By examining the header, your printer can decide whether it will understand the master and how it will decode that master. Because a sequenceInsertMaster references a file with a header, an Interpress master can even be built out of separately encoded pieces.

Character Encoding

Within the master, you are not restricted to a particular character-encoding scheme. A particular character encoding is just the mapping used by a font to arrive at the character mask and metrics. The only restriction here is that individual numbers map unambiguously into characters. You can support the character encoding you desire simply by installing fonts, which understand that encoding, at your printer. Your printer can even support several different encoding schemes by including the corresponding fonts. When you create masters, however, you must be sure that the current font matches the encoding of the strings you are producing.

Inserting External Files

The sequenceInsertFile mechanism is designed to be vague about the inserted file's format. In fact, the file need not contain Interpress. What is required is that the printer understands and can deal with the file and that the net result is equivalent to having inserted a sequence of Interpress instructions. This flexibility allows you to develop precompiled forms that can be inserted with the sequenceInsertFile mechanism. The standard suggests that, if you do develop your own form for inserted files, you begin the file with a header string. The printer can use the header to distinguish your file format from other possible formats (such as the standard Interpress fragment).

The Printer's Environment

A number of things (fonts, colors, operators) may be found in the printer's environment. They are always identified by universal names, so that their names are unique. You can structure your printer's environment to meet your needs.

Among the objects most often acquired from the environment are fonts, which are located by the FINDFONT operator. Although you can also construct a font in the master by means of the MAKEFONT operator, finding a font usually will be far more efficient. So you should determine the set of fonts you will need and install them in your printer's environment.

You can also choose any image format or compression scheme you wish by installing a corresponding decompressor in the printer's environment. Some decompressors are described in the Xerox Raster Encoding Standard; also, you can design your own. You can access your decompressor by the

FINDDECOMPRESSOR operator—remember to apply this operator to the image samples before using them in a pixel array.

The FINDCOLOR operator allows you to install named colors as part of the printer's environment. It may be useful to have colors such as Xerox/Blue or Kodak/Yellow readily available.

The FINDCOLOROPERATOR and FINDCOLORMODELOPERATOR commands let you install your own model for specifying colors. Color images can be encoded in the most convenient manner, and the corresponding model can be made available at the printer.

Finally, the FINDOPERATOR command is a powerful escape mechanism that allows you to extend Interpress by adding your own specialized operators.

Printing Instructions

The printing-instruction mechanism accommodates extensions. The instructions are presented in a property vector so that you can easily include new instructions. A printer ignores instructions that it does not understand, so you can even use the printing instructions to save information about a document that the printer does not use. Universal names are used for printing instructions to avoid name conflicts.

Registering Names

If you wish to define your own environment objects, such as colors, fonts, decompressors, or printing instructions, you need to name them. Using universal names avoids name conflicts. To form universal names, you should register a universal identifier. Your names should be vectors of identifiers that begin with your registered universal identifier. Since no one else should begin their names in this way, you need to control the uniqueness of your own names to avoid conflicts. To register a universal identifier, write to:

Xerox Corporation
Xerox Systems Institute
475 Oakmead Parkway
Sunnyvale, CA 94086

A Word of Caution

Interpress offers the means to configure your printer to fit your needs best. The price, though, is the device independence of your masters. If your masters rely on special operators, fonts, colors, or encodings found only on your printer, then they cannot be printed elsewhere. To maintain device independence, you should try to minimize references to the printer's environment.

Software-Development Tools

The degree of difficulty you will face in developing Interpress software depends, in large part, on the tools you have available. Several are essential: one is a full-capability Interpress printer. You need a device that displays an image obtained from an Interpress master. Your printer should also generate complete and explanatory error messages, preferably indicating the error's position in the Interpress file. This is the primary vehicle for testing your Interpress programs; you send them to a printer to see if they work.

You may need both a printer with a full implementation of Interpress and a printer with the implementation set you are targeting. This allows you to distinguish between an error in your master and a limitation in your printer. You may end up altering your program in either case, but it helps to know where the problem is.

Another essential pair of tools is an Interpress disassembler and an assembler. The disassembler converts from the standard encoding to a human-readable form. This lets you look at what has been generated. It also lets you examine other people's Interpress masters for comparison.

With an editor and an assembler, you can construct test cases by hand, test fixes to a faulty master, and remove portions of a master that you know are correct to isolate the part that contains the problem.

Another useful tool is an Interpress debugging interpreter–a program that executes an Interpress master primarily to find the bugs. It can check rules, such as whether the arguments are of the correct type, the limits are not exceeded, and bodies are well formed. The tool also may allow setting of break points, single stepping, and display of stack, frame, and imager variables.

If you are creating Interpress masters, a library of encoding routines will be helpful. These are routines that take strings, or numbers, and generate the proper Interpress encoding for operands. The library also may include procedures for output of the various Interpress operators.

If you are writing the software for an Interpress printer, you may find useful the Interpress Printer Certification Software, a collection of Interpress masters that test the printer.

Tools such as these are available through the Xerox Systems Institute. For more information, see the section entitled "Further Reading" at the end of this book.

What Can Go Wrong

When an Interpress master is printed, a number of things can go wrong. There are two broad classes of problems: those related to the particular printing request made, and those resulting from the Interpress master itself.

Various operational problems may occur, such as a broken printer, a paper jam, an incorrect routing of the printed document, and so on. The printer may reject a job because its supply of the right kind of paper is exhausted, because a data error has been detected during the transmission of the master to the printer, or because the requestor has exceeded his or her alotted printing funds. Some operational problems are transitory, such as a delay when the printer's job queue is full. In this case, the requestor can try again later.

Once you get past operational impediments, you may face problems that result from the construction of the master. Interpress printers minimize the disastrous effects of errors in a master: often, the interpretation of a master can continue without spoiling more than the one page where an error occurred. However, some errors, such as those detected when the preamble is executed, may prevent printing the entire document.

Error Categories

Printing errors are divided into two classes: appearance and master. Appearance errors are those that affect only the appearance of a page; master errors signal problems that arise as the master is decoded and interpreted.

As we saw in the section on Error Recovery in Chapter 2, errors are further divided to yield four categories: appearance warning, appearance error, master warning, and master error.

Error Logging

An Interpress printer should provide diagnostic information about each error it encounters. This information often is printed on the break page but may be presented in other ways as well. An error indication should include:

- The location of the error in the master.
- The page number and position on the page (if applicable).
- The class of the error (appearance warning, appearance error, master warning, or master error).
- An indication of the nature of the error.

The error listing should be meaningful. Suppose, for example, that the master makes 503 calls to the SETGRAY operator, and that 304 of them cause appearance errors because they specify a gray color, whereas black is the only color the printer can handle. Printing 304 error messages is not a good idea. Most users would be content with one error message showing that the printer could not handle gray, perhaps with a list of pages that will not be correctly printed. By contrast, each font approximation made should be clearly indicated in the error listing, giving the name of the requested font and the name of the one used.

A printer may give more comprehensive diagnostic information for the benefit of a programmer who needs to track down the cause of the error. The information might include, for example, the location in the master where the error occurred, the stack's contents at the time, or the name of the primitive operator that caused the error. Since most users will not want such detailed information, the printer might give it only if commanded by a printing instruction.

Error Recovery

Besides logging an error, the printer must recover and continue interpreting the master, if possible. For appearance warnings, appearance errors, and master warnings, the interpreter can continue as usual. For master errors, the interpreter may need to take drastic action before resuming interpretation.

The MARK mechanism, explained in Chapters 2 and 8, indicates points in the master where interpretation can continue as usual after a serious error. Each page body is executed with mark protection, so that, if a master error occurs within a page body and no further marks are present, the remainder of the page body is not interpreted, but interpretation of the next page body can proceed without difficulty. Note that, even if a page body is not interpreted completely, a page should be printed that contains any output successfully generated before the error occurred. If a master error occurs while interpreting the preamble, the printer might not be able to generate any output besides a break page that indicates the error.

Examples of Errors

General discussions of errors are useful and reassuring but fail to give a feeling for all the things that can go wrong. In this section, we list the most common types of errors. Each error is annotated with a code that indicates whether it is an operational error (O), an appearance warning (Aw), an appearance error (Ae), a master warning (Mw), or a master error (Me). Some printers may not classify these errors in the ways indicated by the codes.

Although this incomplete list of errors may seem imposing, in practice, many of the errors occur infrequently. Not counting operational problems, the only errors likely to occur often are appearance warnings resulting from font approximations.

Starting a Printing Job
- The printer's job queue is full (O).
- The printer encounters a data error while reading the master from the medium that transmits it to the printer (O).

- An error occurs when the printer tries to interpret the external printing instructions that accompany the master (O).
- The printer is not working (O).
- The printer lacks necessary supplies, such as paper or staples (O).
- Insufficient funds are available in the account to be charged for the printing job (O).
- The printing job cannot be handled because of operational restrictions, such as limits on the maximum number of pages printed in a job (O).

Printer Capabilities

- The printer's interpreter implements the wrong *set*, as indicated by invoking a primitive operator that is not available (Mw or Me).
- One of the printer's *limits* is exceeded, such as the maximum stack depth (Me).
- A printer resource, not given explicitly as a *limit*, is exhausted (Me). For example, storage for composed operators and vectors might be exhausted.
- The master requests a capability that the imager does not have, such as printing gray color, or scaling a pixel array or a character using a transformation that is not among the easy net transformations of the printer (Ae).
- The printer is *limited*, and one or more of the pages specified in the master are so complex that the image-generation hardware cannot keep up with the printer mechanics (Ae).

Master Errors and Warnings

- The Interpress master is not well-formed (Me). That is, the header, BEGIN, END, and well-formed page bodies cannot be found.
- The Interpress master is not encoded properly (Me). For example, a primitive operator code or a sequence type may be out of range, or the rules about encoding body operators have not been followed.
- A reference to the environment cannot be honored (Mw or Me).
- One of the arguments passed to a primitive operator is not of the correct type or in the correct range (Me). For example, −1 IGET and 1 SHOW will generate master errors.
- The master "program" does not terminate (Me). To detect whether a master is looping, printers usually take steps, such as establishing a maximum interpretation time or noting the absence of calls to imager operators that actually generate output.
- A computational error occurs (Me). Division by zero and GETCP applied to poorly conditioned transformations are examples.

Appearance Errors and Warnings
- A font approximation is made (Aw).
- The master has been created in such a way that the image is greatly distorted in the presence of font approximations. *This causes no error beyond the appearance warning that accompanies a font approximation.*
- A font that is requested can be neither matched nor approximated (Ae).
- Part of the image lies off the page (Ae).

Troubleshooting

What do you do when the master you have created causes an error message, or the wrong image, or a blank page? There are no hard and fast rules for debugging but techniques that have proved helpful include:
- *Disassemble and look at the master.* Disassembly usually reveals encoding problems. Look for unreasonable values, strange, or unexpected operators, and items that appear out of place.
- *Isolate the problem.* Edit the disassembled program to remove irrelevant portions. Remove all page bodies except the one with the error. Remove innocent instruction groups. Try to remove everything except the problem area, to simplify the analysis and avoid confusion. Assemble the simplified master and try it to make sure you have not disturbed the error. If you do not actually know where the error occurs in the page body, employ a binary search technique by dividing the page into halves, printing each, and noting which has the error. Note, however, that dividing the page in half is not simply dividing the code, since there is usually some setup at the start of the page (establishing the master coordinate system, setting up fonts, and so on) that must be duplicated for both halves. One way to do this is to duplicate the entire page body and then remove portions to see whether the error is contained in the remainder.
- *Desk check the code.* If you have a small disassembled listing that contains the error, step through it by hand, keeping track of the stack, frame, and imager variables. This process often reveals problems such as missing or disordered operands, erroneous transformations, wrong fonts, and so on. If everything seems to work by hand, it may be that the printer does not act the way you think it should.
- *Insert "print statements."* You can add instructions to the faulty Interpress master to trace its execution. You can print either in the error log or on the page image, but the error log (where supported) is usually preferable, since this will not interfere with the image you are constructing. A statement can be entered in the error log with the

ERROR operator using a code value of 100 to indicate a comment. Messages can be printed on the page using the SHOW operator. In Appendix C, we have provided routines that will print on the page, the values of numbers on the stack and the types of other operands. You can construct similar operators that write into the error log. By using these instructions to trace the program, you can compare what occurs at the printer to your desk execution. This comparison should help you determine the location of the problem. (Some printers may provide an extended set of operators for debugging. Operators that print the stack, frame, or imager variable contents can be quite useful.)

- *Add to a working program.* Another way to find a bug is to start with an Interpress program that you know works, and add instructions to it, one by one, until you encounter a problem. You may want one set of print statements to display the final state of each iteration. One way to get a working program is to comment out everything questionable. You can then remove the comments, one by one, until the problem point is located.

The Likely Errors

A bug can crop up in several ways. The most obvious is an error message from the printer; another is a page with ill-formed images; a third is a page with images missing entirely. A descriptive error message may be the easiest to deal with because it can give you some idea as to what went wrong and where.

One common error message, "unknown operator," is usually symptomatic of an encoding problem that has resulted in data being treated as operators. Problems such as padding being added to records during file transmission or byte-order reversal can cause this kind of error. Usually, disassembly reveals encoding problems.

Another common error message, "bad operand type," usually indicates a stack problem, such as an extra operand, a missing operand, or a bad ordering of the operands. Printing the stack contents at the point of error often reveals the problem.

An ill-formed image can also indicate that you have stack problems or that you are generating the wrong values for operands. Again, printing the operands is useful.

A poor image may be caused by printer limitations, and could be out of your control. Hardware limitations can cause round-off errors and aliasing effects (nonuniform spacing, jagged lines, varying line widths, moiré patterns, or variations in color). There may also be limitations in what the printer has implemented. Look for appearance warnings, and check your printer's specification. You can also try sending the master to a different class of printer.

The image will also be ill-formed if it is too complex for the printer. The effect depends on the particular printer and just how its limits are exceeded. For example, white bands may appear on the page, or portions of the image may be missing. The printer may–or may not–notify you of the problem. If you can divide the page body and print each half separately, your page may be too complex. You may have to worry about the number of objects on a scan line, and not just about the total number of objects on the page.

A frustrating problem is a job that completes normally, but prints a blank page. There are several bugs that can cause this, but you should pay particular attention to transformations. It is easy to rotate the image off the page. Negative scales and large translations also will cause a blank page. You may have scaled the image so small that it cannot be seen, or so large that it is clipped away. For sequenceInsertFiles, there is the danger of going through the MCS-to-ICS transformation twice. For graphics, you should check that the strokeWidth is not at its default zero value. Also check that you are not using white ink.

Summary

In this chapter, we have considered topics beyond the basic understanding of the language that concern the Interpress software implementor. We have seen how to generate efficient Interpress masters, and how to match the Interpress masters generated to the printer's capabilities. We have discussed the flexibility of Interpress that allows you to adapt this language to your needs. A list of tools that are helpful in developing your software was presented. We also discussed the bugs and errors that can arise and explained how to cope with them.

In Chapter 10, we shall consider how Interpress fits into the context of printing systems and applications.

Chapter 10
INTERPRESS AND THE FUTURE OF ELECTRONIC PUBLISHING

*"It is only from
the man with the
machine that
I can hope for any
amelioration
of my lot as a
reader."*

ALDOUS HUXLEY

The latest generation of raster printers can print any combination of text, graphics, and pictures, just as a traditional printing press can. These printers use various devices and techniques, including lasers, ink jets, thermal transfer, ion deposition, electrographics, and the like, allowing great versatility in the type and quality of the finished product. Interpress, as we have seen, is an ideal language for describing the appearance of page images in a document and can exploit this versatility effectively.

Getting the most out of computers, networks, and raster printers for electronic-publishing applications, however, calls for additional high-level protocols and standards so that documents can be printed immediately; stored for later use; sent to remote sites by local-area networks, telephone lines, or magnetic media; or printed on different printers at different sites anywhere in the world. It also requires standards for representing the alphabets of different languages, compressing bitmap images, and describing colors.

Well-suited to stand-alone desktop publishing jobs, Interpress also has been designed to fit well into all in-house publishing applications and network and host environments such as the International Standard Organization/Open Systems Interconnect (ISO/OSI), Systems Network Architecure (SNA), or Xerox Network Systems (XNS). The Interpress printing architecture offers the additional protocol and standards definitions to support an even greater range of printing and publishing applications.

In this chapter, we shall describe some of the general characteristics of the Interpress printing architecture that ease its use as an open system for a wide range of applications, networks, and printers. We shall also examine some of the main types of in-house applications that can be developed using Interpress. The chapter ends with a few comments on Interpress' future in electronic publishing.

Interpress Printing Architecture: An Open System

As an open system, the Interpress and related standards have been made available free of any royalty or licensing fees. Interpress is now supported by many major vendors of electronic publishing systems. The Interpress printing architecture is a collection of standards for representation, management, and electronic transport of documents.

Character Codes and Fonts

Interpress provides extensive printer-environment capabilities through the use of different character codes, fonts, raster-compression techniques, and colors. The user, who is not tied to a specific characteristic, can use any of the facilities supported by the printer. Xerox itself has adopted the multilingual Xerox Character Code standard, an Interpress-based Font Interchange Standard, and a Raster Encoding Standard (for image compression). However, to promote consistency of printing in diverse environments, major font vendors have agreed to offer a standard set of fonts in Interpress, using the Xerox Font Interchange and Character Code standards. This open-system approach frees the user of Interpress from dependence on any specific vendor for computer, printer, or fonts.

The Xerox Character Code Standard provides representations for most major language alphabets of the world, including Roman, Greek, Russian, Japanese Kanji, Chinese, Hebrew, and Arabic. These alphabets can be intermixed in the same document. This standard also uses an encoding scheme that makes document transmission and storage more efficient and compact. The character-code standard also facilitates compactness and high-quality typography by providing for technical symbols and by rendering characters such as ligatures. Further, the Xerox encoding is compatible with a large number of national and international character-code standards, including ASCII, ISO 646, and JIS-C-6226. Interpress users, of course, can also use any of these other character-code standards.

Similarly, any variety of raster-compression techniques or colors may be used merely by referencing that property by name. The printer attempts to find the property in its environment; if it cannot find the property, it may choose to approximate it (for example, by font substitution or shades of gray). These printer-environment capabilities provide great flexibility in the construction of high-quality images, and suit Interpress for a wide variety of publishing applications and in-house environments.

Raster and Color Encoding

The Raster Encoding Standard (RES) is a general-purpose encoding scheme that permits an image to be used as a document, either by itself or as a part of an Interpress document. RES uses Interpress encoding rules and terminology. This simplifies printer software that handles raster-image files specified by

Interpress masters. RES image descriptions, like Interpress, are intended to be processed by machines and not directly by people, so no attempt has been made to encode the information in a form that humans can read.

In RES, each raster image, whether binary, continuous tone, or color, is described as a single entity (file). A raster-scan pattern is assumed, and allowance is made for the possibility of nonrectangular image areas. The representation is flexible enough to permit simple images to be described with little overhead, yet considerable related information can be included (especially to facilitate editing and modification) when necessary. Specifying the encoding rules rather than supplying a rigid format for the data gives this flexibility. Raster-image data, which can require a great deal of memory, is described in compressed form with provision for several standard compression schemes, including the CCITT Group 4 compression scheme (an international standard for facsimile equipment).

The Color Encoding Standard (CES) describes how colors are to be specified in a variety of color document-processing applications (such as creation, editing, printing, storage, scanning, interchange, and mail). For example, Interpress, as well as RES, represents color using CES. The purpose of CES is to provide color specifications that precisely describe color in a manner that allows the user of a description to understand the intent of the creator of that description. For this document, "color" means the attributes related to the spectral distribution of the light reflected from or emitted by an object, such as lightness, hue, and saturation. Gray is a color, as are red, green, and blue, for example. "Full color" covers those cases where there are so many different colors possible that they must be described by nearly continuous multidimensional scales. On the other hand, "named colors" (for example, Xerox/Blue or Kodak/Yellow) describe specific values of the continuous scales used for full color. Products that use large but limited (for example, indexed) sets of colors can handle them with named colors or with the map type of color model operators that are already part of the Raster Encoding Standard.

In keeping with standards such as the Interpress standard, the CES is intended to describe colors by how they look to a human observer, not by how they are physically created. It is based on an international standard observer (the CIE 1931 Standard Colorimetric Observer, Official Recommendations of the International Commission on Illumination, CIE Publ. No. 15.2, 1986) for describing how a color looks.

Color, mostly in the sense of shades of gray, is already described in Interpress and in RES. For this reason, CES is an extension of current descriptions to include full color. For ease in coupling to existing and future black-and-white systems, primary emphasis is given to color descriptions compatible with black-and-white printing.

Network and Mainframe Environments

Interpress also has many facilities that enhance its suitability for networks. For example, the sequenceInsertFile function makes possible the inclusion of files accessible by the printer. Such files can contain Interpress masters, fragments of Interpress masters, or even printer-dependent object code that represents previously decomposed Interpress masters (such as forms). The printer can use the full network file pathname, so an Interpress master can "reach out" into an entire internetwork connected to the printer's local-area network. Interpress also takes explicit steps to establish a universal name space (for fonts and so on), and to provide for a central registry mechanism for the distribution and control of names in this space. This offers a way to establish a uniform environment for an extended family of printers in large, diverse network applications.

Other protocols defined include the printing protocol to transmit Interpress masters to printers; the clearinghouse directory protocol for locating printers, workstations, and other network resources; the authentication protocol for information security; and the time protocol for a uniform time-stamp. Transport of the electronic documents can be accomplished via local-area networks, telephone lines, direct-connect channels, or a variety of magnetic media. Initial network applications of Interpress were on XNS environments, using XNS protocols. Later applications have been on personal computers, workstations, and mainframe environments, using various transport means and protocols. The Xerox Printer Access Facility (XPAF) enables IBM host computers using MVS/370 and MVS/XA operating systems to "speak" to Interpress printing systems.

The Interpress standard, the result of over a decade of research on printing technologies, evolved during Xerox' many years of experience using it in a distributed network environment. Interpress proved to be gracefully extensible so that as new printing technology, new applications, and other new requirements emerged, Interpress was extended without requiring the modification of existing encoded masters—a testimonial to the standard's reliability and extensibility. Combined with other related standards and protocols, Interpress represents a complete and open architecture for printing.[†]

[†]All these standards, published by Xerox Corporation, are available from the Xerox Systems Institute; see the section entitled "Further Reading" at the end of this book for more information.

Using Interpress for In-House Applications

In today's business world, the role of electronic printing is rapidly changing. Expectations of end users for new applications rise as new capabilities become available. Interpress can play a key role in meeting the demands of these new applications.

Manuals Composed from Many Sources

It is an often-repeated story that the documentation for all the parts of a commercial airplane such as the Boeing 757 occupies more space than the plane itself. Without a doubt, an immense amount of documentation is written and printed to support today's technological products.

Typically, when a technical manual is prepared, the information comes from many sources. Tables of data may be taken from a host computer. Text entered in a personal computer is merged with computer-aided design (CAD) graphics captured from an engineering workstation. Still other existing or hand-drawn graphics are scanned in. Usually, some type of page-composition software, often running on a minicomputer, pulls it all together.

In some cases, the page-composition software takes all the relevant information and converts it into a format that the software understands and can edit. In many other cases, however, it merely accepts the data and merges it with overall formatting styles to specify the overall description of the printing job; and that overall description can be Interpress, which can describe efficiently the input from a wide variety of sources.

While such a document is being created, it may be previewed on a workstation screen at 72 spots per inch, printed as a proof copy on a 300-spot-per-inch laser printer, and prepared for offset press at 1200 spots per inch.

Again, Interpress makes this possible. Because it is device-independent, its output can be directed to all the various output devices that might be used. Indeed, in the future, such manuals may even be stored electronically and read on screen at workstations that can decompose the stored Interpress master and present it.

In addition, Interpress' page independence makes it convenient to print documents cover-to-cover at production speeds and with page imposition. The actual printing can be one- or two-sided, and even two or more up for booklets or large printing signatures. Interpress makes it possible to print such technical manuals in customized form for specific users.

Desktop Publishing

Desktop publishing has moved much of the power of the scenario outlined in the previous section into personal computers (PCs) or workstations such as the IBM PC, the Xerox 6085, and the Apple Macintosh. The advent of desktop publishing (inexpensive PCs and laser printers) combined with ubiquitous copiers and duplicators has potentially moved the Gutenberg press into any office. The user has control over the design of a page previously associated only with expensive typesetting and layout equipment. The traditional roles for the person who sets the type, the person who lays out the page, the person who strips in the artwork, and the person who shoots the board have all been merged into one role—played by a single person with one software program.

As a result, newsletters that were once typed on a typewriter, in-house communications once expensively produced in an outside shop, and even magazines formerly typeset in the traditional manner are being produced quickly, efficiently, and inexpensively with traditional quality.

Page-description languages are essential to this achievement. Interpress not only supplies a vehicle to describe complicated page images but also does so in a way that allows you to send the output file to a low-resolution laser printer for a proof and to a high-resolution typesetting device for camera-ready copy, with the assurance that the pages produced on the two different devices will be essentially the same.

Demand Publishing

Any publisher of information (such as the technical-manual publisher previously described) could theoretically function as a demand publisher. To date, most demand publishers have been manufacturers or service providers who need to supply vast amounts of documentation for their end users. The traditional approach for such in-house publishers was to prepare a low-cost master (perhaps from a laser printer, perhaps directly from an impact printer). They then reproduced and bound one thousand or more copies or used an offset press to print several thousand copies. (In the latter case, they might also have used a higher-quality typeset master.) Copies were printed and stocked in sufficient numbers to meet the expected demand of the next year or two.

Unfortunately, product demand changes, updates to information occur, and new versions of manuals need to be printed. Users are stuck with dozens of corrected pages to insert into three-ring binders, or vendors are left with out-of-date documents to discard. In addition to the loss involved in discards, the publisher also has inventory carrying costs.

In demand publishing, information is stored electronically. Only a small number of copies are printed on an as-needed basis. Inventory costs as well as wastage costs are eliminated. The electronic version of the document is continuously updated, supplying current information at each printing.

Interpress contains the commands to support the whole range of document output, including high typographic quality, line drawings, and photographs. It allows demand-publishing applications to be stored electronically in a single file. In addition, the Interpress view of the the master as a document (and not just single pages) offers a vehicle to carry the information needed for demand publishing (for example, collation and binding information).

Demand publishing often involves multiple printers at different locations. For example, a company may print documents as needed in several regional centers. Because Interpress is device-independent, printers of different speeds and capabilities can be used in various locations to meet more closely the print demand of that area.

Printing Unique Documents in High Volume

Think for a moment of the printing requirements of a large insurance company. On a daily basis, the company issues hundreds of new policy statements. Each one of those statements is different, with different riders, varying limits, and so forth.

Traditionally, the preparation of such statements required a clerk's "shopping spree" through a warehouse of standardized forms. The policy preparer collected the forms needed for a particular policy from standardized ones. Additions and corrections were typed in. The bunch was stapled together and mailed out as the policy. It was a labor-intensive process, prone to error.

Today, thanks to high-speed printers and Interpress, individual documents can be custom printed. Application programs in the mainframe computer at the head office pull together various Interpress fragments stored in the environment, such as a scanned-in logo for the insurance company and standard boilerplate material for various coverages, and merge these with an Interpress file containing the information for that customer.

The entire job might then be rotated and reduced in size to print as a 5.5- by 8.5-inch signature page. The result is a personalized policy printed with a high degree of professionalism—and dozens of these policies can be printed per minute at the main data center or in any of the branch offices.

Interpress supports this application in several ways. First, its design supports implementation on high-speed printers. Without that control, the required speed of this application could not be guaranteed. Further, Interpress can merge files from its environment (through a command such as sequenceInsertFile), so it can bring together efficiently, at the time of printing, both the standard, stored information and the new data. Finally, the basic page-independent Interpress model supports rotation and translation of text and images, as well as pages. This makes it possible to print the document as a folded booklet.

Distributed Printing

Increasingly, offices are becoming electronic: PCs and workstations are found on more and more office desks. As such machines proliferate, corporations try to integrate them through local-area networks. Such networks are then tied together into a larger internetwork.

The results of this networking of corporate America affect traditional applications. For example, a company may decide not to distribute its personnel manual automatically but instead to store it electronically in a central file-storage device. The manual can then be accessed by all employees on an as-needed basis and printed on a local convenience printer.

To make this possible, you need several capabilities, all of which Interpress has. First, you want to store documents in a final format—one not intended to be edited. Otherwise, an enterprising employee might amend the printed version to his or her advantage. Also, because a large, distributed environment is likely to have a variety of printers with different characteristics, device independence is required. Another important factor is the ability to allow shared use of these distributed printers. A master defined in Interpress cannot interfere with these printers' environments or performance in a way that would affect the next user.

Future Directions

Interpress is a far-reaching architecture for printing that is making possible new applications as well as enhancing the interoperability and integration of products, often provided by more than one vendor. The architecture is being enhanced in new areas (such as provision for full color) to enable new applications to meet customer demands.

Another application of Interpress especially important to Xerox Corporation is electronic reprographics. Hard copy is normally reproduced by conventional copiers and duplicators or printing processes that use optical imaging systems. Another way to make copies is to scan a document electronically and then print the scanned image on an electronic printer. Thanks to relatively low-cost, high-resolution, fast electronic scanners and printers, reproducing hard copy electronically not only becomes practical but also offers a user added capabilities and improved productivity. It gives greater flexibility in input and output documents, including variable page types and sizes, one- or two-sided impressions, and so on. The quality of the printout is improved; demand and custom publishing are possible; and hard copy and electronic information can be combined in imaginative ways, bridging the gap between the conventional and the electronic office.

In the future, multivendor integration in network environments will increase, enabled by the international OSI standards. Interpress will play an important role in this integration by allowing the consistent printing of high-quality documents on a variety of output devices. Many software programs and application tools already are easing this integration in the most popular operating environments, including MS-DOS (IBM PCs, and so on), UNIX (AT&T, Berkeley, and so on), VMS (DEC Vax and Microvax), and MVS (IBM and other mainframes), as well as many specialized publishing packages. Because of the network orientation and advantages of Interpress, the number and variety of devices supporting Interpress will increase greatly in the future, and Interpress capability will be available for virtually every environment.

Summary

We have discussed just a few of the ways Interpress can be used. Throughout the industry, users are making more complex demands—they want to cut costs—of printing, of storing documents, and of preparing masters. They want interoperability among products supplied by the same or different vendors. They want greater control over their documents and equipment, and they seek increased visual sophistication in documents that once were only typewritten.

In this chapter, we have examined the vital role Interpress has played in these and other changes—especially the significance of the open Interpress printing architecture for in-house applications.

Appendix A
INTERPRESS
FUNCTION SETS

Interpress, a complete and powerful document-description language, supplies functions to create almost any two-dimensional image. Because it is so extensive, however, some printer manufacturers may prefer to support only part of it (perhaps to reduce development time and cost or to improve performance). Recognizing this and also recognizing the potential for chaos if every printer were to implement a different portion of the language, Interpress designers have defined three standard function sets: the Commercial Set, the Publication Set, and the Professional Graphics Set. The intent is that a printer manufacturer will support all the operators in one of these sets. The sets provide a common ground, telling programmers responsible for Interpress-creation software which operators they can use with assurance of support and telling printer manufacturers which operators they must implement to print the document produced by a given program. For example, if you create documents that adhere to the limitations of the Commercial Set, then any printer that supports the Commercial Set prints them. Furthermore, the Commercial Set is a subset of the Publication Set, which in turn is a subset of the Professional Graphics Set. So a printer supporting either of the more comprehensive sets also prints your document.

The Commercial Set

The Commercial Set is designed for text- and form-printing applications, such as might be required in a data center. It includes all the base-language operators and all the encoding facilities. Transformations are supported, but only for 90-degree rotations; so you can print in portrait or landscape mode, but the printer does not have to support arbitrary rotations of fonts or pixel arrays. Font and text operations are supported, except that you cannot construct your own characters and fonts.

Line graphics are limited to horizontal and vertical rectangles. This allows you to construct forms, underlines, and simple boxlike graphics. Binary pixel arrays are supported, so you can include scanned logos, forms, or signatures.

Constant colors can be located by FINDCOLOR or synthesized from a pixel pattern with MAKESAMPLEDBLACK, but MAKEGRAY and SETGRAY are not included.

The Commercial Set does not support nested blocks, so only single-level skeletons should be used. The following operators are supported:

Arithmetic
> ABS, ADD, CEILING, DIV, FLOOR, MOD, MUL, NEG, REM, ROUND, SUB, TRUNC

Vector
> GET, GETP, GETPROP, MAKEVEC, MAKEVECLU, MERGEPROP, SHAPE

Stack
> COPY, COUNT, DUP, ERROR, EXCH, MARK, NOP, POP, ROLL, UNMARK, UNMARK0

Frame
> FGET, FSET

Imager State
> IGET, ISET

Test
> AND, EQ, GE, GT, NOT, OR, TYPE

Control
> IF, IFCOPY, IFELSE

Operator
> DO, DOSAVE, DOSAVEALL, DOSAVESIMPLEBODY, FINDOPERATOR, MAKESIMPLECO

Current Position
> GETCP, SETXY, SETXREL, SETXYREL, SETYREL

Transformation
> CONCAT, CONTATT, MAKET (if b and d or a and e are zero), MOVE, ROTATE (for angles that are multiples of 90 degrees), SCALE, SCALE2, TRANS, TRANSLATE

Character
> FINDFONT, MODIFYFONT, SETFONT, SHOW, SHOWANDXREL, SHOWANDFIXEDXREL

Corrected Mask
> CORRECT, CORRECTMASK, CORRECTSPACE, SETCORRECTMEASURE, SETCORRECTTOLERANCE, SPACE

Pixel Array

    FINDDECOMPRESSOR, MASKPIXEL (with black color), MAKEPIXELARRAY (samplesPerPixel $= 1$, maxSampleValue $= 1$, samplesInterleaved $= 1$)

Color

    FINDCOLOR (may return black), MAKESAMPLEDBLACK, SETSAMPLEDBLACK (clear $= 1$)

Graphics

    MASKRECTANGLE, MASKUNDERLINE, MASKVECTOR (with $x_1 = x_2$ or $y_1 = y_2$), STARTUNDERLINE

Perhaps the operators that printer manufacturers are most reluctant to support are IFCOPY, MAKESAMPLEDBLACK, and SETSAMPLEDBLACK. The IFCOPY operator complicates the internal representation of page images (the copy-dependent portions must be included). The MAKESAMPLEDBLACK and SETSAMPLEDBLACK require both mask and color channels (for example, for patterned text); supporting only a mask with black color is not sufficient. Because of these difficulties, some printers may fail to conform to the Commercial Set in these areas. So, although they are included in the set, you may wish to avoid these operators if possible.

The Publication Set

The Publication Set is designed to support in-house publishing applications. It includes all the Commercial Set operators, and in addition supplies synthetic graphics and gray-level color capabilities. It supports nested blocks in the skeleton, allowing documents to be constructed from other documents. Rectangular clipping is also included.

The following operators are supported in addition to those of the Commercial Set:

Color

    MAKEGRAY, SETGRAY, MAKESAMPLEDBLACK, SETSAMPLEDBLACK (no restrictions)

Graphics

    ARCTO, CONICTO, CURVETO, LINETO, LINETOX, LINETOY, MAKEOUTLINE, MAKEOUTLINEODD, MASKDASHEDSTROKE, MASKFILL, MASKSTROKE, MASKSTROKECLOSED, MASKTRAPEZOIDX, MASKTRAPEZOIDY, MASKVECTOR (no restrictions), MOVETO

Clipping

    CLIPRECTANGLE

The Professional Graphics Set

The Professional Graphics Set is the full Interpress language. All the Interpress facilities are available. This adds color, arbitrary rotations, and full clipping to the operators of the Publication Set.

The following operators are supported in addition to those of the Publication Set:

Transformation

> MAKET (no restrictions), ROTATE (no restrictions)

Character

> MAKEFONT, MASKCHAR

Pixel Array

> MAKEPIXELARRAY (no restrictions)

Color

> FINDCOLORMODELOPERATOR, FINDCOLOROPERATOR,
> MAKESAMPLEDCOLOR, SETSAMPLEDCOLOR

Clipping

> CLIPOUTLINE

Appendix B
ELEMENTS OF
INTERPRESS

This appendix contains a handy reference to the elements of the Interpress language. You will find in it sections on primitive operators, the skeleton or overall structure of an Interpress master, printing instructions, and imager variables. The first section, however, describes how you can encode various Interpress elements in a master.

Encoding

To make Interpress concepts useful, you must express them in a form that the machine can understand. In other words, you need an encoding for the language that specifies how to express operators, skeleton tokens, numbers, and identifiers. Many encodings are possible and Interpress does not restrict the encodings that you can use. One reason for the header string at the start of each master is to allow the printer to identify which encoding the master uses. Of course, for the document to print, it must be expressed in an encoding that the printer understands.

Xerox has included a standard encoding as part of Interpress. The header string "Interpress/Xerox/3.0 "at the start of a master identifies it as using the Xerox standard encoding for Interpress Version 3.0. This encoding is designed to make Interpress files compact, reducing transmission time and storage requirements. The tricks that reduce the file size result in an encoding that is a little more complicated than the minimum one. For example, there are two ways to express operators, five ways to express numbers, and several ways to represent large vectors of numbers.

There are five token formats in the standard encoding (see Figure B.1). The leftmost bit indicates whether the item is a number or something else. If the leftmost bit is 0, then the item is a number. If it is 1, then you look at the next two bits to select between a Short Op, a Long Op, a Short Sequence, or a Long Sequence.

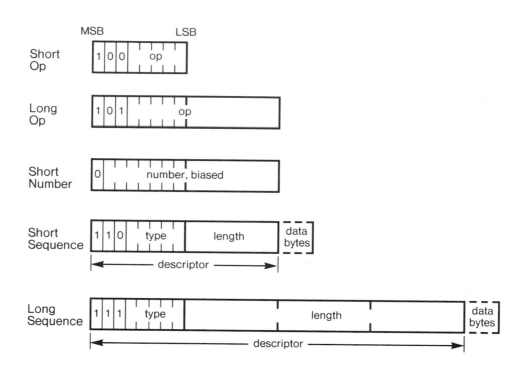

Figure B.1 Standard encoding formats.

Numbers

There are several ways to represent numbers. The Short Number form, the most compact, describes small integers, which are used for Boolean values, for indexing imager and frame variables, and even for coordinates if you choose a suitable master coordinate system. This representation uses 2 bytes and is identified by a 0 in the most significant bit of the first (most significant) byte. This leaves 15 bits to represent the number. To represent both positive and negative integers, the 15-bit value is biased by 4000. For example, the number 0 is represented by the value 4000.

$$
\begin{aligned}
0 \ \text{is encoded as} \quad &4000 = 0FA0 \text{ hex} \\
1 \ \text{is encoded as} \quad &4001 = 0FA1 \text{ hex} \\
-1 \ \text{is encoded as} \quad &3999 = 0F9F \text{ hex}
\end{aligned}
$$

$$-4000 \text{ is encoded as } 0000 = 0000 \text{ hex}$$
$$28767 \text{ is encoded as } 32767 = 7\text{FFF hex}$$

The biasing allows you to represent numbers between -4000 and $28,767$. Because it allows much larger positive integers than negative integers, the biasing provides for the large positive numbers that may be needed for the coordinates of points on the page. Integers outside this range and rational numbers are expressed as sequences; they are discussed in the following section.

Although the Xerox encoding does not directly support floating point numbers, you can use rational numbers to represent or approximate them. For example, 0.5 is equivalent to the rational number 1/2; 0.00035278 can be approximated by 24/68031. This approach generally leads to a more compact encoding, with no significant loss in precision.

Sequences

A sequence is a series of bytes used to encode items whose representation needs 3 or more bytes. Examples are identifiers, large numbers, comments, file names, and certain special vectors, such as a string of character codes or the samples of a pixel array.

The first byte of a sequence is a token indicating whether the sequence is long or short. The three most significant bits are "110" for a Short Sequence and "111" for a Long Sequence. The remaining five bits in both tokens identify the type of sequence. There are 32 possible types, but only 13 are defined (refer to Table B.1).

Table B.1 Sequence types by value.

Value	Name
1	sequenceString
2	sequenceInteger
3	sequenceInsertMaster
4	sequenceRational
5	sequenceIdentifier
6	sequenceComment
7	sequenceContinued
8	sequenceLargeVector
9	sequencePackedPixelVector
10	sequenceCompressedPixelVector
11	sequenceInsertFile
12	sequenceAdaptivePixelVector
13	sequenceCCITT-4PixelVector

A short sequence descriptor consists of a Short Sequence token and a byte specifying the length of the data part of the sequence in two's-complement form. Therefore, a short sequence can have at most 255 data bytes. This is adequate for most character strings, large integers, and rational numbers.

A long sequence descriptor consists of a Long Sequence token and three bytes containing the length of the sequence data in two's-complement form. Therefore, a long sequence can have up to $2^{24}-1$ data bytes. Long sequences are typically used to encode pixel array sample vectors.

The sequence data follows the sequence descriptor. The interpretation of the data bytes depend on the sequence type. The 13 defined sequence types are described below in alphabetical order. For each, we give the sequence type, the Short and Long Sequence token values, and the type of operand it encodes.

sequenceAdaptivePixelVector

12   Short Token = CC   Long Token = EC
→ < samples:Vector >

The data bytes contain a compressed sampled image in the [Xerox, Adaptive] format, as described in the Xerox Raster Encoding Standard. This compression scheme represents the image as a run-encoded sequence of error values, where the error is the difference between true and predicted sample values. There are 15 different predictors, and the one used is the one that would have worked best on the previous scan line. The sequence encoding automatically invokes the proper decompression operation, and explicit decompression of the samples vector is *not* required. The decompressed samples vector is placed on the stack.

sequenceCCITT-4PixelVector

13   Short Token = CD   Long Token = ED
→ < samples:Vector >

The data bytes contain a compressed sampled image in the [Xerox, CCITT-4] format, as described in the Xerox Raster Encoding Standard. This is the coding scheme designed by the CCITT as part of the Group 4 facsimile equipment standards. The sequence encoding automatically invokes the proper decompression operation, and explicit decompression of the samples vector is *not* required. The decompressed samples vector is placed on the stack.

sequenceComment

6   Short Token = C6   Long Token = E6
→ < >

The data bytes are ignored and the stack is unchanged.

sequenceCompressedPixelVector

10   Short Token = CA   Long Token = EA
→ <samples:Vector>

The data bytes contain a compressed sampled image in the [Xerox, Compressed] format, as described in the Xerox Raster Encoding Standard. This is a specialization of the [Xerox, adaptive] format. The sequence encoding automatically invokes the proper decompression operation, and explicit decompression of the samples vector is *not* required. The decompressed samples vector is placed on the stack.

sequenceContinued

7   Short Token = C7   Long Token = E7
→ <result depends on previous sequence>

The data bytes of the sequenceContinued construction are appended to the data bytes of the immediately preceding sequence. This allows you to extend sequences. For example, you could encode a large sample vector in several pieces: the first piece is a sequence of the appropriate type for encoding the samples, and the remaining pieces use sequenceContinued.

sequenceIdentifier

5   Short Token = C5   Long Token = E5
→ <id:Identifier>

This is the way all identifiers are expressed. The data bytes contain the ISO 646 character codes for the letters, digits, and minus characters that make up the identifier. For example, the short sequence encoding for the identifier "Xerox" is C5 05 58 65 72 6F 78 in hexadecimal. Uppercase letters may be included but are mapped to lowercase. All printers should support identifiers up to 100 characters in length.

sequenceInsertFile

11   Short Token = CB   Long Token = EB
→ <result depends on the contents of the file>

The data bytes give the name of a file containing Interpress literals or some representation of the effect of executing a sequence of literals. When a sequenceInsertFile is encountered, the input stream switches to the referenced file, and execution proceeds using that file as the source of Interpress instructions. When the end of the file is reached, the input stream reverts back to the tokens following the sequenceInsertFile. Because the referenced file can also use sequenceInsertFile, it is possible to nest sequenceInsertFiles. SequenceInsertFile may only occur within a body.

sequenceInsertMaster

3   Short Token = C3   Long Token = E3
→ does not apply

The data bytes of the sequence provide the name of a file that contains a complete Interpress master. The effect is to insert the outermost block of the referenced master, including the enclosing BEGIN and END tokens, at the point of sequenceInsertMaster. A sequenceInsertMaster must *not* occur within a body. SequenceInsertMasters may be nested if the inserted master also contains a sequenceInsertMaster construct.

sequenceInteger

2   Short Token = C2   Long Token = E2
→ <n:Number>

The data bytes contain the two's-complement representation of an integer. The bytes are ordered from most significant to least significant in the master. The sequence may be used to specify integers outside the range from −4000 to 28,767. For example, the short sequence encoding for 32,767 is C2 02 7F FF in hexadecimal. The specified integer is placed on the stack.

sequenceLargeVector

8   Short Token = C8   Long Token = E8
→ <v:Vector>

This sequence constructs a large vector of integers, such as might be used for a pixel-array sample vector. The sequence encoding lets the printer avoid the overhead of parsing each number, and may also allow it to circumvent its limitations on stack size. The first data byte of the sequence tells how many bytes should be used for each number in the vector. If the value of the first byte is b, then the remaining data is considered in b-byte groups. Each group is interpreted as a two's-complement integer. If there are ℓ data bytes in the sequence, then there will be $(\ell - 1)/b$ integers in the vector. The vector lower bound is 0.

sequencePackedPixelVector

9   Short Token = C9   Long Token = E9
→ <samples:Vector>

The data bytes contain a sampled image in the [Xerox, Packed] format, as described in the Xerox Raster Encoding Standard. The first and second data bytes form a 16-bit number that specifies the number of bits in each sample. The third and fourth bytes form a 16-bit integer that gives the number of samples in each scan line. The remaining bytes are also grouped into 16-bit quantities from which the sample values are extracted, high-order bit first. Padding is added to make each scan line a multiple of 32 bits. The sequence encoding automatically invokes the proper unpacking of the sample values, and explicit decompression is *not* required. The decompressed samples vector is placed on the stack.

sequenceRational

4   Short Token = C4   Long Token = E4
→ <n:Number>

This sequence provides the means for expressing rational numbers. There should be an even number of data bytes. The first half of the data is the two's-complement representation of the numerator. The last half of the data is the two's-complement encoding of the denominator. The resulting rational number is placed on the stack. For example, the short sequence encoding for 24/68031 is C4 06 00 00 18 01 09 BF in hexadecimal.

sequenceString

1   Short Token = C1   Long Token = E1
→ <v:Vector>

The sequenceString encoding offers a way to create the vector of character codes required by the SHOW operator. The data bytes determine the character codes. A run-encoding scheme is used that allows 16-bit character codes, while usually requiring only 1 byte per code in the sequence. The encoding is defined in the Xerox Character Code Standard and also in the Xerox Interpress Electronic Printing Standard. Informally, the character codes are grouped into 255 character subsets. A data byte in the sequence selects a character code from the current subset (which is subset 0 at the start of the sequence). If the data byte has the value 255, then the following byte (if it is between 0 and 254 inclusive) selects a new current subset. If the byte following the 255 value also has the value 255, then the next byte must be 0, and a mode is entered where the following bytes are considered in pairs and give 16-bit character codes. The sequenceString places the vector of resulting character codes on the stack. For example, the short sequence encoding for the character string "beta β" is C1 08 62 65 74 61 20 FF 26 62 in hexadecimal.

Operators and Skeleton Tokens

Operators and skeleton tokens are represented as either Short Ops or Long Ops. A Short Op token has 1 byte and a Long Op token, 2. The three leftmost bits of a Short Op token are "100," which leaves 5 bits to represent the encoding values of up to 32 operators. Currently, only the 17 most frequently used operators can be encoded as Short Op tokens: FGET, FSET, GET, IGET, ISET, LINETO, LINETOX, LINETOY, MASKSTROKE, MOVETO, NOP, SETXREL, SETXY,

Table B.2 Encoding values and token names.

Dec	Hex	Name	Dec	Hex	Name
1	01	NOP	148	94	MODIFYFONT
10	0A	SETXY	149	95	FINDDECOMPRESSOR
11	0B	SETXYREL	150	96	MAKEFONT
12	0C	SETXREL	151	97	SETFONT
13	0D	SETYREL	154	9A	SETCORRECTMEASURE
14	0E	LINETOX	155	9B	SETCORRECTTOLERANCE
15	0F	LINETOY	156	9C	CORRECTMASK
16	10	SPACE	157	9D	CORRECTSPACE
17	11	GET	159	9F	GETCP
18	12	IGET	160	A0	MAKET
19	13	ISET	162	A2	TRANSLATE
20	14	FGET	163	A3	ROTATE
21	15	FSET	164	A4	SCALE
22	16	SHOW	165	A5	CONCAT
23	17	LINETO	166	A6	SCALE2
24	18	MASKSTROKE	168	A8	CONCATT
25	19	MOVETO	169	A9	MOVE
102	66	BEGIN	170	AA	TRANS
103	67	END	180	B4	POP
105	69	CONTENTINSTRUCTIONS	181	B5	DUP
106	6A	{	183	B7	COPY
107	6B	}	184	B8	ROLL
110	6E	CORRECT	185	B9	EXCH
114	72	MAKESIMPLECO	186	BA	MARK
116	74	FINDOPERATOR	187	BB	UNMARK
120	78	DOSAVESIMPLEBODY	188	BC	COUNT
140	8C	MASKCHAR	192	C0	UNMARK0
145	91	SHOWANDFIXEDXREL	200	C8	ABS
146	92	SHOWANDXREL	201	C9	ADD
147	93	FINDFONT	202	CA	AND

SETXYREL, SETYREL, SHOW, and SPACE. You can optionally use the 2-byte Long Op format for these operators. All other operators and the skeleton tokens use the Long Op format. The three leftmost bits of a Long Op are "101": the 5 bits remaining in this byte and the 8 in the next allow 13-bit encoding values.

Table B.2 lists in numerical order the 117 currently-defined encoding values in both decimal and hexadecimal. The Short Op token value (in hex) is simply the sum of the encoding value and 80 hex; the Long Op token value is the sum of the encoding value and A000 hex.

Table B.2 Encoding values and token names (cont'd).

Dec	Hex	Name	Dec	Hex	Name
203	CB	CEILING	404	194	CONICTO
204	CC	DIV	409	199	MASKFILL
205	CD	EQ	410	19A	MASKRECTANGLE
206	CE	FLOOR	411	19B	MASKTRAPEZOIDX
207	CF	GE	412	19C	MASKTRAPEZOIDY
208	D0	GT	413	19D	STARTUNDERLINE
209	D1	MOD	414	19E	MASKUNDERLINE
210	D2	MUL	416	1A0	MAKEOUTLINEODD
211	D3	NEG	417	1A1	MAKEOUTLINE
212	D4	NOT	418	1A2	CLIPOUTLINE
213	D5	OR	419	1A3	CLIPRECTANGLE
214	D6	SUB	421	1A5	FINDCOLOROPERATOR
215	D7	TRUNC	422	1A6	FINDCOLORMODELOPERATOR
216	D8	REM	423	1A7	FINDCOLOR
217	D9	ROUND	424	1A8	SETGRAY
220	DC	TYPE	425	1A9	MAKEGRAY
231	E7	DO	426	1AA	MAKESAMPLEDBLACK
232	E8	DOSAVE	427	1AB	MAKESAMPLEDCOLOR
233	E9	DOSAVEALL	428	1AC	SETSAMPLEDBLACK
239	EF	IF	429	1AD	SETSAMPLEDCOLOR
240	F0	IFCOPY	440	1B8	MASKSTROKECLOSED
241	F1	IFELSE	441	1B9	MASKVECTOR
282	11A	MAKEVECLU	442	1BA	MASKDASHEDSTROKE
283	11B	MAKEVEC	450	1C2	MAKEPIXELARRAY
285	11D	SHAPE	451	1C3	EXTRACTPIXELARRAY
286	11E	GETP	452	1C4	MASKPIXEL
287	11F	GETPROP	600	258	ERROR
288	120	MERGEPROP			
402	192	CURVETO			
403	193	ARCTO			

ISO 646 Character Codes

The Xerox standard encoding for Interpress uses the ISO 646 7-bit character codes for encoding the header string, identifiers, messages, and file names. The matrix on the next page shows the ISO 646 character codes. The shaded spaces are reserved for control characters. The hexadecimal code for a given character is the sum of the numbers heading the column and row that it occupies. For example, the code for "b" is $60 + 2 = 62$.

Matrix of ISO 646 7-bit Character Codes

	00	10	20	30	40	50	60	70
0			space	0	@	P	`	p
1			!	1	A	Q	a	q
2			"	2	B	R	b	r
3			#	3	C	S	c	s
4			$	4	D	T	d	t
5			%	5	E	U	e	u
6			&	6	F	V	f	v
7			'	7	G	W	g	w
8			(	8	H	X	h	x
9			)	9	I	Y	i	y
A			*	:	J	Z	j	z
B			+	;	K	[	k	{
C			,	<	L	\	l	|
D			–	=	M	]	m	}
E			.	>	N	^	n	~
F			/	?	O	_	o	

Operators

This section presents a summary of all the operators of the Interpress language in alphabetical order. In some cases, the descriptions are less precise than the more formally structured and mathematically precise definitions in the Interpress standard, which is the final authority. For each operator, we give the name, the encoding value in decimal and hex, the Long Op token value in hex, the Short Op token value (if any), and the syntax of its use, as well as a brief description of the semantics.

ABS

200   C8   Token Value = A0C8
$<$a:Number$>$ ABS $\rightarrow$ $<$c:Number$>$

Pops the number a and returns its absolute value $c = |a|$ on the stack.

ADD

201   C9   Token Value = A0C9
$<$a:Number$>$$<$b:Number$>$ ADD $\rightarrow$ $<$c:Number$>$

Pops the numbers a and b and returns their sum $c = a + b$ on the stack.

AND

202   CA   Token Value = A0CA
$<$a:Cardinal$>$$<$b:Cardinal$>$ AND $\rightarrow$ $<$c:Cardinal$>$

If both a and b are nonzero, returns $c = 1$ on the stack; otherwise, returns $c = 0$.

ARCTO

403   193   Token Value = A193
$<$t$_1$:Trajectory$>$ $<$x$_1$:Number$>$ $<$y$_1$:Number$>$ $<$x$_2$:Number$>$
$<$y$_2$:Number$>$ ARCTO $\rightarrow$ $<$t$_2$:Trajectory$>$

Extends the trajectory t_1 by appending a circular arc starting at the last point of t_1, passing through the point (x_1,y_1) and ending at (x_2,y_2). The resultant new trajectory t_2 is returned to the stack. If the point (x_2,y_2) coincides with the last point of the trajectory t_1, ARCTO appends a circle, traced counterclockwise, with (x_1,y_1) diametrically opposite (x_2,y_2).

CEILING

203   CB   Token Value = A0CB
$<$a:Number$>$ CEILING $\rightarrow$ $<$c:Number$>$

Returns the number c, the least integer $\geq$ a, on the stack.

CLIPOUTLINE

418   1A2   Token Value = A1A2
$<$o:Outline$>$ CLIPOUTLINE $\rightarrow$ $<$ $>$

Intersects the outline o with the current clipping region to produce a new clipping region, which it installs in the clipper imager variable. A point is inside the new clipper only if it lies inside both the old clipper and the outline o.

CLIPRECTANGLE

419   1A3   Token Value = A1A3

$<x_1:Number> <y_1:Number> <x_2:Number> <y_2:Number>$
CLIPRECTANGLE $\rightarrow$ $< >$

Creates a rectangular outline with corners at (x_1,y_1), (x_1,y_1+y_2), (x_1+x_2, y_1+y_2) (x_1+x_2,y_1) in the master coordinate system. This outline is then intersected with the current clipping region to form a new clipping region, which is installed in the imager variable clipper.

CONCAT

165   A5   Token Value = A0A5

$<t_1:Transformation> <t_2:Transformation>$
CONCAT $\rightarrow$ $<t_3:Transformation>$

Computes the transformation $t_3=t_1\times t_2$ (the composite of transformation t_1 followed by transformation t_2), and returns it on the stack.

CONCATT

168   A8   Token Value = A0A8

$<t:Transformation>$ CONCATT $\rightarrow$ $< >$

The transformation t is left concatenated with the current transformation T to form $t\times T$, which then replaces the current transformation in the imager variable T.

CONICTO

404   194   Token Value = A194

$<t_1:Trajectory> <x_1:Number> <y_1:Number> <x_2:Number>$
$<y_2:Number> <s:Number>$ CONICTO $\rightarrow$ $<t_2:Trajectory>$

Extends the trajectory t_1 by appending a conic curve segment defined by the last point of the trajectory t_1, the point (x_1, y_1), the point (x_2, y_2), and a shape parameter s. The resultant trajectory t_2 is returned to the stack.

COPY

183   B7   Token Value = A0B7

$<x_1:Any> <x_2:Any>...<x_n:Any> <n:Cardinal>$
COPY $\rightarrow$ $<x_1> <x_2>...<x_n> <x_1> <x_2>...<x_n>$

Pops the number n and the next n operands from the stack and then pushes the same n values back onto the stack twice, each time retaining their order.

CORRECT

110   6E   Token Value = A06E
CORRECT < b:Body > → < >

Adjusts the spacing of the characters imaged in the body b so that the change in current position is within correctTolerance of the correctMeasure value.

CORRECTMASK

156   9C   Token Value = A09C
< > CORRECTMASK → < >

When included in a composed operator, makes the image created by the operator behave like a mask-correcting character under CORRECT.

CORRECTSPACE

157   9D   Token Value = A09D
< x:Number > < y:Number > CORRECTSPACE → < >

When included in a composed operator, makes the image created by the operator behave under CORRECT like a space-correcting character with width in master coordinates specified by the operands x and y.

COUNT

188   BC   Token Value = A0BC
< m:Mark > < x_1:Any > < x_2:Any > . . . < x_n:Any >
COUNT → < m:Mark > < x_1 > < x_2 > . . . < x_n > < n:Cardinal >

Counts the number n of operands above the uppermost mark on the stack, and pushes the value n onto the stack.

CURVETO

402   192   Token Value = A192
< t_1:Trajectory > < x_1:Number > < y_1:Number >
< x_2:Number > < y_2:Number > < x_3:Number > < y_3:Number >
CURVETO → < t_2:Trajectory >

Extends the trajectory t_1 by appending a Bézier curve whose control points are the last point of t_1 and the points (x_1,y_1), (x_2,y_2), and (x_3,y_3) in master coordinates. The resultant trajectory t_2 is returned to the stack.

DIV

204   CC   Token Value = A0CC
< a:Number > < b:Number > DIV → < c:Number >

Returns $c = a/b$, the rational signed quotient of a and b, on the stack.

DO

231   E7   Token Value = A0E7

<o:Operator> DO → <effect on the stack depends on o>

Executes the composed operator o. Any imager variable changed by the execution of the composed operator is left in its changed state upon completion of the operator.

DOSAVE

232   E8   Token Value = A0E8

<o:Operator> DOSAVE → <effect on the stack depends on o>

Executes the composed operator o. Upon completion of the operator, all nonpersistent imager variables are restored to the state they had before the execution of the operator; persistent variables changed by the operator are left in their changed state.

DOSAVEALL

233   E9   Token Value = A0E9

<o:Operator> DOSAVEALL → <effect on the stack depends on o>

Executes the composed operator o. Upon completion of the operator, all imager variables are restored to the state they had before execution of the operator.

DOSAVESIMPLEBODY

120   78   Token Value = A078

DOSAVESIMPLEBODY <b:Body> → <effect on the stack depends on b>

Converts the body b into a composed operator, and executes it in a DOSAVE manner.

DUP

181   B5   Token Value = A0B5

<x:Any> DUP → <x><x>

Pops the top element from the stack and then returns two copies of it to the stack.

EQ

205   CD   Token Value = A0CD

<a:Any><b:Any> EQ → <c:Cardinal>

Returns c=1 if a and b are both numbers or both identifiers, and a is identical to b; otherwise, c = 0 is returned.

ERROR

600   258   Token Value = A258
<m:Vector of Cardinal> <c:Cardinal> ERROR → < >

Prints the error message m, expressed as a vector of ISO 646 character codes, and the severity code c in the printer error log. The five possible values for the severity code are

0	master error
10	master warning
50	appearance error
60	appearance warning
100	comment

EXCH

185   B9   Token Value = A0B9
<a:Any> <b:Any> EXCH → <b> <a>

Exchanges the positions of the top two elements on the stack.

EXTRACTPIXELARRAY

451   1C3   Token Value = A1C3
<pa:Pixel Array> <select:Vector of Cardinal>
EXTRACTPIXELARRAY → <p:Pixel Array>

Creates a pixel array p from a subset of the samples of pixel array pa and returns it on the stack. The vector *select* gives the indices of the samples in pa that are used to form p. If the original pixel array pa has n samples per pixel, then the operand *select* must be a vector of cardinals with values between 0 and n. The width, height, samplesInterleaved, and transformation parameters are the same for both pixel arrays.

FGET

20   14   Token Value = A014   Short Token Value = 94
<j:Cardinal> FGET → <x:Any>

Pushes a copy of the operand x stored in frame location j onto the stack. The contents of frame location j are not affected.

FINDCOLOR

423   1A7   Token Value = A1A7
<v:Vector of Identifiers> FINDCOLOR → <col:ConstantColor>

The vector of identifiers v contains the universal name of a specific color. The specified constant color col is returned to the stack if the color is found in the printer's environment. Otherwise, an approximation to the color is returned and an appearance warning is generated.

FINDCOLORMODELOPERATOR

422   1A6   Token Value = A1A6
<v:Vector of Identifiers>
FINDCOLORMODELOPERATOR → <colorModelOp:Operator>

The vector of identifiers v contains the universal name of a specific color model operator. The operator colorModelOp is returned to the stack if it is found in the printer's environment; otherwise, a master error is generated.

FINDCOLOROPERATOR

421   1A5   Token Value = A1A5
<v:Vector of Identifiers> FINDCOLOROPERATOR → <colorOp:Operator>

The vector of identifiers v contains the universal name of a specific color operator. The specified operator colorOp is returned to the stack if it is found in the printer's environment; otherwise, a master error is generated.

FINDDECOMPRESSOR

149   95   Token Value = A095
<v:Vector of Identifiers> FINDDECOMPRESSOR → <decomp:Operator>

The vector of identifiers v contains the universal name of a decompression operator decomp, which is returned to the stack if it is found in the printer's environment. Otherwise, a master error is generated.

FINDFONT

147   93   Token Value = A093
<v:Vector of Identifiers> FINDFONT → <f:Font>

The vector of identifiers v contains the universal name of a specific font f, which is returned to the stack if the font is found in the printer's environment. Otherwise, an approximation to the font is returned and an appearance warning is generated.

FINDOPERATOR

116   74   Token Value = A074
<v:Vector of Identifiers> FINDOPERATOR → <o:Operator>

The vector of identifiers v contains a universal name of a specific operator o, which is returned to the stack if it is found in the printer's environment. Otherwise, a master error is generated.

FLOOR

206   CE   Token Value = A0CE
<a:Number> FLOOR → <c:Number>

Returns the number c, the greatest integer ≤ a, on the stack.

FSET

21   15   Token Value = A015   Short Token Value = 95
<x:Any> <j:Cardinal> FSET → < >

Pops the operands x and j from the stack and stores x in frame location j.

GE

207   CF   Token Value = A0CF
<a:Number> <b:Number> GE → <c:Cardinal>

Returns the value c = 1 on the stack if a ≥ b; otherwise, returns c = 0.

GET

17   11   Token Value = A011   Short Token Value = 91
<v:Vector> <j:Cardinal> GET → <x:Any>

Pops the vector v and index value j from the stack and returns the operand x, which is component j of the vector, to the stack. A master error occurs if j is not in the index range of the vector.

GETCP

159   9F   Token Value = A09F
< > GETCP → <x:Number> <y:Number>

Converts the device coordinates of the current position, stored in imager variables DCScpx and DCScpy, to master coordinates and returns them to the stack. A master error is generated if the current transformation T cannot be inverted.

GETP

286   11E   Token Value = A11E
<v:Vector> <propName:Any> GETP → <value:Any>

Assumes the operand v is a property vector and returns the value of the first entry in the vector with the property name propName. The operand propName should be a cardinal, identifier, or vector of identifiers. If a matching entry is not found, a master error is generated.

GETPROP

> 287   11F   Token Value = A11F
>
> <v:Vector> <propName:Any>
> GETPROP → <value:Any> <1:Cardinal> or <0:Cardinal>
>
> Assumes the operand v is a property vector. If a property name matching the value of the operand propName is found, the corresponding value is returned to the stack, followed by the cardinal value 1. If no match is found, only the cardinal value 0 is returned. The operand propName should be a cardinal, identifier, or vector of identifiers.

GT

> 208   D0   Token Value = A0D0
>
> <a:Number> <b:Number> GT → <c:Cardinal>
>
> Returns c = 1 to the stack if a > b; otherwise, returns c = 0.

IF

> 239   EF   Token Value = A0EF
>
> <i:Cardinal> IF <b:Body> → <effect on the stack depends on i and b>
>
> If i = 0, IF pops the operand i and bypasses the body. If i = 1, IF pops i and converts the body b to a composed operator, which it immediately executes in a DO manner using a copy of the current frame for its work space.

IFCOPY

> 240   F0   Token Value = A0F0
>
> <testCopy:Operator> IFCOPY <b:Body> → < >
>
> IFCOPY pushes the copyNumber and copyName on the stack and then executes testCopy in a DOSAVEALL manner. The operand testCopy is a composed operator that consumes the copy name and copy number values from the stack and returns a cardinal value to the stack. If it returns the value 0, IFCOPY bypasses the body b. Otherwise, IFCOPY converts b to a composed operator and executes it in a DOSAVEALL manner.

IFELSE

> 241   F1   Token Value = A0F1
>
> <i:Cardinal> IFELSE <b:Body> →
> <effect on the stack depends on i and b>
>
> If i = 0, IFELSE bypasses the body b and returns a cardinal c = 1 to the stack. If i = 1, IFELSE converts b to a composed operator, executes it in a DO manner, and then returns a cardinal c = 0 to the stack.

IGET

18   12   Token Value = A012   Short Token Value = 92
$<$j:Cardinal$>$ IGET $\rightarrow$ $<$x:Any$>$

Pushes a copy of the operand x stored in the imager variable with index j onto the stack. The imager variable is not affected by this operation. A master error occurs if j is outside the range of imager variable indices.

ISET

19   13   Token Value = A013   Short Token Value = 93
$<$x:Any$>$ $<$j:Cardinal$>$ ISET $\rightarrow$ $<>$

Pops x and j from the stack and stores x in the imager variable with index j. A master error occurs if the type of operand x does not match the type of imager variable j, or j is outside the range of imager variable indices, or an attempt is made to set one of the medium or field imager variables (indices 6 through 11).

LINETO

23   17   Token Value = A017   Short Token Value = 97
$<t_1$:Trajectory$>$ $<x_2$:Number$>$ $<y_2$:Number$>$
LINETO $\rightarrow$ $<t_2$:Trajectory$>$

Extends the trajectory t_1 by drawing a line from its endpoint (x_1,y_1) to the point (x_2,y_2). The resultant trajectory t_2 is returned on the stack.

LINETOX

14   0E   Token Value = A00E   Short Token Value = 8E
$<t_1$:Trajectory$>$ $<x_2$:Number$>$ LINETOX $\rightarrow$ $<t_2$:Trajectory$>$

Extends the trajectory t_1 by drawing a line from its endpoint (x_1,y_1) to the point (x_2,y_1). The resultant trajectory t_2 is returned on the stack.

LINETOY

15   0F   Token Value = A00F   Short Token Value = 8F
$<t_1$:Trajectory$>$ $<y_2$:Number$>$ LINETOY $\rightarrow$ $<t_2$:Trajectory$>$

Extends the trajectory t_1 by drawing a line from its endpoint (x_1,y_1) to the point (x_1,y_2). The resultant trajectory t_2 is returned on the stack.

MAKEFONT

150   96   Token Value = A096
$<$fd:Vector$>$ MAKEFONT $\rightarrow$ $<$f:Font$>$

Creates an object f of type Font using the information in the vector fd and returns it to the stack. The operand fd must be a fontDescription vector.

MAKEGRAY

425   1A9   Token Value = A1A9

<f:Number> MAKEGRAY → <col:ConstantColor>

Generates the shade of gray specified by the number f, which lies between 0 and 1, and returns it as an object col of type Color (subtype Constant-Color) on the stack. Informally, MAKEGRAY linearly maps f onto a range of gray intensities between white (f=0) and black (f=1).

MAKEOUTLINE

417   1A1   Token Value = A1A1

<t_1:Trajectory> <t_2:Trajectory>...<t_n:Trajectory> <n:Cardinal> MAKEOUTLINE → <o:Outline>

If any of the n trajectories t_i is not closed, it is first converted to a closed trajectory by adding a line between its start and endpoints. The n closed trajectories thus produced are combined into an object o of type Outline, which is returned to the stack. The interior of the outline is the collection of all points with a nonzero winding number.

MAKEOUTLINEODD

416   1A0   Token Value = A1A0

<t_1:Trajectory> <t_2:Trajectory>...<t_n:Trajectory> <n:Cardinal> MAKEOUTLINEODD → <o:Outline>

If any of the n trajectories t_i is not closed, it is first converted to a closed trajectory by adding a line between its start and endpoints. The n closed trajectories thus produced are combined into an object o of type Outline, which is returned to the stack. The interior of the outline is the collection of all points with odd winding numbers.

MAKEPIXELARRAY

450   1C2   Token Value = A1C2

<xPixels:Cardinal> <yPixels:Cardinal> <samplesPerPixel:Cardinal> <maxSampleValue:Cardinal or Vector of Cardinal> <samplesInterleaved:Cardinal> <m:Transformation> <samples:Vector of Cardinal> MAKEPIXELARRAY → <pa:PixelArray>

Creates an object pa of type PixelArray from the operand *samples*, a vector of image samples, and returns it on the stack. The pixel array is a rectangle xPixels wide and yPixels high in the pixel-array coordinate system. The operand samplesPerPixel gives the number of samples in each pixel of the array. The operand maxSampleValue gives the maximum value of the samples. If maxSampleValue is a vector of cardinals, then its ith component gives the maximum value of the ith sample of a pixel; if it is a cardinal, then all samples have the same maximum value. The image samples themselves are contained in the operand *samples*. If the samplesInterleaved operand is 0, the samples are not interleaved and the ith samples of all the pixels occur consecutively in the vector *samples*; otherwise, the samples are interleaved and all the samples of each pixel occur consecutively in the vector. The transformation m converts from pixel-array coordinates to master coordinates and is used for orienting, sizing, and positioning the pixel array.

MAKESAMPLEDBLACK

426   1AA   Token Value = A1AA
< pa:PixelArray > < um:Transformation > < clear:Cardinal >
MAKESAMPLEDBLACK → < col:Color >

Creates a black-and-white sampled ink col from the binary pixel array pa and returns it on the stack. The pixel array pa must be created with the operands samplesPerPixel, maxSampleValue, and samplesInterleaved all set to 1. The transformation um maps the pixel array pa to device coordinates. The operand clear specifies the behavior of zero-valued pixels when the ink is used. When clear is 0, zero-valued pixels write white on the page; otherwise, they are transparent and leave the page unchanged.

MAKESAMPLEDCOLOR

427   1AB   Token Value = A1AB
< pa:PixelArray > < um:Transformation > < colorOp:Operator >
MAKESAMPLEDCOLOR → < col:Color >

Creates a colored sampled ink col from the pixel array pa and returns it on the stack. The transformation um maps the pixel array to device coordinates and the color operator colorOp converts the samples of each pixel to a color.

MAKESIMPLECO

114   72   Token Value = A072
MAKESIMPLECO < b:Body > → < o:Operator >

Creates a composed operator o with body b and returns it on the stack. Associated with the operator is a copy of the frame made at the time MAKESIMPLECO is executed.

MAKET

160   A0   Token Value = A0A0
< a:Number > < b:Number > < c:Number > < d:Number > < e:Number >
< f:Number > MAKET → < t:Transformation >

Builds and returns to the stack a transformation with the following matrix representation:

$$\begin{bmatrix} a & d & 0 \\ b & e & 0 \\ c & f & 1 \end{bmatrix}$$

MAKEVEC

283   11B   Token Value = A11B

$<x_1{:}Any> <x_2{:}Any>\ldots<x_n{:}Any> <n{:}Cardinal>$
MAKEVEC $\rightarrow$ $<v{:}Vector>$

Pops the value n and the next n operands from the stack and combines the n operands into an object v of type Vector which it returns to the stack. The components of the vector v can be accessed by integer indices between 0 and $n-1$; the operand x_1 has index 0 and the operand x_n has index $n-1$. A null vector results if $n \leq 0$.

MAKEVECLU

282   11A   Token Value = A11A

$<x_1{:}Any> <x_2{:}Any>\ldots<x_n{:}Any> <l{:}Cardinal> <u{:}Cardinal>$
MAKEVECLU $\rightarrow$ $<v{:}Vector>$

Pops the values l and u and the next $n = l - u + 1$ operands from the stack and combines the $l - u + 1$ operands into an object v of type Vector which it returns on the stack. The components of the vector v can be accessed by integer indices between l and u inclusively; the operand x_1 has index l and the operand x_n has index u. A null vector results if $l > u$.

MARK

186   BA   Token Value = A0BA

$<x_1{:}Any> <x_2{:}Any>\ldots<x_n{:}Any> <n{:}Cardinal>$
MARK $\rightarrow$ $<m{:}Mark> <x_1> <x_2> \ldots <x_n>$

Pops the value n and the next n operands from the stack, pushes a mark m on the stack, and then pushes the n operands back on the stack in their original order.

MASKCHAR

140   8C   Token Value = A08C

$<fd{:}Vector> <i{:}Cardinal>$ MASKCHAR $\rightarrow$ $<fd>$

The vector fd must be a fontDescription vector. MASKCHAR executes the character mask operator with index i in vector fd at the current position, which is left unchanged. The fontDescription vector fd is returned to the stack so that the MASKCHAR operator can be repeated with other character index values to construct compound characters from the existing characters of a font. The current transformation in effect when MASKCHAR is called transforms font-description coordinates to device coordinates.

MASKDASHEDSTROKE

442   1BA   Token Value = A1BA
<t:Trajectory> <pattern:Vector of Number> <offset:Number>
<length:Number> MASKDASHEDSTROKE → < >

Images a dashed line with alternating strokes or dashes and spaces whose centerline is the trajectory t. The operand *pattern* is a vector describing the lengths of the dashes and spaces in master coordinates: the first element is the length of the first dash; the second element, the length of the first space; the third element, the length of the second dash; and so on. The vector is repeated as many times as needed to supply dash and space lengths. The operand *offset* specifies the starting position in the pattern. A pattern with a positive-valued length as specified by the operand *length* is stretched or shrunk to match the actual length of the trajectory t. If the value of *length* is 0 or negative, then the lengths of the dashes and spaces as specified by the operand *pattern* are not adjusted. The current color, strokeJoint, strokeWidth, and strokeEnd imager variables apply to each dash.

MASKFILL

409   199   Token Value = A199
<o:Outline> MASKFILL → < >

Transforms the outline o to device coordinates using the current transformation T, creates a mask defined by the interior of the transformed outline (the interior of the outline is determined by the winding-number convention used to create the outline o), and then applies the current color to the page image through the mask.

MASKPIXEL

452   1C4   Token Value = A1C4
<pa: Pixel Array> MASKPIXEL → < >

The operand pa must be a binary pixel array, created with the operands samplesPerPixel, maxSampleValue, and samplesInterleaved all set to 1. MASKPIXEL transforms the pixel array to device coordinates using the current transformation T, converts the pixels in the transformed array with value 1 into a mask, and then applies the current color to the page image through them.

MASKRECTANGLE

410   19A   Token Value = A19A
$<$x:Number$> <$y:Number$> <$w:Number$> <$h:Number$>$
MASKRECTANGLE $\rightarrow$ $<>$

Creates a rectangular outline with corners located at the points (x,y), (x+w,y), (x,y+h), and (x+w,y+h) in the master coordinate system. This outline is then mapped to device coordinates, using the current transformation T. The interior of the transformed outline is converted to a mask and the current color applied to the page image through it.

MASKSTROKE

24   18   Token Value = A018   Short Token Value = 98
$<$t:Trajectory$>$ MASKSTROKE $\rightarrow$ $<>$

Creates a mask whose centerline is the trajectory t, by thickening the trajectory to the width specified by the imager variable stokeWidth, and maps it to device coordinates. It then applies the current color through the mask to the page image. The imager variable strokeJoint describes the joints between trajectory segments and the imager variable strokeEnd describes the end caps of the mask.

MASKSTROKECLOSED

440   1B8   Token Value = A1B8
$<$t:Trajectory$>$ MASKSTROKECLOSED $\rightarrow$ $<>$

This operator is identical to MASKSTROKE, except that if the trajectory t is not closed, it is first closed by adding a line segment joining the start and endpoints of the trajectory. It uses a stroke joint between the first and last segments instead of the end caps used by MASKSTROKE.

MASKTRAPEZOIDX

411   19B   Token Value = A19B
$<$x$_1$:Number$> <$y$_1$:Number$> <$x$_2$:Number$> <$x$_3$:Number$>$
$<$y$_3$:Number$> <$x$_4$:Number$>$ MASKTRAPEZOIDX $\rightarrow$ $<>$

Creates a trapezoidal-shaped outline whose vertices are located at the points (x_1,y_1), (x_2,y_1), (x_3,y_3), and (x_4,y_3). The parallel sides of the trapezoid are parallel to the x axis of the master coordinate system. This outline is mapped to device coordinates, using the current transformation. The interior of the transformed outline is then converted to a mask and the current color applied to the page image through it.

MASKTRAPEZOIDY

412   19C   Token Value = A19C

$<x_1:Number> <y_1:Number> <y_2:Number> <x_3:Number>$
$<y_3:Number> <y_4:Number>$ MASKTRAPEZOIDY → $< >$

Creates a trapezoidal-shaped outline whose vertices are located at the points (x_1,y_1), (x_1,y_2), (x_3,y_3), and (x_3,y_4). This operator is identical to MASKTRAPEZOIDX, except that the parallel sides of the outline are parallel to the y axis of the master coordinate system.

MASKUNDERLINE

414   19E   Token Value = A19E

$<dy:Number> <h:Number>$ MASKUNDERLINE → $< >$

Creates a rectangular outline with corners located at the points $(x_s,$ $y_{cp}-dy-h)$, $(x_s,y_{cp}-dy)$, $(x_{cp},y_{cp}-dy)$, and $(x_{cp},y_{cp}-dy-h)$. The operands dy and h are specified in master coordinates. The current position is (x_{cp},y_{cp}) and x_s is the starting x position in the imager variable underlineStart. The outline is mapped to device coordinates, using the current transformation T. The interior of the transformed outline is converted to a mask and the current color applied to the page image through it.

MASKVECTOR

441   1B9   Token Value = A1B9

$<x_1:Number> <y_1:Number> <x_2:Number> <y_2:Number>$
MASKVECTOR → $< >$

Creates a mask whose centerline is the line segment joining the points (x_1,y_1) and (x_2,y_2), maps it to device coordinates, and then applies the current color through the mask to the page image. The imager variables strokeWidth and strokeEnd determines the thickness and end caps of the mask, respectively.

MERGEPROP

288   120   Token Value = A120

$<v_1:Vector> <v_2:Vector>$ MERGEPROP → $<v_3:Vector>$

The operands v_1 and v_2 must be property vectors. Constructs a property vector v_3 that includes every propertyName-propertyValue pair that is in either of the vectors v_1 or v_2. If the property name is found in both v_1 and v_2, the property value found in v_2 is included in v_3, and the property value found in v_1 cannot be reached. The number of components of v_3 and their order are printer dependent.

MOD

209   D1   Token Value = A0D1

$<$a:Number$><$b:Number$>$ MOD $\rightarrow$ $<$c:Number$>$

Pops the numbers a and b and returns the number $c = a - (b \times i)$ to the stack, where i is the greatest integer less than or equal to the quotient a/b. A master error is generated if b is equal to zero.

MODIFYFONT

148   94   Token Value = A094

$<$f$_1$:Font$><$m:Transformation$>$ MODIFYFONT $\rightarrow$ $<$f$_2$:Font$>$

Creates an object f$_2$ of type Font by applying the transformation m to the font f$_1$ and returns f$_2$ to the stack.

MOVE

169   A9   Token Value = A0A9

$< >$ MOVE $\rightarrow$ $< >$

Modifies the current transformation T so that the origin of the master coordinate system is at the current position.

MOVETO

25   19   Token Value = A019   Short Token Value = 99

$<$x:Number$><$y:Number$>$ MOVETO $\rightarrow$ $<$t:Trajectory$>$

Creates a zero-length trajectory with the same start and endpoint (x,y) in the master coordinate system and returns it on the stack.

MUL

210   D2   Token Value = A0D2

$<$a:Number$><$b:Number$>$ MUL $\rightarrow$ $<$c:Number$>$

Pops the numbers a and b and returns their product $c = a \times b$ to the stack.

NEG

211   D3   Token Value = A0D3

$<$a:Number$>$ NEG $\rightarrow$ $<$c:Number$>$

Pops the number a and returns $c = -a$ to the stack.

NOP

1   1   Token Value = A001   Short Token Value = 81

$< >$ NOP $\rightarrow$ $< >$

Executing this operator has no effect on the stack or on the state of the machine.

NOT

212   D4   Token Value = A0D4

$<$a:Cardinal$>$ NOT $\rightarrow$ $<$c:Cardinal$>$

Returns $c = 1$ on the stack if $a = 0$; otherwise, returns $c = 0$.

OR

213   D5   Token Value = A0D5

$<$a:Cardinal$>$ $<$b:Cardinal$>$ OR $\rightarrow$ $<$c:Cardinal$>$

Returns $c = 0$ on the stack if both a and b are zero; otherwise, returns $c = 1$.

POP

180   B4   Token Value = A0B4

$<$x:Any$>$ POP $\rightarrow$ $<$ $>$

Pops the top element from the stack and discards it.

REM

216   D8   Token Value = A0D8

$<$a:Number$>$ $<$b:Number$>$ REM $\rightarrow$ $<$c:Number$>$

Pops the numbers a and b and returns the number $c = a-(b \times i)$ to the stack, where i is the integer part of the quotient a/b. A master error is generated if b is equal to zero.

ROLL

184   B8   Token Value = A0B8

$<$x$_1$:Any$>$ $<$x$_2$:Any$>$ ... $<$x$_n$:Any$>$ $<$n:Cardinal$>$ $<$a:Cardinal$>$
ROLL $\rightarrow$ $<$x$_{a+1}$$>$ $<$x$_{a+2}$$>$ ... $<$x$_n$$>$ $<$x$_1$$>$ $<$x$_2$$>$ ... $<$x$_a$$>$

Pops the values n and a and the next n operands from the stack. The first a of these operands $x_1, x_2, \ldots, x_a$ are set aside and the next $n-a$ operands $x_{a+1}, x_{a+2}, \ldots, x_n$ are pushed on the stack, retaining their order. Then the operands $x_1, x_2, \ldots, x_a$ are pushed back on the stack. Informally, the ROLL operator exchanges the order of two groups of operands on the stack, without changing the order of the operands within each group; the first group is the top $n-a$ operands on the stack and the second group is the next a operands on the stack.

ROTATE

163   A3   Token Value = A0A3

$<$a:Number$>$ ROTATE $\rightarrow$ $<$t:Transformation$>$

Pops the number a, which it interprets as an angle expressed in degrees, then builds and returns to the stack the transformation t with the following matrix representation:

$$\begin{bmatrix} \cos a & \sin a & 0 \\ -\sin a & \cos a & 0 \\ 0 & 0 & 1 \end{bmatrix}$$

ROUND

217   D9   Token Value = A0D9

$<$a:Number$>$ ROUND $\to$ $<$c:Number$>$

Returns the number c, equal to the integer part of $a + 0.5$, on the stack.

SCALE

164   A4   Token Value = A0A4

$<$s:Number$>$ SCALE $\to$ $<$t:Transformation$>$

Builds and returns on the stack the transformation t, with the following matrix representation:

$$\begin{bmatrix} s & 0 & 0 \\ 0 & s & 0 \\ 0 & 0 & 1 \end{bmatrix}$$

SCALE2

166   A6   Token Value = A0A6

$<$a:Number$>$ $<$e:Number$>$ SCALE2 $\to$ $<$t:Transformation$>$

Builds and returns on the stack the transformation t, with the following matrix representation:

$$\begin{bmatrix} a & 0 & 0 \\ 0 & e & 0 \\ 0 & 0 & 1 \end{bmatrix}$$

SETCORRECTMEASURE

154   9A   Token Value = A09A

$<$x:Number$>$ $<$y:Number$>$ SETCORRECTMEASURE $\to$ $<$ $>$

Transforms the displacement (x,y) from master coordinates to device coordinates and stores the results in the imager variables correctMX and correctMY, which contain the desired shift in current position for a collection of images in a CORRECT body.

SETCORRECTTOLERANCE

155   9B   Token Value = A09B

$<$x:Number$>$ $<$y:Number$>$ SETCORRECTTOLERANCE $\to$ $<$ $>$

Transforms the displacement (x,y) from master coordinates to device coordinates and stores the results in the imager variables correctTX and correctTY, which contain the acceptable error in the x- and y-coordinate positions of the current position at the end of a CORRECT body.

SETFONT

151   97   Token Value = A097
< n:Cardinal > SETFONT → < >

Copies the font stored in frame location n to the imager variable font. A master error occurs if frame location n does not contain an object of type Font.

SETGRAY

424   1A8   Token Value = A1A8
< f:Number > SETGRAY → < >

Creates the same gray color as f MAKEGRAY and places it in the imager variable color.

SETSAMPLEDBLACK

428   1AC   Token Value = A1AC
< pa:PixelArray > < vm:Transformation > < clear:Cardinal >
SETSAMPLEDBLACK → < >

Creates a black-and-white sampled ink from the binary pixel array pa and stores it in the imager variable color. The pixel array pa must be created with the operands samplesPerPixel, maxSampleValue, and samplesInterleaved all set to 1. The product vm×T of the transformation vm and the current transformation T maps the pixel array pa to device coordinates. The operand clear specifies the behavior of zero-valued pixels when the ink is used. When clear is 0, zero-valued pixels write white on the page; otherwise, they are transparent and leave the page unchanged.

SETSAMPLEDCOLOR

429   1AD   Token Value = A1AD
< pa:PixelArray > < vm:Transformation > < colorOp:Operator >
SETSAMPLEDCOLOR → < >

Creates a colored sampled ink from the pixel array pa and stores it in the imager variable color. The concatenation vm×T of the transformation vm with the current transformation T maps the pixel array to device coordinates and the color operator colorOp converts the samples of each pixel to a color.

SETXREL

12   0C   Token Value = A00C   Short Token Value = 8C
<x:Number> SETXREL → < >

Converts the displacement (x,0) from master to device coordinates using the current transformation and adds the result vectorially to the contents of the current-position imager variables, DCScpx and DCScpy.

SETXY

10   0A   Token Value = A00A   Short Token Value = 8A
<x:Number> <y:Number> SETXY → < >

Converts the point (x,y) from master coordinates to device coordinates and stores the result in the current-position imager variables, DCScpx and DCScpy.

SETXYREL

11   0B   Token Value = A00B   Short Token Value = 8B
<x:Number> <y:Number> SETXYREL → < >

Converts the displacement (x,y) from master to device coordinates using the current transformation and adds the result vectorially to the contents of the current-position imager variables, DCScpx and DCScpy.

SETYREL

13   0D   Token Value = A00D   Short Token Value = 8D
<y:Number> SETYREL → < >

Converts the displacement (0,y) from master to device coordinates using the current transformation and adds the result vectorially to the contents of the current-position imager variables, DCScpx and DCScpy.

SHAPE

285   11D   Token Value = A11D
<v:Vector> SHAPE → <l:Cardinal> <n:Cardinal>

Pops the vector operand v from the stack, obtains its lower bound value l (the index value of the first element) and the number n of elements it contains, and returns them to the stack.

SHOW

22   16   Token Value = A016   Short Token Value = 96
<v:Vector> SHOW → < >

The operand v is a vector of integer character codes that index the character-shape-generating mask operators of the font stored in the imager variable font. SHOW adds the image of the character string described by the vector v to the page image. Each character is imaged at the current position, which is then incremented by the character's width or escapement. "Imaging a character" means transforming its mask to device coordinates using the current transformation and then applying the current color to the page image through the transformed mask.

SHOWANDFIXEDXREL

145   91   Token Value = A091
< v:Vector > < x:Number > SHOWANDFIXEDXREL → < >

The operand v is a vector of integer character codes that index the character-shape-generating mask operators of the font stored in the imager variable font. SHOWANDFIXEDXREL adds the image of the character string described by the vector v to the page image. Each character is imaged at the current position, which is then incremented by the sum of the character's escapement and the displacement (x,0), expressed in master coordinates.

SHOWANDXREL

146   92   Token Value = A092
< v:Vector > SHOWANDXREL → < >

The vector v is a vector of alternating integer character codes and displacement values. For each character code-displacement value pair, starting with the first pair in the vector v, the character in the current font indexed by the character code is imaged at the current position, which is then incremented by the character's escapement. The x-coordinate value of the current position is then moved again by an amount, expressed in master coordinates, equal to the displacement value, modulo 256, less 128.

SPACE

16   10   Token Value = A010   Short Token Value = 90
< x:Number > SPACE → < >

Increments the x-coordinate value of the current position by the value of operand x, expressed in master coordinates, and then calls CORRECTSPACE to make it a space-correcting displacement under CORRECT.

STARTUNDERLINE

413   19D   Token Value = A19D
< > STARTUNDERLINE → < >

Stores the x-coordinate value of the current position (in master coordinates) in the underlineStart imager variable.

SUB

214   D6   Token Value = A0D6
<a:Number> <b:Number> SUB → <c:Number>

Pops a and b and returns c = a–b, their algebraic difference, to the stack.

TRANS

170   AA   Token Value = A0AA
< > TRANS → < >

Modifies the current transformation T so that the origin of the master coordinate system is at the printer grid point nearest the current position.

TRANSLATE

162   A2   Token Value = A0A2
<x:Number> <y:Number> TRANSLATE → <t:Transformation>

Builds and returns on the stack the transformation t, with the following matrix representation:

$$\begin{bmatrix} 1 & 0 & 0 \\ 0 & 1 & 0 \\ x & y & 1 \end{bmatrix}$$

TRUNC

215   D7   Token Value = A0D7
<a:Number> TRUNC → <c:Number>

Pops a and returns c, the integer part of a, to the stack.

TYPE

220   DC   Token Value = A0DC
<x:Any> TYPE → <c:Cardinal>

Pops the operand x and returns the cardinal c, whose value is the type code of x, to the stack. The Interpress operand types and type codes are given in Table B.3.

UNMARK

187   BB   Token Value = A0BB
<m:Mark> <x_1:Any> <x_2:Any> ... <x_n:Any> <n:Cardinal>
UNMARK → <x_1> <x_2> ... <x_n>

Pops the value n and the n next operands from the stack. It then pops the next operand, m: it must be a mark placed on the stack by a MARK operator that was executed in the same context as the UNMARK operator. If it is, then the n operands x_1, x_2, ..., x_n are pushed back onto the stack,

Table B.3 Type codes.

Type Code	Type
1	Number
2	Identifier
3	Vector
4	Operator
5	Transformation
6	PixelArray
7	Color
8	Trajectory
9	Outline
10	Font
11	Clipper

retaining their order. A master error occurs if operand m is not a mark, or it is a mark but was not placed on the stack within the current context, or one of the operands $x_1, x_2, \ldots, x_n$ is a mark.

UNMARK0

192   C0   Token Value = A0C0
< m:Mark > UNMARK0 → < >

Pops the top element from the stack. A master error occurs if it is not a mark, or if it is a mark but was not placed on the stack within the current execution context. The effect of UNMARK0 is identical to 0 UNMARK.

Skeleton

The Interpress skeleton structure delimits the pages, preambles, and printing instructions in a master. This section will present and explain the Backus-Naur form (BNF) definition of the skeleton structure and describe how you encode the skeleton in an Interpress master.

Five special tokens describe the skeleton in a master. These tokens delimit blocks and bodies, and indicate the presence of content instructions.

BEGIN

102   66   Token Value = A066

This token indicates the start of a block. BEGIN and END tokens are always paired. Blocks are described later in this section and in Chapter 8.

CONTENTINSTRUCTIONS

   105   69   Token Value = A069

This token immediately precedes a body containing content instructions.

END

   103   67   Token Value = A067

This token indicates the end of a block and is always paired with a BEGIN token.

{

   106   6A   Token Value = A06A

This token indicates the beginning of a body. Left and right brace tokens are always paired. Bodies are described in this section and in Chapter 2.

}

   107   6B   Token Value = A06B

This token indicates the end of a body and is always paired with a right brace token.

Bodies

A body is a sequence of Interpress operators and operands enclosed in the token denoted by braces:

{ operands and operators }

A body can have other bodies nested within it, but the braces that delimit the bodies are always paired (left preceding right). At the skeleton level, there are four uses for bodies: a body can contain the Interpress commands for a page (page body), the commands for the preamble (a preamble body), or the commands to build printing instructions (document-instructions body and content-instructions body). In the BNF form, we can write

pageBody ::= body
preambleBody ::= body
instructionsBody ::= body
contentInstructionsBody ::= body

Blocks

Bodies are collected into groups called blocks. A block is delimited by BEGIN and END tokens:

$$\text{block} ::= \text{BEGIN} \quad \text{preambleBody} \quad \text{nodelist} \quad \text{END}$$

The first thing that follows the BEGIN token is always a preamble body. In fact, the way that you recognize a preamble body is that it follows a BEGIN token. Every block must contain at least one preamble body, even if it is empty.

A block also contains a *nodelist*, which might be empty. Informally, a nodelist is a list of pageBodies or blocks and their content instructions. More formally,we have

$$\text{nodelist} ::= \text{node} \mid \text{node} \quad \text{nodelist}$$

$$\text{node} ::= \text{content} \mid \text{CONTENTINSTRUCTIONS}$$
$$\text{contentInstructionsBody} \quad \text{content}$$

$$\text{content} ::= \text{block} \mid \text{pageBody}$$

You can see that a nodelist is a list of nodes, and each node has a *content* and, optionally, some instructions. A content is either a block or a pageBody. Thus, where you have a pageBody in the Interpress skeleton, you also can have an entire block. So, our original block contains a nodelist, which can include page bodies, or other nested blocks, or some combination of them.

Besides a pageBody or a block, a node may have printing instructions. If the instructions are present, they are found in a contentInstructionsBody preceding the block or page body. A contentInstructionsBody is introduced by a CONTENTINSTRUCTIONS token, which indicates that the following body contains content instructions and not the Interpress commands for a page.

Finally, we have

$$\text{skeleton} ::= \text{instructionsBody} \quad \text{block} \mid \text{block}$$

An Interpress skeleton has a top-level block, and, optionally, some document instructions. If instructions are present, they precede the block. So, if you encounter a left brace at the start of the master, you know you have instructions. If the first entry you encounter is the BEGIN token, then document instructions are absent.

An Interpress master is composed of a header (a sequence of bytes that identifies the file as Interpress and indicates the encoding) followed by the skeleton. Chapter 8 presents further discussion of the skeleton and examples.

The sequenceInsertMaster Encoding

One additional encoding construct, called sequenceInsertMaster, though not part of the skeleton definition, occurs only at the level of the skeleton tokens. It gives a reference to a block contained in a file. A master can then be constructed out of references to other masters. The details of the sequenceInsertMaster encoding are discussed in the section on sequences, and examples of its use are given in Chapter 8.

Printing Instructions

This section lists the standard printing instructions. We first list document instructions and then consider content instructions.

Document Instructions

For each document instruction, we give the name, the form of the value, the default value (if any), its precedence behavior, and a brief description. The precedence tells you where the values come from if instructions arrive from several sources (for example, both the master's instruction body and some external source). The steps the printer takes in establishing the document instructions are shown in Figure B.2.

breakPageFont
> Value: Vector of Identifier
> Default: chosen by the printer
> Precedence: document master

> The value is the universal name of the font used to print the break page.

breakPageType
> Value: Identifier or Vector of Identifier
> Default: chosen by the printer
> Precedence: external source

> The possible identifier values, *none*, *terse*, and *verbose*, indicate whether no break page or a break page with minimal or maximal information, respectively, is printed. A vector of identifiers would be the universal name of a printer-specific break-page type.

copyName
> Value: Run of Identifier
> Default: [10^7, null]
> Precedence: external source

> The expanded vector, indexed by copy number, assigns each copy a name.

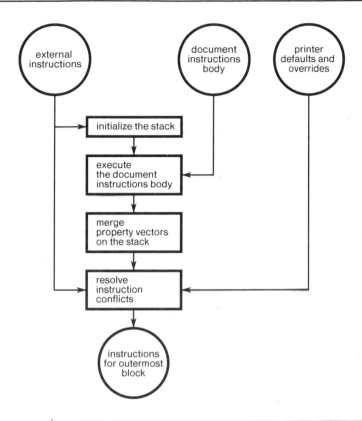

Figure B.2 Resolution of instruction conflicts.

copySelect
>   Value: Run of Cardinal
>   Default: [1, 1]
>   Precedence: external source

>   The expanded vector, indexed by copy number, says which copies of the document should be printed. A value of 1 means the copy should be printed; a value of 0 means it should be skipped.

docComment
>   Value: Vector of Cardinal
>   Default: empty vector
>   Precedence: document master

The value is a vector of character codes for a string containing a comment to be printed on the break page using the break-page font.

docCreation Date

Value: Vector of Cardinal
Default: empty vector
Precedence: document master

The value is a vector of character codes for a string giving the document's creation date and time. The string may be printed on the break page.

docCreator

Value: Vector of Cardinal
Default: empty vector
Precedence: document master

The value is a vector of character codes for the name of the document's creator, which may be printed on the break page.

docEndMessage

Value: Vector of Cardinal
Default: empty vector
Precedence: document master

The value is a vector of ISO 646 character codes for a message, which is to be delivered to the printer operator (where applicable) as soon as possible after imaging the master.

docName

Value: Vector of Cardinal
Default: empty vector
Precedence: document master

The value is a vector of character codes which specify a name for the document. The name may be printed on the break page.

docStartMessage

Value: Vector of Cardinal
Default: empty vector
Precedence: document master

The value is a vector of ISO 646 character codes for a message, which is to be delivered to the printer operator (where applicable) before, and as close as possible to, the time of imaging the master.

environmentNames

Value: Vector of Vector of Identifier
Default : empty vector
Precedence: external source

Each vector of identifiers is the name of an object that the master tries to find in the printer's environment. The instruction is useful in routing the print job to a printer with the necessary resources or enabling the printer to collect the resources that it needs.

finishing

Value: Identifier or Vector of Identifier
Default: printer dependent
Precedence: external source

The identifier values are *none* and *cornerstaple*. A vector of identifiers would specify the universal name of a printer-dependent finishing option.

insertFileMapping

Value: Vector of Mapping
Default: empty vector
Precedence: external source

A mapping is a two-element vector, each element of which is a vector of cardinals. Each two-element vector is a mapping between a file name, which might be found in a sequenceInsertFile encoding, and an alias file name, which should actually be used instead.

insertFileNames

Value: Vector of Vector of Cardinal
Default: file names in the printer's environment
Precedence: document master

This instruction is a way of listing file names found in sequenceInsertFile and sequenceInsertMaster encodings within the document master. After any replacements indicated by insertFileMapping are carried out, the list gives the file requirements of the print job.

media

Value: Vector of Property Vector
Default: [[mediumName, defaultMedium]]
Precedence: external source

This instruction lists the various media that are used in printing the master. A property vector is used to describe each medium. The property names mediumName, mediumXSize, and mediumYSize are defined, as well as mediumMessage, whose property value is a message string that describes the medium to the printer operator. Additional properties described by universal names also can be included.

mediaSelect

Value: Run of (Run of Cardinal)
Default: $[10^7, [10^7, 1]]$
Precedence: external source

The inner vector, indexed by page number, says which medium to use for each page. The medium is described by an index into the vector value of the media instruction. The outer vector is indexed by copy number and allows different copies to have different page-medium mappings.

onSimplex

Value: Run of Cardinal
Default: $[10^7, 1]$
Precedence: external source

The expanded vector is indexed by page number: a value of 1 in the expanded vector means that the corresponding page should be printed when printing simplex; 0 means it should be skipped.

outputPosition

Value: Run of Cardinal
Default: $[10^7, 1]$
Precedence: external source

The expanded vector is indexed by copy number, with each cardinal value indicating the output position (for example, sorting bin or stacking offset) of the copy.

pageSelect

Value: Run of (Run of Cardinal)
Default: $[10^7, [10^7, 1]]$
Precedence: concurrence required; see below

The inner vector when expanded is indexed by page number. A value of 1 in the expanded vector means the corresponding page should be printed; a value of 0 means it should be skipped. The outer vector is indexed by copy number and allows you to select different pages for different copies. If this instruction is found both in the document master and the external source, the page will be printed only if it is selected in both places.

pixelArrayTransformationUses

> Value: Vector of Transformation
> Default: any transformation is assumed possible
> Precedence: external source
>
> The instruction provides a hint as to the transformations that the master uses to convert from pixel-array coordinates to Interpress coordinates.

plex

> Value: Identifier
> Default: printer dependent
> Precedence: external source
>
> The two possible values are *simplex* and *duplex*, indicating that printing should occur on only one side or on both sides of the paper, respectively.

set

> Value: Identifier or Vector of Identifier
> Default: professionalGraphics
> Precedence: external source
>
> This instruction says what Interpress facilities are used by the master. The possible identifier values are *professionalGraphics*, *publication*, and *commercial*. The value may also be a vector of identifiers specifying the universal name for some other set of Interpress facilities.

xImageShift

> Value: Number
> Default: 0
> Precedence: external source
>
> The value specifies the distance in meters that each page image is to be shifted in the x direction. If the value is positive, odd pages are shifted to the right and even pages to the left; if it is negative, then odd pages are shifted to the left and even pages to the right.

Content Instructions

This section lists the content instructions. For each, we give the name, the form of the value, the precedence behavior, and a brief description. Content instructions do not have default values and if they do not appear in a master, then the master's document instructions apply. As a general rule, content instructions have precedence over document instructions for the scope of the content. The determination of instruction values when external and content instructions both appear is depicted in Figure B.3.

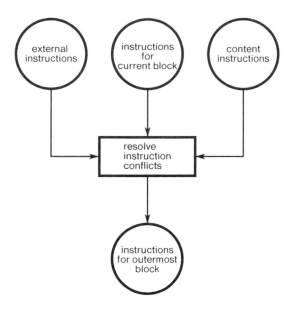

Figure B.3 Resolution of conflicts from content instructions.

contentInsertFileMapping

Value: Vector of Mapping
Precedence: not applicable; see below

The instruction allows file-name mappings to occur for each content. A mapping is a two-element vector, each element of which is a vector of cardinals representing a string, as in the insertFileMapping document instruction. When contents are nested, contentInsertFileMapping instructions are applied sequentially from the innermost out. After the contentInsertFileMappings are applied, the insertFileMapping is applied.

contentOutputPosition

Value: Run of Cardinal
Precedence: external source

The expanded vector is indexed by copy number, with each cardinal value indicating the output position of the pages in the content. This instruction allows the output position of pages to be controlled and to vary across copies. It takes precedence over the outputPosition document instruction, but an external instruction takes precedence over both.

contentPageSelect

Value: Run of Cardinal
Precedence: external source

When expanded, the resulting vector is indexed by copy number and indicates whether the pages in the content should be printed for that copy. This instruction can cause pages to be included that had been excluded by the pageSelect document instruction.

contentPlex

Value: Identifier
Precedence: external source

The possible values are *simplex* and *duplex*, telling the printer whether pages within the content are to be printed on one side or on two sides of the paper.

pageMediaSelect

Value: Cardinal
Precedence: document master

The value is an index into the media vector, selecting the media to be used for the pages in the content.

pageOnSimplex

Value: Cardinal
Precedence: document master

A value of 0 means the pages in the content should be skipped if printing in simplex mode: a value of 1 means the pages should be printed.

Imager Variables

Interpress has 25 imager variables. These variables contain imaging-state information; that is, data for creating images, such as current page position (DCScpx, DCScpy), the ink to use (color), the thickness to make lines (strokeWidth), and the font to use for showing text (font). This information typically applies to several of the objects imaged so that it is stored as state, rather than being explicitly specified with each object. Table B.4 lists the index values and names of the imager variables.

The imager variables are global in the sense that any mask operator or composed operator can access them. A mask operator does not affect the values of the imager variables, but a composed operator can use any of the Interpress primitive operators available for setting or changing imager variable values.

Table B.4   Imager variable indices.

Index	Name
0, 1	DCScpx, DCScpy
2, 3	correctMX, correctMY
4	T
5	priorityImportant
6, 7	mediumXSize, mediumYSize
8, 9	fieldXMin, fieldYMin
10, 11	fieldXMax, fieldYMax
12	font
13	color
14	noImage
15	strokeWidth
16	strokeEnd
17	underlineStart
18	amplifySpace
19	correctPass
20	correctShrink
21, 22	correctTX, correctTY
23	strokeJoint
24	clipper

You have the option of executing a composed operator with either a DO, DOSAVE, or DOSAVEALL command. If you use DO, then the changes the composed operator makes to the imager variables remain in effect when the operator finishes. On the other hand, if you execute a composed operator with DOSAVEALL, the imager variables are saved and then, upon completion of the composed operator, restored to their former values. As a result, a composed operator, when executed by DOSAVEALL, can freely alter the the imager variables with the assurance that, when it has completed, they will be restored to the state in which the operator found them.

DOSAVE provides an option intermediate between restoring all of the imager variables (DOSAVEALL) and restoring none of them (DO). DOSAVE saves and restores all but four imager variables: the current page position (DCScpx, DCScpy) and the desired size of a line of characters (correctMX, correctMY). Since any changes to the values of these variables persist after the completion of a composed operator, they are called *persistent* imager variables. All other imager variables are *nonpersistent*; changes made to them by a composed operator executed with DOSAVE do not persist after the completion of the operator.

To see why this feature of DOSAVE is useful, consider constructing your own composed operators for drawing characters. Your operator might want to alter imager variables such as the line thickness (strokeWidth) and current transformation (T) to draw a character. When its done however, the only change you want to see is in the current page position, which is advanced to the page position at which you would draw the next character.

You might be tempted to use IGET and ISET operators (instead of DOSAVE and DOSAVEALL) to save and restore imager variables directly. This practice is discouraged for two reasons. First, many imager variable values are not saved or restored directly; rather, the variables store the result of some printer computation in an internal form. The second reason is that the printer may have other "hidden" imager variables besides those listed in Table B.4. These variables, also part of the printer's internal state, are not accessible using IGET and ISET but are saved and restored by DOSAVEALL.

The rest of this section describes the individual imager variables in alphabetical order. For each, we give its name, its index value, the type of object it stores, its initial value, and a brief description of its properties, including how the values are set or modified.

amplifySpace

18   Type: Number   Initial value = 1

This variable contains a multiplication factor that is applied to the widths of all amplifying characters. The amplifying characters in a font are usually the spaces. By changing the amplifySpace value, you can alter the effective widths of spaces, expanding or shrinking them to justify text lines. It is changed by the ISET operator.

clipper

24   Type: Clipper   Initial value: see below

This variable holds the definition of the clipping region; only the portions of a mask that lie within it are imaged on the page. In instruction bodies and preambles, its initial value is the maximum field; at the start of a page body, the printer sets the clipper to the usable field. The clipper should be modified by the CLIPOUTLINE and CLIPRECTANGLE operators.

color

13   Type: Color   Initial value = 1 MAKEGRAY

This variable describes the color or ink that is pressed through a mask to form page images. Colors can be either constant (subtype ConstantColor for uniform colors or shades of gray) or sampled (derived from a pixel array). The color imager variable is initialized to black and is changed by the ISET, SETGRAY, SETSAMPLEDBLACK, and SETSAMPLEDCOLOR operators.

correctMX

2   Type: Number   Initial value = 0

correctMY

3   Type: Number   Initial value = 0

These two imager variables are persistent and contain the expected change in the current position (in device coordinates) for a CORRECT body; that is, the desired length of the text line. The CORRECT process computes where a line of text would end, compares it against the desired end position, and uses the difference to rejustify a line of text. These imager variables are set indirectly by the SETCORRECTMEASURE operator.

correctPass

19   Type: Cardinal   Initial value = 0

This variable says whether the CORRECT mechanism is on the first pass, computing where a line of text would end, or on the second, adjusting and imaging the text. The CORRECT mechanism uses this variable to obtain different behavior from operators on the first and second pass. It can be set directly from the master with ISET; a value of 0 disables correction.

correctShrink

20   Type: Number   Initial value = 1/2

The CORRECT process uses two mechanisms for shrinking the length of a line. It will reduce the width of space-correcting characters to some limit, specified by the correctShrink variable. (Beyond that limit, it will reduce the width of mask-correcting characters.) Space-correcting characters are not allowed to shrink to less than $(1 - \text{correctShrink})$ times their former size. The initial value allows CORRECT to shrink spaces by as much as half their width; correctShrink can be modified by the ISET operator.

correctTX

21   Type: Number   Initial value = 0

correctTY

22   Type: Number   Initial value = 0

The imager variables correctTX and correctTY are used by the CORRECT process to specify the maximum absolute x and y device coordinate differences, respectively, between the actual length of a line text and the desired length, as specified by the correctMX and correctMY imager variables. They should be set indirectly by the SETCORRECTTOLERANCE operator.

DCScpx

0 Type: Number   Initial value = 0

DCScpy

1 Type: Number   Initial value = 0

These two imager variables contain the device coordinates of the current position; DCScpx contains the x-coordinate value and DCScpy contains the y-coordinate value. They are persistent imager variables and both are initially set to 0. They are set indirectly by the SETXY, SETXREL, SETYREL, and SETXYREL operators and modified by the SHOW, SHOWANDXREL, and SHOWANDFIXEDXREL operators. They can be read indirectly by GETCP.

fieldXMax

10 Type: Number   Initial value: see below

fieldXMin

8 Type: Number   Initial value: see below

fieldYMax

11 Type: Number   Initial value: see below

fieldYMin

9 Type: Number   Initial value: see below

These four imager variables describe the field or area of the page that is available for imaging. The lower-left corner of the area is at the point (fieldXMin, fieldYMin) in the Interpress coordinate system (meters); the upper right corner is at (fieldXMax, fieldYMax). The printer initializes them to 0 at the start of instructions bodies and preambles and then sets them at the start of page bodies to show the actual size of the field. They are read-only variables; the master cannot set them, but it can read their values in meters using IGET. You can further reduce the area of the page available to your master for imaging with the clipper imager variable.

font

12 Type: Font   Initial value = [ ] MAKEFONT

The font variable indicates which font should be used to image characters. It is initialized to a font with no characters so that it must be changed before any character imaging takes place. It is set by the ISET and SETFONT operators

mediumXSize

6   Type: Number   Initial value: see below

mediumYSize

7   Type: Number   Initial value: see below

The printer uses the mediumXSize and mediumYSize imager variables to describe to the master the x and y dimensions of the medium or page in the Interpress coordinate system. This is different than the field size since the printer might not be able to image over the entire page. They are initialized to zero at the start of instructions bodies and preambles and to the actual page size at the start of page bodies. These variables are read only; the master cannot set them but can obtain their values in meters using the IGET operator. For example, an 8.5- by 11-inch page in portrait orientation would give the following values:

$$\text{mediumXSize} = 8.5 \text{ inches} \times 0.0254 \text{ meters/inch} = 0.2159 \text{ m}$$
$$\text{mediumYSize} = 11 \text{ inches} \times 0.0254 \text{ meters/inch} = 0.2794 \text{ m}$$

noImage

14   Type: Cardinal   Initial value = 0

This variable is a flag that can turn off the imaging of mask operators, allowing you to execute operators and note their side effects without actually imaging them. No changes to the page image occur when the noImage variable has a nonzero value. Its value is initialized to zero, allowing imaging, and can be changed by the ISET operator.

priorityImportant

5   Type: Cardinal   Initial value = 0

The priorityImportant variable controls the order in which imaging operators are executed in a master. While it has a nonzero value, masks are said to be *ordered* and the printer executes them in the same order that they occur in the master. This allows precise control of the imaging of overlapping masks. This variable is initialized to zero so that masks are *unordered* and the printer is free to reorder them for the most efficient imaging. The value is set by the ISET operator.

strokeEnd

16   Type: Cardinal   Initial value = 0

The strokeEnd variable specifies the style of end cap in strokes imaged by the MASKSTROKE, MASKDASHEDSTROKE, and MASKVECTOR operators. The legal values are 0 for square ends, 1 for butt ends, and 2 for round ends. The values are changed by the ISET operator.

strokeJoint

23   Type: Cardinal   Initial value = 0

The strokeJoint variable specifies the style of joint when strokes are imaged by MASKSTROKE, MASKDASHEDSTROKE, and MASKSTROKECLOSED. The legal values are 0 for mitered joints, 1 for beveled joints, and 2 for rounded joints. It should be changed by the ISET operator.

strokeWidth

15   Type: Number   Initial value = 0

The strokeWidth variable specifies the thickness of strokes imaged by the operators MASKSTROKE, MASKSTROKECLOSED, MASKDASHEDSTROKE, and MASKVECTOR. The value is expressed in terms of master coordinates. Since the initial value is 0, this variable must be changed to a positive value before any strokes will be visible. It is changed by the ISET operator.

T

4   Type: Transformation   Initial value: see below

The imager variable T contains the current transformation, which converts from the master coordinate system to the device coordinate system. The printer initializes it to 1 SCALE for instructions bodies and preambles, and to the transformation from Interpress coordinates to device coordinates at the start of page bodies. To use something other than Interpress coordinates in your master, you can modify T by concatenating transformations with it using the CONCATT operator. The MOVE and TRANS operators also change the value of T.

underlineStart

17   Type: Number   Initial value = 0

This variable saves an x-coordinate value, which is used in constructing underlines. The value is expressed in terms of the master coordinate system in effect at the time the variable is set. It is set by means of the STARTUNDERLINE operator.

Appendix C
PRINT
OPERATORS

This appendix contains the definitions of some "magic" Interpress operators with which you can print stack values and types. You may find them useful in displaying the results of the base-language operations of Chapter 2. Operators such as these may also be useful for debugging. Most procedures display the results on the page image through SHOW, which means that they require a current font in the font imager variable. You can write versions, however, that display their results as comments with the ERROR operator, in which case no fonts are required. You replace SHOW with 100 ERROR. The operators, stored in frame variables 40 through 49, can be defined within the preamble of the master.

The operators in 46 through 49 call the earlier operators with DOSAVEALL to recover the current position, and then shift it down in y. This has the effect of a carriage-return and linefeed. The downward shift is 4 millimeters, assuming Interpress coordinates. If different coordinates are used, the shift value will be adjusted accordingly. If the earlier routines are revised to use the ERROR operator rather than the SHOW operator to display results, then these last four operators are not needed.

Descriptions of the operators and their definitions follow:

operator 40   number-to-string

<n:Number> 40 FGET DO → <v:Vector>

The vector v is the vector of character codes for the string representation of the number n (followed by two spaces). The string includes a minus sign if the number is negative, the integer part, a decimal point, and five digits of the fraction part.

```
MAKESIMPLECO              --build the number-to-string operator--
{
  1 MARK                  --mark to count characters in vector--
  DUP 0 GE NOT            --test a copy of the the number n--
  IF                      --to see whether it is negative--
  {
```

```
    45 EXCH                             --if so, need a minus sign--
    NEG                                 --use -n--
}
DUP 39 FSET                             --save a copy of the number--
0 EXCH                                  --initialize a digit count to 0--
TRUNC                                   --next consider the integer part of n--
MAKESIMPLECO                            --define a recursive op to take n apart--
{                                       --assume stack has op, n, count--
  3 2 ROLL                              --roll the op out of the way--
  DUP 0 EQ NOT                          --quit if number is zero--
  IF
  {                                     --number is not zero--
    DUP 10 MOD                          --extract a digit and make it a character--
    48 ADD
    3 1 ROLL
    DUP 1 ADD                           --increment the character count--
    4 3 ROLL
    4 ADD
    DUP 1 SUB
    ROLL                                --roll character into place--
    10 DIV
    TRUNC                               --remove the digit from n--
    3 1 ROLL
    DUP DO                              --recursive call to convert rest of n--
  }                                     --end of the nonzero case--
}                                       --end of the recursive procedure --
DUP DO                                  --initial call to convert integer part--
POP                                     --zero left from integer part of n--
EXCH
POP                                     --remove the conversion operator--
NOT
IF                                      --if no integer part--
{
  48                                    --then create a leading zero--
}
46                                      --code for the decimal point--
39 FGET                                 --get n for converting fraction--
DUP TRUNC
SUB 10 MUL DUP TRUNC DUP 48 ADD 3 2 ROLL    --convert five digits--
SUB 10 MUL DUP TRUNC DUP 48 ADD 3 2 ROLL    --of fraction--
SUB 10 MUL DUP TRUNC DUP 48 ADD 3 2 ROLL
SUB 10 MUL DUP TRUNC DUP 48 ADD 3 2 ROLL
SUB 10 MUL TRUNC 48 ADD
32 32                                   --add two trailing spaces--
COUNT MAKEVEC                           --return a vector of all character codes--
1 UNMARK                                --remove counting mark--
} 40 FSET                               --save this operator in frame[40]--
```

operator 41   print-number

$<$n:Number$>$ 41 FGET DO $\rightarrow$ $<$ $>$

This operator converts the number on the top of the stack to a string and then shows the string at the current position. The current position is left at the end of the string.

```
MAKESIMPLECO                 --print-number operator--
{
  40 FGET DO                 --convert the number to a string--
  SHOW                       --show the string--
} 41 FSET                    --save this operator in frame[41]--
```

property vector 42   call-table

This is not an operator but rather a property vector that serves as a call table for the print routines used for different operator types. It is defined such that, for numbers, the value of the number is printed; for anything else, the type is printed.

```
--call table of actions to take for each operand type--
1 41 FGET                    --if type is number, print the value--
2 MAKESIMPLECO               --otherwise, print the type--
  {POP 73 100 101 110 116 105 102 105 101 114 32 11 MAKEVEC SHOW}
3 MAKESIMPLECO
  {POP 86 101 99 116 111 114 32 7 MAKEVEC SHOW}
4 MAKESIMPLECO
  {POP 79 112 101 114 97 116 111 114 32 9 MAKEVEC SHOW}
5 MAKESIMPLECO
  {POP 84 114 97 110 115 102 111 114 109 97 116 105 111 110 32
  15 MAKEVEC SHOW}
6 MAKESIMPLECO
  {POP 80 105 120 101 108 65 114 114 97 121 32 11 MAKEVEC SHOW}
7 MAKESIMPLECO
  {POP 67 111 108 111 114 32 6 MAKEVEC SHOW}
8 MAKESIMPLECO
  {POP 84 114 97 106 101 99 116 111 114 121 32 11 MAKEVEC SHOW}
9 MAKESIMPLECO
  {POP 79 117 116 108 105 110 101 32 8 MAKEVEC SHOW}
10 MAKESIMPLECO
  {POP 70 111 110 116 32 5 MAKEVEC SHOW}
11 MAKESIMPLECO
  {POP 67 108 105 112 112 101 114 32 8 MAKEVEC SHOW}
22 MAKEVEC                   --make into a property vector--
42 FSET                      --which is saved in frame[42]--
```

operator 43   print-any

$<$x:Any$>$ 43 FGET DO $\rightarrow$ $<$ $>$

This operator uses frame[42] to print any type x. When x is a number, its value is printed; for everything else, the type is printed. Printing takes place at the current position, which is then left at the end of the string.

```
MAKESIMPLECO              --print-any operator--
{
  DUP TYPE                --get the type of the object on the stack--
  42 FGET                 --get the operator for that type--
  EXCH GETP DO            --execute the operator to print--
} 43 FSET                 --save this operator in frame[43]--
```

operator 44   print-nth-stack-item

$<$x$_n$:Any$>$ $<$x$_{n-1}$:Any$>$ ... $<$x$_1$:Any$>$ $<$n:Cardinal$>$
44 FGET DO $\rightarrow$ $<$x$_n$$>$ $<$x$_{n-1}$$>$ ... $<$x$_1$$>$

This operator prints the nth item on the stack, counting down from the operand n. The operand n is consumed by this operator, but x$_n$ is not. The current position is left at the end of the printed string.

```
MAKESIMPLECO              --operator to print nth stack item--
{
  DUP 1 ADD 1 ROLL        --roll the item to the top--
  DUP 43 FGET DO          --print a copy of it--
  EXCH DUP 1 SUB ROLL     --roll it back in place--
} 44 FSET                 --save this operator in frame[44]--
```

operator 45   print-top-n-stack-items

$<$x$_n$:Any$>$ $<$x$_{n-1}$:Any$>$ ... $<$x$_1$:Any$>$ $<$n:Cardinal$>$
45 FGET DO $\rightarrow$ $<$x$_n$$>$ $<$x$_{n-1}$$>$ ... $<$x$_1$$>$

This operator prints the n stack items below the operand n. All items are printed on a line, with the top item printed on the right. Only the operand n is consumed by the operator. The current position is left at the end of the line.

```
MAKESIMPLECO              --operator to print top n stack items--
{
  MAKESIMPLECO            --recursive operator to print every item--
  {
    EXCH DUP 1 GE         --see if there is at least one item--
    IFELSE
```

```
  {
    DUP 2 ADD 44 FGET DO        --if so, print it--
    1 SUB EXCH                  --one less item to print--
    DUP DO                      --recursively print the rest--
  }
  IF                           --if no more items on stack--
  { POP POP }                  --remove count and operator--
}                              --end of recursive operator--
DUP DO                         --execute recursive operator--
} 45 FSET                      --save this operator in frame[45]--
```

operator 46   print-number-CRLF

$<$n:Number$>$ 46 FGET DO $\rightarrow$ $<>$

This operator prints the number n and leaves the current position 4 millimeters below its original value, assuming Interpress coordinates are in effect.

```
MAKESIMPLECO                   --print-number-CRLF operator--
{
  40 FGET DOSAVEALL            --print the number saving state--
  -0.004 SETYREL               --y moves to next line--
} 46 FSET                      --save this in frame[46]--
```

operator 47   print-any-CRLF

$<$x:Any$>$ 47 FGET DO $\rightarrow$ $<>$

If x is a number, this operator prints its value; otherwise, it prints its type. The current position is left 4 millimeters below its original value, assuming Interpress coordinates are in effect.

```
MAKESIMPLECO                   --print-any-CRLF operator--
{
  43 FGET DOSAVEALL            --print the object saving state--
  -0.004 SETYREL               --y moves to next line--
} 47 FSET                      --save this in frame[47]--
```

operator 48   print-nth-stack-item-CRLF

$<x_n$:Any$>$ $<x_{n-1}$:Any$>$ ... $<x_1$:Any$>$ $<$n:Cardinal$>$
48 FGET DO $\rightarrow$ $<x_n>$ $<x_{n-1}>$ ... $<x_1>$

The nth item on the stack, counting down from the n operand, is printed. The current position is left 4 millimeters below its original value, assuming Interpress coordinates are in effect.

```
MAKESIMPLECO                    --print-nth-stack-item-CRLF operator--
{
  44 FGET DOSAVEALL             --print the object saving state--
  -0.004 SETYREL                --y moves to next line--
} 48 FSET                       --save this in frame[48]--
```

operator 49   print-top-n-stack-items-CRLF

$<x_n:Any> <x_{n-1}:Any> \ldots <x_1:Any> <n:Cardinal>$
49 FGET DO $\rightarrow <x_n> <x_{n-1}> \ldots <x_1>$

This operator prints the top n items on the stack, counting down from the
n operand. The top item is printed on the right. The current position is left
4 millimeters below its original value, assuming Interpress coordinates
are in effect.

```
MAKESIMPLECO                    --print top-n-stack-items-CRLF operator--
{
  45 FGET DOSAVEALL             --print the object saving state--
  -0.004 SETYREL                --y moves to next line--
} 49 FSET                       --save this in frame[49]--
```

GLOSSARY

absolute positioning: determining position or placement in terms of the MCS.

absorptance: the proportion of incident light absorbed by a material.

accent: a mark or symbol added to a letter.

amplifying characters: characters whose escapement can be modified easily by the amplifySpace imager variable.

amplifySpace: image variable 18; indicates the fractional adjustment of amplifying characters.

appearance error: an error in the appearance of the page image; usually occurs because the master invokes a function that the imager cannot accommodate.

appearance warning: notification of a content-preserving approximation to the ideal image.

approximation: finding an external color or font close, but not identical, to the one requested.

arc: a segment of a circle.

argument: a value popped from the stack by the execution of an operator.

ASCII: American National Standards Institute's American Standard Code for Information Interchange.

base language: the syntactic and semantic framework of Interpress, without any imaging operators.

baseline: a horizontal line just under the "bottom" of nondescending characters in Latin alphabets.

Bézier curve: a parameterization of a curve used for cubic curves in Interpress.

binary sample: sample with only two possible values, interpreted as ink or no ink.

binding: fastening printed pages together.

binding offset: a shift in the position of the coordinate axes on a page to leave room for the binding (staples, perfect, and so on).

black-and-white compatible: a characteristic of a color representation that allows it to be used directly by a black and white system.

block: a sequence of Interpress nodes enclosed in BEGIN and END tokens.

body: a sequence of literals bracketed by { and }.

body height: the nominal distance between lines of text for a given font.

body operator: a primitive operator that immediately precedes a body.

break page: a page automatically printed at the beginning of a job to identify the output of the job and to separate it from that of adjacent jobs.

B-spline: a parameterization of a curve.

cardinal: a nonnegative mathematical integer in a limited range: one of the subtypes of the base language.

CCITT: Comité Consultatif International Télégraphique et Téléphonique or International Telegraph and Telephone Consultative Committee, a body that sets facsimile image standards.

CCS: abbreviation for character coordinate system.

character: a graphic shape for the representation of visual information.

character code: see character index.

character coordinate system: a standard coordinate system in which each character operator is defined.

character index: a cardinal, sometimes called a "character code," that identifies a particular character; used to index a font.

character mask: an operator that generates the mask for imaging a character.

characterMasks: a property in a fontDescription, the value of which is a vector of character operators for the font.

character metrics: the measurements of the critical dimensions of a character.

characterMetrics: a property vector in a fontDescription specifying the character metrics for a font.

character set: the correspondence between character codes and letterforms.

CIE: Commission Internationale de l'Éclairage or International Commission on Illumination, a body that sets color standards.

clipper: imager variable 24, which defines the region of the page that can be altered by mask and ink; also, the type of objects that may be used as the values for this imager variable.

clipping: not imaging the portion of a figure that lies outside a specific region.

closed trajectory: a trajectory that forms a closed curve without endpoints.

color: the ink used to show a primitive image; also, imager variable 13, which specifies the current color; the type of an object which may be used as a value for this imager variable.

color map: a mapping between index values and color specifications; a table of color values.

color model: a system for associating numbers with the subjective or objective attributes of a color perception or stimulus.

color model operator: an operator that constructs a color operator according to a particular color model.

color operator: an operator that converts numbers into an Interpress color.

Commercial Set: a set of Interpress instructions for support of text (with 90-degree rotations), forms, and scanned binary images for typical office documents and text produced in a computer data center.

composed operator: an operator defined in the master.

compression: a computation that reduces the number of bits required to specify some data, usually a vector of image samples.

concatenation (of transformations): forming a new transformation that has the same effect as the sequential application of the concatenated transformations; when the transformations are represented by matrices, the concatenation can be carried out by matrix multiplication.

conic segment: a section of an ellipse, parabola, or hyperbola.

constant color: a subtype of data type color where the color is the same at every point.

content: either a block or a page body.

content instructions: a body of printing instructions associated with a content.

context: a particular execution of a composed operator.

control points: points that define the shape of a curve.

convenience operator: a redundant operator, usually introduced to reduce the number of steps in a frequently-occurring sequence.

coordinate system: conventions to describe locations in space.

correct: to compensate for differences between the escapements of character operators used by the printer and those assumed by the creator.

correctMX: imager variable 2; the desired measure of a text line in the DCS x direction.

correctMY: imager variable 3; the desired measure of a text line in the DCS y direction.

correctPass: imager variable 19; indicates the stage in the correction process.

correctShrink: imager variable 20; limits the fraction by which space-correcting characters may be reduced.

correctTX: imager variable 21; gives the tolerance for CORRECT in the DCS x direction.

correctTY: imager variable 22; gives the tolerance for CORRECT in the DCS y direction.

creator: the program that constructs an Interpress master.

current position: a point on the page image, often indicating where the origin of the next character should be placed.

current transformation: a transformation that converts from master coordinates to device coordinates.

dash pattern: the length of the dashes and the gaps between them in a dashed line; also, the vector of numbers describing the lengths of the dashes and spaces for a dashed stroke.

DCS: abbreviation for device coordinate system.

DCScpx: imager variable 0; the x component of the current position in device coordinates.

DCScpy: imager variable 1; the y component of the current position in device coordinates.

decompression: expanding compressed data into its original form.

decompression operator: an operator that accepts a vector of compressed data and yields a vector of expanded data.

demand publishing: an approach to the production of a document in which current editions of the document are produced quickly when needed (as opposed to stockpiling copies of the document and issuing change lists).

density: see optical density.

device coordinate system: a device-dependent coordinate system suitable for driving a printing device.

device independence: avoidance of explicit and implicit reference to the device used; for example, a description is given as an ideal image, independent of the printing device, so that any device can then make its best effort at producing the image.

device independent: does not depend on properties of the printing device.

document-description language: a computer language for describing the content, layout, assembly, and properties of an entire document.

dot: a printer pixel; see spot.

dpi: abbreviation for dots per inch; a measure of resolution, the same as spots per inch.

duplex: a mode of printing in which images are placed on both sides of a sheet of paper; also, a printing-instruction value.

easy transformation: a net transformation that the printer can handle efficiently for fonts or pixel arrays.

element: one of the values that make up a vector.

encoding: a particular representation of Interpress masters.

end cap: the shape of a stroke at its end (square, butt, or round).

environment: the set of objects made available to a master by a printer; for example, fonts, colors, and decompression operators.

escapement: of a character, the spacing from one character to the next.

external instructions: those printing instructions supplied by mechanisms outside an Interpress master.

external value: a value not defined in the master, but obtained from the printer by a FIND operator.

field: the printable area of the medium.

fieldXMax: imager variable 10; gives the maximum x value of the printable field.

fieldXMin: imager variable 8; gives the minimum x value of the printable field.

fieldYMax: imager variable 11; gives the maximum y value of the printable field.

fieldYMin: imager variable 9; gives the minimum y value of the printable field.

finishing: actions applied to a document after the pages are imaged, such as folding, stapling, and stitching.

font: a collection of character definitions; also, imager variable 12, which defines the current font; the type of object that may be a value of this imager variable.

font-definition coordinate system: the coordinates used by the font designer in defining the character-mask operators of the font.

fontDescription: a property vector that defines a font.

font metrics: the measurements of the critical dimensions of a font.

frame: an array of local variables associated with an execution of a composed operator.

frame variable: an element of the frame.

function set: a characterization of the capabilities of an Interpress printer.

grid points: a grid overlaid on the device coordinate system for describing the spatial resolution of the printing device.

header: an identifying string at the beginning of an encoded Interpress master.

hierarchical name: a vector of identifiers that represent a structured name.

hierarchical name space: a tree-structured naming system, in which each name is a sequence of simple names that traces out a path from the root of the tree.

ICS: abbreviation for Interpress coordinate system.

ideal image: an image that results from ideal (infinite) precision interpretation of arithmetic and imaging operators.

identifier: a sequence of characters that usually name an external value; one of the types of the base language.

image: a two-dimensional pattern created at a workstation, described by an Interpress master, and printed on a medium as output.

image fidelity: how close the actual image is to the ideal image.

imager: the software module that interprets imaging operators to build page images.

imager state: 25 variables that control the functioning of many mask operators.

imager variable: one of 25 variables that control the functioning of many mask operators.

imaging model: the process whereby primitive images specified by a color, a mask, and a clipper are built up on a page image.

imaging primitives: the basic image components supported by the language, from which complex images are synthesized.

inflection point: a point at which the second derivative of a curve changes sign.

initial frame: a vector that is part of a composed operator; used to initialize the frame for each execution of the operator.

ink: the color in the Interpress imaging model.

instance: usually refers to an image of a standard symbol on the page; for example, the word "SHIPS," when printed, contains two instances of the symbol "S."

instructions body: an optional body in a master that contains printing instructions.

Interpress coordinate system: a device-independent coordinate system for specifying locations on the page image.

joint: the point where one segment abuts another segment of a stroke; Interpress supports three types: miter, bevel, and round.

justify: to space characters such that text-line boundaries are aligned. Often both left and right boundaries are justified to produce a column of text.

kern: the portion of a typeface that projects beyond the body or shank of a character.

landscape orientation: orientation of a medium with the long edge at the bottom.

laser printer: a type of raster printer that defines the raster by scans of a laser beam and produces spots by means of variations in the beam's intensity.

last point: the endpoint of the last segment of a trajectory.

leading: the space between lines of text.

letterform: the shape of a character.

letterspacing: spacing adjustments between letters.

ligature: a character combining two or more letters.

limit: a restriction on the size of some object.

literal: a representation in a master of a value.

lower bound: the integer that names the first element of a vector.

luminance: the response of the Standard Observer to the total amount of light emitted by a visual stimulus; a tristimulus value.

mark: a value that can be popped from the stack only by certain operators.

mark recovery: an error-recovery procedure that pops the stack to the topmost mark and finds a matching point in operator execution.

mask: a description of the shape of a primitive image that will be added to the page image.

mask correcting: the property of allowing uniform reduction in width when required to correct the positioning of text; usually applied to the characters that form words.

mask operator: an operator that constructs a mask and uses it to alter the page image; an imaging operator.

master: an Interpress program.

master coordinates: coordinate information specified by the master as arguments to imaging operators.

master coordinate system: the coordinates in the specification of imaging operations; the coordinates specified by the current transformation.

master error: the result of executing a primitive without meeting the conditions stated in its definition.

master warning: notification of a problem found in the master that did not interrupt processing.

matrix: a representation of a transformation.

MCS: abbreviation for master coordinate system.

measure: the length of a text line.

medium: the identity of the material on which a page image is printed.

mediumDescription: a property vector that determines a medium.

mediumXSize: imager variable 6; gives the size of the medium in the x direction.

mediumYSize: imager variable 7; gives the size of the medium in the y direction.

metric master: an Interpress master that conveys information about the fonts on a printer.

metrics: of a character or font, the measurements of its critical dimensions.

name: a cardinal or identifier used to specify an element of a property vector.

net transformation: the total transformation from a pixel array's or character operator's standard coordinate system to the Interpress coordinate system.

node: a content and its content instructions.

noImage: imager variable 14; controls whether or not imaging takes place.

normalized pixel-array coordinate system: a coordinate system for describing a pixel array where the height of the array is one unit.

normal viewing orientation: the standard orientation of a page (or other form of image output).

NPCS: abbreviation for normalized pixel-array coordinate system.

number: a rational number in a particular subset; one of the types of the base language.

open trajectory: a trajectory that does not close in on itself; the trajectory has two endpoints.

operand: an argument value for an operator.

operand stack: a last-in-first-out data structure from which operators retrieve arguments and on which they place results.

operator: a value that can be executed to cause state changes and output.

optical density: a measure of light absorptance; the common log of the reciprocal of the transmittance or reflectance.

origin: the point of intersection of coordinate axes; also, a reference point on a character mask.

ISO 646: International Standards Organization's Seven-Bit Coded Character Set for Information Processing Interchange.

outline: a set of closed trajectories, usually used to define the outline of a region.

output: result of executing a master.

page: a unit of output.

page-description language: a computer language that can express page images.

page image: the image built by a page body, which will be printed.

page body: the portion of a master that generates the output for a page.

page independence: the definition of a page image does not affect the definition of any other page image.

page initial frame: the values defined by the preamble that initialize the frame at the start of every page.

parametric form: expressed in terms of a parameter; for example, a curve in the x-y plane can be expressed in terms of a parameter t as x = f(t), y = g(t).

PCS: abbreviation for pixel-array coordinate system.

persistent variable: an imager variable, the value of which is not reset by DOSAVE.

pixel: an element of a pixel array; a point in an image.

pixel array: a two-dimensional array of samples that defines the color everywhere in a rectangular region.

pixel-array coordinate system: a standard coordinate system in which a rectangular array of samples is defined.

point: a printer's unit of distance, usually 1/72 inch; also, a position in space.

portrait orientation: orientation of a medium with the short edge at the bottom.

postfix notation: an instruction syntax in which operators follow their operands.

preamble: the part of the skeleton that establishes the initial frame for execution of the page bodies.

primitive: an operator built into Interpress and defined in the standard.

printer: a device that accepts Interpress masters and produces the corresponding images.

printer dependent: that part of Interpress whose detailed interpretation is not standardized, but instead is left to individual printer manufacturers or operators to specify.

printing instructions: commands that control the printing of an Interpress master.

priority: the property that determines which of two overlapping primitive images will appear to be "on top."

priorityImportant: imager variable 5; indicates whether the printer must preserve priority.

Professional Graphics Set: all of Interpress 3.0.

property name: an identifier, number, or vector of identifiers used in a property vector to name a corresponding value.

property vector: a vector formatted to describe (property name, value) pairs.

Publication Set: a set of Interpress instructions supporting most text, graphics, and scanned images, including all of the Commercial Set, and, in addition, straight and curved lines (both solid and dashed), filled outlines, and constant gray-scale color.

raster: a rectangular grid on which image samples are located.

raster encoding fragment: an Interpress fragment in the form specified by the Xerox Raster Encoding Standard (RES).

raster printer: a printer that produces images from the spots on a raster.

reflectance: the proportion of incident light reflected by a material.

registry: a set of identifiers that controls a particular point in a hierarchical name space.

relative positioning: determining position or placement in terms of, or relative to, the current position.

result: a value pushed onto the stack and left there by the execution of an operator.

rotation: a transformation that moves every point about the origin in a circular arc.

rounding: usually, finding the grid point closest to a device coordinate.

run: an encoding of a repeated element that uses its run length; for example, [4,1] is the run encoding for [1,1,1,1].

run length: the number of times something is repeated.

sample: a record of the color at a pixel; for example, a point in an image.

sampled color: an ink in which each pixel can have its own color.

scale: a transformation that changes the unit of distance of the coordinates.

scan conversion: the act of converting geometric or sampled intensity information into a raster image.

scan line: a straight-line sequence of pixels as sampled by a scanner or imaged by a printer.

scanned image: see pixel array.

scanner coordinate system: a coordinate system in which a scanned image is defined; equivalent to the pixel-array coordinate system defining a scanned image not yet oriented upright.

SCS: abbreviation for scanner coordinate system.

segment: basic element of a trajectory (line segments, arcs, conics, and cubic Bézier curves).

signature: a sheet of paper that folds into a certain number of pages (usually 8, 16, or 32) of a book.

simplex: a mode of printing in which an image is placed on only one side of each sheet of paper; also, a printing-instruction value.

skeleton: the global structure of a master, down to the level of the outermost bodies.

space correcting: the property of allowing proportional adjustment of width to correct the positioning of text; usually the white space between words is adjusted.

spi: abbreviation for spots per inch; a measure of resolution, the same as dots per inch (dpi).

spot: a small region of the output image the color of which can be controlled by the printing device independently of all other regions.

stack: see operand stack.

Standard Observer: the CIE definition of average human spectral response curves.

state: the information that can affect further execution of master.

stroke: a mask obtained by broadening a trajectory to a uniform width.

strokeEnd: imager variable 16; indicates the end-cap style for strokes (square, butt, or round).

strokeJoint: imager variable 23; indicates the joint style for strokes (miter, bevel, round).

strokeWidth: imager variable 15; indicates the width of strokes.

symbol: a graphic shape; several instances of a symbol may appear in a page image.

T: imager variable 4; the current transformation.

T$_{ID}$: the transformation from the Interpress coordinate system to the device coordinate system.

token: a primitive element of an Interpress master.

trajectory: a set of connected segments that define a curve or path.

transformation: a conversion of co-ordinate information from one coordinate system to another; one of the types of the base language.

transition function: a mapping from states into states and output, which defines the meaning of an operator.

translation: a transformation that shifts the position of the coordinate axes.

transmittance: the proportion of light transmitted by a material.

trapezoid: a four-sided figure with two of the sides parallel.

tristimulus values: the amounts of three primary color stimuli that when added together match a given color stimulus.

two-up printing: two page images printed side-by-side on a single, landscape-oriented page.

type: one of the classes of values.

underlineStart: imager variable 17; remembers the MCS x coordinate to be used as the start of an underline.

universal identifier: an identifier defined in the Interpress universal registry.

universal name: a vector of identifiers in which the first identifier is a universal identifier.

universal property vector: a property vector that can be extended using property names that are universal names.

universal registry: a registry of unique identifiers assigned to organizations that wish to create structured names of objects in a printer's environment.

upper bound: the integer name of the last element of a vector.

value: data associated with a name in a property vector.

vector: a sequence of values named by integers; one of the types of the base language.

white: the neutral or gray stimulus with maximum luminance under given observing conditions.

winding number: a count of the number of times a point is surrounded by an outline.

wrap number: see winding number.

FURTHER
READING

Standards Documents

A number of standards documents related to electronic printing and publishing are available from Xerox Corporation. All are consistent with Interpress. The Xerox standards documents listed here may be obtained by writing to:

Xerox Systems Institute
Xerox Corporation
475 Oakmead Parkway
Sunnyvale, CA 94086

Interpress itself is defined by:

- Interpress Electronic Printing Standard, Version 3.0; Xerox System Integration Standard XNSS 048601. Stamford, CN: Xerox Corporation (Jan. 1986).

Related standards that define the font structures, character sets, decompression operators, colors, and color operators that can be used with Interpress are:

- Font Interchange Standard, Version 1.0; Xerox System Integration Standard XNSS 238512. Stamford, CN: Xerox Corporation (Dec. 1985).

- Character Code Standard; Xerox System Integration Standard XNSS 058605. Stamford, CN: Xerox Corporation (May 1986).

- Raster Encoding Standard; Xerox System Integration Standard XNS 178506. Stamford, CN: Xerox Corporation (June 1985).

- Color Encoding Standard: Xerox System Integration Standard. Stamford, CN: Xerox Corporation (in preparation).

The Xerox Systems Institute also makes available the Interpress Toolkit, a collection of software to aid in writing Interpress generators, and a library of Interpress programs called the Interpress Printer Conformance Software.

For certain messages, Interpress makes use of the following standard:

- Seven-bit Coded Character Set for Information Processing Interchange. ISO 646–1983 (E), International Standards Organization.

Color definitions are based on the following standard:

- *Colorimetry*, 2nd ed., Publication CIE No. 15.2. Vienna: Central Bureau of the CIE (1986).

Typography

The following book is a helpful introduction to typography:

- Craig, J. *Designing with Type*. New York: Watson-Guptill Publications (1980).

Some collections of typefaces may be found in the following:

- *Digital Types and Non-Latin Alphabets*. Newbury Park, CA: Autologic Inc. (1985).
- *A Portfolio of Text and Display Typefaces*. Wilmington, MA: Compugraphic Corporation (1980).
- Holthusen, B. *Scangraphic Digital Type Collection*, 2d ed., Hamburg, West Germany: Scangraphic Dr. Böger GmbH (1985).
- Jaspert, W. P., Berry, W. T., and Johnson, A. F. *The Encyclopedia of Typefaces*. Poole Dorset, United Kingdom: Blandford Press (1983).
- Weinberger, N. S. *Encyclopedia of Comparative Letterforms for Artists and Designers*. New York: Art Directions (1979).
- *The Type Specimen Book*. New York: Van Nostrand Reinhold Company (1974).

Computer Graphics

The basic imaging model incorporated in Interpress is described in:

- Warnock, J. and Wyatt, D. K. A Device Independent Graphics Imaging Model for Use with Raster Devices. *Computer Graphics*, Vol. 16, No. 3, pp. 313-319 (1982).

An introduction to synthetic graphics may be found in:

- Harrington, S. *Computer Graphics: A Programming Approach*, 2d ed. New York: McGraw-Hill (1987).
- Foley, J. D., and VanDam, A. *Fundamentals of Interactive Computer Graphics*. Reading, MA.: Addison-Wesley (1984).

Conic curves are discussed in:

- Pavlidis, T. Curve Fitting with Conic Splines. *ACM Transactions on Graphics*, Vol. 2, No. 1, pp. 1-31 (1983).

- Pratt, V. Techniques for Conic Splines. *Computer Graphics*, Vol. 19, No. 3, pp. 151-159 (1985).

Bézier curves are described in:

- Gordon, W. J., and Riesenfield, R. F. Bernstein-Bézier Methods for the Computer-Aided Design of Free-Form Curves and Surfaces. *Journal of the ACM*, Vol. 21, No. 2, pp. 293-310 (1974).

A survey of cubic curve techniques is given in:

- Boehm, W. On Cubics: A Survey. *Computer Graphics and Image Processing*, Vol. 19, No. 3, pp. 201-226 (1982).

A discussion of winding numbers is given in:

- Newell, M. E., and Sequin, C. H. The Inside Story on Selfintersecting Polygons. *Lambda*, Vol. 1, No. 2, pp. 20-24 (1980).

The following is one of many references on image scanning and processing:

- Schreiber, W. F. *Fundamentals of Electronic Imaging Systems*. Berlin: Springer Verlag (1986).

Color

A general introduction to the industrial use and measurement of color is:

- Billmeyer, Jr., F. W., and Saltzman, M. *Principles of Color Technology*, 2d ed. New York: John Wiley & Sons, (1981).

Details of color models mentioned in Chapter 7 may be found in the following:

- Munsell, A. H. *A Color Notation*, 12th Ed. Baltimore: Munsell Color, Inc., (1971).
- *Munsell Book of Color*. Baltimore: Kollmorgen Corp.
- *Pantone Color Specifier*, Designers' Edition. New York: Pantone, Inc.
- *Color: Universal Language and Dictionary of Names*, U.S. National Bureau of Standards Special Publication 440. Washington, DC: U.S. Department of Commerce (1976).

Preliminary work on the Xerox Color Encoding Standard can be found in:

- Buckley, R. R., Interpress Standard for Color Printers and Workstations. Anaheim, CA: *Conf. Proc. Lasers in Graphics*, Vol. 2, pp. 24-28 (1986).

INDEX

PRODUCTION
NOTES

Besides a reference and source for Interpress, this book is also a model of its use as a page- and document-description language. The entire book was put together under the direction of one of the authors (Robert Buckley) using Interpress tools.

The manuscript was typed and formatted using a Xerox 6085 workstation with ViewPoint software; strings were included in the manuscript where the Interpress masters for the figures were to be inserted. Composing the book required converting all the material—both text and figures—into Interpress. The figures themselves originated from a number of sources; most were generated by an interactive illustrator program that used Interpress primitives. The figures generated by the examples were already in the form of Interpress and all that was required was converting the text encoding of the examples into the standard Xerox encoding. Finally, the scanned images were either input on a variety of scanners or generated by a computer program, and then converted into Interpress. As a result, everything between the covers of this book, including the color plates, exists in the form of Interpress masters.

Interpress tools then integrated the text and figures, using the techniques described in Chapter 8. The masters for the figures, along with a transformation to position them on the page, were combined with the masters for the text to produce Interpress masters for each chapter. Proof copies were generated on a 12-page-per-minute 300-spot-per-inch Xerox 8044 laser printer using Interpress 3.0 software; the entire book was printed in less than 4 hours. Camera-ready copy was then produced on a 1200-spot-per-inch Interpress output device and delivered to the publisher.

ABOUT
THE AUTHORS

Steve Harrington is a member of the research staff of Xerox Corporation in Webster, New York. Steve grew up in Portland, Oregon, and has a BS in Mathematics and Physics from Oregon State University. Besides a PhD degree in Physics, he has MS degrees in both Computer Science and Physics from the University of Washington. Before joining Xerox, Steve was a post-doctoral fellow at the University of Utah, and taught computer science at the State University of New York, Brockport. His last foray into print was "Computer Graphics: A Programming Approach."

Rob Buckley is a member of the research staff of Xerox Corporation in Pasadena, California. Rob grew up in Canada and has a BSc in Electrical Engineering from the University of New Brunswick. He has a BA in Physiology and Psychology from the University of Oxford, where he was a Rhodes Scholar, and obtained SM, EE, and PhD degrees in Electrical Engineering from the Massachusetts Institute of Technology. Rob's expertise lies in the field of color image processing, and he has given several talks on color in electronic publishing systems at industry conferences.